The Logic of Sufficiency

The Logic of Sufficiency

Thomas Princen

The MIT Press
Cambridge, Massachusetts
London, England

MIT Press books may be purchased at special quantity discounts for business or sales promotional use. For information, please e-mail special_sales@mitpress.mit.edu or write to Special Sales Department, The MIT Press, 55 Hayward Street, Cambridge, MA 02142.

This book was set in Sabon by SNP Best-set Typesetter Ltd., Hong Kong. Printed and bound in the United States of America.

Printed on recycled paper.

Library of Congress Cataloging-in-Publication Data

Princen, Thomas, 1951–
    The logic of sufficiency / Thomas Princen.
        p.   cm.
    Includes bibliographical references and index.
    ISBN 0-262-16232-6 (alk. paper)—ISBN 0-262-66190-X (pbk. : alk. paper)
    1. Sustainable development.   2. Nature—Effect of human beings on.   I. Title.

HC79.E5P6925   2005
338.9′27—dc22
                                                                    2005042802

10 9 8 7 6 5 4 3 2

Contents

Preface

I go to lots of environmental talks, at my university, at academic conferences, and at governmental and activist meetings. Typically, they follow a pattern: The first fifty-five minutes of the one-hour presentation details an environmental trend or describes the state of some piece of the environment—a forest being deforested, a lake level lowering, a persistent toxic substance accumulating, a climate system destabilizing. In the last five minutes, sometimes in the very last minute, the speaker says, You know, this really isn't a biological problem, nor a chemical or geologic problem. It's a human problem.

And then the speaker, abandoning any pretense of scientific analysis, proposes solutions: People have to be less greedy. They have to think long term, and global. Politicians have to marshal the political will. Consumers have to buy green. Citizens have to vote green. And so on.

As a social scientist focusing on behavior and organization, it's a bit frustrating. Vast resources have been expended in recent decades to document the state of the environment, and the results are nearly always the same: a few success stories, usually anecdotal, and then an overwhelming body of data showing unmistakable and portentous trends. More data and more sophisticated computer models refine and clarify but ultimately confirm the pattern: humans are undermining the life-support systems of other species and their own. What we are now doing is not sustainable. It's a dilemma, these analysts proclaim, a crisis, a really big fix we're in. We really ought to do something. And we can. If only we would be less greedy, buy green . . .

It's gloom-and-doom plus platitude; sky-is-falling plus wishful thinking. Certainly serious students of environmental change can do better.

Many do, of course—natural scientists, social scientists, journalists, business-people, policymakers, and citizens. These are people who appreciate the intricacies of human behavior as much as the dynamics of ecosystems. To go beyond the facile prescriptions, they say that, one way or another, humans must rethink how they relate to nature. We must restructure industry to internalize costs and close material loops. We must reorient consumers to value that which markets ignore.

"Restructuring" and "rethinking" are certainly in order. Yet the proposed solutions tend to be more of the same: use resources more efficiently. Recycle more. Form partnerships. Tax the bads, subsidize the goods. Promote spiritual awakening. Adapt. When things get bad enough people will change; they always do.

Missing are principles of social organization consonant with long-term, sustainable resource use. It is from such principles that ecologically sensitive patterns of use can emerge. *Sufficiency* is one such broad principle.

So this book represents some ten years of concerted "rethinking." It undoubtedly has some of the same pitfalls of the trend watchers and the rethinkers. A central premise is that, indeed, industrial society must reorganize, but it need not create development patterns de novo. People are perfectly capable of living within ecological constraints and, in fact, have a long history of doing so. To get contemporary society on a sustainable path, it must rediscover these patterns and adapt them to the current environmental predicament.

The voluminous literature on sustainability might seem a good place to start. Authors target inadequate laws and regulations, ineffectual bureaucracies, and shortsighted business practices. Others pin blame for unsustainable ways on capitalism or industrialism or, simply, on "the market." But very few address how industries or markets or communities should be organized. There's very little on principles and practices that are actually congruent with sustainable resource use.

Sufficiency is often mentioned in environmental critiques and in calls for new thinking and new directions. But nowhere, to my knowledge, has it been developed in a systematic way. In part, this lack of development is due to the sheer difficulty of doing so. Ecological economist Herman Daly has probably done more than anyone to promote the idea of "enough" or optimal scale. Even so, he finds the concept of sufficiency, let alone its application in economic life, daunting. "It will be very difficult to define sufficiency and build the concept into economic theory and practice," he writes. "But I think it will prove far more difficult to continue to operate [as if] there is no such thing as enough."[1]

Sufficiency's absence is also due to the fact that the idea is absolutely contrary to efficiency, the dominant principle of material social organization today. This book accepts the challenge of building the concept of sufficiency, contrasting it with efficiency, and grounding it in everyday, organized practice. The data are not the kind that fill spreadsheets. The concepts are not the kind that political and economic leaders can fit into their greened-up, business-as-usual approaches to environmental problems. Some readers will find the stories and ideas fanciful, even quaint or nostalgic. Their search for hard-nosed, realist solutions where current patterns of resource use and human mobility are taken as given, where the interchangeability of human and natural capital is assumed, and where technological fixes, maximized outputs, and unending economic growth are presumed possible will not be satisfied here. They will dismiss these ideas as utopian or Pollyannaish or wishful thinking. But this book isn't for such self-proclaimed realists and pragmatists. They will not change their minds on the basis of argument or evidence. They will, I am convinced, disappear as the inconsistencies mount.

This book is instead for those who accept the world's ecological constraints and see utopianism in contemporary beliefs, in notions like the following: increasing population and consumption can continue indefinitely; prices reflect all significant costs; lower prices are always better; well-being correlates with gross domestic product; technology solves more ecological problems than it creates; more economic growth solves the problems of economic growth. Such are the fanciful ideas of the contemporary global ecological crisis. These are the myths that justify unending increases in material and energy throughput on a finite planet, that absolve from responsibility those responsible for irreversible change.

I would like to think that this book wholly discards such myths and presents *the* alternative, that it covers it all, across levels, across cultures and time. Such would be the demand by those who see the contradictions but can't see a way out. Certainly I would like to think that a new economy—an ecological economy, a modern (or postmodern) moral economy—could emerge from these pages. But of course no single work can do all that. Here I can only point in a direction, what I consider to be a fruitful direction, given the facile prescriptions that come from the natural scientists, from the environmental community, and from the policymakers. The prescriptions here, I hope the reader will agree, are grounded. They are grounded not just in what is conceivable (people *can* be less greedy; they *can* have the political will) but in what collectivities have actually done. And they are grounded in established understandings of human capacity. As I will argue throughout the pages to come, I reject prevailing assumptions about humans' inherent short-term thinking, about their inability to self-organize for restrained resource use, about the insatiability of their consumption, about their incapacity to do much more than work (for others) and spend (on what others make).

My approach is to take many cuts at the problem of unsustainability and the need to build sufficiency into decision making. For all the talk in environmental studies about multiple perspectives and interdisciplinary approaches, most research and teaching, I dare say, is narrowly focused, highly specialized in scope and method. Working for years in avowedly multidisciplinary environments, I have come to appreciate why. Every foray outside one's domain of mastery is risky. One just cannot master it all, the biological and physical, the behavioral and social, the historical and contemporary, the cross-cultural. And yet the nature of environmental problems demands it.

What to do? Study more? Be assertive? Retreat to that single, comfortable approach? At times, I certainly do these things. But I also occasionally admit to colleagues, even to a student or two, that I feel like I am always walking on thin ice. Systems theory, the sociology of work, industrial organization, economics, ecology, nutrition, history, linguistics, philosophy, social commentary. These and more can be found in the following pages. Separately, each is indeed thin. Together I hope to have constructed more than thin patches of randomly floating ice. I hope to have driven a few pilings, erected a platform or two, some conceptual, some empirical. And I hope to have steered an icebreaker into some old floes—especially the ones labeled efficiency—that have piled up over the last couple of centuries to give the appearance of solid ground.

The challenge, I have found, is not so much mastering all the necessary perspectives and approaches. It is to keep the problem—the global ecological crisis—in perspective, a perspective that must be at once conceptual and practical, realistic and ethical. The challenge, for me, is to focus a decade of "rethinking" and many more trying to "relive" the good life in North America, trying to be a responsible citizen, educator, parent, husband, and son. For perspective, one can hardly do better than turn to Donald Worster, Wendell Berry, and Donella Meadows.

Worster is an environmental historian who, like few others, can navigate ecology and economics and technology yet never lose sight of the underlying current, power. Worster's immediate context is water in the Western United States. The real issue, though, is domination and conquest, total use and absolute efficiency—in short, empire:

If history teaches us anything unequivocally about empires, it is that sooner or later they begin to falter. The illusions on which they are constructed eventually begin to lose their hold over the minds of the people. The promises they have made are simply too grand to be delivered. Contradictions begin to mount, legitimacy to crack and flake away. The unanticipated social and ecological consequences of empire become increasingly unmanageable, just as they always have, and Leviathan starts to wobble, clutching more and more frantically at panaceas.[2]

Economies expand indefinitely on a finite planet. Efficiencies reduce energy use. Green consumption saves the environment. Worker productivity improves well-being. Such are the illusions of economic and environmental progress. The Leviathan promises more of the same, just better. But a single planet cannot support "total use," as the hydraulic engineers described their aims for the rivers of the American West, any more than those rivers can be endlessly dammed and diverted and loaded with salts and synthetic chemicals.

The logic of empire is the accumulation of private wealth, efficient extraction, and technological mastery, says Worster, a "techno-economic order" that, like irrigation canals, highways, and power lines, runs in "straight line[s] toward maximum yield, maximum profit."[3] That logic has delivered a lot. Now that the planet is ecologically full, though, it must give way to alternative logics, ones that twist and fall, that have mystery and surprise, that do not maximize anything. They must be at once economic and ecological, rational and self-limiting, innovative and humble. One such logic might be sufficiency.

Wendell Berry, essayist, social critic, and farmer, finds sufficiency in the discipline of work. His immediate context is agriculture, not the production of crops as much as the husbandry of the land. "The model figure of this agriculture," Berry writes,

is an old man planting a young tree that will live longer than a man, that he himself may not live to see in its first bearing. And he is planting, moreover, a tree whose worth lies beyond any conceivable market prediction. He is planting it because the good sense for doing so has been clear to men of his place and kind for generations. The practice has been continued because it is ecologically and agriculturally sound; the economic soundness of it must be assumed. While the planting of a field crop, then, may be looked upon as a "short-term investment," the planting of a chestnut tree is a covenant of faith.[4]

Economic soundness, says Berry, follows ecological soundness. Modern industrial agriculture, and much else in contemporary society, has it the other way around. The dominant institutions—the market, the factory, the laboratory—do so with the aid of a powerful principle: efficiency. "Nearly all the old standards, which implied and required rigorous disciplines," continues Berry,

have now been replaced by a new standard of efficiency which requires . . . a relentless subjection of means to immediate ends. . . . Instead of asking a man what he can do well, it asks him what he can do fast and cheap. Instead of asking a farmer to practice the best husbandry, to be a good steward and trustee of the land and his art, it puts irresistible pressures on him to produce more and more food and fiber more and more cheaply, thereby destroying the health of the land, the best traditions of husbandry, and the farm population itself.[5]

Quick and cheap. Produce more, consume more. Faster and better. The incentives and pressures come from all directions. They are ubiquitous, just the way things are. Positive feedback. Perfectly natural. It's the system.

Not necessarily, Donella Meadows, systems analyst, writer, teacher, farmer, and business consultant, would say. It is *just* a system. And systems do change; they have to, especially when the contradictions mount. Positive feedback loops may be positive for some—more income, prestige, and power, say. But "they drive growth, explosion, erosion, and collapse in systems," writes Meadows. "A system with an unchecked positive loop ultimately will destroy itself." But in well-functioning systems "a negative loop [usually] kicks in sooner or later." Slowing positive feedback loops "gives the many negative loops, through technology and markets and other forms of adaptation, time to function."[6] New flows of information and accountability along with different rules and norms enhance that functioning. This book is about checking positive loops, improving accountability, and getting the rules of the game right, right for long-term social and ecological sustainability.

My intention is to leave the reader not with gloom and doom or with business as usual, greened up to improve the environment, but with signs of hope. The fragility of empire, the potential of discipline, the possibility, indeed likelihood, of systems change all are such signs. Stories and ideas, including organizing principles, are further signs. But before delving into the argument for sufficiency (part I), a word about the cases of part II is in order.

I imagine few readers of this book are, or intend to be, loggers or fishers or even neighborhood activists. I do assume, though, that when readers worry whether their water source is secure or wonder whether that new road will ease traffic congestion or question whether a new engine design will really alleviate climate change (let alone question whether their leaders' *denial* of climate change is based on science), they will find lessons in these cases.

I did not choose these cases to suggest reform in the timbering and fishing industries, or changes in political action per se. Rather, I chose them because I have found in my own working and learning and teaching that it is in such stark settings, in such day-to-day activities that the sufficiency principle most clearly reveals itself. It is in grounded activities such as timbering and fishing and transporting (and water pumping and irrigating and a host of similar direct-use activities) that one can sense the intuition—and the rationality—of seeking enough and not too much. It is here that "ecological rationality" and "real working" come to life, acquiring the immediacy, the sensitivity of practical human behavior and organization. It is here that it makes sense for an old man to plant a tree. It is here that the social system meets the biophysical system, where feedback loops become concrete, where new norms and principles change the system. It is here, above all, that competing forms of knowledge reveal their strengths and weaknesses, that human longings for the good life either promote or stymie sustainable practice.

Of course, I can only hope that the lessons of these cases will be generalizable, that readers will find applications in *their* daily lives, in their professional engagements, in their struggles to effect a more sustainable world. But such is the hope of an educator, a parent, a citizen. Others will have to decide whether such hope is visionary thinking or just wishful thinking. So some readers will want to proceed straight to the cases, coming back, if at all, to the arguments that undergird, and derive in part from, these cases.

Acknowledgments

A decade-long project like this, indeed a life's project, incurs many intellectual and emotional debts, some personal, some distant via writings, reports, interviews, and talks. Dwight Clark got me started years ago, asking some fundamental questions about daily life and social purpose. Dennis Criteser and James Arthur continued the conversation. In more recent years, Raymond De Young, James Crowfoot, and Michael Maniates have been kindred souls on matters of "enoughness" and "too muchness." All inspired me through their dedication, their thought, and their action.

Like all complex adaptive systems, research projects require feedback—positive and, especially, negative. For valuable comments on the entire manuscript I am very grateful to Matthew Paterson, Henry Regier, and three anonymous reviewers. For comments on individual chapters I owe much to Bina Agarwal, Arun Agrawal, Samuel Barkin, Steve Brechin, Jennifer Clapp, James Crowfoot, Raymond De Young, Mary Durfee, Horace Herring, Willett Kempton, Stuart Kirsch, Gabriela Kutting, Michael Maniates, Jack Manno, Donald Mayer, Ian Robinson, Andrew Rudin, Harvey Sachs, Dulcey Simpkins, Paul Steinberg, Paul Tinkerhess, Richard Tucker, Paul Wapner, Paul Webb, and Marc Williams. Rudolph Becking, Terrence Bensel, Angela Cacciarru, Gordon Enk, Wes Jackson, Baylor Johnson, Bobbi Low, Joan Nassauer, Elinor Ostrom, Ivette Perfecto, Andrew Rudin, Jack Stevens, Christopher Uhl, Julia Wondolleck, and Donald Worster were influential in the early stages of research, helping me shape the design and suggesting sources. Numerous students read drafts, commented on presentations, or discussed key ideas and data. Among them were Michael Cohen, Nicholas Cucinelli, Gary Davis, Michael DiRamio, Jason Duvall, Keith McDade, Christopher Schreur, Michael Shriberg, Karl Steyaert, Cari Varner, and Elizabeth Wilson.

For invaluable research assistance I thank John Callewaert, Moushimi Chaudbury, Michael Diramio, Carmencita Princen, Judith Robinson, Michael Shriberg,

Karl Steyaert, and Elizabeth Wilson. For their labors and skills in manuscript preparation, I thank Michael Diramio, James Mudd, Carole Shadley, and Elizabeth Wilson. Librarians and curators at the Bancroft Library, University of California, Berkeley, the Humboldt County Library in California, the Maine State Archives, the Monhegan Museum, the Toronto Island archives, and the University of Michigan provided valuable assistance. Bill Bertain, Albert Fulton, Wiley Lacy, Lt. Daniel B. Morris, John and Winnie Murdock, Mary Hay, and Merline Williams were especially generous sharing their materials from personal files.

Many of my sources in the case histories were interviewed confidentially and thus remain anonymous. I am deeply grateful for their willingness to talk and to share their insights, their lessons, and, at times, their dreams and their pain. They, and so many like them, provide the ultimate inspiration that makes a project like this worth doing.

I wish to thank Clay Morgan at The MIT Press for his leadership in encouraging and stewarding through publication so many important works on the environment, and Sandra Minkkinen and Elizabeth Judd for their careful attention to the editing and production of this book.

The John D. and Catherine T. MacArthur Foundation provided substantial financial support midway through this project. The School of Natural Resources and Environment, the Horace H. Rackham School of Graduate Studies, and the Corporate Environmental Management Program, all of the University of Michigan, provided institutional and financial support at crucial times.

And behind the scenes, as always, were Carmencita, Maria, and Paul, who kept it all going.

1

The Idea of Sufficiency

Imagine a major metropolitan city in North America. Downtown, cars are bumper to bumper. Overhead, on the expressway, trucks roar by. As a pedestrian, it's a struggle walking even a few blocks. Crossing a major intersection takes forever. And you worry about walking through the underpass where it's dark, even in daytime; litter is everywhere, and it's so noisy no one would hear a call for help.

So you head for a residential district, not by private automobile as most people do, but by public conveyance, most likely a bus. If you were in Toronto, Canada's largest city, you could take a ferry to one neighborhood. It's called Ward's Island, a remnant piece of sandy spit less than a kilometer offshore in Lake Ontario. When the ferry lets you off and pulls away, the silence is almost deafening. It's an urban neighborhood all right, but very quiet. It's not that there are no people; they are everywhere. There are just no cars, or very few anyway. And it feels safe. With a bit of inquiry you discover that residents don't lock their doors.

City historians and longtime residents know that geography explains only part of this scene, the silence and the safety. The other part is the relative absence of cars. That absence was not serendipitous nor a simple consequence of being remote. Connecting the island to the mainland via bridge or tunnel was straightforward technically and, in fact, city planners tried again and again throughout the twentieth century. Rather, the reason for the neighborhood's character is that residents and some public officials consistently rejected the development schemes of others, electing—sometimes fighting in court and on the streets—to retain their community as a community, without immediate automobile access.

In mid-twentieth century, the Toronto Islands, of which Ward's is one, was a vibrant community with stores, restaurants, hotels, and, from shacks to mansions, houses. But the postwar period brought a new vision of city life, a new approach to progress: urban planning. The can-do, publicly minded spirit of the times led to grand public works projects. "Urban renewal," vast parks, and major roadways would transform not just Toronto but cities across North America. In Toronto, a prime target for such progress was the Toronto Islands, city land only partially developed as a city park and, unfortunately for those with grand schemes, leased to a curious collection of upscale wealthy summer-cottage owners and year-round, mostly working-class, shanty dwellers. In 1951 the city planning board, with help from the federal government, established an overriding goal: "the maximum use of this natural asset for the largest number of the citizens, to serve the 'many' not the 'few.' "[1] Islanders would be among the "few"; visitors, including motorists, would be among the "many."

By 1960, 261 houses, some 20 stores, and a number of hotels—a third of all island buildings—were bulldozed and burned. In their place, the city added picnic grounds, a petting zoo, and a concrete mall with fountains and flower gardens. Only 260 houses were left standing, all on the two easternmost islands. All this in the name of "urban renewal," "progress," and, of course, efficiency, the greatest good for the greatest number.

Ward's Island survived, but so did plans for roads and parking, lots of parking, and a tunnel or bridge. The planners always promised the residents more convenience, more time saving, more labor saving with automobile access. And the residents were tempted: ready access to jobs and shopping. No more waiting for the ferry, no more packing into the island bus in the dead of winter when the ferry was iced in. Yes, more efficient use of time. So they could have cooperated with the planners and developers, worked out a deal—traffic signals and crosswalks, for example. But they said no, deciding against the easy access, against the "savings" and the efficiencies, and *for* restrained automobile use, *for* a different kind of urban life.

Theirs was a choice to establish what is *enough* in everyday automobile use. When the prevailing approach both privately and publicly for a century has been to *promote* automobile use, expand roadways, increase parking, connect populations, and facilitate commerce, here is an instance, albeit tiny, where people collectively bucked the trend. Here people managed not just development but developers and the very idea of development. And they managed not just cars and roadways, but themselves, their access, their mobility, their convenience. The choice was not one of indulgence versus abstinence or convenience versus hardship. For them, it was a "first best" choice, not second best, not a concession, not a sacrifice. It was one of *sufficient* use, of some automobility but not too much, enough to meet basic transportation needs but not so much as to compromise basic community needs.

Now imagine a timber company in North America. Just about any company on the continent and just about any time in the last couple of centuries will do. Chances are it operated by finding rich stands of timber, cutting as fast as technologies and markets allowed, and then moving on. Or it grew a single species of tree—Douglas fir or loblolly pine, for example—in neat rows with fertilizer and herbicides. Just another crop, like corn and soybeans. From early in the ninetieth century, timber companies cooperated with suppliers and buyers and government agencies, all to get the cut out, to do their bit to build a great nation. There was never enough, though, no harvest rate that was too much, only more land, more cutting, and more return on investment.

But if you had picked Pacific Lumber Company midcentury, you would have seen something quite different. There, on private land in northern California, were mostly intact forests—redwoods it turns out, very large trees yielding straight, fine-grained, rot-resistant wood. There you could have seen harvesting techniques that leave enough trees to allow regrowth, and then some, and a mill with state-of-the-art equipment, a company town with a waiting list, and, in the bank, a generous pension fund. The key to the company's success, its officials regularly told stockholders, workers, and community leaders, was "restrained harvesting"—cutting less than what was possible, less than the industry norm. "The Company . . . has had many years of practice in restraining itself from overharvesting its timber resource, limiting itself to a harvest equivalent to the amount of growth," concluded two company historians, articulating what, by the 1980s, had become gospel among timber managers at Pacific Lumber Company. "It has been exercising this restraint for several decades, reducing production in some cases even in times of good markets of its products, which is most unusual in this industry whose sales are largely cyclical."[2] Harvesting not what the market will bear, but what the forest will bear. Cutting enough and not too much.

Sufficiency here was hardly sacrifice. The owners and workers and their families were not merely surviving, but, by their own descriptions, thriving.

Now "scale up," shift to the regional and the international. The Great Lakes, a fifth of the world's surface freshwater shared by Canada and the United States, have suffered one environmental insult after another. Sewage, pesticides, canals, diversions, and industrial wastes of every imaginable sort have disrupted the basin's ecosystem, sometimes irreversibly. In the first half of the twentieth century it was not hard to decide that sewage discharges were too much: the stench, they say, was overpowering and the sight, well, unsightly. And the algal mats stretched for miles on end, slimy rafts of green that no swimmer or boater would dare venture near. So the two countries, with guidance from their binational boundary board, the International Joint Commission (IJC), promoted sewage treatment locally and restricted phosphates nationally. It worked. The smell and the floating "nuisances" largely disappeared. Sewage is still discharged, but in limited amounts, as much as the system can absorb as a waste sink, it appears, but not too much. Sufficient for the basin's population and its human wastes.

Persistent, bioaccumulative toxic substances are another matter in the Great Lakes. Mercury, lead, dioxin, and polychlorinated biphenyls (PCBs) cannot be treated at a local plant. They enter the basin from land, water, and air, they disperse, and they concentrate in the fatty tissues of grazers and predators such as mussels, salmon, eagles, and humans. A salmon in Lake Michigan can have a million times the concentration of mercury in its blood as the water in which it swims. Toxicologists, epidemiologists, psychologists, and wildlife biologists are churning out the studies. The U.S. Agency for Toxic Substances and Disease Registry released one in 1998 titled "Public Health Implications of Persistent Toxic Substances in the Great Lakes and St. Lawrence Basins." "The collective weight of evidence indicates that certain PCB/dioxin-like compounds found in fish in the Great Lakes–St. Lawrence Basin (and elsewhere) can cause neurobehavioral deficits," it reported. Children's short-term memory, neuromuscular coordination, IQ, and reading comprehension were all found impaired, attributed to in utero and early childhood exposure. These hormone-mimicking substances were transmitted from the mother to the fetus via the womb and breast milk at crucial times of development.[3] Other studies document increased hyperactivity and fear among children and reduced sperm counts among adult men (as much as 60 percent in some populations).

Although there is no technological fix, the IJC weighed the scientific evidence and concluded that there is also no "acceptable assimilative capacity for persistent, bioaccumulative toxic substances.... The only appropriate water quality objective is zero." And this is not simply a biological or economic issue, or even strictly a health issue, the IJC told its clients, the governments and publics of the two countries: "The production and release of these substances into the environment must ... be considered contrary to the [Great Lakes Water Quality] Agreement legally, unsupportable ecologically and dangerous to health generally. Above all, it is ethically and morally unacceptable."[4] Former IJC cochair, Gordon Durnil, a self-described conservative businessman, fed up with all the excuses for doing nothing, put it bluntly: "Why not just get on with the important business of creating a process to *sunset* ... the manufacture, distribution, storage, and use of persistent toxic substances? Why continue the charade?"[5] The charade is the pretense that some level of these substances is tolerable. The evidence says there is no such level, only zero.

So zero discharge and virtual elimination have become the watchwords for Great Lakes water-quality managers. Negotiators in a more famous case—the Montreal Protocol, which bans ozone-depleting substances—came to a similar conclusion: these substances have no place in the upper atmosphere. They thin the ozone layer, which increases ultraviolet radiation, and they disrupt global climate. In both cases, scientists and policymakers alike decided there is no trade-off, no cost-benefit analysis that tells us how to exchange economic goods for public health or ecosystem integrity. Any amount is too much. This, too, is sufficiency.

An urban neighborhood eschews the car, a timber company holds back on its harvests, two industrialized countries find that treated sewage is enough, persistent toxics too much, and international society bans ozone-depleting substances. Unusual cases, perhaps, but rather sensible, one might think. A similar story can be told about lobster fishing in Maine and, no doubt, about countless other practices in countless other places, in North America, Europe, and other "advanced industrial countries." Each instance may represent a trivial portion of that country's overall economy. But the "advances" of these economies—the technologies, the stock markets, the transportation and communication systems, the conveniences and time-saving devices—represent something else, namely, *ever-increasing throughput of material and energy.* That throughput—the extraction of resources, the manufacture and use of products, and the disposal of wastes—supports, and now threatens to undermine, those very economies. Such throughput cannot be sustained. So these instances of sufficiency may be trivial by conventional measures—municipal budgets, industry outputs, gross domestic product, trade flows, stock market indices. But they are harbingers of a different economy, I contend, one that puts ecological and social constraint with a long-term view at the center of economic and political life.

And so it is stories like these that need telling. Members of so-called advanced societies, and those elsewhere who aspire to have such "advances," need to know that even at home, where unending economic growth is an unquestioned "good thing," essential for progress, cherished for its ability to solve all problems, even those of growth itself, that even here people have learned to say enough. And they need to know that saying enough need not be a matter of sacrifice or do-gooderism. Saying enough, indeed, *practicing* enough, in the neighborhoods, in the woods and on the water, is not just a means of surviving. It is a means of thriving.

So I will leave the details of the Toronto neighborhood and of the timber company and the lobster story to part II. The Great Lakes and ozone cases are amply told elsewhere.[6] Here and in part I, I address another need of concerned citizens, people who, like IJC chair Durnil, are fed up with ever-increasing throughput, with the open-access, free-for-all assault on the planet's natural resources, with the 24/7 work-and-spend mentality, with the commercial promises of the good life—the efficiencies and conveniences and the stuff, more and more stuff. This is the need for a language consonant with "enoughness" and "too muchness," not just words, but concepts and organizing principles. In an ecologically constrained world, people need the rhetorical and political means for turning a silencing hand to the barkers and boosters, to the marketeers, to the spinmeisters and political handlers, all of whom tell us that the good life comes from purchasing goods, and that because goods are good more goods must be better.

From Idea to Principle

Sufficiency as an idea is straightforward, indeed simple and intuitive, arguably "rational." It is the sense that, as one does more and more of an activity, there can be enough and there can be too much. I eat because I'm hungry but at some point I'm satiated. If I keep eating I become bloated. I go for a walk because it feels good, because I enjoy the movement and the fresh air, but if my physical exertion begins to override my pleasure, I've had enough. If I keep walking to the point where all my attention is on my aching feet and tired legs, I've had too much. I can sense the excess.

Sufficiency is also a commonsense idea at the collective level when risks are readily perceived and serious. A farmer knows that everyone on the homestead wants increased yields. But the uncertainties of weather and markets mean that one cannot push the land and the workers too hard without risking soil quality and worker reliability. A lumber executive knows that a big cut this year will please shareholders and mill hands alike. But with new timberland unavailable, the executive holds back the harvest to ensure a cut the next year and the next decade, maybe even cuts through the next century. A college president knows the funds and the space for expansion can be obtained but decides the college's mission would be compromised with more bureaucratization and more encumbered funding sources.

The *idea* of sufficiency begins to shift to the *principle* of sufficiency when structure is needed for enactment, when more than sensory perception of "enoughness" or "too muchness" is needed to recognize excess and to act. If I crave chocolate, I know I must stop eating it well before the craving ends if I am to avoid a severe headache. If I feel especially strong willed that day, I just stop myself after one chocolate bar and a couple chocolate chip cookies. Otherwise, I have to arrange things in my house so only one chocolate bar and two cookies are available; to get more

I'd have to make a trip to town, a considerable inconvenience. And I'd have to so arrange my chocolate supply *in advance* of my craving. I'd have to plan ahead.

All this arranging is management or, better, *self-management*. I anticipate my craving and I plan to indulge it because, in fact, I know chocolate doesn't just taste good, it stimulates creative thinking. But I also know there are risks. I can have too much. A few chocolate bars too many and a debilitating headache puts me in bed for an entire day.

In situations like this, I'm just being human; I want more of a good thing. I know I'd enjoy every additional ounce of chocolate. But with chocolate, as with so many good things, I cannot rely on immediate perception and rational response. I cannot wait until I'm satiated to stop eating. Rather, the management of such desires requires guidelines—rules of thumb, criteria, norms—in short, *principles*. This is especially so in situations where individuals or collectivities confront risks to long-term well-being. Sufficiency as an idea, as a personally and intuitively sensible goal, thus becomes a *principle of management*.

A principle is socially useful when it routinely generates particular questions. And it does so not as experiments or occasional challenges to the status quo, but as a continual means of raising and espousing critical values. A management principle broadens to a *social organizing principle* when rules and procedures regularize collective behavior, allowing such questions to arise normally and, hence, protecting and enhancing those critical values. In the process, other values are submerged.

Sufficiency as a principle aimed at ecological overshoot compels decision makers to ask when too much resource use or too little regeneration jeopardizes important values such as ecological integrity and social cohesion; when material gains now preclude material gains in the future; when consumer gratification or investor reward threatens economic security; when benefits internalized depend on costs externalized.

Historically, societies have developed related notions—moderation, thrift, frugality, prudence, temperance, reverence—all to restrict the otherwise human tendency to want more of a good thing. The risks were to social cohesion, self-defense, and survival. Among those directly dependent on the land or the seas, the farmers and fishers, for instance, the risks were to future harvests. But other principles of social organization have ascended and eventually dominated, including power, caste, divine right, and expansion. Since the advent of industrialization, the ascendant and now-dominant principle in the marketplace—and increasingly elsewhere—is efficiency. Societies the world over increasingly orient themselves to its precepts, including the values of specialization and mobility. Notions like frugality and prudence have been rendered subordinate, acceptable as a guide for individual behavior perhaps but irrelevant to the designs of society's major institutions: the factory, the laboratory, the market.

These three institutions more than any are responsible for the ever-increasing throughput of modern society.[7] They have been fabulously successful in generating material wealth, extracting raw materials from all corners of the globe, and creating products people will buy. They have made it appear that there is always room for more automobiles, always another forest to harvest, always a body of water or an expanse of air to absorb the wastes. Now they are making it appear that fresh water is like other valuable liquids such as oil: with effort and new technologies, prospectors can always find more and, with market pricing, it can always be moved to its most productive use.[8] In times of abundance, the risks of such endeavors were only foregone opportunities—investments and discoveries that someone else would get to first. In an ecologically "empty world," a world in which human impact was minuscule relative to the extent and regenerative capacity of resources and waste sinks, there were, after all, always more forests to cut, more swamps to drain, more grasslands to plow, more rivers and lakes and airsheds to dump in. For the entrepreneurs and pioneers, being *resourceful* meant getting the most from nature's bounty, using resources efficiently to be sure, but for immediate gains, for power, or for the sheer pleasure of playing high-stakes games, but not for long-term sustenance. Mistakes might bring financial ruin but resources abounded elsewhere. One just had to pack up and move on. There was always another frontier.

The risks are different now, profoundly serious from the individual to the societal to the global level. Not only are there few true frontiers left but the biophysical underpinnings of human life are in jeopardy. The litany of issues—global warming, species extinctions, bioaccumulative toxics, water shortage—is long, well known, and well documented. More of the same, however fine-tuned to be efficient, even "eco-efficient," will not reverse the trends. In fact, in an ecologically "full world" every incremental increase in human impact jeopardizes life-support systems. Squeezing out yet another production efficiency is of little benefit if throughput still increases.

Social organizing principles attentive to excess, to risks displaced in time and place, are desperately needed. Sufficiency principles such as restraint, respite, precaution, polluter pays, zero, and reverse onus (chapters 2 and 9) have the virtue of partially resurrecting well-established notions like moderation and thrift, ideas that have never completely disappeared. They also have the virtue of being highly congruent with global ecological constraint, a congruence not shared by efficiency. By asking how much is enough and how much is too much, one necessarily asks what is excessive, what the risks are, not just risks in the short term and for immediate beneficiaries, but risks to those unlikely to realize the benefits, both for the immediate and the long term.

Sufficiency, then, is a commonplace notion, self-evident, even intuitive, at the personal level (ingestion, walking, sleep), sensible at the organizational level (managing intensified cropping, containing organizational growth). What is more, it has historical antecedents. A paradox remains, however. How can an idea like sufficiency be so straightforward yet so alien in modern society? How is it that I can rationally develop a chocolate-consumption regime for myself yet run into one brick wall after another arguing for optimal scale in my university? How is it that the world's scientific community, its environmental community, and even much of industry know that climate change is real, that caps on greenhouse gases are eminently sensible (as are, everyone seems to agree, caps on SO_2 emissions), yet leaders of some of the largest CO_2-emitting countries—the United States, China, and Canada—insist that the economy (and hence emissions) must continue apace? The explanation for these apparent contradictions lies in part with personal or political struggle. My colleagues employ techniques like mine to contain their personal urges, yet in their professional lives, they must function in a university that equates progress with new programs and bigger budgets. Many leaders know fundamental change must occur. But they also know that pursuing such change would be political suicide in a society wedded to scientific and technological knowledge, in a society that embraces freewheeling markets and promotes the proliferation of goods and services those markets generate.

A deeper explanation, however, must go to expectations and norms, indeed, to the *principles* around which such a society is organized. To develop this deeper explanation and to set the stage for articulation of sufficiency as a broad social organizing principle in an ecologically constrained world, not just as a personal idea, the next chapter takes up the social concern—critical environmental threats—and the policy goal—sustainability—that informs this study. I frame them in decision-making terms, as "ecological rationality." I then show how sufficiency contrasts with society's dominant principle, efficiency, tracing its history and rhetorical use. Work and consumption are elementary contexts for sufficiency. These chapters constitute part I. Part II shows through original case histories that sufficiency is quite possible. Some readers will want to proceed straight to those cases. They show through the detail of everyday decision making, through personal challenge and collective struggle, how sufficiency makes sense, how the logic of sufficiency plays out on the ground, in the water, and along the streets. Other readers, though, will want to know how all this sufficiency talk fits into the social and natural sciences. They will want to know what kind of exercise I am leading them into: Is it descriptive, predictive, or prescriptive; is it explanatory or normative? They will want terms defined, concepts justified, and the theoretical and applied context set. These readers should read on.

In Principle

Global timber harvesters are squeezing more and more fiber out of a hectare of forest, yet deforestation proceeds unabated. The automobile and petrochemical industries are creating more wealth for each unit of pollution, yet emissions continue to grow. And the world's water managers seem to agree on most things, including the need for treaties and more water, yet freshwater availability is dropping to critical levels. Contrary to conventional wisdom, there is actually quite a lot of efficiency and cooperation in today's political and ecological economy. Where there are problems—for example, deforestation, greenhouse gas buildup, water scarcity—practitioners and scholars alike call for more efficiency and more cooperation. It might just be that the principles themselves—efficiency and cooperation—are part of the problem. It might be that entirely different principles are needed to address critical environmental threats.

Today's environmental problems are of a wholly different order from those presumed in many environmental and economic institutions. The laws and regulations of countries, as well as the treaties and understandings between countries, are constructed as if a little adjustment here, a bit of retooling there will reverse the trends. They will not.

Critical environmental threats entail irreversibilities and nonsubstitutabilities; they threaten vital life-support systems. Overconsumption—resource use beyond regenerative capacities that threatens entire species, including humans—is a real possibility.[9] Saving a species or slowing CO_2 emissions (let alone slowing the rate of growth in CO_2 emissions) only postpones tough choices. To make such choices, to construct institutions from the local to the global, from the tiny inshore fishery to the global atmospheric commons, requires principles attuned to such threats. Analysts and practitioners who take seriously the trends and accept social responsibility for contributing to the reversal of such trends must go beyond marginal improvement, beyond efficiency and cooperation, and beyond the descriptive and predictive. They must be prescriptive. They must find principles that speak directly to critical environmental threats. *Sufficiency* is one class of such principles.

A premise of this book is that prevailing principles of social organization—efficiency, cooperation, equity, sovereignty—are not up to the task. They may have worked in times of resource abundance, in an ecologically "empty world," a world where human impact is minor, where there is always another frontier, but they do not work now. They do not guide decision makers—not elite global managers, not farmers and fishers, not corporate leaders, not consumers—in reversing the biophysical trends and getting on a sustainable path.

The perception of critical environmental threats has spawned an abundance of critiques—of environmental policies, of business practices, and of the environmental movement. The critiques often end by insisting that economic expansion and growth at any cost cannot continue, that society must recognize its self-generated predicament and accept that enough is enough. Society must scale back. It must return to the old virtues, frugality and moderation, for instance, as if such notions are self-evident by themselves, let alone meaningful in the modern, industrial, and postindustrial context. But recall ecological economist Herman Daly's words: "It will be very difficult to define sufficiency and build the concept [of sufficiency] into economic theory and practice. But I think it will prove far more difficult to continue to operate [as if] there is no such thing as enough."[10]

Modern society has, of course, found it all too easy to act as if there is never enough and never too much. In the marketplace, where much is decided about resource extraction and waste disposal, there are myriad financial, managerial, and political ways of displacing costs in time and space, all contributing to the apparent absence of sufficiency. Such market "failures" are driven by an imperfect, often-strategic use of a prevailing principle of social organization: *efficiency*. In the civic realm, formal laws and regulations as well as informal norms are governed by another prevailing principle: *cooperation*. By themselves, efficiency and cooperation are unalloyed "good things." But one can find efficiencies in mining a renewable resource just as readily as in sustaining that resource; one can cooperate to displace costs, just as readily as one can cooperate to conserve. The two principles lack direction, especially with respect to long-term ecological context. They need to be unpacked and put in their place.

The Efficiency Principle

The idea of getting more benefit for a given effort or of investing less to get the same outcome is age-old. It has arguably informed a good deal of biological and cultural evolution. Individuals who can acquire resources with the least expenditure are more likely to survive and to reproduce, passing along their genes and cultural traits. A selection bias for a propensity to seek efficiencies is thus reasonable to infer.

This natural propensity toward efficiency-seeking made a huge cultural leap with industrialization. The rewards for an efficiency gain were no longer a boost in immediate satisfaction—more meat from a hunting expedition, say—or even a boost in annual yield—more corn from a hectare of land. Rather, the rewards were substantial surpluses, enough to ensure sustenance or even prosperity, and most significantly, enough for further investment and trade, leading to yet more surplus. For the cleverest at capturing such efficiencies, it was as if a perpetual-motion machine had been discovered. Prior to industrialization there were always brakes on continuous expansion: population pressures; technical limits on extracting resources and transporting them; physical barriers like oceans, deserts, and mountains. What is more, ecological constraint was ever present: declining yields signaled overharvesting and the need to forgo surplus and shift investments. Now, with advanced metals, steam power, and fossil fuels, all those constraints could be set aside—or so it has seemed for the past few centuries. Efficiencies were everywhere for the taking, like clumps of ripe fruit dangling from heretofore unnoticed branches.

The classic site of such gains was the factory. Ever more finely tuned machines followed by ever more specialized labor made for ever more efficiencies. Each wave of technological and managerial innovation has been an extension of the same theme: from Adam Smith's pin factory and Armor Swift's meat disassembly plants to Henry Ford's automobile assembly line; from a division of labor within the factory to a division of labor across the globe; from vertical integration to outsourcing; from real goods to virtual goods. All as if there were no end in sight, no equivalent to uncrossable deserts and insurmountable mountains.

But the process never stopped with technical-efficiency gains on the factory floor. Giddy with the cornucopia opened by manufacturing, modern societies have pushed the efficiency principle to other realms, including to some of the most unlikely institutions. Governments must be "streamlined," waste cut, and budgets tightened to perform in a businesslike manner, as if technical changes will produce wiser legislation, better administration, and more justice. The news media must find "synergies" with other knowledge-based industries, including entertainment, as if journalistic ideals in a free society will never be compromised by marketeering and centralized ownership. Schools and universities must find "economies of scale" by getting larger, consolidating neighborhood schools into school districts, and expanding colleges into major research universities, as if the fundamentals of a good education, not to mention the search for truth, can be so managed. Communities must relieve traffic congestion so drivers can make better use of their time, as if expanded roadways have no significant effect on other modes of transportation, on personal safety, or on residential life. Families must practice time management at home and minimize the daily drudgery of cleaning and cooking so as to maximize work, education, and recreation, all as if free time is "wasted time" and self-provisioning is the lowly activity of the poor and backwards.

What was once a useful guide to factory organization has now become a pervasive principle of social organization. Efficiency claims abound, often unquestioned and unexamined. Perhaps most pernicious is the power of the efficiency principle to justify public policies, especially those that skew benefits toward the powerful and away from the weak, and those that displace true costs, especially ecological costs, in time and place. If, for example, a legislator wants to promote factory hog farming, the most "productive" way of getting pounds of pork from an acre of land, he need only argue that this advanced method is more efficient than free-range hog rearing. Public funds are then justified via tax abatements and zoning variances. The actual efficiencies are rarely spelled out, let alone questioned. If they were, they would have to include threats to groundwater, spread of livestock disease, public health effects of antibiotics, displacement of family farms, and dissolution of communities. *Net* gains would be highly questionable. Similarly, if a university administrator wants to spur energy research, she need only show that the expected "return" in grants and patents will exceed the outlay of public and private funds. Such an efficient use of funds would likely ignore the attendant increases in student tuition, decreases in teaching commitments for selected faculty, and elimination of inefficient (read financially uncompetitive) programs.

In the contemporary era, then, efficiency criteria have insinuated themselves into nearly every facet of daily and professional life. As a principle, efficiency has become hegemonic in the sense that it is so universal, so internalized by nearly everyone in nearly all realms of life, that one hardly thinks about it, let alone questions it. Having moved from its most obvious and possibly most useful application, the factory, to so many others, even child rearing and leisure, it has overspilled its boundaries. It is used to skew market benefits, appropriate public funds, and mine resources, all in the name of "growth" or "development" or "progress," even environmental protection. Efficiency has become nearly synonymous with "good" and "better." It has a scientific and technological ring to it and is thus invoked to promote and legitimize nearly any agenda, immune from questioning. It is, moreover, a principle that impinges on other principles, including those critical to sustainable resource use, principles I put under the rubric of *sufficiency*.

The Cooperation Principle
An antidote to efficiency, one might think, would be cooperation. If efficiency is used to expand endlessly, to claim value for a few, cooperation steps in to even the score, to make sure everyone is in the game and everyone wins something. Unfortunately, even if cooperation serves this purpose, the game, as played on a finite planet, cannot deal with critical environmental threats. Global water is a case in point.

A vast amount of research on trends in freshwater availability seems to have come to a resounding, and disturbing, consensus: societies around the globe are facing or will soon face dire water scarcities. By the year 2015, some estimate, 3 billion people, 40 percent of the world's population, will not have enough water to meet basic needs. The spillover effects via poverty and migration on international and human security, as well as on human and ecological health, could be horrendous.[11]

At the same time that water scarcity is becoming a prominent global environmental and security issue, a variety of water regimes from the local to the global have attempted to grapple with the shortage. In a survey of international water regimes, global water expert Peter Gleick identifies six prevailing principles:

1. Equitable utilization
2. Prevention of significant harm
3. Obligation to notify and inform other parties
4. Obligation to share data among parties
5. Cooperative management of international rivers
6. Obligation to resolve disputes peacefully.[12]

One would have to stretch point 2, no significant harm, to get anything close to a notion of water capacity. Otherwise, these agreements, as written, are simply cooperative measures. They say the parties should share data, inform each other of new development projects, and try hard to resolve differences peacefully. And, following these measures, the parties can do all this cooperating as they permanently draw down aquifers, salinize soils, destroy fisheries, spread disease, and eliminate species. Very few cooperative regimes confront the fact that water, a potentially renewable resource, can be consumed, irreversibly drawn down, permanently diverted or contaminated.

Of course, these agreements, as practiced, are replete with competition, including competition to get every last drop out of a water system. The Western states in the United States develop their economies and populate their deserts by extracting Colorado River water in ever-greater volumes, leaving a trickle at best for Mexicans. The Mexicans complain and the Americans listen. And they sit down together periodically to work on the problem (generally, the problem of getting more water, that is)—all in a spirit of cooperation. The Israelis and Palestinians pump water from the West Bank, sending drill rigs ever deeper. The equity principle is violated when the Israelis control access to that water, allocating it first to themselves. But even here in this conflict-ridden part of the world, the two parties can claim a degree of cooperation under the Israeli-Palestinian Joint Water Committee.

Cooperation is not only possible, it may be the norm in water institutions. "Between the years 805 and 1984, countries signed more than 3,600 water-related treaties, many showing great creativity in dealing with this critical resource," write two other water experts, Sandra Postel and Aaron Wolf. They add that "an analysis of 1,831 international water-related events over the last 50 years reveals that two thirds of these encounters were of a cooperative nature."[13] Cooperation is ubiquitous. Living within the capacities of the respective water systems is quite another matter.

Existing international water regimes and proposals for new regimes put great faith in the ability of leaders to steer efficiency gains and cooperative relations in a novel direction—that is, *away* from conventional development goals (economic growth, increased population, more foreign currency) and the ever-increasing water consumption that tends to accompany such goals, and *toward* restrained water consumption, consumption that falls safely within hydrologic capacities. It is a leap that would be credible if the principles for collective action, extant or proposed, were grounded in the biophysical conditions that define water scarcity: *water is finite and locally depletable.* Those principles would have to incorporate biophysical constraint and social restraint. Such principles would complement, if not entirely supplant, the otherwise all-popular principles of efficiency and cooperation. This would be a first-order condition for an institution of sustainable practice.

All this is not to say that efficiency and cooperation have no place in a sustainable society. In organizing for collective action, efficiency principles are useful because they are especially sensitive to technical and economic aims—avoiding waste and matching technological possibility to human wants and needs. Cooperation principles are useful because they are sensitive to conflict, especially to the defusing of tension and prevention of violence, and to democratic ideals—fairness, nondiscrimination, and human rights.

But to arrest declines in ecosystem functioning, cooperation and efficiency are not enough. As intuitive and popular as these principles are, both suffer from "normative neutrality." One can find efficiencies in harvesting a forest so as to save trees just as well as one can find efficiencies to get every last bit of fiber off an acre of timberland. One can cooperate to protect a forest just as well as one can cooperate to clear-cut it. When incentives line up on the side of return on investment and growth, cooperation and efficiency lean toward clear-cutting and fiber extraction, toward ever more economic activity, spurring material and energy throughput in the economy. The pursuit of these principles may actually thwart ecological restoration and sustainable use by helping key actors disguise, displace, and postpone true costs. Squeezing out yet another production efficiency, even in the spirit of cooperation, is of little benefit if throughput still increases.

Efficiency and cooperation are thus no more suited to reversing the trends and promoting sustainable practice than they are at stimulating those trends and thwarting sustainable practice. The two principles do not distinguish between environmental improvement and sustainability (chapter 2). They do not address two defining characteristics of contemporary environmental trends:

1. *The increasing criticality of environmental threats, problems characterized by irreversibility and nonsubstitutability, threshold and synergistic effects ("surprise"), long time lags between cause and effect, and, therefore, limited predictability and limited control.* Climate change, biodiversity loss, topsoil erosion, persistent toxics, and declining freshwater availability are examples of such threats.

2. *The increasing ease of exporting the risks of critical threats and escaping responsibility for their creation.* Globalization, privatization, and diminishing state capacity conspire with technological innovation and market manipulation to skew the benefits and costs of economic activity, creating the illusion of environmental progress. Examples would include local pockets of pristine and healthy environments, especially among those who can buy their way out of degraded environments. At the same time vast areas around the world are being degraded and huge waste sinks such as the oceans and atmosphere are being filled.

Sufficiency in Practice

To observe that efficiency and cooperation are hegemonic in economic and ecological regimes, that they contribute more to excess throughput than to limiting that throughput, is not to say that sufficiency does not exist in expansive societies. Certainly it does at the individual level and in some circumstances at the organizational level. I have given a few examples already, ranging from the personal and community to the regional and global.

But consider American business, the paragon of efficiency-driven, growth-oriented, technologically determined organization. This might seem like the most incongruous place to find sufficiency in practice. Publicly traded corporations, for instance, exhibit an imperative to constantly grow, to generate ever-greater returns on investment. There are other firms, though—many of them small and privately held with secure market niches—that act otherwise. These firms are attentive to the problems of bureaucratization through growth, or of spreading thin through diversification, or of compromising strengths by taking on new lines of production, or of damaging reputation by advertising carelessly. The family farm, the locally owned hardware store, the owner-operated fishing boat, and the timber company with no place to expand are all profit-making enterprises that in one form or another embody the sufficiency principle. Whether or not they consciously employ or explicitly articulate the principle, their actions speak to their sensitivity to scale, to overstepping natural boundaries or social norms, to exceeding capacity, to jeopardizing good will. I develop two such cases—the Pacific Lumber story and a fishing story, Monhegan—in part II.

Another unlikely place for sufficiency would be the planning and development departments in rapidly growing cities. Here, mobility is sacrosanct. Private access, especially access via cars and trucks, is paramount in the push to develop, to become a great city. With the help of citizens concerned about residential life, however, even such departments can embody the sufficiency principle. Here is where the island neighborhood in Toronto—Ward's Island—comes in, the third case of part II.

Because these examples of private business and public planning exist in societies known for their obsession with squeezing out efficiencies in personal, professional, and public life, societies where one would otherwise never expect to find models for "sufficient living," each represents the *hard case* analytically. The easy case would be isolated hunter-gatherer tribes or religious cults or rejectionist sects or even, say, countries like Norway or Costa Rica. It is too easy, and ultimately too ineffectual, to point to such societies as models, as if to say, look, they can do it, they can hold back, they can be attentive to scale, they can live within their means, so why can't we? It is a much harder case to show that even in the most efficiency-driven, growth-oriented societies of North America, sufficiency can make sense. Sufficiency does exist here. These three cases and various shorter ones sprinkled throughout the book are indeed "hard cases," sites where one would otherwise expect to find that suffi- ciency and operational subprinciples like restraint and respite have been completely subsumed by efficiency and its subprinciples, specialization and mobility. These examples suggest that even under such highly competitive, ultimately destructive conditions, a different path is possible. It is possible, moreover, without top-down coercion, without elite, technocratic knowledge. And it is possible among those who are otherwise mainstream, who are just trying to make a living or maintain a com- munity. It is possible, these cases suggest, to both manage and self-manage under ecological constraint. Indeed, my aim throughout this book is to show through argu- ment and story that, although efficiency and cooperation still reign supreme in such a society, sufficiency is logical and will become increasingly so, indeed increasingly imperative, as its members are forced to come to grips with the realities of ecolog- ical constraint.

A final word on usage. In this book I use *sufficiency* to mean a sense of "enough- ness" and "too muchness," a quality where concern for excess is paramount in the life of an individual, an organization, or a nation. But in everyday English the term often means or implies "good enough" or "second best." In economics, psychol- ogy, and other fields, *satisficing* appears to have similar connotations. "Human beings . . . *satisfice* because they have not the wits to *maximize*," wrote psycholo- gist Herbert A. Simon in a work that landed him a Nobel Prize in economics. "Administrative man," as opposed to the superrational "economic man," satisfices "because he treats the world as rather empty and ignores the interrelatedness of all things . . . ," Simon wrote.[14] My use of sufficiency could not be more contrary.

In the context of primary concern, namely, human resource appropriation under ecological constraint, the effective decision maker is precisely the one who has the wits to engage the interrelatedness, to avoid excess, to take long-term impacts and displaced costs into account, and to avert irretrievable diminution of ecological integrity. Such wits enable the "sufficient person" to comprehend the world not in a mechanical, utility-maximizing, information-processing, data-crunching way, but in an intuitive, experiential way. The sufficient person seeks connection and is sen- sitive to unintended consequences. The sufficient person exercises restraint and respite not because he or she can't perform in a scientifically prescribed, economi- cally rational manner and therefore must be content with second-best outcomes. Rather, the sufficient person exercises restraint and respite because such principles are consistent with a world that is ultimately unknowable and uncontrollable, a world where cause-and-effect relationships are deeply problematic, a world where limited predictability, system surprise, threshold, and synergistic effects are the norm, not the exception. In short, the sufficient person manages oneself and manages others in a totally different way from the way one manages in the factory or laboratory. In this messy, complex, constantly adapting world, a world simultaneously resilient and fragile, a world full of humans and human impacts, one must have wits galore to function.

Efficiency and cooperation may have served humans well. But they have done so under conditions unique to the resource and waste-sink availabilities of the last 300 years. Under other conditions—namely, environmental criticality—a different set of principles are needed, a set that embodies *social restraint* as the logical analog to *ecological constraint*, a set that guides human activities when those activities pose grave risks to human survival. *Sufficiency* is a class of principles sensitive to critical environmental risks, to the needs of management and self-management, when it is otherwise all too easy to evade responsibility for such risks. Sufficiency is an idea, a principle, indeed an ethic for sustainability.

I

Sufficiency in Principle

2

Ecological Rationality: Management and Self-Management in an Ecologically Constrained World

Every spring, as the snows melt and the edelweiss blooms, Swiss farmers coax their dairy cows out of the valleys and up into Alpine meadows to graze. In each village, the farmers decide collectively how many cows each farmer can send to the mountain commons. That decision is based on the number of cows the farmer can overwinter, which is, in turn, based on the farmer's valley pasturage and barn space. Overwintering capacity has little connection, if any, to the meadow's grazing capacity but somehow the system works. And it has worked year after year, with no evidence of overgrazing, for at least 500 years. A reasonable candidate, I'd say, for sustainable practice.

In the Lofoten Islands in the far north of Norway, a portion of the cod fishery is set aside for sail-powered boats. Factory trawler ships are prohibited entirely. These Norwegians know perfectly well that modern techniques would bring them greater yields. But they're not so sure modern techniques will ensure them fish for their lifetime and that of their children and grandchildren. Despite repeated attempts by the government to emphasize revenues, the fishermen's primary goal is not maximum yield or profit; it's a secure fishery. The result is a relatively "inefficient" management regime, but one with a track record: 100 years of successful management (two government reviews concluded that it worked and should not be changed) and some 500 years of cod exports to the Mediterranean. Similar stories can be told for long-standing small-scale, inshore fisheries around the world. Again, reasonable candidates for sustainable practice.

On Marajo Island, a large chunk of land in the mouth of the Amazon River, ranchers graze beef cattle on native grasses, getting respectable but not great yields of meat. Nearby, on the mainland, ranchers use modern methods of feeding to produce superior quantities of beef. The land and water in the mainland ranches are degrading, though, making uncertain whether their practices can continue. Meanwhile, the Marajo ranchers are expected to continue their relatively low-yield practices for a long time to come. After all, they've been doing it for some 400 years. Sustainable practice again, it would seem.

Tenant farmers in the Philippines irrigate their fields by damming rivers with sticks and mud. Every year, sometimes two or three times a year, floods wash out the dams. The farmers rebuild after each flood and continue to plant and harvest. They know, and the landowners know, that more permanent structures would do the job better but by some kind of joint decision making they stay with the mud and sticks. The river "wins" but the farmers get their crops, too, again and again, year after year. And they've been doing so, some estimate, for centuries. Yet another candidate, perhaps, for sustainable practice.[1]

Great cases, conservationists might say. But they're so . . . so . . . inefficient. Alpine meadow grazers are hardly the basis of the Swiss economy. Rebuilding stick-and-mud dams—let alone grazing cattle in the middle of the Amazon River—is hardly the stuff of a successfully developing nation. These systems may have persisted for centuries, weathering economic downturns, flood and fire, peace and war, but are they *rational*? Wouldn't well-defined property rights, an effective judicial system, and a thorough marginal analysis of costs and benefits, not to mention some finely tuned technologies, allow them to do better? Wouldn't the Amazon island ranchers get more meat for their efforts, the Norwegian fishers spend less time on icy, storm-plagued Arctic waters?

By conventional standards there is only one rationality. It derives from modern economistic and legalistic thought, forms of reasoning that emphasize the efficient and the judicial. Pick up a journal or textbook in public policy or business administration and chances are it will be replete with such reasoning. Observe a legislature in session or a court hearing, attend a World Trade Organization ministerial meeting or a council of business leaders, and, again, one will find that decisions are judged for their adherence to economic and legal criteria. Does the expected outcome—the new airport, the revised regulation, the trade deal, the next generation of software—make the most efficient use of resources—financial, human and natural? Does it help maximize social welfare or return on investment? Does it respond to consumer preferences as expressed through price? Does it respect property rights and follow the rules set out in law and regulation? Are disputes resolved peacefully? To ask different questions, especially competing questions, to reason otherwise, is quite unimaginable to participants and observers. For that matter, they may ask, why should one reason otherwise? If lawmaking and rule setting are imperfect, they should be improved, not replaced.

Granted, there may be something in other forms of reason, the hard-core realists seem to say, something to strategic calculation, artistic expression, mother's intuition. But the preferred forms, indeed, the higher forms, and necessarily the dominant forms, are those grounded in science and law, bodies of thought that have developed over decades, even centuries, and have contributed more than anything to the progress we see in the world. This is material progress and progress in self-governance, progress fighting disease and eliminating slavery, progress setting universal norms for civilized life. Because a free people, so progressive thought goes, require institutions of open markets and representative democracy, all other forms of reasoning must necessarily be subordinate, interesting perhaps as historic artifacts, as curious representations of a bygone era, but not the stuff of real policymaking, of progress in advanced industrial and postindustrial societies.

I take a different position in this book, what one might term *rational pluralism*. There are many kinds of rationality besides the economistic and legalistic. Just as educators now accept different kinds of intelligence and risk analysts accept different kinds of risk, I contend that people employ different rationalities in their day-to-day personal and professional lives. A priori, no single rationality is superior to another, only better suited to a particular purpose and decision-making setting. Economic rationality is certainly appropriate in the federal banks and labor ministries, in the offices of the bond and commodity traders, especially in countries committed to free enterprise and open markets. Legalistic rationality is appropriate in the courts and legislatures of a constitutional democracy. There, precedence, due process, and constitutionality are uppermost in people's minds. But on the farm and in the fishhouse and at the water authority, as well as in the halls of international climate-change and biodiversity deliberations, a different rationality is appropriate, indeed imperative. In these settings, to promote ecological integrity an appropriate rationality is one attuned to the dynamics of ecological systems. Most importantly, that rationality must be attuned to the peculiarities of the interactions between the two systems, the biophysical and the human.

What makes sense in such settings with respect to the goal of long-term ecological integrity I call *ecological rationality*.[2] Decisions that appear backward or inefficient or wasteful can be, once the reasoning is played out, perfectly reasonable, indeed rational. That rationality assumes that the common good, especially with respect to the "commons" of global climate stability and biodiversity, of local clean water and fertile soil, cannot be achieved by simply aggregating individual private "goods." Adam Smith's "invisible hand" works marvelously for commodities—wheat, vegetable oil, petroleum—and manufactured goods—shoes, cars, computers. And one can generally assume that societal welfare increases as well-informed, competent buyers and sellers voluntarily enter such transactions. But the "good" of environmental public goods is natural capital, the ecosystem services that all economic transactions, all economies, rest on. Just as markets in human vital organs and in children are prohibited because of their threat to individual and societal health, an ecologically rational society resists trade in its foundations, in the material building blocks and structural configurations that undergird that society's economy. An ecologically rational society conditions individual decisions so as to be attentive to ecosystem fragility and to enhance ecosystem resilience, at the same time that its members extract resources and deposit wastes.

In Adam Smith's time, human impact on natural systems was minor or highly localized. There was always another forest to cut, a grassland to plow, a fishery to trawl, always an upstream, an upwind, a place that was "away." That's changed dramatically in the intervening two centuries. Human population, technologies, transportation, and communication have combined to make humans the preeminent force for environmental change on the planet. The world is "full." It is full of humans whose reach extends into every nook and cranny of the planet, from fertile valleys to mountain forests, from deserts to tundra, from the deep ocean to the upper atmosphere. Most significantly, this fullness is creating irreversibilities of immeasurable, indeed unimaginable, long-term effect: species loss, genetic homogenization, topsoil erosion, climate change.

Adam Smith and his immediate followers can hardly be faulted for not foreseeing such massive human impacts. The same cannot be said for those today—policymakers, media leaders, and academics—who witness the massive impacts, yet continue to appropriate Smith's name to champion free markets and unending economic growth (which is tightly coupled with material and energy growth), and dismiss or choose to ignore the ecological fullness. Indeed, in the eyes of contemporary policymakers whose lenses are overwhelmingly economistic and legalistic, little has changed: the answer to economic decline is more consumption, to pollution more technology, to energy shortages more supply. Some value the environment more than others, but their reasoning is essentially the same: Get the prices right. Internalize the external costs. Improve market information. Reduce transaction costs. Enforce property (read, private property) rights. Such is the mantra of mainstream policymaking, from the local to the global, from the North to the South, from business to law to environmental protection.

For such adherents, the reasonableness of ecological rationality, indeed its usefulness, let alone its superiority in particular decision-making settings, will be a hard sell. By contrast, those who interact directly with natural resources—the grazers, the fishers, the ranchers, the irrigators—need no convincing. The rationality of direct users, especially if it is grounded in practice over long periods and entails a dependency on the regeneration of a particular, placed-based resource, is self-evident. Science does not always have the answer for the practitioners; markets do not always offer the "right" price; courts do not always determine what's fair, especially across generations. If these users develop habits of use, rules of thumb, operational procedures and principles, and if the resource persists as they utilize it, we have prima facie evidence that they are employing a rationality tied to the biophysical and social conditions of that resource. In other words, they are employing ecological rationality. And, I assume, it is from such rationality that principles of social organization can be derived, principles that guide practitioners and the policymakers who construct the broader institutional environment for practitioners.[3]

The analytic and prescriptive challenge is to tease out that reasoning, to reveal the assumptions, the understandings, the perceptions that lead to the practice. For some—the Marajo ranchers, perhaps, or my neighbor who gardens for the love of it—that practice will be a simple matter of individual choice. For others, and this is the real concern of this study, it is a *collective choice*, a group or societal effort that establishes norms, principles, rules, and procedures consonant with ecological constraints—the Norwegian fishers and the Swiss and Filipino farmers organizing among themselves, the negotiators of the Montreal Protocol banning ozone-depleting substances, the scientists of the Intergovernmental Panel on Climate Change (IPCC) building the scientific basis of a climate-stabilization regime.

Of course some people will never be convinced. They will cling to empty-world assumptions about resource and waste-sink availability, trusting human technological cleverness to get society out of its predicament. They will act as if such cleverness always trumps another kind of human cleverness, namely, the propensity to highlight and internalize benefits while shading and externalizing costs.[4] Society may only change when the true believers in economistic and legalistic rationality die off, as science historian Thomas Kuhn once observed with respect to paradigm shifts in science. Meanwhile, others, the intended audience for this book, will see the anomalies in current practices and policies, anomalies and contradictions that do not go away, only multiply. They will see that economic growth does not "decouple" from the growth in resource extraction and waste-sink filling, that technological fixes often create yet worse problems, that prices do not reflect long-term, intergenerational scarcity, let alone the system "surprises" that come when biophysical thresholds are exceeded. And more often than not, they will see that administrative rule and court rulings do not challenge prevailing practices and concepts, but reinforce them.

Those who see the anomalies and crave truly new thinking need a language, and some good stories. They need a set of analytic concepts and organizing principles, theoretically sound and empirically grounded. They need to know, intellectually and intuitively, that ecological rationality is legitimate, even preferred in an ecologically full world, in situations where critical environmental values are at risk. As an initial step, I distinguish three approaches to environmental problems—frontier, environmental protection, and sustainability—and show that a complexity perspective is one means, a scientifically oriented means, of conceiving ecological rationality. Experiential knowledge and thermodynamic/ecological notions of value are two more. A long-term orientation is a necessary precondition. Along the way, decision criteria for an ecological rationality emerge.

Just Managing: Three Approaches to Environmental Problems

On a frontier, the environment is the set of resources available for immediate exploitation. The central environmental problem is how to extract the resource in the most profitable manner, including when to cease extraction and move on to the next frontier. Politically, a frontier economy is one devoid of jurisdictional authority. Resource users are those who claim rights but do not need to accept responsibilities for the resource. Resistance by downstream recipients of exported costs is insignificant. Economically, a frontier provides free resources and waste sinks. Equivalently, there is always another frontier to move to when the resource is exhausted. Ecologically, a frontier economy has infinite regenerative capacity or its resources can always be replaced or substituted. Negative feedback (see below) takes the form of financial returns on investment, not ecological costs returning to the user.

At one time, humans inhabited or could readily find such frontiers. Sometimes they had to partially create them by eliminating resistant populations. Using resources for immediate needs or for commerce often meant finding and exploiting such conditions. Arguably, the lure of the frontier has not disappeared. Business strategy with respect to resource use can be viewed as a search for approximations of this ideal. Being competitive means entering resource frontiers early to extract and exiting promptly when political resistance mounts or true costs return. What has changed, however, is the ability of ecosystems and social systems to withstand such use. A little frontier exploitation may not hurt and, in fact, may spur innovation and adaptation. Too much, though, brings irreversible loss and the diminution of essential ecosystem services. Nonresponsibility in a frontier economy becomes irresponsibility in an ecologically constrained economy.

A second approach to managing environmental problems is *environmental protection*. Here the environment is taken as something "out there," something that either provides amenities—clean air and water, wildlife for hunting or viewing, scenic vistas—or is the source of necessary inputs for industrial production—raw materials and energy. Because all human activity has environmental impacts, the central environmental problem is deciding how much impact society will accept to obtain the benefits of economic prosperity. Dealing with environmental problems is thus viewed as a trade-off against other benefits, most notably economic outputs— goods, services, and jobs. The benefits of environmental protection are construed as luxuries, whereas the benefits of human-created values (especially the value added in production) are construed as necessities. Incorporating a "hierarchy-of-needs" notion of human motivation, environmental protection as enhancement of amenities is sought only when basic needs like food, shelter, and clothing are met. Similarly, environmental protection as a contribution to industrial production is pursued only when resource inputs are threatened—timber supplies have dwindled or water is too polluted for residential and industrial use. In such cases, markets do not clear and substitutes do not arise or collective action problems make solutions intractable.

In short, the environmental-protection approach begins with humans' existing patterns of material and energy use and the resource users or managers seek improvements. The users or managers do not challenge the existing political economy. Environmental protection is responsive to strongly expressed public desires (for public parks or for air-pollution control, for instance) and to cost-effective industrial measures (e.g., pollution prevention or green marketing). It is much less responsive to, even resistant to, attempts to change established practices such as logging public lands or trawling open seas or driving private automobiles. And there is always a trade-off, always an exchange rate between social values (e.g., high employment) and ecological values (e.g., the survival of a species). There are no absolutes, no critical ecological values that transcend trade-offs (e.g., irreversibilities such as loss of a species or loading of a heavy metal). One never has too much, just better, better trades at the margin.[5]

The third approach to environmental problems centers on the concept of *sustainability*, a term that can mean many things. Because it has been used to suggest everything from total nature preservation to continuous corporate profits, many analysts and practitioners have rejected it. But as an analytic concept and a policy goal, it does, or can do, what no other term in the environmental realm does. And because a strong and meaningful notion of sustainability is the context for this entire study, the overarching goal to which sufficiency principles apply, I develop it at more length.

Sustainability

Sustainability is a term much used and much abused. With roots in forestry's sustained yield and the international development community's sustainable development, the concept has been debated, conceptualized, and appropriated for sundry concerns. Preservationists use it to describe their plans for permanent parks; city planners and economists for unending growth. One prominent newspaper columnist wrote about sustainable globalization; a planner in my town proclaimed the need for sustainable parking; a nearby concrete company markets sustainable pavement (its permeable components reduce runoff).

The many uses and abuses, the lack of consensus on a single meaning, and the incessant bickering about what sustainability *really* is have led many to give up on the term. As if to throw up their hands in exasperation, they dismiss it as yet another buzzword, a term rendered meaningless through overuse and co-optation.

The uses and abuses indeed seem endless. I will not review the vast literature nor attempt to adjudicate competing claims. I will, though, stake out a position, one both theoretical and normative, one that establishes the goal of ecological rationality and provides the context for the logic of sufficiency.

Sustainability is a "big idea," a global concept that has arisen to meet a contemporary challenge, one unlike anything humanity has faced in the past: global ecological crisis. No other term—conservation, preservation, environmental protection, pollution control, or global environmental management—captures the essence of a meaningful response to that crisis.

Like peace, democracy, progress, and other "big ideas" of modern times, sustainability is broad, overarching, in some respects all-encompassing. And like those other big ideas, sustainability is, quite naturally, debated and constantly adjusted to meet new threats and new understandings. For those of us deeply concerned about environmental trends, especially those entailing irreversibilities, the task is not to get the one right definition. It is to continually refine the idea to meet the threats, especially the novel threats, those like overpopulation and overconsumption that human society has not faced in the past (certainly not on a global scale) and does not fully face now. The central task is to take what is self-evident at two extremes of scale—the limits of ever-expanding activity for the individual and for the planet—and to locate limits in human organization.

It's about at this point in the lecture that my students squirm and wrinkle their brows. One brave soul pipes up: Okay, so what *is* sustainability? I am tempted to give a standard two-handed answer, the kind we academics are so fond of—on the one hand . . . on the other . . . —but I resist. Instead I give them a four-handed answer or, maybe more aptly, a four-pronged answer. For the purpose of guiding ecological decision making I offer these four prongs: establish what is distinctive about sustainability, embed it in complexity theory, connect it to experiential knowledge, and articulate a set of principles for social organization at many levels and in many contexts. That, in a nutshell, is the task of this book. I sketch the first three here, leaving the fourth, a set of sufficiency principles, to other chapters.

Distinctly Sustainable

Sustainability is not mining. My students chuckle at this statement: well, of course! The reasoning, though, is a bit trickier than it appears. Mining will be part of a sustainable society; *what* is mined is the issue.

Consider this thought experiment. I am the first human to traverse a vast desert. Along the way I see a bright nugget of gold. I stoop down, pick it up, and am unavoidably confronted with a stark, binary choice: do I put it back on the ground only to have it covered by the next sandstorm, or do I take it home and work it into a nice gold ring? To leave it there is to forgo all possible value from that gold. To make a ring from it is to enjoy it for my lifetime and to pass it on to my children and grandchildren. To use a gold ring is also to wear down the gold, to send atoms of gold dissipating daily into the environment, never to be recovered by anybody ever again. It is to irreversibly consume the gold, to mine it.

Few of us would have trouble with this binary choice. We would take the gold and then watch it entropically disappear over the years and generations. And in a sustainable society we would do so as we are simultaneously extracting the surplus growth from our forests and fisheries and grasslands. But in an *un*sustainable society, we would mine those resources right along with the minerals, with the gold and iron ore and petroleum. In an *un*sustainable society we would irreversibly change ecosystems, extinguish species, erode soil (beyond its regeneration), and pump groundwater (beyond recharge, allowing geologic cavities to collapse). In a *sustainable* society we would *mine minerals, not renewables*. This is the first distinguishing feature of sustainability.

A second is a *long-term* decision-making orientation. Modern resource managers tend to ignore ecologically relevant time frames, say biological ecologist Crawford S. Holling and political scientist Steven Sanderson. These managers operate "as if change were continuous and predictable, or they think of the world 'in normal times' as the base management state. . . . They expect that what exists now will persist." A short-term orientation makes sense because what is "normal" now—a forest with a thick canopy yet only one species of tree, a river running smoothly, well-contained by dams and dikes, an upper atmosphere that protects us from ultraviolet light yet continues to be bombarded by ozone-depleting substances—is presumed to continue. And working from such a baseline allows further experimentation on natural systems, further attempts to increase human wealth. The expectation of " 'Normal times,' " say Holling and Sanderson,

allows us to ignore the degree to which human intervention itself perverts natural dynamics in ways that may play themselves out beyond the manager's time horizon. . . . The overriding temptation of modern human societies is to maximize for a narrow range of values, so that maximum . . . yield of forest or fishery or rice field forces managers to ignore the importance of long-term successional dynamics, in favor of short-term output.

In a sustainable system, this "management myopia," as Holling and Sanderson call it, gives way to a time frame consonant with biological and physical cycles.[6]

A long-term orientation is thus not just a few more years than the business cycle, not a term or two more than the election cycle. It is periods of time that are ecologically meaningful—several generations of key species, for instance. In the soil that might be a few years, even months, given the reproductive cycles of microorganisms. On the African savanna it might be a century or more given the life span of the elephant, a keystone species. But for most practical purposes, for guiding humans' resource use and management, the life span of one species in particular is most relevant, especially in light of environmental impact: for sustainable use of resources and waste sinks, *human decisions* must be framed in a time scale that spans many *generations of humans*. To accept such a time scale is to construct a normative framework that values future generations and future needs, however unimaginable they may be. It is to build structures that acknowledge the role of discount rates in the financial realm while asserting the role of farsightedness and experiential knowledge and, dare I say, wisdom in the social and ecological realms. It is to graze Alpine meadows and Amazonian grasslands, to fish Arctic waters and irrigate Asian rice fields in ways that respect ecological and managerial constraints over long periods of time.

The choice of a specific number of years is the *time scale*. A strong notion of sustainability goes beyond specific time periods, though. It *frames* time in a way that compels risk-averse decision making with respect to humans' critical, life-sustaining resources. It does so not by choosing a particular number of years, but by orienting to the *indefinite future*. When people write their country's constitution, preserve a work of art, erect a memorial, invest in children, or defend their country's flag, they do not do so for a decade or even a century. They do so for forever, or at least for as long as one can imagine. These are high-value, high-stakes issues for which people risk their lives. They are issues with a certain uniqueness, a quality of irreversibility. Should they be violated, a sense of security and fundamental identity is put at risk.

And so it is with ecosystems, the life-support system of planet earth. Decisions aimed at sustainable practice must, on a daily basis, from the individual to the collective, from the citizen to the polity, be *risk averse with respect to the biophysical underpinnings of life*. The long term as indefinite future is a necessary ingredient, and thus a first-order criterion of ecological rationality.

The third defining feature of sustainability is decision making that aims at the *intersection of the biophysical and social systems*. Conservation, preservation, and pollution control have typically treated the environment as "out there," as an entity to be managed. Whether the goal is high-production yields, pristine nature, or minimized health threats, "the modern organization and management of nature," say Holling and Sanderson, derives "from single equilibrium, short-time horizons, and maximization of ecological system outputs."[7] Humans are set apart from natural systems.

But when the environment "out there" is brought "in here," when decision making is as much about managing human behavior as it is about managing biophysical dynamics, questions of excess become legitimate. Imagine a fertile river bottom when it is first brought under the plow, producing crop yields that exceed all prior experience. If such yields are good for the farmer and for the consumer, then, according to the conventional wisdom of a "productive" economy, more must be better; there can be no such thing as too much. Squeezing ever more product out of a hectare of that bottomland becomes the name of the game. To ask if, in so doing, the soil itself is jeopardized is to ask not just about productive capacity but about human practice—farming techniques and consumer preferences, say. It is to ask about humans' twin desires to want more now and to want some in the future, too. It is to ask not just about maximum gain now, but gain now *and* into the future, the far future, many years or decades or, with high-stakes items like soil fertility, the indefinite future. Bringing the environment "in here" is to ask about sufficiency.

The Complexly Adaptive

Sustainability has little meaning when a mechanistic and reductionist perspective is taken, the worldview underlying economistic and legalistic reasoning. In this view, the world is a complicated machine: it's billiard balls bouncing off each other distributing energy and creating material form. A bit of study, especially mathematical study, the kind that fits things into solvable linear equations, allows one to predict just about anything: a ball will roll down the board in this direction with this acceleration; a carbohydrate will yield these calories with oxidation; a tree will grow so high with so many board feet with these amounts of light and nutrients. And when all is predictable (or nearly so, short of the right data and models), all is also controllable: human interventions into natural systems can be designed to enhance human values.[8]

But when the world is not so viewed, when the world is seen as a complex adaptive system, one that has multiple interconnections and many equilibrium states, one that changes discontinuously, predictability is highly limited, sometimes impossible.[9] "There are points in any system's development where several possible directions of radical change are open," write systems analysts James J. Kay and Eric Schneider, "and it is not possible to predict, with certainty, which one will occur." And, then, when interactions accumulate, predictability is even more difficult. Advances in meteorology have led to vast amounts of data feeding into sophisticated computer models. Yet weather forecasts are still limited to about five days. The dynamics of land, water, air, and biological activity accumulate, creating chaotic behavior of such proportions that no amount of data or sophistication of modeling can capture it. "Computers cannot substitute for crystal balls," say Kay and Schneider, "except for very limited classes of problems that occur over short spatial and temporal dimensions."[10] For ecological rationality, it is precisely the *long* spatial and temporal dimensions that are of interest.

These, then, are the space and time dimensions of complexity. The energy dimension adds organization—from the cellular to the social. Information, especially in the form of feedback loops, is a fourth dimension. Together they assure a system's maintenance and adaptiveness.

The second law of thermodynamics states that energy dissipates and systems tend to run down. But an open system with high-quality energy inputs (low entropy) resists this tendency; it self-organizes. It "responds with the spontaneous emergence of organized behavior that uses the high quality energy to maintain its structure, thus dissipating the ability of the high quality energy to move the system away from equilibrium," write Kay and Schneider. "As more high quality energy is pumped into a system, more organization emerges to dissipate the energy."[11] In the emergence of organized behavior, abrupt change is the norm. The change can take any number of paths, however, which one being an "accident of circumstances." Predictability, once again, is highly limited.[12]

It is from these three aspects of complex systems—time, space, and energy—that one of the most important implications for human interventions into ecosystems emerges. It is an implication that leads directly to the sufficiency principle. Self-organizing systems, write Kay and Schneider,

exist in a situation where they get *enough* energy, but *not too much*. If they do not get sufficient energy of high enough quality (beyond a minimum threshold level), organized structures cannot be supported and self-organization does not occur. If too much energy is supplied, chaos ensues in the system, as the energy overwhelms the dissipative ability of the organized structures and they fall apart. So self-organizing systems exist in a middle ground of *enough, but not too much*.[13]

Change is inherent in complex adaptive systems. But to have integrity, to be self-sustaining, systems must find that *middle ground*, that in-between position of enough but not too much. Put differently, such systems (and, by implication, those who would intervene in such systems) "do not maximize or minimize their functioning."[14] To push a component of the system to its maximum, to spin a wheel at its fastest speed, to reduce forest tree species to only those that have commercial value, to pump water just as fast as the estimated recharge, is to make such systems "brittle," vulnerable to disturbance, and likely to "flip" into a degraded state. A system has integrity, resilience, and adaptiveness when each factor varies within a comfortable range, only rarely exceeding that range. An animal's heart beats rapidly in a fight-or-flight response to a threat; its heart can also lumber along during sleep or hibernation. But if the animal functions at either extreme for long, if its adrenaline pumps constantly (a caribou pursued for hours by a pack of wolves) or it lies about day after day (a zoo specimen), the system deteriorates—or it requires more input, more energy, more nutrients, more protection, more technical fixes. In short, systems must allow for occasional activity at the extremes yet, at the same time, they need mechanisms that keep activity mostly within the safe range. Like governors on a flywheel that automatically engage when the wheel exceeds its safe speed, systems must have built-in mechanisms of *restraint* to keep in the safe range, to operate in the middle ground. Such mechanisms depend on a system's ability to store and channel information, the fourth dimension of complex adaptive systems.

From cells to species, genes convey information within and across levels of self-organization and across generations. Biodiversity is the information database. Humans have an additional databank, culture—skills, histories, and morals, for instance. These information mechanisms, shaped by the particular contexts in which they arose, are "historical track record[s] of success," say Kay and Schneider.[15] They evoke time horizons that reach far back in the organism's evolved history and, with an absence of catastrophic external events, extend into the future. They are inherently long term. A mechanistic perspective, by contrast, tends to be short term, even atemporal. Management myopia is the norm when human-made, mechanistic, and reductionist knowledge dominates.

So if cells, organisms, and ecosystems are to maintain themselves and adapt, these records must be conserved, not held fixed as if suspended in time, but kept as critical, yet ever-changing banks of knowledge. Interventions that compromise such knowledge banks threaten those systems, just as thieves threaten personal security by stealing one's life savings or "thought police" threaten cultural identity by banning books. For all the adaptiveness and resilience of complex systems, they are vulnerable when their information storehouses are tampered with, when their genetic, species, and cultural diversity is upset. "The wildly varied stock of DNA, evolved and accumulated over billions of years," writes systems analyst Donella Meadows, "is the source of evolutionary potential, just as science libraries and labs and scientists are the source of technological potential. Allowing species to go extinct is a systems crime, just as randomly eliminating all copies of particular science journals, or particular kinds of scientists, would be."[16]

Besides information storage, complex systems require information that feeds back on the system to maintain system stability and, at the same time, to enable change. Positive feedback loops are self-reinforcing mechanisms. "The more babies are born," writes Meadows, "the more people grow up to have babies. The more money you have in the bank the more interest you earn, the more money you have in the bank. The more soil erodes, the less vegetation it can support, the fewer roots and leaves to soften rain and runoff, the more soil erodes." Sometimes positive feedback loops are needed for growth or colonization. But unchecked, they destroy a system. They "drive explosion, erosion, and collapse," Meadows says. Slowing them, reducing their positive gains ("positive" in a value-neutral sense, that is) allows negative feedback loops to kick in. A thermostat sends a signal to the furnace to fire up or shut down, maintaining a comfortable range of room temperatures. The signal is negative with respect to the temperature extremes.

In complex adaptive systems self-correcting loops may be inactive much of the time. The emergency cooling system in a nuclear reactor is rarely used. Those of us living in cold regions who have "climate control" in our buildings and cars rarely shiver. An endangered species doesn't appear in danger of extinction as long as zoos keep some breeding pairs alive.[17] Interveners—resource managers, recreationalists, developers—can be unaware of such "latent" feedback loops, or choose to ignore them. A coastal sand spit shifts once a century, when high tides and severe storms coincide. But people build vacation homes there anyway. When they get the feedback from the coastal system, when that rare storm hits, the message to the human system is, in effect, permanent structures do not last on shifting sandbars. It is a message that often comes too late. The social system responds, at best, with disaster-relief payments. A temperate forest withstands decades of clear-cut logging and monospecies replantings. Then a bark-beetle infestation wipes out the entire forest. Information about the need for a diversity of insect-eating birds and a multitude of noncommercial tree species is needed to maintain the system and allow it to adapt to the beetles. Once again, the signal comes too late and, after all, says the land manager, there's nothing one can do about such "natural disasters." City officials build expressways when they see commuters and shoppers stuck in traffic jams. Years later crime in the neighborhoods severed by the expressways forces people to the suburbs. Urban blight "just happens," officials say. They hadn't noticed that, before the expressway, the community, as a high-integrity system, did a lot of its own policing, and did so by its sheer vibrancy, by its residents' concern for neighbors and for the identity of the neighborhood. School officials consolidate schools, closing the little ones, building big, centralized ones so as to make efficient use of building space. Years later, they find that big schools foster delinquency and truancy and that transportation costs are prohibitively expensive.

In the short term we see no effect from doing these things. Why not make the best use of coastal resources? Why allow weed trees to compete with commercial trees? Why leave curves in the road when cars could pass more freely on a straight road without obstructions? Why not fill up every classroom seat? And why have redundant administrative services with lots of little schools?

The "weed trees" and "obstructions" and "redundant services" are seen as inefficiencies. In a society committed to efficiency principles (chapters 3 and 4), cutting out the superfluous, the wasteful makes perfectly good sense: eliminate waste, capture efficiencies, and social welfare increases. In an ecologically rational society, though, one attuned to the connections, to the possibility of unintended consequences, eliminating the apparent inefficiencies can be downright dangerous. "One of the biggest mistakes we make," Meadows says, "is to strip away these emergency response mechanisms because they aren't often used and they appear to be costly. . . . In the long term, we narrow the range of conditions over which the system can survive."[18]

To strip away response mechanisms is to deny or negate negative feedback loops, critical information flows from the biophysical system to the social system, signals of stress on critical variables, portents of looming system change, of "flipping" into a degraded state, of collapse. Open-seas fisheries are overfished because there is no effective negative feedback from the state of the fish population to the decision makers who invest in vessels and nets. Aquifers are drawn down because the information that irrigators do receive—a lowered water table—only encourages drilling deeper wells. To increase fishing effort as stocks diminish, to drill deeper as the water table lowers may make perfectly good economic (and legal) sense: the boat owners get positive returns on their investments; the irrigators get a profitable crop with the water. But from a systems perspective, this is risky behavior. And the risks are far from abstract. Compromised system functioning translates into compromised livelihood. To take such risks may be necessary for survival. But it can also be a form of arrogance, a disregard, even contempt, for others' ability to earn a living or to experience a high-integrity natural system regardless of its extraction value.

The Experiential

Human intervention into ecosystems is necessary for human survival, of course. But from a complexity view and with the goal of long-term sustainable use, caution, temperance, and humility are the bywords that logically accompany such interventions. The complexity view is, to be sure, an abstract construction. Yet, by its derived notions of limited predictability and limited manipulatability, it parallels that of other knowledge bases, those derived from experience—experience tilling the land, hauling the nets, felling the trees, channeling the irrigation water. The sentiments of a farmer in Long Island, New York, one whose family has been working the same 150 or so acres for some 14 generations, is illustrative.

Asked how his practice of farming differs from that of, say, the Iowa farmer with several thousand acres of corn and soybeans, he thought for a moment, then replied:

"I can't control everything. It seems like the big producers, the agribusiness folks, think they can" (personal communication).

This farmer grows over a dozen crops. He knows he's not as productive growing pears as the guy down the road who grows nothing but pears. But when pears are down, when a blight hits or demand dries up or the market is glutted, he has other crops, some of which may be bountiful and in demand the very same year pears are down. In short, he isn't maximizing or minimizing, not squeezing the most crop off an acre, and probably not cutting corners on green manure or fallow either. He senses vulnerabilities in his "environment"—the soil, the water, the product markets, his suppliers and competitors, the economy as a whole—and achieves a degree of security with a diversified portfolio of crops. He exercises caution in his interventions. His approach to the land is not one of mastery, but of careful husbandry.

A sixth-generation fisherman in Maine had a similar view regarding lobstering and what he called "real fishing," as we will see in chapter 7. When the lobster season first opens, all the boats bring in large catches. The lobsters have had a six-month reprieve, they have grown into their new shells, and they are hungry. Anyone can fill a lobster car in no time by just getting the traps in the water and hauling. This is probably akin to what the early European settlers found when they arrived: an abundant frontier resource just waiting to be exploited. Fishing was more like gathering in virgin territory. It took little skill, just some effort. But then, after a few weeks of such bonanzas, the catches diminish. This, explains the veteran lobsterman with emphasis, is when the *real fishing* begins. This is when knowledge of bottom conditions is crucial, as well as the lobsters' movement patterns, the currents and water temperatures, and a host of other factors. A long-time lobster fisher picks up signals from the depth sounders, from the flow of water, from patterns of catches along a string of traps. One does not acquire such knowledge overnight, let alone from formal instruction or books. It is acquired from years, even decades, of being on the water, making a living from fishing and from the know-how passed down from one generation to the next. What's more, it is knowledge acquired by paying close attention—something efficient extractors, people in a rush, are unlikely to do.

The farmer's and fisher's experiential knowledge, derived from lifetimes of practice and from generations of passed-down wisdom, converges with the abstract, mathematically grounded theories of adaptive complexity. The two forms of knowledge overlap precisely where worldview emerges, where attitudes and orientations to the land, to living systems, to the world of material and energy come together. Limited predictability and manipulatability lead, on the one hand, to limited control over nature and markets and world events and, on the other, toward a profound sense of humility. It is a sentiment perfectly natural to these otherwise disparate communities, the theoreticians and the practitioners, the modelers and the tillers.

When humility is brought to bear on critical resource issues, ecological rationality tends to follow. Seasonal harvests, fallow fields, technological limits, days of rest are concrete measures. Rational decision making is not so much managing the biophysical system, extracting all available fiber, using every drop of water, racking up record yields. It is accepting the limitations of complex systems and hence the potential of human interventions; it is husbandry, managing one's interventions with an eye on the distant past and on the far future, all with respect for both the resilience and the vulnerability of those systems. It is, in a word, *self-management*. Kay and Schneider sum up the significance of complexity and ecosystem management:

> Systems theory suggests that ecosystems are inherently complex, that there may be no simple answers, and that our traditional managerial approaches, which presume a world of simple rules, are wrong-headed and likely to be dangerous. In order for the scientific [mechanistic, reductionist] method to work, an artificial situation of consistent reproducibility must be created. This requires simplification of the situation to the point where it is controllable and predictable. But the very nature of this act removes the complexity that leads to emergence of the new phenomena which makes complex systems interesting. If we are going to deal successfully with our biosphere, we are going to have to change how we do science and management. We will have to learn that *we don't manage ecosystems, we manage our interaction with them*.[19]

Science from a complexity perspective and husbandry from an experiential perspective lead to attitudes of respect and humility. In an ecologically constrained world, the sustainability challenge is no longer to manipulate the nonhuman world for maximum human gain. Such gains tend to highlight the near-term benefits while shading the long-term costs. Select groups within present generations reap the bounties while others, present and future, bear the burdens. To practice self-management is to seek mechanisms of restraint. One such mechanism is *problem absorption*, another *buffering*.

Problem Absorption and Buffering

Besides evoking caution and the need to self-manage, ecological rationality implies that all environmental problems are, in some sense, both local and global. With ecological frontiers unavailable, a society's attempt to develop by constantly exploiting resources and moving on bumps up against others' attempts to do likewise. Similarly, attempts to solve one's waste problem by sending it away eventually engenders resistance from those downriver or downwind. Protecting the environment by reducing a pollutant or saving a species often means that the pollutant is transferred to another medium (e.g., from land to air to water) or another species becomes threatened (e.g., a charismatic mammal such as the dolphin is protected, while so-called trash fish are ignored to the detriment of the functioning of the food web).[20] When everything is connected and the planet is finite, seemingly local activities cannot depend on an infinite supply of "other places" nor on an "away" to throw wastes. To truly solve an environmental problem is to *absorb the problem*, not displace it.

When a town's aquifer no longer satisfies growing demands for water, the town doesn't look for new supplies, an untapped aquifer (in a "full world" there are none) or a nearby river. Rather, to contribute to a sustainable society, indeed to be ecologically rational, it looks for ways to develop within the regenerative capacity of its own aquifer. When a near-shore fishery declines, fishers don't move to the next harbor (it's fished, too). Rather, they find ways to reduce fishing pressure. When a timber company can't buy more timberland to feed its mills, it sets milling capacity at a level supportable by existing timberland. When a city's traffic is so heavy that gridlock is a daily occurrence, it doesn't build more parking garages but reduces the incentives for easy access to city center (which may include *reducing* parking). Problem absorption becomes a necessary condition of sustainable practice and thus a decision criterion for ecological rationality.

Buffering is another condition. Human interventions, as noted, are risky but necessary. Arguably any human activity beyond hunting and foraging constitutes an intervention, a manipulation of biophysical systems beyond skimming the surplus as all foragers and predators do.[21] *Buffers* stabilize systems even as interventions push variables toward their extremes. One kind of buffer is a big stock. "Consider a bathtub," writes systems analyst Meadows. "Now think about a small one with fast flows. That's the difference between a lake and a river. You hear about catastrophic river floods much more often than catastrophic lake floods, because stocks that are big, relative to their flows, are more stable than small ones. A big stabilizing stock is a buffer."[22]

Another kind of buffer is a cushion. An endangered species needs more than a few breeding pairs to avoid extinction. A shoe store needs more than today's expected sales on its shelves to be profitable. The extra is not an inefficiency, a waste; nor is it excess capacity or an extravagance. It's insurance, "money in the bank." It's what prevents overshoot, what reduces the possibility of irreversible decline, what enhances stability when interventions are unavoidably destabilizing.

Because the physical stocks in many systems (bathtub, river or lake water, for instance) are given, literally cast in concrete in the case of a dam, the leverage point for system stability or system change is in the design of the system in the first place. Farming on prairie sod, siting a solid-waste facility, or erecting a skyscraper must all self-consciously build in buffers, large stocks and cushions. To maximize anything—crop yield, tons of garbage disposed, building height—is to invite catastrophe by engendering vulnerabilities. Once such interventions are locked in place—the sod is broken, the facility sited, the skyscraper erected—"the leverage," says Meadows, "is in understanding its limitations and bottlenecks and refraining from fluctuations or expansions that strain capacity."[23]

Maximization in this context thus makes little sense, nor does efficiency if by efficiency the intervener means squeezing out every last bit of human use. To maximize a timber harvest one pushes for maximum sustained yield, rolling the ecological dice in effect, hoping that the 100-year flood or the once-in-a-lifetime infestation of bark beetles will not occur. To maximize water withdrawals one estimates the recharge rate and pumps that amount, even more in some years when needs are great. And then, hope against hope, one prays that drought will not come, and that, to restore the aquifer, users will be content to cut back.

To maximize, to push to the limits, is to deny the role of buffers. It is to act as if all is a machine: use it to its utmost and when it breaks just fix it, get new parts, or find another machine. Maximization does make sense in a mining operation: get every last bit of mineral from a vein of ore.[24] And it may make sense in an environmental-protection effort: get the most fiber possible off each hectare while protecting streamside habitat. But sustainable practice requires a balancing act among a suite of ecological elements—nutrient cycles, water cycles, plant and animal populations. Push one nutrient below a threshold, one species beyond what predators or parasites can keep in check, and the system, along with the hoped-for maximized value, deteriorates. To maximize is to act as if all values can be reduced to a single measure. Under economistic and legalistic reasoning, that measure tends to be money. Ecological reasoning demands a plurality of values, including the immeasurables of ecosystem functioning.

Value

A rationality ultimately makes trade-offs between competing values. The values that enter the calculus are determined by the policy goal and one's worldview. Economistic reasoning aims at economic growth and efficient allocation, legalistic at justice and due process. In the contemporary political economy both hold an "empty-world" view of the world: resources and waste sinks are abundant or substitutable. The challenge for resource managers is to make the best use of available resources and sinks in accordance with rules and procedures legislated and adjudicated by duly chosen officials. In practice, difficult trade-offs between, say, economic investment and social safety nets, or between international trade and local autonomy, are resolved through growth. A bigger pie benefits all, however unequally.

Ecological reasoning by contrast aims at long-term resource use, at the integrity of ever-changing biophysical systems over periods of time that span many human generations. The worldview is "full world," a world so dominated by one species (*Homo sapiens*) that life support for that species and others cannot be assumed.[25]

To play out ecological rationality in the context of an ecologically constrained world, then, is to construe value in ways that the economistic and legalistic approaches are incapable of doing. The ecological focus is on the *material*, the biophysical basis of social organization. But the value is not just that which obtains in market transactions (price) or judgments rendered (damages). Consider uninhabited, virgin tropical forests, which have few soil nutrients and yield wood pulp for paper making just as do temperate forests, where soil nutrients are abundant and readily replaced. The two ecosystems and, hence, their ecological values are hardly the same. The pulp may be the most visible manifestation of the resource, but it does not reveal the full range of services—ecological and human—that contribute to the generation of that resource. To derive a final decision criterion for ecological rationality, I compare the economistic perspective of resource value with a thermodynamic and ecological perspective.

From an economistic, factor-input perspective, value attaches to an item like wood when humans apply labor, capital, and technology. A tree is a resource and thus useful only when it becomes lumber or pulp. By contrast, from a thermodynamic perspective, value inheres in an item whenever entropy is lowered, when order increases, when high-quality energy enters a system and that system resists dissipation by self-organizing.[26] Photosynthesis combines high-entropy H_2O and CO_2 to form low-entropy cellulose. The tree grows and, when growth ceases, it maintains itself. Moreover, the ecological component of this "value added"—that is, the *systems* component—is the dependence of such low entropy on a complex set of functions supplied not just by the tree but by the entire forest ecosystem. The ecosystem's ability to create low-entropy cellulose over the long term depends on its *integrity as a forest ecosystem*. Such integrity includes the ability to adapt to disturbance without flipping irreversibly into simpler degraded systems, as when cutover forests on weak soils convert to scrubland without forest regeneration.[27]

So the value of low-entropy material such as wood depends in part on an *organism's functioning* (a tree photosynthesizing) and in part on that particular *ecosystem's functioning* (the forest components interacting, as well as creating, storing, and transmitting information, all functioning as a high-integrity, complex adaptive system). The true, ecologically nuanced value of a resource is, first, that derived from ecosystem functioning and, second, that derived from human application. What's more, every resource is, to some extent, uniquely constituted by the particular combination of the ecosystem and the human application.

A resource-management regime has no ecological content if all that varies is the human interactions—that is, the interactions of humans with each other (buying and selling, for instance) or the human interactions with the resource at the point where human-induced value has been added (logging and milling, for example). To take an ecosystem perspective, the analyst and manager must ask, first, how is low entropy achieved and, second, how are the means—ecological and human—accounted for in decision making. Put as a proposition, if the decision making within the resource regime accords primacy to the human sources of value and thus relegates ecological processes—organismic and ecosystemic—to the periphery, the resource is likely to be overused. The dominance of humans' contribution to value via labor, technology, and capital leads to a devaluation of the ecological contribution of value. When the ecological value approaches zero, we are back to a frontier where short-term expediency—mining—prevails over long-term stewardship.

Resource primacy thus becomes a decision criterion for ecologically rational managers and policymakers. Economic calculation still pertains in the product chain from initial resource extraction to final consumption and disposal. But that chain of decisions and exchanges rests fundamentally on low entropy, on ecosystem integrity, on natural capital. Put differently, the goal of *sustainability is advanced only when managers explicitly account for the intersection of the biophysical and social systems*, not just the social and certainly not just the economic within the social systems, which is conventional practice. Sustainability is advanced when negative feedback from the biophysical system (e.g., a decline in particular species) crosses to the social system and elicits an appropriate response (e.g., reduced human use).

The science of ecological rationality—complexity theory—is one that leads to very unscientific notions like humility and caution, much as the experiential knowledge

Table 2.1
Ecological rationality

	Management	Policy
Goals	economic security; surplus value; long-term resource use	high-integrity, material life-support systems; ecological resilience
Conditions	overharvesting; depletion; waste accumulation; incomplete pricing; hidden costs; unchecked positive feedback	environmental criticality—irreversibility and nonsubstitutability; limited regenerative capacities—resources and waste sinks; overconsumption; excess throughput; unchecked positive feedback

Decision criteria:

- long-term orientation—intergenerational, multiple cycles, indefinite future
- resource primacy
- middle-ground operation
- information preservation
- negative feedback
- problem absorption
- buffering

Decision making for the purpose of sustainable resource use and with respect to critical environmental problems follows criteria attuned to behavioral tendencies and biophysical constraints. These criteria derive from knowledge systems based on theories of complex adaptive systems or on experiential knowledge or both. The scope of decision making is either managerial (managers and users interacting directly with the resource) or political (policymakers setting institutional rules and norms for managers).

of long-standing resource users does. Features of resilient complex systems like middle-ground operation, information conservation, and negative feedback lead to mechanisms like problem absorption and buffering. Resource primacy and long-term orientation govern valuation. These are decision criteria for resource managers. They are the basis of ecologically rational self-management. By rejecting frontier mining and environmental protection as approaches to critical environmental problems, they compel examination of a suite of values, social and biophysical, that extend into the indefinite future (table 2.1).

A More Rational World

Political theorist John S. Dryzek first developed the idea of ecological rationality in a 1987 book titled *Rational Ecology: Environment and Political Economy*, referring in the first instance to the rationality of ecosystems. "An ecologically rational *natural* system is one whose low entropy is manifested in an ability to cope with stress or perturbation, so that such a structure can consistently and effectively provide itself with the good of life support."[28] From this he developed an "anthropogenic life-support approach" emphasizing "basic human interests" as a means of competing with other forms of functional rationality, which he identified as economic, social, legal, and political rationalities.[29] In so doing, he emphasized the intersection of human and biophysical systems, the primary approach taken in this chapter.

Dryzek's book, arguably the most important work on the social-choice processes of sustainability, has been largely neglected, overshadowed it seems by the state-of-the-environment tomes, the critiques, and the pleas for environmentally correct behavior. That neglect may owe to Dryzek's contention that ecosystems have their own rationality, "that, *in the absence of human interests*, ecological rationality may be recognized in terms of an ecosystem's provision of life support to itself."[30] This is a hard conceptual pill to swallow even for scientists who see great order in the universe, let alone for those who are sensitive to circular reasoning. The neglect of Dryzek's work may also owe to the generality of his decision criteria—negative feedback, coordination, robustness, flexibility, resilience—and his failure to convincingly ground his theorizing in practice.

Most likely, though, that neglect owes to the fact that social scientists and the policymakers who employ social science reasoning see no need for an alternative rationality. Economic and legal rationalities prevail in public discourse for good reason. They guide the use of resources to their most efficient ends; they follow rules known to all and deemed fairest for all. They have contributed more than anything to the progress in the world of the last couple of centuries. As a result, economistic and legalistic forms of reasoning have become hegemonic, so pervasive, so exclusive that few question their appropriateness, even in seemingly novel arenas like environmental management and sustainability.

If Dryzek failed to arouse social scientists, he fared even worse with hard scientists and the managers and policymakers who follow their advice. They too see little need for an alternative rationality. For them, good data and political will are what is in short supply. I am convinced, though, that time will right their wrongs, that the need for an alternative rationality will become all but self-evident. The biophysical trends from the local to the global are just too compelling, the anomalies in contemporary discourse too numerous. Yes, adherents of the hegemonic rationalities may have to die off. But those coming along are precisely those who will be paying the price of a century of displaced costs. They will see that the desire for data and political will are desires that only obscure unsustainable practices. The newcomers will crave alternative rationalities, forms of reasoning that are at least as sensible as economistic and legalistic reasoning and yet are attuned to ecological constraint.

So it is a task of this book to show just how rational ecological rationality is, how logical the organizing principles (sufficiency and others) are, how moral a moral economy is that preserves the biophysical underpinnings of its material economy. It is to show that Alpine meadow grazers and Norwegian fishers and Amazonian ranchers and Filipino irrigators are not quaint throwbacks to bygone eras, but highly sensible adapters to complex environments. It is to show that such resource users, far from being at the margins of modern life, are actually at the forefront, especially when "modern" includes the contemporary ecological predicament. It is to show that their experiential knowledge dovetails with an ascendant scientific perspective—complexity theory—to generate insights into sustainable practice.

Here, in part I, I do this via the nature of work and consumption (chapter 5) and, in part II, with detailed case histories. But first I have to expose an emperor. In the next two chapters I undress *efficiency*, the ruling concept of economistic and much of legalistic reasoning. Its history is one of ever-increasing political appropriation, its technics of muddled application, its effects of thwarting sufficiency.

3

Efficiency: A Brief and Curious History

The efficiency of an engine is the proportion which the energy permanently transformed to a useful form by it bears to the whole energy communicated to the working substance.
—W. J. M. Rankine, 1855[1]

The one element more than any other which differentiates civilized from uncivilized countries—prosperous from poverty-stricken peoples—is that the average man in the one is five or six times as productive as the other.
—Frederick Winslow Taylor, 1911[2]

Industrial economies are becoming more efficient in their use of materials, but waste generation continues to increase.
—World Resources Institute, 2000[3]

Societies across time and across cultures organize themselves to use resources. They extract, process, and consume, then they dispose of the wastes. In so doing, they devise rules and procedures guided by general principles. The most prevalent principle has been, and arguably continues to be, power. Those who command the armies, amass the gold, and write the rules get the resources, and it is they who decide who gets what's left. But other social organizing principles have accompanied power, sometimes displacing it, sometimes concealing it. Caste and class determine one's allocation according to one's position in life, whether gained by the karma of rebirth or inheritance. Divine right dictates that those ordained by god must have the resources to do the work of god. Expansion guides exploration, conquest, and conversion, establishing them as noble and worthy enterprises.

Today, the dominant companion principle is efficiency. Extraction, use, and disposal are driven by a calculation of output per unit of input. If cutting trees in 1,000-acre blocks is efficient—that is, if more trees can be cut per day or per worker or per unit of invested capital—such clear-cutting supersedes selective logging. If lopping off the tops of mountains is the cheapest means of getting out coal, deep-shaft mining is abandoned. If mile-long drift nets catch more fish per vessel per voyage, smaller nets and long lines are jettisoned. If a construction company can buy brand-new wooden concrete forms cheaper than it can clean and reuse its old forms, it dumps the new forms after a single use in the nearest landfill.

Efficiency as an idea, an intuitive notion, is age-old. It has arguably informed—or is inherent in—biological and cultural evolution. An individual who extracts more resources for a given effort is more likely to survive, to reproduce, and, hence, to pass on its genetic and cultural traits, including the propensity to seek efficiencies. But the fact that efficiency seeking has made sense for individuals and groups from time immemorial only suggests that it is one of many competing ideas governing behavior. Only when humans organized themselves to extract resources on a large scale for industrial production in the late nineteenth and early twentieth centuries did this particular idea ascend to the status of dominant managerial principle. And then only with mass production and mass consumption did it achieve the status of a broad, pervasive social organizing principle. Efficiency evolved, we will see, from a philosophical element of causation to a mechanical means of measuring to a business principle and, finally, to an overarching social and personal goal.

Having become nearly synonymous with "productive" or "useful," even "good," efficiency has spilled into nearly all realms of modern life. Thus, the central proposition of this chapter is that, in principle and in practice, efficiency seeking thwarts other principles, including sufficiency; it does so by elevating a perfectly commonsensical idea to a dominant social principle, unquestioned and unquestionable. It has become a social goal in its own right, equating with all that is desirable, and then used selectively to promote agendas often unrelated to true efficiency gains.

How did this particular principle ascend? Why not others? Why did it spill into other realms and achieve such exalted status? And why is such ascendancy, indeed, such dominance, dangerous in an ecologically constrained world? To answer these questions it is necessary to turn back the clock on the term itself and catch what linguistic strands exist, recognizing along the way that a comprehensive intellectual history of efficiency has yet to be written. Having laid out such a tentative history, we can then proceed in chapter 4 to current usages, technical and political. From there the purposes of work and the logic of the consumer economy can be elaborated (chapter 5).

A Neat Ratio

If *efficiency* first came into common use in the Middle Ages, as the *Oxford English Dictionary* implicitly suggests (the dictionary's earliest entry is from the sixteenth century), its appropriators had likely turned to the Greeks, Aristotle in particular, for inspiration. Causation, Western tradition has had it, is the key to wisdom, to understanding reality. "Men do not think that they know a thing till they have grasped the 'why' of it," Aristotle wrote long ago. He went on to develop four conceptually distinct and essential causes for rational human use of material resources. In building a house, for instance, there is *causus finalis* (the desire or goal of having a home), *causus formalis* (the blueprint for the house), *causus materialis* (the wood or stone), and *causus efficiens* (the carpenter's labor and tools). The house building would be "caused" by all these. But the house building would be "efficient" if there was an effective match of carpentry skills and tools to the task at hand. It would not be efficient if a stonemason with chisel and trowel had to cut and fit mortise-and-tenon joints in oak beams. The speed of such labor is not the issue, nor is the cost; the fit, the appropriateness of the construction, the *effectiveness* of the builder and of the process of building is.[4]

This equation of efficiency with effectiveness, with the efficacious accomplishment of a task, with the successful achievement of an intended purpose, appears to have persisted through the Middle Ages. It apparently suited those who set the rules, who amassed the fortunes and marshaled the armies, who organized the daily lives of the masses. But a new set of "rulers" emerged in the eighteenth and nineteenth centuries and with them a new linguistic need. These were the people who tinkered with machines and the people who, with entrepreneurial spirit and the daring to upset the established feudal order, transformed the tinkers' contraptions into wealth. The emergent linguistic need was for a term that could capture such industrial magic, a term that combined the best of science and engineering and, soon, economics. Needed was a term that could tell the world that the mechanical clock and the steam engine and the McCormick reaper and the grain elevator were better than their predecessors. Needed was a term that could show that such devices could rightly replace the beasts of burden and relieve the human sweat and toil, all to make life not just more productive, but better, and better for ruler and commoner alike.

The linguistic branch carrying *efficiency*, *effectiveness*, and *efficaciousness* from ancient times through the Middle Ages thus forked. Coincident with the steam engine, great advances in the physical sciences, and an expanding market system,

efficiency became, according to one 1827 usage, "the work done by a force in operating a machine or engine." Construed as work, it is "the total energy expended by
a machine." More than just work performed, though, *efficiency* took on a relative
notion, it became a *ratio* of a desired result, such as light, to an unavoidable constraint, such as electrical power: "the ratio of the total luminous flux produced to
the total power consumed," for instance.[5]

What's more, the ratio was expressed *quantitatively*. Effectiveness, goal achievement, the neat fit of means and ends slipped away as numbers were invoked to
measure, indeed, to define, efficiency. Though apparently first employed only in the
mid-nineteenth century, this technical usage—a ratio of measurable work (motion,
lift, physical or chemical transformation) to measurable constraints (applied
energy)—continues today in engineering, improving machine performance, for
instance, getting more miles for a gallon of gasoline in an internal combustion engine
mounted on a chassis with four wheels. It was then but a simple transformational
step for economists to convert the notions of work and constraint into the notion
of trade-off in market transactions: efficient solutions to problems of production
are those that improve a benefit-to-cost ratio for producer or consumer. An economic efficiency lowers "the cost per unit of output, without sacrifice of quality, in
relation to the value or price of the finished article."[6] The shift to a market economy
is a well-told story but curiously one that, to my knowledge, is mute about the transformation of efficiency from its Aristotelian and physical roots (effectiveness and
mechanical work) to an economic mantra.

A Thoroughly Modern Invention

Until roughly the mid-seventeenth century, industry in Europe was mostly craft
based. Production occurred in homes or small shops. But with growing population,
technological advances, and the relaxation of norms and laws against acquisitive-
ness, production of goods and services became ever more specialized. Land, labor,
and capital became commodities, transferable items with a price. In short, a market
system evolved. The trading of goods became increasingly institutionalized, concentrated in the factory rather than in the home. By the close of the seventeenth
century the stage was set for large-scale industrial manufacturing and capital
accumulation.[7]

Adam Smith's *Wealth of Nations*, originally published in 1776, not only captured
this move toward market-led industrial production but simultaneously laid a conceptual foundation for a rationalized, productive economy. Curiously, he rarely used

the term *efficiency* in his famous 1,000-page treatise. When he did, it was only in the classic sense, a usage quite unrelated to markets: "alehouses are not the *causus efficiens* of drunkenness," reads one index entry.[8]

A modern reader might infer an underlying goal of efficiency in Smith's notions of the "invisible hand," division of labor, and specialization. But for Smith the real goal was economic wealth for all. His aim was as much democratic as economic. The division of labor and specialization and, most generally, economic growth were only means to an end, not ends in themselves. By contrast, efficiency today is, in the words of one economist, "the watchword of the mainstream economist."[9] A solution, a rational choice, a good policy is one that is efficient. It is one that increases a ratio of output (production or "good") to input (constraint or "bad").

As industry increased in scale and power over the course of the eighteenth and nineteenth centuries, the craft- and agrarian-based local economies declined, subsumed by an economic paradigm that equated the "greater good" with increasing production (growth) and with increasing productivity (more efficient use of land, labor, and capital). "Money and the market economy replaced barter and personal relationships in economic transaction," writes demographer Cheryl Russell. "The few long-term economic relationships of farm societies gave way to numerous and fleeting monetary transactions between strangers."[10] Thus, the notion of "market," conceptualized by Smith but mysterious in its operation to most people, even to this day, came to dominate economies; with markets in land, labor, and capital, individual producers abandoned personal relationships for strictly commercial ones.

In this transition, the absence of the term *efficiency*—at least in its economic sense as we now know it—suggests that practice preceded principle. Machines were built and markets developed long before a term emerged to capture their significance. Adam Smith, for instance, derived his seminal ideas by observing factory organization and the flow of goods and services. His empirical base (illustrated by the famous pin factory) represented only a small fraction of the economy of his day (England was still mostly agrarian and even its industry was still mostly craft based). But he could see a trend, one characterized in particular by a separation of tasks among workers, which he labeled a "division of labor" and which we now lump under the term *efficiency*. But in his time, such specialization was only a practice, a logical outgrowth of industry's shift from the cottage to the factory. By identifying and generalizing from this observed practice and building it into a larger framework of industrial, market-led production, Smith began a two-century process of elevating efficiency to the status of economic and managerial principle and, eventually, to a broad social principle.

One branch of his successors was the so-called neoclassical economists who carved out a scientific economics in the late nineteenth and early twentieth centuries. They took Smith's ideas and combined them with long-standing engineering and mathematical ideas to achieve an all-purpose framework centering on efficiency. According to economist Stanley Jevons, "To satisfy our wants to the utmost with the least effort—to procure the greatest amount of what is desirable at the expense of the least that is undesirable—in other words, to *maximize* pleasure—is the problem of economics."[11] Efficiency became a concept applicable not just to pin factories and railroad engines but, in time, to organizations of all sorts, from factories to government agencies to families, and to individuals, soon to be called "consumers." With this marriage, the stage was set for the Progressive Era, otherwise known as the "Age of Efficiency."

But before turning to that era, I must interrupt the story to clarify the significance of this etymology, incomplete as it must be. Its significance lies not just in the account, one that has somehow failed to be told despite the prominence of efficiency in two major disciplines—engineering and economics—but in the prescription for sufficiency.[12] As we will further see, efficiency, far from a universal, age-old notion, evolved continuously. From its ancient origins in philosophical questions of causation to the physicists' notion of work to the economists' concern for market performance to the engineer's desire for a neat, managerial order, efficiency has adapted to meet social needs. In the Age of Efficiency, we'll see, those needs were to understand and promote industrialization, economic expansion, and consumerism.

The idea of efficiency or, better, the *ideas* of efficiency through the ages, were thus socially constructed. Efficiency fit the needs of the times. It explained and justified, infused and promoted. In this respect, efficiency was much like the idea of *personal gain*, the idea that individuals naturally acquire, and should acquire, as much wealth as they can. It is a notion taken for granted today but novel from a historical perspective. "It may strike us as odd," writes historical economist Robert Heilbroner,

that the idea of [personal] gain is a relatively modern one; we are schooled to believe that man is essentially an acquisitive creature and that left to himself he will behave as any self-respecting businessman would. The profit motive, we are constantly being told, is as old as man himself.

But it is not. The profit motive as we know it is only as old as "modern man." Even today the notion of gain for gain's sake is foreign to a large portion of the world's population, and it has been conspicuous by its absence over most of recorded history.... The idea of gain, the idea that each man not only may, but should constantly strive to better his material lot, is an idea that was quite foreign to the great lower and middle strata of Egyptian, Greek, Roman, and medieval cultures, only scattered throughout Renaissance and Reformation times, and largely absent in the majority of Eastern civilizations. As a ubiquitous characteristic of society, it is as modern an invention as printing.[13]

Personal gain and efficiency: thoroughly modern inventions. Perched atop their modern pedestals, they are admired, even venerated, by elites and masses alike. And well they should be. They have served their admirers well, generating unimaginable wealth for a large portion of humanity. Readers skeptical about the possibility of sufficiency achieving a comparable status will do well to keep the evolution of these terms in mind, though. When needs are pressing, when people strive to free the entrepreneurial spirit or to create an ordered world or to save the planet, societies will seek out such notions, organize their productive capacities around them, and move in entirely different directions. And they will do so quite naturally, or so it will appear after the fact, after the struggles of competing ideas and practices have played themselves out.

So the significance of this etymology is this: if the premises of this book are right, today's industrial and industrializing societies will soon adopt sufficiency (or something like it) as a linguistic and political tool. They will do so having come to grips with the impossibility of infinite material growth on a finite planet. They will do so as they change their goals from unending economic expansion and unimpeded technological fiddling to ecological and social sustainability.

The Age of Efficiency

Two powerful developments of the period 1890–1930 converged to create a modern concept of efficiency. One was economists' construction of "economic man," the idealized, hyperrational human who bases all decisions on perfect information to maximize personal gain. This development made economic theory more quantifiable and, as economic boosters hoped, more "scientific." It also created a model for personal and organizational behavior. In this period nearly everyone was seeking to throw off the shackles of tradition and parochialism. One way was to emulate economic man. Although developed by economists as an analytic device, the concept had everything an aspiring modern could want: a scientific aura, an association with business and wealth, and a code of conduct all its own—efficiency.

The second development was the rise of the corporation. Supplanting the family business and the local proprietorship, the corporation became the dominant actor in business and, for that matter, in the economy and society as a whole. Corporate management systems, whether in the form of Montgomery Ward's mail-order catalog or Henry Ford's assembly line, were increasingly revered and imitated. What the corporation did was virtually synonymous with what a modern society did. If business adopted efficiency (and not all did), so would society, its leaders, its public agencies, and its citizens. The corporation, that special form of business designed to maximize financial value for absentee shareholders, didn't just embrace efficiency, it adopted it. It clasped efficiency to its bosom, nurtured it, and sent it out into the world to achieve great things. With help from others in the broader society, it put efficiency atop that pedestal, a champion to be admired and emulated by all.

Classical economists were philosophers, their foremost concerns the satisfaction of basic needs, fair distribution, and the creation of a more just society. But in a struggle of academically epic proportions, they were usurped by the neoclassical economists, those mathematically oriented academics (many with training in engineering or applied mathematics) who largely rejected the discipline's philosophical roots. Instead, the neoclassical economists focused on market performance and wealth generation, supposedly value-free processes made by that all-knowing, ever-calculating maximizer, "economic man." Adam Smith and other classical economists had held that an economy must be grounded in moral behavior. Now, concerns for basic needs and just distribution were consigned to "politics" or, at least, to that old-fashioned line of study, "political economy." The new economics was a science. Wealth for all, Smith's democratically inspired goal, gave way to just wealth.

The new scientists, the neoclassical economists, may have solved one problem, but they created another. America was fast becoming the beacon of hope and freedom, the exemplar of opportunity for all, the enemy of privilege and concentrated power. To champion wealth was, in the time of the much-despised railroad barons and timber tycoons, tantamount to advocating a new aristocracy. The advocates of the new economics, not to mention those of industrial growth and social progress, faced a contradiction. They found resolution in efficiency, not the theoretical construct, as it turned out, but the techniques of perfecting machines and organizing labor to work those machines. Efficiency would, in part, distance the "scientific" economists from the merely "philosophical" ones, and in part it would propel the nation to greatness. And, yes, wealth might gravitate to the wealthy like water to low ground, but efficiency spreads itself evenly, everywhere, benefitting everyone.

If neoclassical economists sought value-free, apolitical analysis in their quest for scientific and public legitimacy, they did so in part by championing efficiency while simultaneously stripping it of its ancient, moral basis. Along with the physicists and engineers, their intellectual brethren, the new economists helped convert efficiency from a qualitative notion to a quantitative one. No longer denoting the accomplishment of a worthy task, the tight fit of means and ends, it would now become a quantitative measure of how well a task is performed, of how well measurable economic inputs are used to generate measurable economic outputs. It was all about how a producer employed raw material, how a consumer satisfied demand, and how society generated wealth. It would substitute the philosopher's concerns for social meaning and purpose for the engineer's concern for mechanical precision. "A special characteristic of efficiency is that it deals only with what can be counted," writes biologist Mary E. Clark. "It asks: How much? How big? How many? How fast? How long? When efficiency takes over, 'goodness' is defined in numerical terms. Whatever is to have value must somehow be converted into a measurable quantity. What cannot be counted is 'of no account'; it is outside the system."[14]

That system, the neoclassical project, was fabulously successful. One indicator is the growth in industrial output and incomes. Another is the sudden rise of the very term *efficiency* as revealed in a content analysis of economic works and major U.S. media (figure 3.1). But the turn-of-the-century spike in usage cannot be attributed solely to neoclassical economics, even as it became the most influential social science discipline.

In the late nineteenth century, American society was buzzing with the trappings of greatness—accelerating industrial output, new technologies, settlement from coast to coast. As economists took their seats at the head of the table of progressive thought (along with the engineers and an assortment of efficiency-oriented business, political, and religious leaders), there was growing and widespread agreement that economic efficiency qualified as one of society's most important ideas, even a goal in its own right. "Efficiency is the goal in industry," wrote economist Norris Brisco in 1914. But it is much more, too: "The nation which nearest approaches this goal in its industrial and business pursuits will be the one which will lead the van of industrial nations. . . . Efficiency methods will make this nation the greatest of all industrial nations, and in an enterprise will be the greatest guarantee of success."[15] Efficiency caught on not just as a term of art, but as a means to greatness.

Still, some economists clung to their classical roots, questioning the equation of efficiency and production with greatness, let alone happiness. In a 1923 book, *The Foundations of National Industrial Efficiency*, economist Vanderveer Custis of Northwestern University wrote that "the highest percentage [ratio] of efficiency is not necessarily conducive to human welfare. . . . Moreover, it must not be supposed that the largest possible industrial product should be made the chief end of human life; and that all human energies that are not used in industry are wasted."[16] Custis's

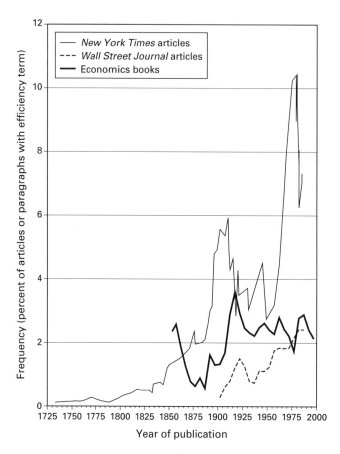

Figure 3.1
Efficiency in economic literature and the media. Until the Progressive Era (the "Age of Efficiency") from the 1890s through the 1920s, *efficiency* was an uncommon term both in economic literature and in news and business media. The first spike in usage corresponds to theoretical developments in economics, most likely following developments in engineering. The ensuing surge in popular usage can be largely attributed to Frederick Winslow Taylor and the efficiency societies.

Through these several centuries the meaning shifted from "effective" to "productive" to "modern" and, simply, to "good." The term's persistence through the twentieth century suggests its widespread adoption, however ambiguous or political its usage.

Data for the newspapers were calculated as the occurrence of articles with one or more efficiency terms relative to the total number of articles in a five-year period (in the available years a total of 19,962,595 articles in the *New York Times*, 4,597,593 in the *Wall Street Journal*). Data for the economic books were calculated as the occurrence of paragraphs with an efficiency term relative to the number of paragraphs per period (39,586 paragraphs total). *Sources:* Proquest Historical Newspapers Library, http://www.cjrlc.org/Discounts/pq_newspapers.htm; The Library of Economics and Liberty, www.econlib.org, accessed May, 2004; both courtesy of the University of Michigan Networked Electronic Resources.

voice was a lone one, though, and remains so. Doubting economists may challenge the doctrine now and then, and mainstream economists may know intellectually that efficiency is not an end in itself. But they and their followers in the policy and business communities still act as if it is. "While economists typically acknowledge the fact that there are several varied objectives possessed by individuals and by societies generally," write environmental economists David W. Pearce and R. Kerry Turner, "they tend to work with only one—economic efficiency."[17] "In the mainstream view," writes another economist, Stephen Marglin, "efficiency considerations dominate: build a better mousetrap and the world will beat a path to your door."[18] And because economics was fast becoming the dominant social science discipline, the field with the most sought-after voice in legislatures and boardrooms, a field vying at times with the hard sciences for prestige and social influence, this one objective acquired a life outside the arcane world of equations and number crunching. As it turned out, though, the most effective proselytizers were not economists, but management-oriented, socially concerned engineers.

That the Progressive Era was also called the Age of Efficiency can be largely attributed to one idea, "scientific management," and to one man, Frederick Winslow Taylor. Taylor, whose name and ideas still resonate in the halls of management schools, delivered the virtues of precision machinery and "economic man" to managers, even to householders, clerics, government officials, and consumers.

Push Worker, Push Product

Scientific management (also known as "Taylorism" or the Taylor system) began on the factory floor where, as a machinist and self-taught engineer, Frederick Winslow Taylor sought the "one right way" to manage production. Through time-and-motion studies, he disaggregated tasks and, with stopwatch in hand, measured them to show managers how they could get more product from their workers.

Taylor initially used the term *efficiency* in a strictly technical sense, extending mechanical efficiency (physical work per energy unit) to labor efficiency (worker's work per day). The "differential piece rate" required that "the shortest possible time for each job be computed and fixed," writes Samuel Haber, a social chronicler of Taylorism. "If the worker finished the job in this time he was given a good price per piece. If he failed, he was given a rate so low that the 'lazy or inferior' worker could not hold the job."[19] Designed to make the worker work harder and faster, the piece-rate system would reward productive workers with higher wages at the same time the employer enjoyed higher profits (see figure 3.2).

INSPECTION OF PERFORMANCE

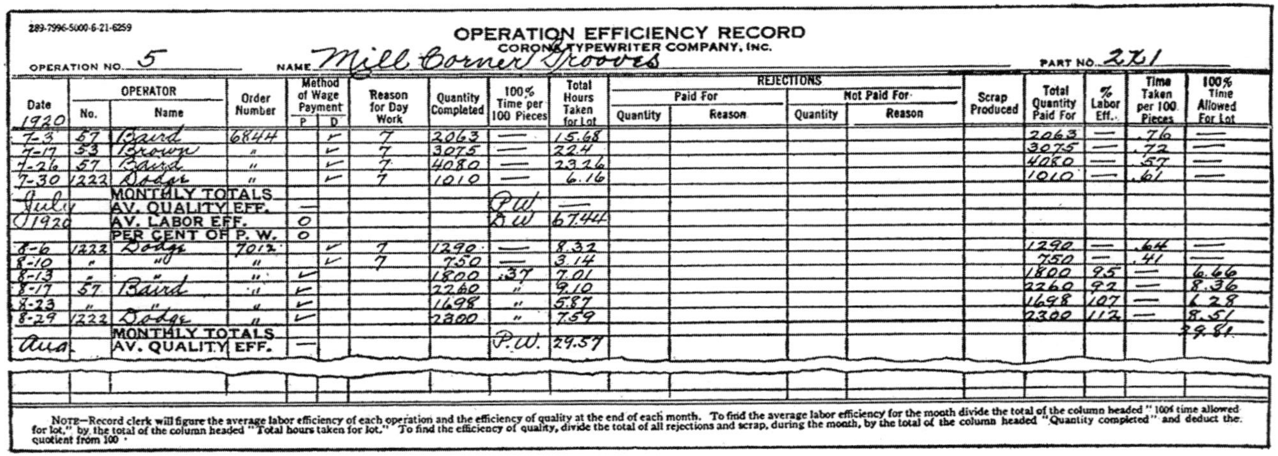

289-7996-5000-6-21-6259

OPERATION EFFICIENCY RECORD
CORONA TYPEWRITER COMPANY, INC.

OPERATION NO. 5 NAME Mill Corner Grooves PART NO. 271

Date 1920	Operator No.	Operator Name	Order Number	Method of Wage Payment P	Method of Wage Payment D	Reason for Day Work	Quantity Completed	100% Time per 100 Pieces	Total Hours Taken for Lot	Rejections Paid For Quantity	Rejections Paid For Reason	Rejections Not Paid For Quantity	Rejections Not Paid For Reason	Scrap Produced	Total Quantity Paid For	% Labor Eff.	Time Taken per 100 Pieces	100% Time Allowed For Lot
7-3	57	Baird	6844		✓	7	2063	—	15.68						2063	—	.76	—
7-17	53	Brown	"		✓	7	3075	—	22.4						3075	—	.72	—
7-26	57	Baird	"		✓	7	4080	—	23.26						4080	—	.57	—
7-30	1222	Dodge	"		✓	7	1010	—	6.16						1010	—	.61	—
July		MONTHLY TOTALS																
1920		AV. QUALITY EFF.		—				P.W.	—									
		AV. LABOR EFF.		O				D.W.	67.44									
		PER CENT OF P. W.		O														
8-6	1222	Dodge	7012		✓	7	1290	—	8.32						1290	—	.64	—
8-10	"	"	"		✓	7	750	—	3.14						750	—	.41	—
8-13	"	"	"	✓			1800	.37	7.01						1800	95	—	6.66
8-17	57	Baird	"	✓			2260	"	9.10						2260	92	—	8.36
8-23	"	"	"	✓			1698	"	5.87						1698	107	—	6.28
8-29	1222	Dodge	"	✓			2300	"	7.59						2300	112	—	8.51
		MONTHLY TOTALS																29.81
Aug.		AV. QUALITY EFF.		—				P.W.	29.57									

NOTE—Record clerk will figure the average labor efficiency of each operation and the efficiency of quality at the end of each month. To find the average labor efficiency for the month divide the total of the column headed "100% time allowed for lot," by the total of the column headed "Total hours taken for lot." To find the efficiency of quality, divide the total of all rejections and scrap, during the month, by the total of the column headed "Quantity completed" and deduct the quotient from 100.

Figure 3.2
Workplace efficiency. The Taylor Society of New York shows manufacturers how to calculate their operational efficiency: combine the average labor efficiency of each operation (hours worked per unit of output as a percentage of time allotted) and average quality efficiency (percentage of output that is not rejected). The theoretical ideal is always 100 percent, which the efficiency experts calculate and managers push workers to achieve.
Source: Reproduced from The Taylor Society, H. S. Person, ed., *Scientific Management in American Industry* (New York: Harper & Brothers, 1929) p. 395, courtesy University of Michigan Library.

Taylor was more than an engineer of labor performance, though; he was a systemizer, an organizer of production, a promoter of industrial betterment. What's more, industrial growth was not the most important thing for Taylor and his followers, nor was profit. Scientific application was what society needed, Taylor believed. Science provided the best standard to judge production, and that standard was not output or revenues; it was efficiency. Not any kind of efficiency, though, certainly not the narrow concept of commercial efficiency—more profit for the invested dollar. Rather, *productivity*—output per worker day—was the name of the game, for the employer, for the worker, and, in time, as Taylor's disciples and much of the populace came to believe, for all of society. Productivity was science at work; profit was for profiteers.

An element of the classic notion of doing a job well thus permeated Taylor's use of efficiency. Only to him a job well done was a job guided by science, designed and judged by those who know science, the "efficiency experts." "First, by way of calculations in foot-pounds, and later with the aid of his techniques of time and motion studies," writes historian Haber,

Taylor went in search of scientific laws of work to answer the closely related questions of how a job could best be done and how much could be produced. He derived a 'science' of shoveling, pig-iron lifting, lathe work, etc., through a controlled variation of the isolated elements of each task. This usually meant the conversion of the task into its physical quantities. Taylor thus passed from commercial to mechanical [and labor] efficiency.[20]

Taylor's efficiency was thus more than tinkering with machines or rewarding and punishing workers for their speed and output. It was at once a technical system and a system of specialization, of separating skills and knowledge. "For one of the most important general principles of Taylor's system," writes Haber, "was that the man who did the work could not derive or fully understand its science. The result was a radical separation of thinking from doing." It may have been the need for exact measurement in the Taylor system that compelled such a sharp demarcation of work and judgment. "The stop watch, an instrument for timing overt action, could gauge only the most routine mental processes," writes Haber. "Therefore, to the extent that Taylor's science strained at strict precision, to that degree it had to externalize work and remove the thinking from it."[21]

In the passage from the owner's concern with the commercial to the scientist's concern with the mechanical and the human (the routinized human), Taylor's efficiency created hierarchy. It was managers, not workers, who would have the decision-making authority. Only managers would develop the expert knowledge that otherwise well-trained engineers (and, presumably, economists) laid claim to.

"Taylor saw the factory hierarchy as one of abilities," writes Haber, "The division of labor did not constrict the worker excessively, because he might rise to that level of competence of which he was capable. Taylor insisted that workers be treated individually and not *en masse*. Each was to be rewarded and punished for his particular deeds."[22]

In practice, in that rewarding and punishing, Taylor relegated workers to an entirely separate—and inferior—status. The scientific expert would measure their productivity and the manager would dish out their just deserts. But the workers were necessarily on one side of the division of labor, the side that took the orders, the side that was constantly pushed to produce more. "The worker was granted an individuality of incentive but not of discretion," concludes Haber. "There was no 'invisible hand' in the factory to bring order out of complexity. This order was to be discovered and realized by the systemizer." Quoting Taylor, Haber continues, "the workers must 'do what they are told promptly and without asking questions or making suggestions. . . . It is absolutely necessary for every man in an organization to become one of a train of gear wheels.' "[23] Adam Smith may have articulated a central efficiency principle—the division of labor—but it was largely Taylor who put it in practice, and with a rationality and scientific distinction that only the most committed traditionalist could resist.

If Taylor or his followers felt any concern for relegating a large segment of society to "a train of gear wheels," they didn't show it. The logic of efficiency took care of such matters. Echoing the goal of classical economists, advocates of Taylorism believed everyone would benefit from scientific management—owners, workers, and managers alike—because the additional wealth from the productivity gains would be distributed to all parties. Mechanical and organizational efficiency, however dehumanizing for some, would erase the divisiveness of distribution. Industrial progress was social progress.

Taylorism can therefore be read as a scientifically sophisticated rendering of Adam Smith's great ideas, a managerial dictum for the division of labor and prosperity for all. Mechanical or commercial efficiency could be value neutral, even value positive—an unambiguous gain for all. But on closer inspection an efficiency of work, indeed of social organization, segregates values; it elevates the position, the status, the power of some actors (notably the efficiency experts and those who hire them), while it denigrates that of others (mostly the workers). Little wonder that, as efficiency gained a hold on the popular imagination, as it shifted from an abstract esoteric idea to a practical guide to action, it became a tool for control and, less obvious, a means of displacing social and ecological costs (chapter 4).

It is not hard to imagine that, as the political uses of efficiency became clear, those who would spread the word drew an important lesson: master the efficiency measures oneself lest one be mastered by them. In a progressive age, one could accept subordination in the workplace (many had little choice anyway). What efficiency offered the body politic, though, was mastery elsewhere. A worker could take orders on the shop floor, straining every day to squeeze the most out of that machine, but at home or in the church pews or in department store aisles, that person, now a consumer, could take charge. All that was needed was the inclination and a bit of skill to get the most out of every meal, every act of devotion, every consumer purchase. The urge to adopt efficiency as both a social and a personal principle was irresistible.

Taylor and his followers did shift from the strictly technical to the managerial, from the standardization and synchronization of work to the very organization of production. Still, for many, Taylor included, this was not enough. In time, they indeed extended the idea beyond, to society as a whole. They offered society a "mental revolution," as Taylor put it. And the public bought it, big time. Self-betterment, we will see, followed industrial betterment. Societal betterment followed the two.

America's Efficiency Craze

The scientific rationality of Taylor's system only partly explains the popularity of efficiency. In the decade preceding American entry into World War I, the high cost of living was a major public issue. Middle-class and professional families were hard hit by inflation, thus creating a political constituency for lower prices. Their concern fixated on what otherwise would have been an obscure issue, the setting of railroad shipping rates, and a legal and regulatory case that would normally have been relegated to the back pages of the business press. The Eastern Rate Case pitted price-sensitive consumers and business interests against railroad owners and unionists who called for a "fair return" on their investments and labor.

Congressional hearings highlighted the polar opposition of the two sides: what railroad interests would have gained by higher rates, others would have lost. Louis D. Brandeis, one of the country's most respected lawyers, represented Eastern business interests who would have been hurt by increased rates. Reflecting the heady optimism and desire for reform typical of his time, not to mention society's faith in expert-led, scientific problem solving, Brandeis came up with the perfect solution: scientific management. Railroads could become more efficient and both groups—

railroad interests and consumers—would gain. Joint gains. Win-win, we would say today.

A widespread efficiency craze followed in the wake of the railroad rate case. "The slogan of the largest segment of those excited by the Eastern Rate Case," says Haber, was " 'efficiency.' "[24] The term caught on in part because it appeared singularly capable of resolving the otherwise inherently conflicting interests of business and citizens—return on investment versus fair (or low) prices. But it also had moral content then, especially among its early proponents, the preachers of personal and social efficiency.

Personal efficiency emphasized hard work, thrift, and willpower. The target was workers, not consumers. Books with such titles as *The Efficient Age, Efficient Living*, and *Personal Efficiency* were immensely popular. Social efficiency held that efficiency was the means to social harmony; it was the logical extension of the Industrial Revolution and the triumph of science. Efficient production leads to high wages and low costs, which "check the greed of the employer and the laziness of the employee."[25] It renders class conflict obsolete. Proponents saw efficiency the way they saw water, not just as desirable, but essential. Experts may be needed to dig the channels and erect the dikes, but otherwise efficiency would just spread across the land and seep into every nook and cranny.

To promote managerial, personal, and social efficiency, "efficiency societies" sprouted up across the country, sown by the pathbreaking work of the efficiency experts. The original, the Taylor Society, was founded in 1911 in Philadelphia, its purpose to promote Taylor's work and serve as a central authority for all questions of scientific management.[26] Its members came from throughout the Northeastern United States, with branches in western Pennsylvania, Cleveland, Chicago, and Tokyo. Although dominated by management engineers, it included businesspeople, academics, and other professionals. The society dealt with both technical issues and questions of public interest. The Efficiency Society of New York included prominent businesspeople, publicists, educators, and economists, as well as engineers. One of its presidents was Melville Dewey, which he often spelled *Melvil Dui* for efficiency's sake. He was a reformer of libraries (he invented the Dewey Decimal System), measurement (he promoted the metric system), and spelling. The society sponsored talks on Salesmanship and Efficiency, Pensions and Efficiency, Dust and Efficiency, and Cheerfulness and Efficiency.

Many of the efficiency societies were dominated by business, in part to promote efficient production, in part to counter organized labor. Such societies tried to eliminate selfishness, promote hard work and clean living, and find ways of boosting

FIRST HOME OF THE EFFICIENCY SOCIETY
THE ENGINEERING SOCIETIES' BUILDING
29 WEST 39TH STREET, NEW YORK

Figure 3.3
Headquarters of the Efficiency Society of New York. Members spoke of the "efficiency movement," offering proof of its success with buildings such as this, well-attended meetings, and publications.
Source: Reproduced from *Efficiency Society Incorporated Transactions, Volume I: 1912* (New York: The Efficiency Society, 1913), opposite title page.

profits. Their bywords were *efficiency* and *cooperation*, terms that still ring loud in the business community and among business educators today.

Efficiency experts and their boosters spared little to spread the word. In 1914 an efficiency exposition was held in New York. With Taylor as its main speaker, 69,000 people attended. A similar event followed in Cleveland. YMCAs around the country offered courses in efficiency. The great lawyer William Jennings Bryan gave an "efficiency reception" to members of the diplomatic corps. Four of the country's major engineering societies worked with the administration of President Theodore Roosevelt to argue that hydroelectric energy should be developed to ease the pressure on coal supplies; that mining could be made more efficient by better utilizing by-products; and that "order, efficiency, and business methods" should be brought "into government."[27]

The efficiency societies and other groups turned out specialized journals and general-interest magazines. There was the *Journal of the Efficiency Society, Efficiency Magazine, Efficiency Magazine and Sales Manager, Bulletin of the Taylor Society,* and *100%: The Practical Magazine of Efficient Management.* Two magazines even used the term twice in their titles, apparently less concerned than Dewey (Dui) with efficient use of the printed page: *Greater Efficiency: Journal of the Efficiency Society,* and *Efficiency: The Magazine of Efficient Management.* Articles in these and less specialized publications spouted titles like "Scientific Management for the One Best Way to Do Work"; "Scientific Management—Progressive and Irresistible"; "The Waste of Getting Tired"; "Social Efficiency"; "The Efficiency of the Cities"; "The Progressive Relation between Efficiency and Consent"; "Efficiency Expert's View of National Outlook"[28] (figures 3.4–3.6).

Popular magazines and books picked up the efficiency theme, touting not only the material benefits of efficiency, but its uplifting qualities. "This new efficiency will ultimately find its way into all departments of American life," claimed *The World's Work* magazine. "It will become a great national educational force. Waste is the great American sin—waste in government, in private life, in agriculture, in the use of natural resources, in business. If, in manufacturing, we can have a far-reaching lesson in efficiency and economy, no one can foresee what tremendous effects it may have upon the national character."[29] The editor of an engineering journal was even more enthusiastic: "The Millennium will have been reached when humanity shall have learned to eliminate all useless waste. . . . When humanity shall have learned to apply the common sense and scientific rules of efficiency to the care of body and mind and the labors of body and mind, then indeed will we be nearing the condition of perfect."[30]

Figure 3.4
Masthead of 100%: The Efficiency Magazine. Notice that the terms *efficiency* and *100%* appear seven times, presumably for emphasis, not efficiency.
Source: Reproduced from January 1918 issue, vol. 10, no. 1, p. 47, courtesy University of Michigan Library.

Millennial perfection may have been a bit much even for devout Taylorites, but the efficiency craze was certainly about reform. Yet whereas old-fashioned reformers appealed to conscience and moral rectitude, Taylorist reformers appealed to science and industry. Uplift came not from denial or right living, or even from hard work, but from eliminating waste and maximizing production, from planning and, eventually we will see, from pushing product and consuming well. Efficiency would destroy laziness, selfishness, and even gender inequality by finding "the best possible man, how to produce the best possible work, and how to secure the best possible effects."[31]

One audience targeted by efficiency reformers was homemakers. The *Ladies Home Journal* ran a series of articles in the early twentieth century about efficiency

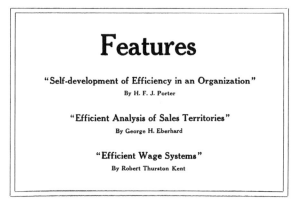

Price 10 Cents   September, 1912

The
Efficiency
Magazine

for the man studying selling, system and advertising

Features

"Self-development of Efficiency in an Organization"
By H. F. J. Porter

"Efficient Analysis of Sales Territories"
By George H. Eberhard

"Efficient Wage Systems"
By Robert Thurston Kent

Published Monthly by **The Business Bourse**
International, Inc.
261 Broadway   Opposite City Hall   New York City

Figure 3.5
The Efficiency Magazine. One of many magazines published in the early years of the Age of Efficiency, this one oriented to business.
Source: Reproduced from the cover of the September 1912 issue, courtesy of the University of Michigan Library.

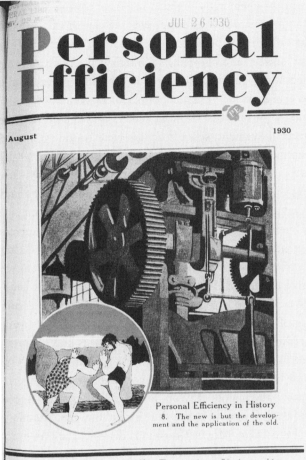

Figure 3.6
Personal Efficiency *magazine at the height of the Age of Efficiency.* Efficiency has now gone beyond manufacturing and business to personal life. The drawing suggests that efficiency seeking in work is age-old. The inset suggests that human labor is primitive and backward, a thing of the past, while work done by machines (without humans) is modern and progressive.
Source: Reproduced from the cover of the August 1930 issue, vol. 20, no. 8, courtesy University of Michigan Library.

in housework and received an overwhelmingly positive response from housewives interested in "domestic engineering." Another audience was the clergy, who saw an opportunity to arrest declining church membership. In New York, a Protestant minister joined the city's efficiency society and chaired its Church Efficiency Committee. Another clergyman called for organizing the church for efficient economic service. One magazine article was entitled, "The Economics of Devotion."[32]

American educators were not to be outdone by homemakers and church reformers. In the broader social reform movement, schoolteachers were routinely singled out for being old-fashioned and ineffective. Consequently, a new profession emerged in the public schools—the school administrator. Seizing on one of Taylor's key efficiency precepts—separating the thinking from the doing—administrators could specialize in the thinking of budgets and buildings; teachers could just teach.

In higher education, a disciple of Taylor, Morris L. Cooke, investigated university organization. He recommended that professors be treated as producers, that lecture notes be standardized, and that the "student-hour" be adopted as a unit of measurement for administrative efficiency. Although heavily criticized at the time, the general thrust of Cooke's prescriptions took root, finding frequent expression in the administrative quarters of today's academe. The language of efficient production (teaching and credentialing) in service to consumers (students and parents), this author knows all too well, is pervasive.[33]

With efficiency so prominent in the public eye, it did not take long for government officials to jump on the bandwagon. Taylor, in fact, had written about government efficiency, recommending among other things that the U.S. president include an efficiency expert in his cabinet. Morris Cooke, his disciple, put it in practice at the municipal level. As Director of Public Works for Philadelphia, Cooke set up a planning department, modeled after Taylor's factory planning department, and a program of "functionalized management." For him, an efficient government was one run by experts. Voting was to be minimized, conducted only for the broader issues. Legislative bodies and juries should be smaller, and terms of administrators (the experts) longer. Administration, as a result, would be divorced from politics. Theodore Roosevelt, who in 1905 appointed a special commission to unearth executive inefficiencies in government, agreed: "There is every reason why our executive governmental machinery should be at least as well planned, economical, and efficient as the best machinery of the great business organizations."[34]

The scientific management of government led to the professionalization of public service. Specialized training via conferences and schools for public service advanced the notion of planning and helped "functionalize work" along the lines Taylor laid out for the factory. Efficiency commissions were convened. At the federal level, President William Howard Taft created a Commission on Economy and Efficiency to bring efficient administration and planning into the federal government. The budget would become a central plan of government, not just a means of accounting. A bureau of central administrative control would draw up the budget, thus exercising "control over the subject of efficiency of personnel and over the character of the results obtained in the several departments."[35] But for all the purported scientific credentials, Congress saw politics in the Taft Commission's proposals, an attempt to weaken Congress's power over the purse. When Woodrow Wilson took office, he dissolved the commission—but he didn't abandon its central goal. Wilson replaced the commission with a "Bureau of Efficiency" tied closely to Congress but performing the same reform mission.

At least sixteen states created similar efficiency commissions. The greatest impact was probably felt in New York state where, in the state's constitutional convention of 1915, the Taft Commission findings were drawn on extensively. Haber concludes that, for whatever efficiencies were actually achieved, such commissions led, over time, to the "consolidation of state agencies, improvement of cost accounting techniques, and, most important, the grant of more power to the governor."[36] Efficiency's ability to divorce politics from administration became a marriage of convenience: those with the means—the efficiency gains—conveniently gained the power.

Of all the arenas in which efficiency took root in government, none was as symptomatic of the era as conservation, especially in the federal government. With decimation of Northern forests, ships blocked by silt-clogged waterways, and fertile land lying fallow for lack of water, waste was a concern of national leaders and the public alike. And, yet, special interests just bickered, always angling for advantage. The efficiency experts had a different way. "Experts, using technical and scientific methods, should decide all matters of development and utilization of resources, all problems of allocation of funds," wrote historian Samuel Hays in his 1959 book, *Conservation and the Gospel of Efficiency*, capturing the sentiments of U.S. President Theodore Roosevelt, his forestry chief Gifford Pinchot, and their followers. "Federal land management agencies should resolve land-use differences among livestock, wildlife, irrigation, recreation, and settler groups. National commissions should adjust power, irrigation, navigation, and flood control interests to promote the highest multiple-purpose development of river basins." This was the scientific way, the one right way, the way that allows science and technology to push politics aside. "The crux of the gospel of efficiency," says Hays, "lay in a rational and scientific method of making basic technological decisions through a single, central authority."[37] Not surprisingly, others were not convinced—at least others who saw politics in the methods and authorities, and feared their interests would be threatened. Congress opposed much of what Roosevelt and Pinchot offered. States and localities had their own ideas about water rights and grazing rights. Railroad owners, shippers, irrigators, and timbermen knew how to develop a nation. Some of the contests played out in legislative lobbies and chambers, some in the courts. But in many respects, the efficiency experts won out, building dams and canals, railroads and, later, highways, all in the name of efficiency.

Injecting Taylorist thinking into government thus had its own politics, not unlike that in the factory: efficiency gains on the shop floor translate into decision-making gains in the upstairs offices; discretion, authority, and power move up the organizational chart.

One challenge to Taylorism in government came from the popular campaign for direct democracy. Scientific management, many political reformers feared, would take yet more authority from the people. But the efficiency reformers again had the answer: "Efficiency provided a standpoint from which progressives who had declared their allegiance to democracy could resist the leveling tendencies of the principle of equality," writes Haber. In other words, "They could advance reform and at the same time provide a safeguard to the college-bred."[38] When efficiency gains take root throughout the society, the reformers assured the critics, the fruits are borne everywhere, consumed by everyone. No one is left behind. No one need worry if some get a bit more.

In a pattern that continues to this day, in and out of government, advocates rarely had to actually demonstrate the efficiency gains; claiming an efficiency—a productivity gain, a faster way of doing things, a conservation measure—was quite enough. "Characteristically," concludes Haber, "there was little talk of where efficient government was going and much rolling-up of sleeves and getting on with the business at hand."[39] The purpose of efficiency measures was given, or assumed, or just ignored. To ask why was tantamount to questioning scientific management and expertise, questioning science itself, even democracy and progress (see box 3.1).

And so efficiency becomes the goal, not the means. And those who can manipulate the techniques, those who can claim the efficiencies, gain the advantage. Far from removing politics from government, let alone from any other realm—the company, the church, the forest, the river—efficiency creates its own politics. That Taylor and a century of his followers have preferred to see it otherwise (or, among the strategically sophisticated, have preferred to act as if there was no politics in

Box 3.1
Efficiency's many guises

As efficiency evolves and permeates modern life it assumes different garbs, each fit for a special occasion. Some of the occasions are strictly technical, others managerial. Still others, possibly most, are political.

The rhetoric varies with the occasion, but the underlying logic is the same: a thing (a new machine, investment, policy) is desirable when more good (more product, wealth, learning, democracy) comes from a given bad (energy and material used up, income forgone, tax dollars spent, policies not pursued). Here are a few of those guises and some contexts in which they typically arise. Some appear more commonly as nouns or verbs, some as adjectives.

Efficiency	Context
improvement	enclosure, economic development
conservation	natural resource harvesting; energy use
productivity	industry, economic growth
economies of scale	production
mobility	factors of production, financial capital
intensification	agriculture, natural resources, pollution
specialization, division of labor	organization of labor
streamline	government
100 percent	business management, resource use
automatic	mechanized services
economical, economize	home maintenance, shopping
convenience	labor-saving devices, transportation
recycling	household and construction waste
multitasking	workplace performance
new and improved	household products
dematerialization	industrial design
synergy	business mergers, consumer products

scientific management and efficiency claims) does not detract from a central truth: efficiency, despite its new clothes of scientific and market-led neutrality, its association with all that's modern and good, even democratic, is, in practice, *political*. It is a means of determining who gets what and how. And it is a means of disguising and displacing costs. It is a way of leading everyone to believe society is marching forward when, in fact, social and natural capital is being consumed. It is a crutch for those who believe that perpetual industrial expansion on a finite planet is possible, indeed, that it is scientific, modern, and just. "It is a peculiar sort of efficiency we worship," writes Mary E. Clark, "since we are encouraged to be wantonly wasteful of the very things we insist be produced efficiently. . . . Modern economies are actually 'uneconomic,' for they encourage ever-increasing *throughput* of goods with an ever-diminishing useful *lifetime*, precisely the opposite of rational economic behaviour!"[40]

Before turning to efficiency's problematic role in a sustainable society (chapter 4), though, we must first understand how efficiency became the linguistic water in which all moderns swim. We must see how efficiency became in modern societies, an unambiguously, unquestionably good thing. A new creature was needed at this juncture of linguistic evolution, not worker or owner, not parent or citizen, but *consumer*.

The Efficient Shopper

Just as the differential piece-rate system would align the interests of workers and employers in a company (higher wages and more profits), efficiency measures would align higher production with greater income and lower prices, thus raising the overall standard of living in society at large. By Taylorist reckoning, productivity, the central efficiency concept in the workplace, served worker, employer, and society alike. Management and labor could, as Taylor put it, "take their eyes off the division of the surplus [because] this surplus becomes so large that it is unnecessary to quarrel over how it shall be divided."[41]

Such was the great promise of the Progressive Era. Battles over distribution, including schemes to share profits between owners and workers, would be rendered obsolete by sheer abundance, by the wealth generated with expert-led productivity gains. It all followed from efficiency's ability to bring science to management, to replace the quirky, egoistic decision making of industrial titans with scientific decision making. To Taylor, science was an "oracle free from human bias and selfishness," a way of knowing and acting that "would point the way to an elevating moral purpose."[42] The bane of industrial production—arbitrary, self-aggrandizing, greedy employers—could be replaced by unbiased, scientific efficiency experts. And the bane of a backward citizenry—tradition, thrift, populism, locality—could be replaced by the efficient organization of society: efficient homemaking, efficient devotion, efficient lawmaking, and, not least we will now see, efficient consuming.

Small wonder Taylorism and, most broadly, the efficiency principle, seeped out of the factory to permeate the homes and offices and playgrounds of people's personal and social lives. Taylor's system was above the pettiness and greed of crass capitalists, beyond the laziness and incompetence of dissolute workers. Taylorism allowed everyone to embrace science and the modern way of life; efficiency could be a personal attribute as readily as a professional technique. Everyone could be a champion. A nation of champions.

Over the years, Taylor's audience just kept widening, a testament to such an appeal. His first paper was published in an esoteric engineering journal; his last paper was serialized in a popular magazine. Over those several decades his language shifted from that of the technical engineer counseling factory owners to the proselytizer converting homemakers and government officials. Taylor and his followers were the messengers of uplift and freedom. Now it was time for everyone to partake. Participation and progress for all. A perfect democracy.

And permeate society it did. "One striking consequence of their concerted effort to fill every corner of social space with the blandishments of management theory," wrote one critic from the vantage point of the 1990s, "was the creation of countless stories about lives uplifted by the gospel of Taylorism, stories directed at a variety of audiences."[43] "In the flood of enthusiasm" for "the principles of scientific management," wrote another, hardly any aspect of American life was exempt, "including the army and navy, the legal profession, the home, the family, the household, the church, and last but not least, . . . education."[44] The message of efficiency "hit like a flash flood," wrote still another, "at first covering almost the entire landscape but soon collecting in various places to be absorbed slowly and to enrich the immediate surroundings."[45]

Perhaps the most insidious permeation of Taylorist reasoning was not in the production of goods or in the making of a home or in the running of a government. It was in production's apparent polar opposite—consumption. In the early decades of the twentieth century, business shifted its emphasis from production to sales. The Taylor Society responded by creating a sales section, discussing how to apply scientific management to the means of influencing consumer demand. "Was there any difference," wrote one efficiency expert in the *Bulletin of the Taylor Society*, "between producing goods and producing orders?"[46] For its part, the National Consumers' League turned from legislation and unionizing to scientific management.[47] "Although the urge for 'social control' of consumers' desires remained a quiet undercurrent in [the 1920s]," writes John Erwin Hollitz in his study of the origins of the consumer economy, "the need to preserve old economic virtues while also recognizing the new imperatives to spend more often led to the embrace of the 'efficient' expenditure of money. . . . Thrift was preserved by defining it not in terms of saving, but rather as proper spending."[48]

To spend efficiently was to shop, to scan retailers' offerings, to monitor prices, and to locate the best and cheapest product on the store shelves. Shopping became the perfect complement to worker productivity. After all, the shopper and the worker are one and the same person. Only now the worker, a serf stripped of discretion and judgment in the factory, could be king or queen in the supermarket. *Consumer sovereignty*, a notion originally developed as a theoretical nicety in neoclassical economics, became the new mantra of business and government leaders. Industrialists only respond to consumers' wants and needs, so the mantra goes. If consumers don't want a product, they won't pay for it and producers can't sell it. What does get produced is therefore only what consumers want. And if there are problems—with safety or pollution, say—it's up to the consumers to demand change. So a firm would be happy to produce wood from well-managed forests or automobiles with safety devices, according to the argument, but it can't do so when the demand isn't there. If the public really wants cleaner production or safer products, preferences will shift and the marketplace will respond. Moreover, say the appropriators of consumer sovereignty, if individual consumer preferences become collectively destructive—if workers are alienated, forests leveled, and rivers fouled— the problem is ethical, it's educational and political, not commercial. Preferences among the mass of consumers can go askew, but the corrections should occur in one's place of worship, in the school, or in the legislature, not in the factory or bank. To suggest that industry should make such corrections is to violate both private choice and public choice, two pillars of an open society and an efficient economy, indeed, of democracy itself.[49]

And so it is that the manager and worker, the homemaker and church official, the educator and government leader, and, not least, the consumer, converged on the idea of efficiency; like desert travelers finding an oasis, they could all agree how terribly desirable it is, how absolutely essential. To be a modern, forward-looking, scientifically oriented person was to accept efficiency as an imperative. People may have jumped on the efficiency bandwagon because it was faddish. But they unwittingly went for a long ride, one with a few bumps—worldwide depression, decimated forests, toxic pollution—but one that promised, and delivered, abundance. In a land of plenty, why ask about the nature of the efficiencies?

Minutes to Dollars

By the early twentieth century in the United States, efficiency had achieved the status of a dominant concept, a widely embraced and routinely invoked ideal, a goal that ranked right up there with American icons such as democracy and progress, a thing that was inherently "good." "By the late 1920's," says science writer Robert Kanigel, "it had begun to seem that all of American society had come under the sway of a single commanding idea—that waste was wrong, that efficiency was the highest good and that eliminating one and achieving the other was best left to the experts."[50] In his comprehensive study of scientific management in the Progressive Era, Samuel Haber concludes that

the Progressive Era is almost made to order for the study of Americans in love with efficiency. For the Progressive Era gave rise to an efficiency craze—a secular Great Awakening, an outpouring of ideas and emotions in which a gospel of efficiency was preached without embarrassment to businessmen, workers, doctors, housewives, and teachers, and yes, preached even to preachers. Men as disparate as Williams Jennings Bryan and Walter Lippmann discoursed enthusiastically on efficiency. Efficient and good came closer to meaning the same thing in these years than in any other period in American history.[51]

Perhaps the meaning of efficiency's remarkable ascendancy in the decades straddling 1900 is best left to a writer of that era. Business Professor Percival White, writing in the *Atlantic Monthly* in 1920, stated that

efficiency is fondly regarded in the American mind as the greatest contribution of this age to civilization. . . . It is deemed an agency for good, a thing one cannot have too much of . . . Efficiency is a lightning calculator, by which you may convert time into anything you like, and read the answer in percentages, to the third decimal place. By its means, for example, you may change minutes into dollars, which is, after all, the thing most of us are trying to do.[52]

Minutes into dollars. Efficiency may have seeped into the lectures of the self-help gurus, the sermons of the clerics, and the commands of the agency heads. But at root it was about commerce, about industrialization and merchandizing; it was about the good life expressed as material abundance for all, as deprivation and self-denial for none. It was about national power and international prestige expressed as industrial output. It was about growth and consumer satisfaction.

"A new business science has grown up in our midst, and it may be called the science of efficiency," wrote economist Brisco in 1914. "Efficiency is the watchword of future industrial progress, growth, and expansion. The nation which produces with the greatest efficiency will be the one who will be able to produce at the least cost, and to command the markets."[53] Natural resource conservation was no exception. In fact, historically in the United States conservation may be an *exemplar* of efficiency, the watchword of industrial growth and consumption. Two unlikely bedfellows, unlikely from a contemporary perspective, anyway, were conservationists and railroad builders. "Conservation leaders felt closer to the spirit of development, typified by the railroad land grants," historian Hays concludes his lengthy treatment of conservation in the age of efficiency,

than to the reaction against the roads. Both railroads and conservationists promoted large-scale economic development. While the conservation movement emphasized greater efficiency in this process, its goal of planned economic growth and its consolidating tendencies closely approximated the spirit of railroad construction. The transcontinental lines, in fact, cooperated closely with conservationists in developing Western resources, and gave special aid to federal irrigation, forest, and range programs. . . .
The broader significance of the conservation movement stemmed from the role it played in the transformation of a decentralized, nontechnical, loosely organized society, where waste and inefficiency ran rampant, into a highly organized, technical, and centrally planned and directed social organization which could meet a complex world with efficiency and purpose.[54]

The Age of Efficiency elevated efficiency from a mere technical device, a means of measuring improvements in machine performance, to a pervasive value. So, yes, the conservation of natural resources was only a part of that age, but, as Theodore Roosevelt proclaimed in 1908, it "is yet but part of another and greater problem . . . the problem of national efficiency, the patriotic duty of insuring the safety and continuance of the Nation."[55] As a principle of social organization efficiency would guide individuals, managers, and policymakers as they overcame tradition and backwardness, as they learned to discipline workers and distribute commodities, as they built a great nation, climbed out of the Great Depression, defeated fascism, and created a cornucopia of goods here on earth. And what are goods if not good. And if goods are good, then more goods must be better. (See figures 3.7 and 3.8.)

Haber says the efficiency craze died with America's entry into World War I. But if the craze died, if the efficiency societies and magazines disappeared, the idea did not. If the term itself is not quite as popular as then, its variants are just as prevalent. With the conclusion of World War II and the postwar economic boom, the idea of efficiency was thoroughly embedded in Americans' language and practices.

100% TRUCK EFFICIENCY

The average motor truck is working at 35% efficiency. The freight car and locomotive shortage is so great that the truck owner should make wider and better use of his transportation facilities.

A horse can pull a heavier load than it can carry. Similarly, a motor truck can pull three times the load it can carry—over the same roads and under the same conditions—if operated with a *King Semi-Trailer*.

A King Semi-Trailer, operated on a 2½ ton motor truck with an average of four trips a day for 300 working days a year, would show a gain of 6,144 tons if operated at only 80% efficiency, carrying the load one way.

If you are working your truck at only 35% efficiency by piling all the load on the truck, adopt the *King Semi-Trailer* method of transportation economy.

Figure 3.7
Trucking company's advertisement, 1918. In the Progressive Era, progress is trucks rolling across North America. Note the claim that average trucks only operate at 35 percent efficiency (not explaining how that's calculated or what exactly it means) and the suggestion that 80 percent efficiency is readily achievable and 100 percent efficiency possible. Reproduced from *100%: The Efficiency Magazine*, vol. 10, no. 6, June 1918, p. 184, courtesy University of Michigan Library.

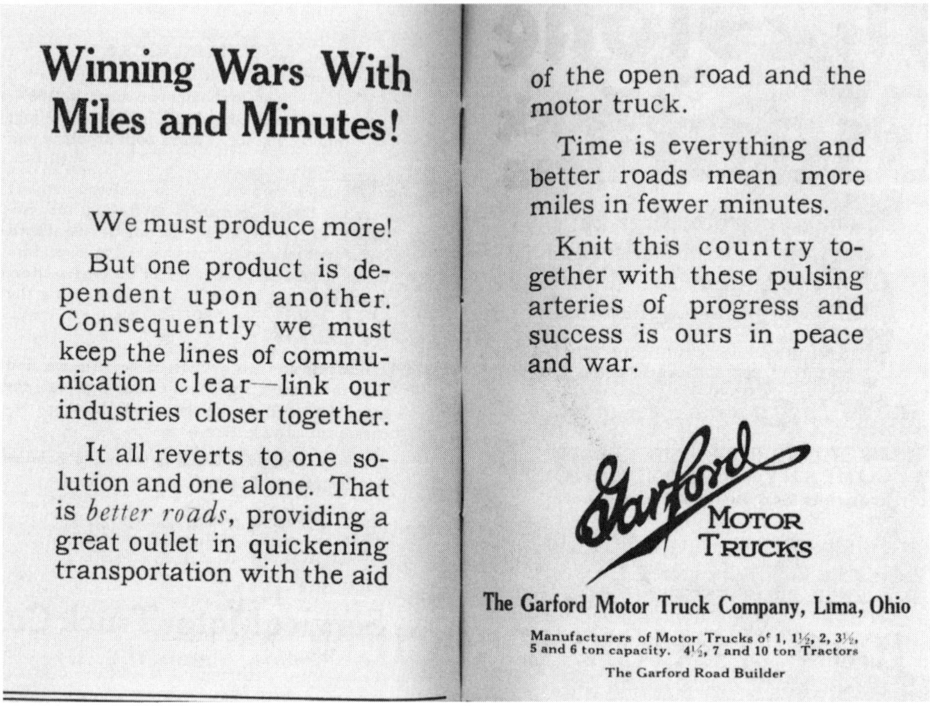

Winning Wars With Miles and Minutes!

We must produce more!

But one product is dependent upon another. Consequently we must keep the lines of communication clear—link our industries closer together.

It all reverts to one solution and one alone. That is *better roads*, providing a great outlet in quickening transportation with the aid of the open road and the motor truck.

Time is everything and better roads mean more miles in fewer minutes.

Knit this country together with these pulsing arteries of progress and success is ours in peace and war.

Garford

MOTOR TRUCKS

The Garford Motor Truck Company, Lima, Ohio

Manufacturers of Motor Trucks of 1, 1½, 2, 3½, 5 and 6 ton capacity. 4½, 7 and 10 ton Tractors

The Garford Road Builder

Figure 3.8
Victory via efficient use of space and time. It was not enough for the trucks themselves to be efficient. Greater production via "quickening transportation" requires "pulsing arteries of progress." Notice there is no mention of who actually pays for such road building, let alone who benefits and who loses. Reproduced from *100%: The Efficiency Magazine*, vol. 10, no. 2, February 1918, pp. 150–151, courtesy University of Michigan Library.

Efficiency Comes of Age

If the Progressive Era was the heyday of efficiency, an adolescent joyride on a linguistic bandwagon that would reform society and relieve the country of its lethargy, its backwardness, its status as a second-rate power, then the 1950s and the decades to follow were the maturing years. No longer novel, no longer an idea that had to be promoted and debated, efficiency receded into the background, not to disappear but to become a *background condition*, the linguistic, analytic, and political water in which we all swim.

After World War II, the consumer society emerged full-blown in the United States and throughout much of the Western world. Advertising and marketing became wildly successful, attracting some of the best minds in psychology and art and design, and raising consumption levels beyond anything previously imaginable. Although the consumerist trend began in the country's early industrialization of the nineteenth century, it was the Taylorist division of tasks and judgment that set the stage. Alienation in the workplace had been legitimated by science and the gains of industrial production. Now it could be further legitimated by consumption: meaning is achieved through consuming the products of other people's work, not through the process of work itself. Individuals maximize utility by choosing from an ever-expanding, ever-changing basket of goods. "To millions today who feel they give up too much to their jobs," writes Kanigel, Taylor "is the source of that fierce, unholy obsession with 'efficiency' that marks modern life."[56] Economic Man metamorphosed into Efficient Consumer.

Logically, efficiency could have accommodated the old virtues of thrift and frugality as it dispensed with the vices of greed and excess. Instead, in those heady days of the roaring 1920s, followed by the booming 1950s and the exuberant 1990s, the only politically acceptable form of efficiency was that of ever-increasing material growth. For an emerging national power, then a competing superpower, and finally the only superpower, population and industrial output are the national crops that have to grow; efficiency is the fertilizer.

From the modern vantage point it is too easy to assume that efficiency has always driven behavior, across cultures and across time, even across species. Like personal gain, it appears universal. Certainly the intuition behind the idea is universal: for most activity, especially material provisioning, one wishes to get the best return for a given effort. "Lose no time," was number 6 on Benjamin Franklin's famous list of personal virtues published in 1783. "Be always employed in something useful; cut off all unnecessary action."[57] Who can argue with that? In fact, schools in the United States now routinely instruct children and their parents on the virtues of efficient time management. "Managing time is a skill that helps people of all ages achieve what they set out to do," say the makers of a daily planner used in middle schools in the year 2003–2004. "To be a successful student, your child needs to develop proper time management habits. . . . Trim activities that take up too much on important activities . . . fine-tune your schedules from time to time"[58] (figures 3.9 and 3.10).

The efficiency virtue has moved up, arguably from number 6 to number 1. And not just as a guide to personal behavior as Franklin intended it, but as an *organizing principle* of social behavior.

Make Your <u>Minutes</u>
Count for <u>You</u>!

1. Carry on your study program at all times—before or during breakfast, too.

2. Minutes on street cars or trains to work may be lost—use them for your own good.

3. Have you an appointment with a man? Precious minutes can be used while waiting.

4. If you're traveling as part of your job, be wise; make leisure minutes pay dividends through study.

5. The noon hour can be used for refreshment purposes—refresh your mind, too, through learning new principles.

6. Spare moments during working hours can be well used by every man who is training for business success.

7. Vacation weeks can be utilized in part for review of previous material.

8. Evening hours are precious hours for the man with determination.

9. Open afternoons and holidays can well contain their quota of extra-study time.

10. It takes only a minute, often, to renew an acquaintance which will prove valuable, as part of your program.

[12]

Figure 3.9
Time management circa 1930. Aspiring businessmen must make efficient use of every minute of every day. Reproduced from *Personal Efficiency*, October 1930, p. 12, courtesy University of Michigan Library.

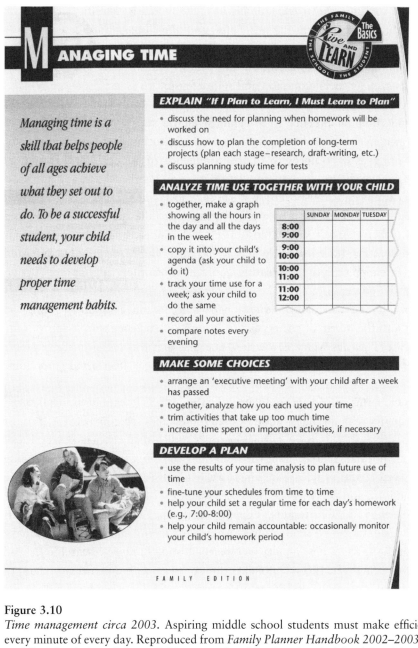

MANAGING TIME

The Family Live and Learn: The Basics — The School The Student

Managing time is a skill that helps people of all ages achieve what they set out to do. To be a successful student, your child needs to develop proper time management habits.

EXPLAIN "If I Plan to Learn, I Must Learn to Plan"

- discuss the need for planning when homework will be worked on
- discuss how to plan the completion of long-term projects (plan each stage – research, draft-writing, etc.)
- discuss planning study time for tests

ANALYZE TIME USE TOGETHER WITH YOUR CHILD

- together, make a graph showing all the hours in the day and all the days in the week
- copy it into your child's agenda (ask your child to do it)
- track your time use for a week; ask your child to do the same
- record all your activities
- compare notes every evening

	SUNDAY	MONDAY	TUESDAY
8:00 9:00			
9:00 10:00			
10:00 11:00			
11:00 12:00			

MAKE SOME CHOICES

- arrange an 'executive meeting' with your child after a week has passed
- together, analyze how you each used your time
- trim activities that take up too much time
- increase time spent on important activities, if necessary

DEVELOP A PLAN

- use the results of your time analysis to plan future use of time
- fine-tune your schedules from time to time
- help your child set a regular time for each day's homework (e.g., 7:00-8:00)
- help your child remain accountable: occasionally monitor your child's homework period

FAMILY EDITION

Figure 3.10
Time management circa 2003. Aspiring middle school students must make efficient use of every minute of every day. Reproduced from *Family Planner Handbook 2002–2003*, Forsythe Middle School, Ann Arbor, Michigan; produced by Premier: A School Specialty Company, Bellingham, WA, 2003, courtesy of Paul Princen.

Beyond the intuition, however, humans have likely employed efficiency only as one among many social organizing principles, and likely one subordinate to power or inheritance or divine right, maybe even equity and justice. At some scale, say the family or community or nation, efficient outcomes were probably always subordinate to goals such as social cohesion and self-defense.

The rise of efficiency in little more than a century, its ascendance from an intuitive idea and common practice to a technical metric and now to a broad social organizing principle, is arguably a product of modernization, maybe a definition of modernization. It is an outgrowth of the confluence of scientific understanding, rapid technological change, human population growth, fossil-fuel use, and advances in communications and transportation. "Those who favor efficiency as the goal of social policy tend to think of it as a grand value that takes up, incorporates, and balances all other values," says philosopher Mark Sagoff.[59] That it now extends from managerial mantra to social policy to personal choice, from education and health care to shopping and childrearing and a host of other "nonmarket" activities, suggests its power in modern life. That few people stop to take notice suggests its *hegemony*, its pervasive and unquestioned value, its universal application. "So interwoven into the fabric of society is this notion of efficiency that it seems 'only common sense,'" writes Mary E. Clark. "The fact that this belief in the supreme rightness of efficiency is just that, a belief based on certain arbitrary assumptions, escapes us."[60]

On its own terms efficiency is an unassailable good. It cannot be challenged because it equates with all that is good or better. It escapes scrutiny because its most common uses, possibly its most pernicious ones, are broadly social and political, not technical, not managerial. As a rhetorical device it is a sure route to claiming value, to asserting authority, to "moving forward," while leaving behind all those mired in tradition and the ways of the past. When I wish to promote a project or a policy, especially one that requires others to pony up, I find a way to frame it as an efficiency gain: the house renovation will allow my family and our guests to make better use of the space; a new faculty member will bring in more research overhead dollars for my university. If my opponents can't counter with an efficiency claim of their own, I win. Questions of fairness or equity or usefulness or excess fall by the wayside. Efficiency trumps all. Efficiency becomes the all-purpose means to all progressive ends. (See box 3.2.)

So in its evolution from shop-floor managerial technique to social imperative, efficiency has achieved the status of a self-evident truth, the gospel truth: as individuals become ever more efficient, they, and the society they comprise, are better off.

Box 3.2
Efficiency saves energy, the nation, the environment

* "The resources of the earth are yet very far from a state of thorough development. There is room for incalculable expansion. . . . The sum to be added to the world's wealth and comfort by the conquest of the waste places is literally beyond the dreams of avarice, even in a day when avarice has large conceptions. . . . The solidarity of the industry with a virtual monopoly at home and advantages abroad . . . would achieve the highest economic efficiency." William Smythe, 1899, 1905.

* "The conservation of resources . . . is yet but part of another and greater problem . . . the problem of national efficiency, the patriotic duty of insuring the safety and continuance of the Nation." Theodore Roosevelt, 1908.

* "No longer the dirty fuel of the past, coal is being burned much cleaner due largely to improved pollution-control technologies. The Environmental Protection Agency says coal-fired electricity plants are 33 percent less polluting than in 1970, even as coal-based electricity has nearly tripled. . . . Electricity is the cleanest and most efficient energy source. The rise in greenhouse emissions concerns all of us. But this should not be permitted to muddle what remains the essential point: We need to recognize the critical contribution of coal to energy supply now and in the future." Aureal T. Cross, professor of geological sciences 2001.

* "There is another way [to fight global warming]: Review the state of science and technology, involve the private sector, set realistic goals and seriously engage developing countries. This is the path toward energy efficiency and progress on the environment." William K. Reily, chairman of the World Wildlife Fund and former EPA administrator, April 2001.

* A triple win from energy efficiency . . . our costs go down, your pocketbook stays fuller, and environmental emissions are lower. . . . In keeping with the desire for conservation, we strive to produce as energy-efficiently as possible. Within ExxonMobil, we have developed a comprehensive Global Energy Management System [that] looks at energy consumption at every link in the supply chain—from production and shipping to manufacturing and transportation. We apply years of experience and the latest technology to optimize energy consumption each step along the way. ExxonMobil, 2003.

Sources: William Smythe, *The Conquest of Arid America* (Seattle, 1969), p. 43; quoted in Donald Worster, *Rivers of Empire: Water, Aridity, and the Growth of the American West* (New York, Oxford University Press, 1985), p. 121; William Smythe, *Constructive Democracy: The Economics of a Square Deal* (New York: Macmillan, 1905), p. 246; *Proceedings of a Conference of Governors in the White House, Washington, D.C.,* May 13–15, 1908 (Washington, D.C., 1909), p. 12; cited in Samuel Hays, *Conservation and the Gospel of Efficiency: The Progressive Conservation Movement, 1890–1920* (Cambridge, MA: Harvard University Press, 1959), p. 125; Aureal T. Cross, "Can We Depend on Coal to Avoid Energy Woes? Cleaner-burning coal promises best way for powering Michigan," *Detroit News*, March 1, 2001, p. 13A; William K. Reilly, "A Climate Policy That Works," *New York Times*, April 1, 2001, sect. 4, p. 17; Advertisement, "Win-Win-Win," *New York Times*, 2003, accessed online at www.exxonmobil.com.

And they are better off unambiguously. Efficiency's offerings are self-evident, a given, a background condition. We hardly notice its role in decision making. And we rarely notice when it's abused, when it's appropriated and contorted to meet the needs of boosters of whatever stripe—commercial, political, educational, religious, environmental. The mental revolution Taylor imagined is complete.

And there efficiency sits, atop its pedestal, dressed in the trappings of science and progress, commanding all to lose no time, to be always useful, to convert minutes to dollars, to push workers and to push product.

It is time to take efficiency down a notch or two. Under conditions of global ecological constraint, other principles need propping up—like precaution and polluter pays and zero discharge and reverse onus and restraint and respite. To further unpack efficiency after this curious history, is, curiously enough, now left to the technical. Efficiency's scientific clothes, its primary source of legitimacy, must be removed. Exposure of the technical side, the very *ratios* efficiency is supposed to represent, reveals efficiency's core limitations, its deliberate ambiguity, its susceptibility to manipulation, and, most significantly for the purposes of this book, its inherent contradiction of the ecological and social conditions necessary for long-term, sustainable resource use.

4

Whose Ratios? From Technic to Rhetoric

Efficiency's exalted status came about in part because of the rhetoric, the proselytizing of Progressive Era leaders such as Frederick Winslow Taylor, Theodore Roosevelt, and Louis Brandeis. Efficiency connotes sophisticated thinking and living, the essence of modernity, progress. It is the problem solver *extraordinaire*, from workplace hazards to global warming to personal time scarcity. In the United States, efficiency is as close to all-round goodness as the proverbial motherhood and apple pie. But its popular appeal, its ability to motivate action and legitimate policies, derives from more than rhetoric, more than a good sell job. It derives from a certain scientific cachet.

For those who probe behind the rhetoric, they can find numbers. But not just any numbers; they can find *ratios*. It is a notion few of us think about in our daily lives. Ratios are a bit mysterious. They are not like everyday measures of weight, height, time, and temperature, for instance—single numbers followed by a unit, like 200 pounds, 6 feet, 5 hours, and 32 degrees. Ratios are two (or more) numbers, each with different units. They are expressed as fractions and can be so manipulated mathematically. We routinely use them, of course—the speed we drive our cars, the price we pay for bread, the wage we get for an hour's work. But we rarely stop to ask why we are using a particular set of numbers and units, let alone deign to uncover their full meaning or challenge the prerogatives of those who successfully appropriate them.

To specify a ratio, let alone to manipulate one, is not an everyday task. Rather, it is something for the mathematically inclined, for those few who, as youngsters, sat in the back of the class, barely listened to the math teacher, and completed the homework assignment before class was out. It is for the scientists, the experts.

So when people hear "efficiency" they hear "better" or "more," yet with a scientific gloss. It's not just any better or more. It's what science has delivered, what the experts, those who could appreciate the elegance, the flow of mathematical relations, could establish as better or more.

But outside the laboratory and lecture hall, one person's elegance can be another's misfortune. Create an efficiency here, displace a cost there. Find an "economy" with the new device, eliminate the old job. Where, in practice, there are efficiencies, there are choices. Thus, taking efficiency down a notch or two as a broad social organizing principle begins with distinctions: technics versus politics; claims versus effects.

The Ratios: Who Decides?

The problem with efficiency as a numerical ratio is that there is no formula, no rule, no general principle for choosing. The choice of a ratio can be quite arbitrary—or, as we will see, strategic. Consequently, the very act of choosing a ratio determines value and the distribution of value.

I may claim my farm is efficient because I get more bushels per acre than my neighbor. But my neighbor claims she is more efficient because she spends less on machines per acre. I'm highlighting the value of production volume; she's highlighting the value of minimizing capital costs. It is impossible to say which of us is doing better. I may like filling my silos to the brim each year; she may like extracting another year's life from her grandparents' old tractor. Both of us may be terribly efficient, given what we value. But without further specification, neither of us can claim to be more efficient than the other. Even if my neighbor and I both claimed our choices were means to, say, maximum profits, the efficiency ratios themselves are incommensurable. I'm measuring volume of grain, she's measuring a machine's usefulness.

On the face of it, a third party resolves things. A mutual friend, an agricultural extension agent, a seed salesperson, a legislator, or simply "the state" steps in and sets the efficiency ratio—say, tons of grain per acre. She and I weigh our harvests, divide by our two farms' acreage, and the third party declares the winner—the one with the largest ratio of weighed grain to the acre.

Complications arise, though, if the third party does more than judge. If it allocates resources to us (for example, farm-support payments or legislative favors), or if it extracts resources from us (say, tax revenues), the third party's judgment is likely to change our behavior. We are likely to think and act strategically (as is the third party, given its interests). Whichever ratio is chosen, she and I will try to improve our production in terms of that ratio. If the ratio is yield in terms of tons per acre,

I order extra fertilizer; she spreads her manure just before it rains. I hire migrant workers; she cajoles family and friends to pitch in. I work late into the night; she works on weekends.

So who's more efficient? I am, of course—assuming my methods are more "productive." But only in the narrow technical sense and only because the third party has designated my preferred efficiency ratio—tons per acre. The values I'm promoting (and, implicitly, the values I'm depreciating) are certainly more complex than that captured in "tons per acre." I want high profits, I want to pay off my loans, and I want to be able to sell my farm to the highest bidder to ensure my retirement. "Tons per acre" is a reasonable proxy for that suite of values. And it probably aligns nicely with the government's desire for revenues: each ton sold generates a percentage for the public coffers.

Alternatively, the third party could set the ratio as tons of grain per unit of capital depreciation (machinery and land). She and I weigh our harvests and divide by our respective depreciation measures. For a given harvest, the farm with the least depreciation—that is, the farm that has best maintained its equipment and soil—is the most efficient. Now who's more efficient? Likely she is. She has used the same tractor for years, maintaining it religiously. And she has put little pressure on the land, fertilizing only with silage from that land, eschewing external inputs. She may get fewer tons of grain per acre than me, but for every ton she does get she has less depreciation than me. With the ratio of grain per capital depreciation, she's more efficient.

Efficiency ratios are thus neither self-evident nor is their increase unambiguously "good." No third party can set an unambiguously precise and comparable measure. Every choice of a ratio reflects a choice of values, a politics. And those values do not just separate along the familiar divides of modern and traditional, new and old, fast and slow, as this farming hypothetical might suggest. They separate along divides of time frame—short term and commercially meaningful versus long term and ecologically meaningful—and cost displacement—the ability to externalize the costs of production and consumption in time and space.

Shifting gears, consider finance. Companies A and B merge to achieve "economies of scale." Each company had its own accounting department and warehouses. And the two companies' shipping routes overlapped. Now, combined, the companies can eliminate redundant services. The cost saving in labor, storage, and transport are the efficiency gains. They are tangible and measurable: jobs, payroll, leases, maintenance expenses. With contemporary financial markets, the gains often translate into bumps in stock price. Shareholder value goes up. On top of this, the fees and salaries of the dealmakers—law firms, CEOs, financial consultants—go up. Every-one is a winner. Joint gains for all. Or so it appears.

Even if the gains from mergers are real (and many doubt that, even in conven-tional terms), these gains are distributed: stockholders and dealmakers do better; laid-off workers do worse. A priori one cannot say if the environment does better or worse with such "economies." If monopoly power increases with the merger, standard economic theory tells us to expect lower output and increased prices. Not-so-standard economic analysis would suggest that lower output lowers overall throughput, thus putting less stress on natural systems. On the other hand, increased economic power can translate into an increased propensity to shade and distance costs (see "Shading" below).

Once again, then, an efficiency is ambiguous in its distribution of value among parties, over time, across space (physical and social), and with respect to environ-mental impact. And yet, in modern society, efficiency is equated with all that is good. And not just good for a few but, the rhetoric has it, good for all: joint gains, gains from trade, win-win, all boats rise, jobs aplenty. The discrepancy between the ambi-guity of value distribution and the definitiveness of rhetorical claims can in part be explained by a failure to specify ratios, as well as a failure to be explicit about what is left out of those ratios.

When All Else Ain't Equal

So what, exactly, is an "efficiency"? In strictly physical terms, it's more work for a given input of energy or the same work for less input or proportionately more work for an increase in energy input. If I get 120 lumens out of a kilowatt of electricity, I will have achieved an efficiency when I get 140 lumens for that kilowatt, or when I get the same 120 lumens from 0.8 kilowatts, or when I get 150 lumens with 1.2 kilo-watts. The original 120:1 ratio increases to 140:1, 150:1, and 125:1, respectively. Efficiency is similar in economic terms: more productive output for the input, or the same output for less input, or proportionately more output for an increase in input.

In practice, though, such efficiencies require one not-so-trivial qualifier: all else equal. That is, an efficiency obtains if one can confidently say that nothing else changes simultaneously. A new car engine is more fuel efficient if, as the engine uses less gasoline per mile, it does not use more oil per mile. A fertilizer improves agri-cultural productivity if, by increasing yields of corn, it does not simultaneously diminish yields of soybeans. A city's street lighting is more efficient if new bulbs do not require more maintenance, which itself consumes more electricity.

If the all-else-equal qualifier pertains, an efficiency gain is an undeniably good thing. In its most general form, an efficiency is, after all, an increase in the ratio good-to-bad. Who can argue with more good for a given bad? Or less bad for a given good? Or accepting more bad so as to achieve even more good? As it turns out, the only ones who can argue against efficiency are those who, in practice, are left out of the gains. Claiming an efficiency, I will show, is at once a technical claim and a political move, an opportunity and a strategic maneuver. It distributes as it creates. A pure efficiency exists only on paper. In the real world, some people gain as others remain the same or lose. Those others may be one's neighbors or fellow citizens. But with increasing environmental criticality, risk export, and responsibility evasion (chapter 2), they are people downstream and downwind or on the other side of the globe, or they are future generations. Before turning to the environmental side of efficiency claims, though, it is necessary to further spell out the technics and the politics, the claims and the effects. Four tendencies in efficiency claims pertain: simplifying, individualizing, saving, and shading.

Simplifying

In choosing from the universe of possible ratios, the more tangible the ratio, the more users see the gains, and the more likely the ratio is to succeed as an efficiency intervention. A new, more efficient car engine might improve gasoline mileage for the vehicle's useful life or its mileage per ton of load or mileage per degree of temperature variance from 25°C. But what is likely to catch the attention of car buyers and regulators alike is simply miles per gallon, what people actually experience driving and filling the fuel tank. Gas mileage over a vehicle's life span may be important to drivers but it is hard to sense, as is gas mileage that varies with load or temperature.

Efficiencies thus have a "simplification bias." A simple, two-element ratio of concrete measures is preferred. Numbers that express lumens per kilowatt, grain per acre, and shoes per worker catch our attention. Scientist and lay citizen alike can understand and work with a ratio that is simple and concrete. The language of efficiency becomes universal when simple measurables are on the table. Immeasurables are for the clergy and the philosopher, sometimes the environmentalist.

And where tangibles are hard to come by, a readily intelligible substitute is often at hand, especially in market-oriented societies: money. An educator can hope to improve the ratio of learning to attendance with a new curriculum. But what administrators and budget makers are bound to look for are children-to-classroom or teacher-to-children ratios, both of which translate readily into monetary terms. A transportation planner may envisage a society of freely flowing traffic with no congestion and few accidents. But municipal authorities will be looking at roadway paved per dollar and vehicles per hour passing through choke points. A business executive may aspire to "social responsibility" in the corporation via the "triple bottom line" (social and environmental performance along with the financial). But when push comes to shove, when sales lag and stock prices drop, everyone simplifies, focusing on productivity (output per labor cost) and return on investment (payout on the invested dollar). (See box 4.1.)

Box 4.1
Managing doctors and beds: Hospitals emulate Henry Ford

In the 1990s health maintenance organizations (HMOs) took over much of health care in the United States. They promised, and in many cases delivered, lower costs, lower prices, and all round gains for consumers (formerly known as patients). How? Efficiencies. The means, as any student of the Progressive Era can guess, was specialization, eliminating waste, and working faster.

Doctors would no longer run a medical practice or conduct surgery by preparing the patient and operating. They wouldn't waste time just talking to patients. Anybody can do that. Rather, doctors would diagnose and treat. Or cut and suture. Or teach interns how to process patients quickly. HMOs would manage the business end and make sure the doctors had ample assistants (read, low-paid medical workers). HMOs would eliminate redundant services, like unnecessary talk and unused beds.

HMOs have captured efficiencies all right. They have compelled doctors to see more patients in a day—that is, they have increased the efficiency ratio of patient-visits per doctor. They have streamlined medical training. And they have cut hospitals' "surge capacity," those extra beds and rooms that are rarely needed.

So how efficient is it really? Pick a ratio, especially one with monetary units, and one can probably conclude that, yes, the health care system is more efficient with managed care. But pick one with surgical death rates or alternative treatments or disaster relief capacity in hospitals and improvement is doubtful. The *quantity* of health care may be increasing—more patients processed, more procedures employed, more revenues generated—but there appears to be a widespread consensus in the United States that the *quality* has declined. Surgery is a case in point.

Joseph R. Wilder, an emeritus professor of surgery at Mount Sinai School of Medicine in New York, was a doctor for some fifty years, twenty as surgical chief of staff. With efficient, high-quantity surgery, he's found errors can happen: "It is common practice in many institutions for a surgeon to start an operation and then leave at some point, letting an assistant finish it. The doctor may rush off to a second operating room, where another assistant has prepared another patient for surgery. All the busy surgeon sees is an operative site—a section of abdomen, for example, where a hernia is to be repaired. The rest of the patient's body is covered by a drape."

That site is what the surgeon knows best, of course. Technically, that is what the surgeon, the specialist, should focus on. But all is not technical in the operating room.

Box 4.1
(continued)

"Suppose the assistant, misreading a chart or working from an inaccurate record, had draped the wrong side of the abdomen," says Wilder. "All the surgeon's skill will be for nothing if he does not make a check of his own before he begins to cut."

An unlikely scenario? Not at all. According to an authoritative study by the Institute of Medicine, between 44,000 and 98,000 Americans die each year from medical errors. It used to be that surgeons would start, carry out, and complete each operation, even place the dressing and see that the patient was moved properly from the operating table. Under health care management, that would be terribly inefficient, a waste of specialized talent and training, not to mention salary paid by the HMO. Assistants should do those things.

For Wilder, the basic rule that minimizes surgical error is trust no one: "A good surgeon cannot conduct any aspect of a case on the word of an assistant alone. And reports from radiology, pathology and the laboratory must be checked by the doctor's own inspection of the records in those departments of the hospital. It is too easy for the test results from one Jones to make their way onto the record of another [Jones], leading, for example, to a doctor opening a patient to remove gallstones that do not exist."

Dr. Wilder also insists that surgeons, no matter how specialized, treat the whole patient: "The way is open to mistakes when, instead of spending a half-hour taking a good medical history in the initial office visit, the doctor has a secretary hand the patient a sheet of paper to fill out, producing a record that is by its nature incomplete and vague."

If Dr. Wilder's prescriptions are valid, no amount of specialization, no division of labor, no supercomputerized record keeping can substitute for the whole-person care of a patient by a single doctor. Only one person can really know the patient, inside and out, so to speak. A sufficient level of specialization means that, although surgeons are highly specialized as doctors, as health care professionals they must perform all tasks, not just the specialized ones. Like the owner-operator company boss who built the enterprise from the ground up, or the fishing captain who maintains the boat, charts the ocean bottom, and sells the fish, the surgeon must perform or monitor everything from check-in to discharge. Sufficiency in the surgical ward is that point at which the benefits of more efficient performance via isolated tasks increase the risk of error.

Doctors in a rush tend to focus on single symptoms and single techniques. Those who take the time to assess what a patient needs—procedures that do not fit into an efficiency ratio—are more likely to probe for underlying causes, to find extenuating circumstances, to look for both the somatic and the psychological, and to treat the patient as a whole person. Hospitals run like factories make doctors and nurses like Frederick Winslow Taylor's line workers. "You can only run so fast and see so many patients and not run an assembly line," says one New York orthopedic surgeon.

Medical training is another area suffering from excess efficiency. "The focus of clinical training has changed drastically, as efficiency has become increasingly important," say Dr. David A. Shaywitz, a research fellow at Massachusetts General Hospital and Dr. Dennis A. Ausiello, physician in chief at Mass General and a professor at Harvard

Box 4.1
(continued)

University. "Our daily experience suggests that in the current preoccupation with speed, something vital to medical education has been lost." New doctors lack basic skills such as performing a routine physical exam.

"Yet, what may turn out to be the most significant casualty of the modern training experience," say doctors Shaywitz and Ausiello, "is also the least obvious: the gradual disappearance of time to think, in an expansive fashion, about an individual patient. Traditionally, such reflective thinking has been a hallmark of teaching hospitals. It was why doctors came to train and why patients came for treatment."

Reflective thinking disappears as HMOs and insurance companies focus more and more on the bottom line, on getting the most return on their invested dollar. "This matters," continue Shaywitz and Ausiello, "because medicine is more than simply the compassionate (and now, efficient) application of received wisdom; it is also the challenging of old customs and the development of new insights."

It was precisely this thoughtful questioning that led to the discovery that stomach ulcers can be caused by bacterial infections and that steroids can effectively treat rheumatoid arthritis.

From the hospital's perspective, "speed medicine" is necessary to cut costs, of course. But even if one could justify the increase in surgical errors and loss of basic doctoring skills and reflection, it's hard to justify the reduction in beds, certainly not from a public health, disaster-response perspective. Before the wave of "efficient" health care swept the country, hospitals routinely kept extra beds—that is, more than they filled on an average day. The reason was to prepare for the nonaverage day, the day when vehicles piled up on the freeway or a mysterious disease broke out or buildings collapsed. It was only after the 2001 attacks on the World Trade Center in New York that public health officials realized that such "surge capacity" in hospitals, what everyone took for granted, had eroded. Such streamlining became another unobvious loss when a system is pushed to maximize one thing—revenues—and minimize other things—waste.

From hyperspecialized surgery to the demise of reflective doctoring to minimal beds, efficiency has overstepped its bounds in contemporary medical care. Doctors know it. Patients sense it. And, it appears, one study after another confirms it.

Specialization, quantity, speed, streamlining: Maybe it's time to ask how much is too much and how much is enough.

Sources: Joseph R. Wilder, "Give Doctors Tougher Rules," *New York Times*, December 10, 1999, p. A35; Dr. David A. Shaywitz and Dr. Dennis A. Ausiello, "The Demise of Reflective Doctoring," *New York Times*, May 9, 2000, p. D7; Linda T. Kohn, Janet M. Corrigan, and Molla S. Donaldson, eds., *To Err Is Human: Building a Safer Health System* (Washington, DC: National Academy Press, 2000); cited in Denise Grady, "Oops, Wrong Patient: Journal Takes On Medical Mistakes," *New York Times*, June 18, 2002, pp. D1, D6; Gina Kolata, "For Those Who Can Afford It, Old-Style Medicine Returns," *New York Times*, March 17, 2000, pp. A1, A18.

Individualizing

Miles per gallon (MPG) figures are plastered on new cars in the United States, right below EPA, the acronym well known to Americans to stand for the Environmental Protection Agency. Car owners know their vehicles pollute and they know the EPA does something about it. It doesn't take much reflection to realize that the higher the MPG number the better that car is for the environment. In fact, the agency, with support from environmental groups and the media, conveys that very message routinely in its public education campaigns: buy a fuel-efficient car and protect the environment.

Few drivers and, it seems, few analysts stop to question the ratio. They don't ask what is left out, such as total miles driven, or the speed driven, or drivers' patterns of acceleration and braking. Drivers and analysts and policymakers take such matters as given—that is, *given by each individual driver*. Consumer sovereignty (chapters 3 and 5) dictates that such matters are questions of individual choice: nobody tells me where I drive or how far I drive or how I apply the accelerator and brake on my car.

What gets left out by "individualizing" environmental problems is the collective choices that enable, indeed, encourage, even require, certain kinds of individual driving patterns.[1] If I want to amble down the expressway at an optimally fuel-efficient speed of 30 mph I can't. I have to "go with the flow"; I can't impede traffic. American drivers rarely have the choice to drive optimally, or slowly, or simply not to drive. Those choices are precluded by the very structure of the transportation system—the roadway, the parking, and, perhaps most significantly, the expectation, the norm that one can and should always drive to one's destination. In fact, rapid driving, the kind that increases traffic flow, is the norm, indeed, the rule (see chapter 8).

The MPG figures capture technological improvements—fuel injection, lightweight materials, aerodynamic body design, for instance. These features are measured by standardized laboratory tests conducted by the EPA to estimate each car's average fuel efficiency. But they do not capture the behavioral changes that accompany such features, let alone the changes that follow from infrastructural changes such as widened roadway.

After the oil shocks of the 1970s, fuel efficiency improved significantly in the United States, from 11.9 mpg in 1973 to 16.9 in the early 1990s. But total fuel consumption increased, too. Each of those cars got more miles for a gallon of gasoline burned. But more cars hit the roads, each car drove farther and faster, and governments built more roads. Between 1970 and 1990, American drivers increased their miles driven from about 1 trillion miles to 2 trillion miles. And the number of vehicles increased 50 percent.[2] All this at the same time American drivers, guided by the EPA's MPG stickers, improved their fuel efficiencies. Technically, the U.S. auto fleet became more efficient. Environmentally, U.S. cars loaded waste sinks for SO_2, NO_x, and CO_2 more than ever.

The difference is behavior: the individual behavior of drivers and the collective behavior of automakers, highway builders, and legislators. The work-to-energy ratios of cars indeed improved. But it wasn't the case that less gasoline was burned for the same miles driven, or even that the same amount of gas was burned for more miles driven. Rather, the efficiency gain was via the third option: proportionately more miles driven for an increase in gasoline consumed and pollutants emitted.

Not only do few people question personal driving behavior, they do not question the impacts of the structure of auto driving. Most people accept a ratio like MPG as an indicator of improvement, of "conserving energy," of "saving the environment" (while driving unimpeded to all points). Most also accept individual choice as the natural order of things, the order that supercedes external impact, especially impact occurring over long time periods. In so doing they ignore collective choices, especially choices regarding cultural norms and underlying structures. And it is evolved norms and structures that constrain individual choices at the same time that they enhance individual choices.

In my town as, it seems, in nearly all others across North America and much of Europe, the automobile reigns supreme. Pedestrians step aside when approached by a car, even if they are in a crosswalk. Bicyclists hug graveled shoulders or dodge pedestrians on sidewalks to keep out of the auto's way. People apologize when they impede the smooth flow of automobile traffic but don't think twice when their driving holds back strollers and wheelchairs and bicycles, let alone pedestrians. And as planners make transit choices, public transportation takes a backseat. A recent airport renovation made car drop-off and pickup exceptionally easy at the same time that airport authorities slapped a tax on buses.

The norm of car driving is evident to anyone who has lived in other, less car-dominated cultures. But here in North America, such a norm is justified by notions of personal freedom, economic growth, and jobs. These indicators of progress play out on the roadways. When drivers are impeded in their movement—when they are "wasting time" in a traffic jam or have to negotiate narrow, winding streets or can't park within a few yards of their destination—policymakers take action. They widen and straighten roads, they repair potholes, they build bridges and parking structures. In the United States, taxpayers spend billions subsidizing auto driving every year. Through federal subsidies and local initiatives, taxpayers, via their elected representatives, extend the water and sewer lines to make urban sprawl possible—and cheap. Planning boards, development agencies, and taxing authorities zone the land and set taxes to facilitate private auto travel (chapter 8).

The EPA's MPG figures thus individualize pollution problems and privilege the car at the same time that society (read, legislators and taxpayers) paves the way for more private automobile travel. The ultimate justifications are efficiency claims. Time saving is probably the most intuitive of these justifications, the one most appealing to each of us, citizen and policymaker alike. (See box 4.2.)

Saving

Have a forest-management problem? You can save trees with our brand-new harvesting method; it's the most productive ever. Fish stocks diminishing? These new food-processing techniques allow you to save the by-catch, making use of everything your nets bring in. Got an electricity crisis? Save energy with these new lightbulbs. Global warming? Save jobs by getting more GDP out of every gigajoule. The river running low? Save water with drip irrigation and showerhead flow restrictors. Save, save, save!

The prescription is ubiquitous. Whether the problem is a supply shortage or overharvesting or excess pollution, the answer is savings via efficiencies. The terms for the efficiencies may vary—productivity, economies of scale, conservation, streamlining—but the answer is the same: *save* resources by getting more use from each tree, from each fishery, from each electrical appliance, from each acre of farmland.

The intuition is straightforward. One "saves" a resource by using it better. I save food and ease my grocery bill (maybe even my waistline) by making use of everything in the refrigerator before the stuff spoils; any excess becomes soup. I save my back and knees by cutting cordwood with a chainsaw rather than with that old bow saw. I save time and drudgery cleaning my house with a vacuum cleaner and quick-acting detergents, rather than a broom and plain soap.

Such ordinary personal measures are indeed "savings"—for me, that is. Without closer examination, though, it is not obvious that my personal savings are not someone else's expenditures, or burden. I could just order the cordwood instead of cutting it myself, for instance, but that would mean someone else would wreck their back. And my short-term gains could result in long-term losses, for me or others. I could hire a maid and let her clean with those potent cleansers, damaging her lungs and perhaps mine, as well as increasing run-off pollution in our waterways.

Box 4.2
From point A to point B: Drive time vs. real time

Ask an automobile driver, transportation planner, or city official why people drive and the almost certain answer is, to save time. Ask them why roads are built, traffic signals installed, and lanes added, and the answer is to facilitate the flow of traffic, which is to say, to save time.

At first glance, such savings are obvious. To get from point A to point B (let's say A and B are at least a few miles apart), I can walk to a bus stop, stand there hoping the bus comes on time, then board the bus, travel to the stop nearest my destination, and walk the rest of the way. Or I can just get in my car and drive there. Since the bus takes the same route or, more likely, a more circuitous route, and travels the same speed (or slower), clearly I save time driving. Few conveyances and few traffic conditions would allow me to get to my destination sooner. The automobile trumps all. It's the most efficient. It saves me valuable time.

Or does it? A few skeptics, this author included, have dared ask the question, even in notable lands of automobilia such as Germany, the United Kingdom, and the United States. The answer, like so many with problems of subtle dimensions, is, it all depends. Depends, that is, on the efficiency ratio.

By my back-of-the-envelope calculation, the savings aren't clear, at least not here in North America. The average monetary cost of owning and operating a car in the United State is, last I checked, $6,500. If the mean income is $30,000 and take-home pay is about $26,000, this means the average American works roughly three months a year (January, February, and March, let's say) just to have one's car. That's a lot of time working to save time.

Other skeptics of time savings have been more systematic in their analysis. Some years ago, social critic Ivan Illich estimated that the typical American male commits 1,600 hours annually to his automobile. That's driving, fueling, and washing it; and it's earning the money to buy, insure, and maintain it. Again, that's a lot of time to save time.

Both these examples involve only private time costs, not public, let alone the costs to the environment. A group of German transportation researchers calculated the speeds of three vehicles—bicycles, small cars, and large cars. When the annual cost of the car and the owners' income were factored in, the researchers found that bicycles are actually faster than small cars and only a few kilometers per hour slower than the larger cars.

The efficiency of time saving via increased speed—that is, the efficiency of increasing the ratio miles:hour—is, at a minimum, suspect. Bring in immeasurables and such saving becomes downright suspicious. These would include the physical space consumed for transport infrastructure (a car with one person going the speed of a cyclist consumes *six times* the space of a cyclist), the loss of social contact among neighbors (and with it, neighborhood safety, self-governance and vitality), and a shift in access toward the wealthy and away from the poor, away from children, from childcare givers, from the elderly and the handicapped.

And yet road building and the traffic that follows it continues apace. The justification is efficient use of people's time via speedier traffic flow. And when "time is money,"

Box 4.2
(continued)

> saving time is saving money. Along the way, a few private interest groups succeed in urging governments to spend public monies on roads and bridges. (See chapter 8.)
>
>   "The monetarization of motorists' time savings," says John Whitelegg, Head of the Geography Department at Lancaster University, "is a convenient fiction that enables the evaluation process to come up with the desired answer—build the road." When individuals choose the fastest means of getting from point A to point B, they "not only restrict their own lives [by missing social contact], but also those of other people," says Whitelegg. Neither a sustainable transport system nor a sustainable economy can be founded, Whitelegg concludes, on efficiency notions, on
>
> > economic principles which, through their monetarization of time, orientate society towards higher levels of motorization, faster speeds and greater consumption of space. The fact that these characteristics produce energy intensive societies and pollution is only part of the problem. They also distort value systems, elevate mobility above accessibility, associate higher speeds and greater distances with progress and dislocate communities and social life.
>
> *Sources*: John Whitelegg, "Time Pollution," *The Ecologist* 23/4 (July–August 1993): 131–134; Jane Jacobs, *The Death and Life of Great American Cities* (New York: Random House, 1961).

Shifting from the personal to the organizational, the timber industry claims it is saving the forest by managing it more intensively. Companies get more board feet or more fiber off an acre of timberland as they shorten rotations with fast-growing plantations of jack pine and eucalyptus. Rather than *extensively* using vast tracts of timberland, the industry says, it *intensively* uses a limited number of acres, leaving the rest for recreation and watershed services. Internationally, foreign aid projects designed to integrate environmental conservation and economic development assume that if poor farmers adopt more intensive practices they will encroach less on nearby protected areas.

In the forestry and conservation realms, the reasoning is deceptively simple: double the yield of one acre and some other acre can be set aside. I am unaware of any institutional mechanism that actually implements such an exchange, or of evidence of a direct connection between an increment of intensification and an increment of preserved forest. There is abundant evidence, though, of increasing consumption of wood products and disappearing primary forests. And where studies have been done in the international development and conservation arena, the benefits of agricultural intensification are seen as doubtful. Tropical-forest researchers

Arild Angelsen and David Kaimowitz conducted eighteen studies in a variety of countries, places with different types of agriculture and technology. They found that forest cover can improve with new agricultural technologies. But "anything that makes agriculture in forested areas more attractive runs a big risk of being bad for forests," Angelsen and Kaimowitz say. That "anything" includes cattle ranching and soybean production, particularly profitable activities where export markets exist. More efficient farming can actually "encourage or permit existing farmers to clear additional land or attract new farmers." Where this is not the case, conservation is due not to efficiencies but to other measures. "The experience of western Europe and the United States shows that attractive off-farm employment opportunities and effective regulation of forest conversion greatly reinforce the positive effects of agricultural productivity improvements on forest cover."[3]

The timber industry's claim for "saving" forests by intensively managing plantations is just that, a claim, but one that holds considerable credence in many circles, industrial and environmental circles included. It is a claim that derives its sway from a basic efficiency notion: getting more product from an acre of land, by improving the ratio of goods (wood products) to necessary bads (harvesting, processing, risking invested capital). If efficiencies are a good thing, the "savings" must be real.

Housing developers, especially those sensitive to the environmental concerns of their target communities, make similar assertions. They cluster their houses on a portion of the former farmland, and "save" the rest as "open space," a park, say. Initially, the parkland is indeed "saved"—that is, spared the ax and the bulldozer. A scenario of incremental conversion over time is not hard to imagine, though. The houses are built and the park is set aside. Ten years later the next developer requests a zoning variance just like the previous one, this time to develop "only a portion" of the open space while setting the remainder aside as, yes, parkland. And so it goes. One person's saving (in the short term) is another's progress (in the long term)— conversion of open, undeveloped space. And all justified as saving, as an efficient use of land.

Government reorganization is another example of efficiency as saving. Every new administration in the United States brings in a cadre of reformers. These latter-day efficiency experts, often from business or academe, have a mission. They set out to "streamline" government, to "trim the fat" from bloated bureaucracies, to put the public on a "sound business footing." In so doing, the reformers proclaim, taxpayers' hard-earned money will be "saved." Once again, the reasoning is deceptively simple: eliminate waste and the cost of government service goes down. Putting aside the fact that few reformers of this ilk actually accomplish anything (they are quick to blame inefficient government and its apologists), a gain in one realm typically is a loss in another. The police department splits its two-person patrols so the same number of cops can cover more territory or fewer cops can cover the same territory. In so doing, though, each cop is more vulnerable to attack and, understandably, avoids high-crime areas. Crime goes up, the courts fill, and prisons bulge. Savings in one part of the criminal justice system translates into new costs elsewhere in that system.

Why is "saving" so seductive? Maybe it has a virtuous ring to it. Maybe it harks back to those days (real or imagined) when frugality and thrift were notions integral to everyday life, when saving was more than getting a bargain at the superstore. Maybe it is because most savings are tangible: it is easy to imagine forestland "saved" as other land is cut, parkland preserved, budgets reduced, tax bills diminished.

Whatever the psychology of saving via efficiency, the claim typically escapes scrutiny because ratios are rarely spelled out, rarely examined for what's put in and what's left out. The claim escapes scrutiny in part because the politics of efficiency claims are susceptible to highlighting benefits while shading costs. (See box 4.3 and table 4.1.)

Shading

If a software manufacturer tells me I can send my messages faster and more easily with e-mail than with stationery and the postal service, the benefit is clear—clear to me, that is. My ratio of messages per hour of writing increases either because I can now send the messages I always wanted to send and didn't have the time (i.e., more messages per hour) or because I use less time sending my usual messages (i.e., the same number of messages in less time).

What the e-mail manufacturer does not highlight is the fact that electronic message sending is a two-way street. The ease of sending messages means more messages come to me, solicited or not. As I spend increasing time answering or filtering or deleting, at some point my enhanced efficiency ratio as a sender (messages per hour) is offset by the burdens of being a receiver. It's the aggregate of everyone else's "efficient" sending that overwhelms.[4]

So in my decision to adopt the technology, I can't know ex ante whether the narrow efficiency gain for me will be offset by the broader efficiency gains (or, better, the access gains) of others. Once dependent on the medium, however, I have little choice. Today's efficiency is tomorrow's dependency.

Box 4.3
Efficiencies light the way

Table 4.1
Street lighting in the United Kingdom

Year	Lamp efficiency (lumens/watt)	Lamp type	Street-lamp electricity consumption (GWh)	Miles of lighted street
1923	11	Incandescent	71	37,952
1928	12	Incandescent	130	40,808
1933	12	Incandescent	221	43,211
1938	60	LP sodium	298	44,501
1947	60	LP sodium	188	45,397
1951	80	LP sodium	415	45,460
1955	100	LP sodium	627	45,553
1960	120	LP sodium	922	45,782
1965	125	LP sodium	1260	46,185
1970	150	LP sodium	1682	47,047
1975	175	LP sodium	2073	48,328
1980	190	LP sodium	2252	49,136
1985	195	LP sodium	2335	49,949
1990	200	LP sodium	2558	50,896
1995	205	LP sodium	2443	51,254
1996	205	LP sodium	2578	51,439
Percentage increase, 1923–1996	1764%		3530%	35%
Percentage increase, 1955–1990	100%		307%	12%

Sources: Horace Herring, "Does Energy Efficiency Save Energy? The Debate and its Consequences," *Applied Energy* 63/3 (July 1999): 209–226; table adapted from table 1, p. 218. Herring's sources are listed as: Transport Statistics, GB; Digest of UK Energy Statistics; Handbook of Electricity Supply Statistics; Lamp guide, 1990. Lighting Industries Federation Limited.

The early manufacturers of florescent lightbulbs faced a dilemma. They knew their bulbs would save customers energy—a florescent bulb would use fewer watts of electricity than an incandescent bulb for every lumen of light. But they didn't know if their customers would take those savings in reduced electricity bills or increased lumens.

Box 4.3
(continued)

> Both would be more efficient than continuing with incandescent bulbs. The choice all hinged on how the new florescents would be marketed.
>
> Power generators in England, fearful of losing sales, prevailed on the florescent manufacturers to market the bulbs as light enhancing devices—more lumens for the kilowatt. Sure enough, florescent bulb sales resulted in increased lighting, but no savings—that is, no *reduction* in energy consumed. For example, writes energy analyst Horace Herring of the Open University in the United Kingdom, "the designed illumination level for offices rose five fold" from before the 1940s to the 1970s.
>
> It seems the pattern was not unique to florescent bulbs and offices, though.
>
> The efficiency of street lamps in the United Kingdom increased dramatically over a seventy-year period: for every watt of energy consumed, more lumens of light are emitted. But energy consumption has increased, too, even controlling for increased miles of road lit. And even with increasing efficiencies in low-pressure sodium lamps (LP sodium), consumption continued to rise: a doubling in technological efficiency was accompanied by a quadrupling in consumption from 1955 to 1990. Herring concludes that the considerable efficiency improvements in lighting have "been taken in the form of higher levels of service, both in more miles illuminated and in higher illumination levels, not in the form of lower consumption."

Like so much else in a technologically and commercially driven world, boosters have an incentive to highlight benefits and shade costs.[5] Adopters have limited information. And even the boosters, let alone the regulators, cannot anticipate all the consequences of their new gadgets and ever more convenient foods and transportation. What the boosters can do, though, is invoke an efficiency claim, highlight the numerator (the "good"), shade the denominator (the "bad"), and leave it to users and others to assess gains and losses. Efficiencies sell.

It is quite a separate issue, though, whether efficiencies do anything to enhance personal well-being or to ensure long-term social and ecological security. Despite all the claims for saving and improving, such efficiencies may contribute little to the sustainability of a firm, community, or society. In fact, to the extent efficiencies enable boosters to shade costs, to displace them over time and space, those efficiencies may detract from sustainability. One step toward such an assessment is to examine efficiency claims as they impart environmental harm. Here is where the ambiguities of technical change, systemic effect, and the decision authority of key actors enter. (See box 4.4.)

Box 4.4
Productivity

In the march of progress, efficiency assumes many guises (box 3.1). In national economic policymaking, none is so prevalent as productivity, the drum major of modern economies. Invoked almost as much as growth (and often *with* growth), it is the answer to all things bad in a modern economy. "As we have witnessed so clearly in recent years," Federal Reserve chair Alan Greenspan said in 2002, "advances in technology have enhanced the growth in productivity, which in turn has been essential to lifting our standards of living." Productivity explains the exuberant 1990s (but not the 1990s bubble that burst) and is the antidote for the lackluster 2000s.

Productivity, like so many efficiency ratios, is deceptively simple. It is the output of the economy per hour of work. An increase in productivity is an unambiguously good thing: more "goods" (products, services) for a unit of "bad" (labor).

But with only two elements in the ratio, it does leave out a few things—like questions of whose standard of living is lifted and whose depressed, whose jobs are gained and whose lost, which resources (financial, human, natural) are enhanced and which diminished.

Champions of productivity rarely mention that that simple ratio—output per work hour—can increase (*improve* is the term of choice) in two ways: more goods are produced for a given labor input or the same goods are produced with less labor input. In other words, productivity can go north when jobs go south.

But these concerns seem not to arise in the thriving field of productivity studies and in the growth-is-the-solution policy environment. In those places, the tide always rises. Joint gains always obtain. And, besides, it must be satisfying, and lucrative, bashing traditionalists: "The biggest drag on Japan's anemic economy of the 1990s," says the economic consulting firm The McKinsey Global Institute, "is low productivity." And nowhere is that more apparent than in retailing. "Overall retail productivity in Japan," the amount of sales per retail worker, says McKinsey and company, "is 50 percent of that in the United States."

And why is that? The *shotengai*, the local shopping districts composed of little mom-and-pop stores. These "highly unproductive traditionals," says McKinsey and company, are just too labor intensive.

Retail is efficient when sales per worker is high. Back in 1924, management guru Paul Mazur emphasized scale in his prescriptions for American retailers: "Retail mergers must continue because they offer management efficiency, overhead reduction, and the economy of purchasing large volumes. Large-scale operations will be most effective not through the building of an unlimited number of new retail units, but though the consolidation of existing stores and chains." Now the message is the same only consumer benefit is added: "The shortage of large-scale retailers is particularly acute in food retailing," say McKinsey and company with respect to Japanese retailing. "Large-scale formats are more productive than traditionals—particularly in food retailing—because they offer more choice for lower price and manage to serve many customers with relatively few personnel."

Those Japanese retailers who have taken the message to heart are, in fact, very productive. Discount stores, supermarkets, and general merchandise stores in Japan are

Box 4.4
(continued)

84 percent as efficient as the U.S. retail average, says McKinsey and company. But "traditionals" are only 19 percent as efficient. Clearly, it is Japan's turn to catch up to America.

Nevermind that these same shotengai stores were the domestic undergirding of the Japanese economy throughout the booming 1960s, 1970s, and 1980s, a time when nearly all major industrial countries, the United States included, were trying to catch up with Japan. Nevermind that the shotengai shopkeepers have "traditionally been the backbone of the Japanese neighborhood," as one reporter puts it. "They organize festivals that make the long hot summers here [in Japan] tolerable. They are active in school affairs and community sports. They hang out in front of their shops, chatting with patrons and handing out candy or small toys to children." They might even contribute to the low per capita levels of energy consumption in Japan. From my visits there, it is clear that most residents walk or bicycle to these stores.

But all that, the productivity experts proclaim, is just tradition. Productivity is the way to get ahead say the high-powered consultants, the megastore owners, and not a few politicians. Bigger stores, more sales, more parking, more driving. That's the name of the game. All this because labor is just another factor input, the denominator that must be minimized in an efficiency ratio. For a good many Japanese (and not a few Americans), though, labor is a part of livelihood, part of what makes communities vibrant and what gives people meaning and identity, and not for what they buy, but for what they contribute (chapter 5).

So when Japan's economy was booming and observers feared it was "overheated," the solution was productivity: produce more goods for the labor, prices will drop, consumers will buy more goods thus absorbing any excess productive capacity. Now, with the Japanese economy "anemic," "flat on its back" (a curious diagnosis given that in conventional terms it has been growing but at *only* one percent annually), now the answer to its economic problems is, yes, productivity: more sales per worker means lowered costs and higher profits which attracts investment so that more can be produced, all of which lowers prices to consumers and "lifts Japan's standard of living."

It's all very logical, of course. Especially when pesky details about worker dislocation and community deterioration and resource depletion don't enter the productivity ratio. One can only wonder if the growing gap between rich and poor, the loading of toxic substances and the emissions of greenhouse gasses could really improve with productivity gains—or are exacerbated by them.

If the retail world is impervious to such "externalities," maybe the financial world is more open; investment dollars are at risk, after all. But if reports to the federal reserve by economists from prestigious universities and think tanks are any indication, such optimism would be misplaced. "When productivity rises, employers can pay higher wages because they are producing more with less," conclude experts in 2002. "The Federal Reserve doesn't have to fret as much about inflation because output grows without straining resources. Ultimately, that results in a bigger pie."

No strain on resources. When financial analysts conduct financial studies for financial institutions and they are reported in financial papers like the *Wall Street Journal*,

Box 4.4
(continued)

"resources" means finances. And the economic pie is the one measured by wages, interest rates and GDP. It is not the one that houses the soil that nourishes the crops, the water that cools the turbines, the atmosphere that absorbs the CO_2. That pie stays the same—or, if you believe even half the reports that come out yearly on the state of the environment—it is shrinking. Natural capital is receding as financial capital is expanding.

Don't fret, though. Productivity—getting more for less—raises all boats and washes away all concerns. Productivity increases, the economy grows, workers and investors earn more, inflation is tamed. With productivity, it never floods. And that other pie, the one that actually doesn't grow was, by this financial view, never very important anyway, certainly not to an economy that lives on efficiency gains.

So if the financial world is no better than the retailing world accounting for the uncountable, maybe the natural resource sector is more enlightened.

"Pollution intensity" is the environmental equivalent of labor productivity. Improvement, greater intensity, is getting more output, more GDP, for each unit of input—energy and its accompanying pollutants. Equivalently, pollution intensity is emitting less pollution for each unit of GDP.

When United States President George W. Bush rejected the Kyoto Protocol, which limited greenhouse gas emissions, his alternative plan sounded good, at least to devotees of a productivity-led economy. He proposed a target of an 18 percent drop in CO_2 emissions per dollar of GDP over ten years. Such productivity gains, it turned out, would only continue a trend, a trend with a decreasing ratio of pollution to economic output and *an absolute increase in total emissions*. The proposal would do nothing to restrict, let alone reduce, United States carbon emissions, the only thing that matters to "the environment."

Productivity claims, like so many other efficiency claims, always sound good. At first. More goods, lower prices, higher wages, less environmental burden—indeed, a better "standard of living." The devil of that living standard, though, is in the ratios.

Sources: "MGI Report: Why the Japanese Economy is Not Growing," report of the McKinsey Global Institute, copyright 1996–2003; accessed at http://www.mckinsey.com/knowledge/mgi/Japan/cases/retail.asp; Paul Mazur, "Future Development in Retailing," *Harvard Business Review* 2 (July 1924): 434–446; quoted in William Leach, *Land of Desire: Merchants, Power, and the Rise of a New American Culture* (New York: Pantheon Books, 1993), 289; Stephanie Strom, "As Japan Deregulates, Quality-of-Life Laments: Mom and Pop Do Battle with Discounters," *New York Times*, August 8, 2000, pp. C1, C10; Steven Liesman, "The Outlook: Productivity Growth May be Here to Stay," *Wall Street Journal*, January 7, 2002, p. A1; describes a report to Atlanta Federal Reserve Bank, 2002.

Bringing the Environment In

It's Not Technics

In physical terms an efficiency gain is simply the increase in the ratio of useful work to energy expended. For example, a horse hauls one cord of wood in a wagon with hexagonal wheels. The wagoner rounds off the wheels and that same horse pulls two cords of wood. The original work-to-energy ratio of 1:1 (1 cord to 1 horsepower) increases to 2:1 (2 cords to 1 horsepower)—an efficiency gain.

Alternatively, by rounding the wheels the wagoner can haul the same one cord of wood and just hitch up a pony, which generates ½ horsepower, eats half the feed, and requires half the maintenance. The wagoner gets the same efficiency gain; the original work-to-energy ratio of 1:1 (1 cord to 1 horsepower) increases to 2:1 (1 cord to ½ horsepower).

And then there's a third option. With the newly rounded wheels, the wagoner hitches up both the horse and the pony (now 1½ horsepower), and hauls three cords of wood. The efficiency gain is still 2:1; the original work-to-energy ratio of 1:1 (1 cord to 1 horsepower) increases to 2:1 (3 cords to 1½ horsepower).

From a strictly technical perspective, the three efficiency gains are the same. The work-to-energy ratio goes from 1:1 to 2:1. But from an environmental perspective, from the perspective of ecological carrying capacity, they may not be the same at all.

Let's say environmental impact (harvesting and land-conversion pressure) is a function of the workhorse. The more horsepower the wagoner employs, the more the feed and pasturage and, hence, the more the clearing of forest and draining of wetland. The 2:1 efficiency gain achieved by hauling two cords with the same horse is neutral with respect to this environmental impact. The 2:1 efficiency gain achieved by hauling the same one cord with the pony is clearly a gain for the environment. And the third option, the 2:1 efficiency gain of hauling more wood with more horsepower, is a detriment to the environment. What is technically equivalent—converting a work-to-energy ratio from 2 to 1—is environmentally ambiguous. An efficiency gain can, as is routinely claimed, lessen environmental impact. But it can just as easily increase it, or have no effect.

The environmental difference between the first two efficiency gains (neutral and positive improvement) and the third (negative) is, once again, human behavior; it's personal and societal choice. Whether an efficiency gain translates into an environmental gain is *not*, in the first instance, *a technical* matter. What matters environmentally is the wagoner's choice of load and power, not wheel rounding.

It's the System, Too

Here's another way to disentangle efficiency ratios and behavioral change as they relate to environmental impact. Imagine two societies equal in all respects—population, land area, income distribution, and environmental concern. They also have the same transportation choices: for their private vehicles individuals can choose either huge gas guzzlers or little fuel misers.

It just so happens that in society A, everyone drives the fuel misers and they only drive a short distance to work. In society B, where the roads are especially bad, a few people commute long distances driving the guzzlers while everyone else walks to work. The total emissions for each society are the same.

By conventional measures (that is, fuel-efficiency standards) people in society A are the environmental good guys. For each gallon of gasoline burned, the A folks get more miles than those profligate B folks with the guzzlers. And by conventional *prescription*, society B should convert to the more fuel efficient vehicles, to the little misers that all of society A uses.

So society B, being just as environmentally concerned as society A, begins improving its roads to accommodate the little cars. A few gas-guzzling commuters trade in their behemoths for the misers. But walkers see new options, too. With the little cars, they can now choose, on a daily basis, whether to walk or drive. So a few walkers buy cars—the misers, of course. As more and more B folks choose the little cars, society B builds more roads and parking lots. Walking becomes increasingly difficult with all the vehicles, so yet more walkers make the transition to vehicular commuting.

Soon society B is a driving society. A few gas guzzlers remain, but everyone else has a fuel-miser car. As a result, society B's car fleet, as a whole, has become more efficient: each vehicle, on average, gets more miles per gallon than the guzzlers. But total gasoline consumption and, hence, pollution, has increased: now everyone drives and spews out a potpourri of gases that irritate the lungs and mess with the climate. But now they do it with fuel-efficient cars; they, too, are environmental good guys.[6]

The efficiency gain of the vehicle translates into more consumption, into more impact on the environment. Understanding how this occurs, along with the role of technics and power, is essential to unpacking efficiency claims with respect to individual behavior and collective choice and constructing an alternative principle such as sufficiency. A little systems theory helps immensely (chapter 2).

In society B, individual values held constant but behavior changed, prompting a collective response that in turn prompted more individual behavior change. A few walkers started driving, officials responded with infrastructure, and still more people drove. A positive feedback loop with respect to driving (and, eventually, a negative one with respect to walking) came into play. In short, the transport *system* changed, not just a variable or two within that system, not just miles driven for a gallon of gasoline consumed. System-level changes—numbers of drivers and walkers, driving behavior, and infrastructure—overshadowed what gains might have occurred within the system if all had remained the same, if society B's gas-guzzling drivers had chosen the little fuel misers while the walkers kept on walking. If this had happened, if the numbers of drivers and walkers, the driving behavior, and infrastructure remained constant (i.e., truly *all else equal*), the relative efficiency of the fuel misers would have reduced total impact.

But in this story there was no such single-variable change, no reduction in gallons of gasoline consumed as miles driven stayed constant. Instead, individual and collective behavior and all the infrastructure and taxes and regulations and social norms changed. Individuals may choose their mode of transport and how they drive, but the transport system determines the *collective* impact.

In real life, in societies where efficiency is routinely invoked to "save" the environment or to spur the economy or to enhance national security, the system usually changes, too. It changes not just as a society naturally evolves, but as a direct consequence of interventions designed to save or protect or clean up. And those interventions unavoidably favor some while they disadvantage others. What appear to be mere technical choices (more fuel-efficient engines, for instance) are value choices. They are political choices. They distribute private benefits and costs through the population and they distribute environmental impacts across space and time. Walkers, in the hypothetical example (and in many not-so-hypothetical examples) are shunted aside, the atmosphere is loaded with yet more gases to assimilate, and future generations must deal with degraded landscapes and climate instability. Today's drivers may find advantages in their newfound mobility, but tomorrow's may miss the walking (or the neighborliness and different kinds of access that come with walking) and resent the respiratory problems and floods and droughts.

The details may vary in practice, but the pattern appears universal. To paraphrase energy-management expert Andrew Rudin, it's not the lamp, it's the switch . . . and it's the windows and the shading and the wiring and the building code and the electric grid and the power plants. It's not the car engine, it's the roads and the parking and the speed limits and the status of walking and bicycling and busing. It's not the speed of the message, it's the combination of e-mail, fax, telephone, and postal mail. It's not the productivity of farms, it's the food network.[7]

Efficiencies narrowly target a single variable, sometimes two, in a system otherwise made up of multiple variables interacting in complex, often-unpredictable ways. If the system were *complicated* like a clock, the variables and their interactions would be predictable. Break a tooth in a gearwheel and the machine stops. But when the system is *complex*, like an organism or a weather system or a stock market, perturbations are largely unpredictable, or of limited predictability. A push here produces a ripple there. A ripple produces a wave. Some waves dissipate, others join other waves to produce storms. Some variables may follow the laws of nature—gravity and thermodynamics, for example. But others follow the vagaries of human behavior with all its quirks and manipulations.

Efficiency claims rest on a worldview that is at once mechanistic and cornucopian. The mechanistic perspective handles mechanical problems well: the engine is wasting fuel so a new design, one that gets better mileage with a smaller engine and better fuel delivery, solves the problem. And if, in the end, ever more resources are consumed and waste sinks filled, then yet more efficiencies will handle those problems, too. A complex systems perspective, by contrast, is well suited to environmental problems. The output—power, convenience, even pollutants—of a given engine is immaterial. "The environment" does not respond to engine size and fuel injection. It responds to the total loading coming from all vehicles used over a significant period of time—that is, over a time period for which cause and effect connect biophysically and feedback loops are realized socially. Moreover, total loading is a function not just of engine efficiency but of a host of individual and collective choices: car size and design; bus, rail, and air options; walking, bicycling, and pushcart options; and the infrastructure choices that privilege some modes of transport over others. If I live in Los Angeles I must drive a private automobile to meet the most basic needs—food, jobs, schooling. In many places, if I dare walk I risk life and limb. But if I live in New York City or Tokyo it's foolish to operate a car when roadway and parking are so limited and so expensive.

From a mechanistic and cornucopian perspective, individual drivers make choices to serve their individual needs. As their choices improve (more mobility, cheaper gas), the aggregate results in overall social-welfare gain. And new fuels can always be developed to provide the power. Sufficiency is an alien concept.

From a complex systems perspective, the transport system sets boundaries in which people's behavior occurs. The transport system interacts unavoidably over time with the biophysical system, which itself sets boundaries because of its limited regenerative capacities. There can be enough and there can be too much. The resiliency of both systems—social and biophysical—improves as negative feedback loops emerge and as redundancies are built in. Such redundancies, which organizational theorists would call "slack," make systems adaptive. From the mechanical perspective, redundancies are *inefficiencies*.

The intervener—the booster of industry, the enforcer of the law, the savior of the environment—may have the best of intentions. The efficiency is designed to improve things. It must. The ratio of good to bad increases. You can see it, feel it, or at least easily imagine it.

What is a little harder to imagine is that systemic effects may be impossible to see or anticipate, certainly impossible if only a variable (gallons of gasoline consumed for each mile driven, for example) is the target. And maybe even more impossible when the targeted variable is the most visible or tangible or the one that converts most readily to money. When the numbers on top are clearly good (miles driven to work and shopping) and those on bottom bad but necessary (dollars spent and pollutants emitted), the intervener appears right.

Ask the target audience members if they'd like more miles driven (or, better, more mobility) and if they'd like to purchase less gasoline (or, better, spend less money on fuel), and they are bound to say yes. Such questions are routinely posed in public opinion surveys and they work their way into policymaking. They may get at management—of machines, infrastructure, and nature—but they do not get at self-management. Such questions neglect the system and the behavior of people as variables, individually and collectively, within that system. They neglect feedback loops, especially positive self-reinforcing loops: sure I'd like more mobility or a lower gas bill (actually, I'd like both) and, by the way, I'll need more roadway and parking, too. Maybe most significantly, they neglect external effects, including systemic effects on the environment and strategic interaction, the inevitable jockeying for advantage and power. Adoption of a technology and the resulting organizational change reveals such effects. (See box 4.5.)

And It's Power

A timber company is cutting trees like everyone else in the industry—with "misery whips," two-person handsaws. Along comes an entrepreneur with a gas-powered chainsaw to sell.

He first approaches the loggers, those who sweat and toil every day, risking life and limb, and cutting, on average, two trees per logger per day. The entrepreneur shows them how the chainsaw works and makes his pitch: you're pushing yourselves hard every minute of the day, taking risks and wearing out your bodies. With

Box 4.5
Recycling: Doing good or doing well?

Progressive societies can still debate the merits of saving a species of salamander or cleaning up a toxic hotspot. But what is beyond debate, it seems, is recycling. If there was ever a universal, environmentally correct activity, one endorsed by consumers and manufacturers alike, it's recycling. In the United States, it rivals motherhood and apple pie as an indisputably good thing.

As an efficiency measure, recycling allows more use for a given unit of resource. When fiber is extracted from high quality writing paper and used as newsprint then cardboard and finally roofing, its use value goes beyond the original product, the writing paper. Rather than consigning the original fiber to the waste heap of industrial excess, it gets an extended life. The more the fiber's life is extended the larger is the ratio of use:fiber (or value:tree or utility:human-effort-and-cost-of-harvesting-and-processing-fiber).

Because an instance of recycling is deemed an efficiency gain, overall efficiency increases as more material is recycled. Recycling is a good thing. So more recycling must be better. Or so it would seem.

There are two ways to get more recycling. One is to divert a larger proportion of the existing waste stream from landfills and incinerators to recycling. The other way is to simply increase the waste stream, keeping the proportion of recycled material the same. It takes me three weeks to fill my city's recycling crate with bottles and cans. If I buy more processed foods, more carbonated beverages and more canned vegetables, I can fill it in two weeks. I'd be recycling more. Recycling is good and more must be better so if I do fill the crate in two weeks I must be doing better for the environment. Right?

Wrong. No one needs to conduct a life cycle analysis or calculate the ecological footprint to see that more processed foods circulating through my household puts *more* stress on the environment, *not less.*

Meanwhile, waste management authorities trumpet the success of recycling—that is, that Americans are recycling more. The United States Environmental Protection Agency notes, however, that between 1990 and 2000 the total quantity of products and packaging generated as waste *increased* nearly 20 percent while the population increased only 13 percent. More recycling, more waste. More per capita and, most relevant to environmental impact, more in total.

The ambiguities of recycling, like that of other efficiency claims, are matched by their vulnerability to manipulation. When African and Asian leaders objected to waste shipments from wealthy industrialized countries to their poor agricultural countries, shippers simply relabeled their operations and their cargo: the shippers, now "recycling agents" and "waste management experts," would provide valuable recycled materials to resource-starved countries. And at a bargain. "It is often cheaper to recycle such items in poorer countries where environmental regulations for recycling are more lax," says political scientist Jennifer Clapp, an expert in hazardous waste trade. "Latin America and Asia are key locations for the recycling of lead-acid batteries, while Asia seems to dominate the recycling of both computers and plastics."

Some 100,000–150,000 tons of plastic waste collected in local recycling programs in the United States and Germany went to Indonesia every year in the early 1990s.

Box 4.5
(continued)

Only about 60 percent of this waste was actually recycled, however, and the rest, some of which was toxic, was disposed of in landfills. "The plastic recycling operations in Indonesia operate under extremely unsafe conditions," says Clapp. "Plastic wastes often contain residues from their original contents, such as toxic cleaners, pesticides, and fertilizers. Protective clothing is seldom given to employees, mainly women and children. Moreover, the importation of plastic wastes has been implicated in diminishing the livelihood of some 30,000–40,000 scavengers of local plastic waste (supporting some 200,000 dependents) who supply local, small-scale plastic recycling operations." Although Indonesia has banned the import of plastic wastes, China, the Philippines, Korea, India, and Taiwan, and other countries continue the imports.

"Indeed," concludes Clapp, "the Asian market for post-consumer plastic waste has been a big part of the economic viability of plastic recycling in the United States, with the United States exporting to Asia some 200,000 metric tons of plastic waste for recycling in 1995."

As with all efficiency claims, the promised gain obtains only when all else is held constant. All else includes material and energy throughput and human behavior. If one person's efficiency is another's dumping ground, it's unlikely that recycling is reducing human environmental impact.

I still fill my recycling crates, though. I think I'm doing good. But I can't help worrying that the ease of recycling is just encouraging more overall resource use, that some folks—in particular, miners, manufacturers, packagers, shippers, waste haulers, maybe my neighbors (but certainly not my family)—are doing well while the environment groans under the strain of more and more stuff—including recycled stuff.

Sources: U.S. Environmental Protection Agency, cited in "Managing Planet Earth," *New York Times* August 20, 2002, p. F1; Society Promoting Environmental Conservation, "Beyond Recycling: The Future of Waste," *Enough Magazine*, April 10, 2003; accessed online at http://www.spec.bc.ca/article/article.php?articleID = 172, *June 14, 2004*; Jennifer Clapp, "The Distancing of Waste: Overconsumption in a Global Economy," in Thomas Princen, Michael Maniates, and Ken Conca, eds., *Confronting Consumption*, 155–176 (Cambridge, MA: MIT Press, 2002).

this chainsaw you can cut your two trees each day, all right. But you'll cut them so fast you will have more time to size up each tree for felling and bucking, making your job safer. You'll even have time to rest.

The loggers, needless to say, are sold—sold on the efficiency gain of less cutting time (and hence less injury and less physical wear) for the same output of logs.

Next the entrepreneur goes to the company's lumber-mill managers. After demonstrating the newfangled saw, he makes his pitch: like all mill operators, you have downtime. The logs don't always come in when you and your salespeople need them. You can't always keep your workforce fully employed. On top of this, some day you'll have to expand because demand continues to go up, and with it, lumber prices. Labor costs are likely to rise as well. With this saw your company can cut trees when you need them. And to do so, you don't have to hire more loggers or millworkers. The chainsaw does the extra work.

The mill managers are sold—sold on an efficiency gain of more logs for a given crew.

Next the entrepreneur goes to the company's board of directors, who represent shareholders. He shows pictures and graphs demonstrating the chainsaw's capabilities. He makes his pitch: you're not getting the most product out of your logging crews and millhands. Your bottleneck is cutting; it holds up your sawyers, your planers, your stackers, your shippers, and, most important, your salespeople. How many times, do you think, does a sales rep tell a customer, sorry we can't deliver that load 'til we get the trees out? Too many times, I'd say. With these chainsaws you can cut all the trees you need, when you need them. Now, of course, it'll cost you. But consider this: if you only need two trees per logger per day then, with the cutting speed of this device, you can reduce your labor costs, your biggest cost of production by far. In fact, with these, you can hire fewer loggers and cut *more* than you do now.

The directors are sold—sold on getting the same or more trees for lower labor costs; sold on reducing total operating costs so as to get a better return on every dollar their shareholders invest.

The company's decision? There's no question. The efficiencies are too great not to adopt the new technology. Moreover, all major players are sold on the idea—loggers, mill operators, stockholders. There are just two problems, both revealed by closer examination of the efficiency ratios.

Each of the three sets of players sees, with the aid of the entrepreneur, a different ratio or a different change in ratio. The loggers see fewer hours cutting but the same number of logs cut and the same hours of employment. That is, the efficiency *ratio* of relevance to the loggers—logs per day's work—would increase with the chainsaw by holding the numerator constant (and hence their jobs) and reducing the denominator, their time on the job actually spent cutting trees.

The mill operators also see the ratio, logs per day, but the efficiency gain is to be achieved by *increasing the numerator*, the logs, while holding overall working hours (including millworkers' hours) constant.

The stockholders see an entirely different ratio—dollar return on dollar invested—expressed by dollar value of lumber sold per total cost of logging and milling. This ratio could be improved with the chainsaw by reducing the workforce, hardly what either the loggers or the millworkers have in mind.

The ambiguity of the efficiency ratios enables the entrepreneur to sell the product by appealing to different expectations. The loggers expected to hold constant the labor force and the number of trees cut. The mill operators expected to hold constant their jobs, too, while varying the logs coming into the mill. The shareholders expected to vary any set of factors—loggers, millworkers, trees cut—that increases their return on investment.

So what happens once the chainsaw is adopted? Whose ratio prevails? Enter power—decision authority, managerial influence, the ability to hire and fire, to supply or withhold capital. My bet is that, in practice, the efficiency ratio that prevails with the adoption of a new technology like the chainsaw is return on investment. Workers are laid off; those who remain change their work pattern, sometimes working harder than ever. And production increases. My wager rests only on the simple observation that owners, not managers or workers, have the last word, and they decide, more than anything, on their immediate interests, not on the managers' interests, not on the workers', and not on the condition of the forest ecosystem. It is this last point—environmental impact—that brings us to the second problem with efficiency and organizational change.

The entrepreneur never approached the timberland manager. This is the guy who, because of temperament and professional training, is in the habit of saying no. It's not that he's a contrary sort of fellow. Rather, it's the nature of his job to be conservative. He marks trees for cutting, but only trees that are ready. "Ready" is a judgment call, though, one that derives in part from collecting large amounts of scientific data on tree size and growth, soil and water conditions, and the like. And it derives from a sense that one develops after many years working the land, a sense of the regenerative capacity of each patch of forest as it varies by conditions of soil and water and light and species diversity. What this manager knows, no logger or mill operator and certainly no stockholder knows. And what they need—easier cutting, more logs to the mill, a more flexible supply of logs, less operating costs—is of little concern to this gentleman. An efficiency in the lumber camp or on the mill floor is of no account. Forest health matters to him.

The timberland manager's job is thus to maintain the resource base to produce harvestable timber for as long as customers and owners want the lumber. As often as not, he turns down the request of the loggers or mill operators. But he rarely says no to the owners. When the owners say more trees, he finds them, ready or not. So if the entrepreneur's efficiency ratio is attractive to the owners and more trees must be cut to realize the efficiency gains, the timberland manager's sense of "ready" will be overridden. When ratios with tangible outcomes—especially outcomes that can be readily simplified, converted to a monetary measure—when such ratios are pitted against measures that reflect ecological capacity and integrity, the tangible and monetary tend to win out, certainly as today's political economy is structured. Pressure on the resource increases, all in the name of efficiencies, all when power rests with those who can manipulate the ratios via ambiguous efficiency claims. (See box 4.6.)

An Article of Faith

It is a curious position that environmentalists, policymakers, and industrialists have latched onto. Efficiency, they seem to agree unanimously, even enthusiastically, is the antidote to society's environmental problems. From overharvesting to polluting to despoiling, if we just did things more efficiently, with less waste and better use, we'd solve these problems.

Perhaps even more curious is the huge investment of material and human resources designed precisely to capture efficiencies, to *save* resources. And, then, after all is said and done, no one bothers to evaluate, to see if the gains exceeded the investments, let alone if some people, some regions, some environments benefited while others lost. Instead, they're on to the next efficiency. And it's called progress.

A bit of history might have set things straight long ago. It might have helped us all to know that efficiency was appropriated a century ago to serve a particular set of social objectives: to modernize industry and increase output; to train and discipline a workforce; to rid the farm and the government and the church and the school of their backward ways; to squelch the politics in favor of the scientific. We can debate the objectives and the means but, with scrutiny, we cannot ignore the fact that efficiency, as practiced, is, for all its scientific pretensions, deeply political.

Box 4.6
Intensely agricultural, extensely environmental: efficiency meets meat

American agriculture is widely acclaimed as the most productive in the world. The evidence is *yield*—bushels of wheat per acre, say. It could also be total harvest or total crop value or, however preposterous, grain produced with the least environmental impact. But the preferred measure of greatness is yield, that neat and tidy ratio of bushels per acre, or pounds per animal, or tons per invested dollar. It is a ratio that neglects external costs and long-term impacts.

In agriculture the logic of efficiency is the logic of *intensification*. The story of meat epitomizes industrial agriculture's obsession with maximizing a ratio.

Decades ago, free-range cattle grazing gave way to fenced ranching because one could get more head of cattle to the acre. Fenced pasture gave way to feedlots because, again, one could get more head to the acre and, with high protein feeds, more meat for the inputs (especially labor). And now, with external factors (grassland, pasture, stockyard) at their physical limits (the pens can't get any smaller than the animals) the cowboy efficiency experts have turned inward, to growth enhancers, specially formulated feeds and antibiotics. Along the way, the time to reach slaughter weight has dropped from four or five years a couple generations ago to fourteen or fifteen or sixteen months now. Grow 'em faster and fatter is the mantra.

Fishing has gone through a similar transformation. Roaming the high seas for wild fish is dangerous. Stocks deplete readily and inexplicably. A lot of time and effort can be wasted chasing such slippery prey. So fish farming is more efficient. Thousands of fish can be raised in moored, floating cages and harvested after a year or two of feeding. With genetically engineered fish (perhaps the ultimate form of intensified production) they grow faster and bigger than wild fish. The state of Maine in the United States, for example, has some 800 acres of salmon pens resulting in a $100 million industry.

There's a logic, of course, to all this agricultural intensification. The financial side is straightforward: more pounds of meat to the square yard translates to more revenue for the invested dollar, especially with the uncertainties of free-range grazing and open-seas fishing mitigated. The vagaries of nature—population shifts, migrations, disease—make factory livestocking not only economical of space, but low in search and repair costs. It's predictable and controllable.

That's the financial logic. The environmental logic is equally compelling but, as with so many efficiency measures that concentrate benefits for a few, it ignores the dispersed costs to the many. As farmers and fishers get more harvest off an acre of land or water, so goes the efficiency-oriented environmental argument, other areas can be left alone. Shifting cultivators need not clear new land because they can get more product from their existing land. Fishers need not chase down the last fish in the fishery because, as aquaculturalists, they can stay home and raise fish, meeting consumers' needs as depleted stocks recover. Intensification is conservation.

Like so many "advances" in productivity, the logic is appealing. It appears win-win. The economy and the environment do better.

Unfortunately, the facts speak differently, at least those facts that account for systemwide effects over the long term.

Livestock may be compatible with many grassland ecosystems. And fish may do well for awhile in cages and aquariums. But when the efficiency logic is pushed to its logical

Box 4.6
(continued)

extremes, when stockyards bulge with fast-growing animals and fish cages are packed like the proverbial sardines, the unintended consequences can overwhelm what benefits producers claim and consumers realize.

By one estimate, over 26 million pounds of antibiotics are used in livestock each year in the United States. Only 2 million pounds of that is used to treat sick animals. The rest is for growth enhancement, for increasing the ratio of pounds of meat per unit of livestock per year. Disease organisms become resistant to these antibiotics, and not only to the specific antibiotic, but to others in the chemical class, rendering many disease-fighting drugs for humans ineffective.

Floroquinolones are a case in point. Antibiotics in this class are among the most powerful known. They are used to treat a number of human diseases including anthrax. In 1995, the U.S. Food and Drug Administration approved one variety of floroquinolone for use in chickens. Resistance among bacteria that cause food-borne illness in humans rose from almost nothing to 17 percent in less than four years. By one estimate, some 5,000 people with foodborne disease can no longer be treated. Three studies in the New England Journal of Medicine confirmed links between antibiotic overuse and drug-resistant bacteria found in meat and poultry products.

Still, defenders of non-therapeutic use of antibiotics say it's worth it: the consumer benefits. How? Efficient production keeps prices low and choices abundant.

Aquaculture has followed a similar path. A highly contagious virus appeared in Norwegian and Scottish fish farms in the 1980s and in salmon pens of Canada and the state of Maine in the 1990s. Officials have killed millions of farm fish (presumably at public expense) to contain the spread of the virus. Although little is known about the virus, some biologists believe it has long existed in wild populations. Because it moves in water and from fish to fish, the disease outbreak is likely due to the forced concentration of these animals.

The efficiency claims for intensified production—more pounds of meat per acre or per invested dollar—is not the efficiency of public health management, nor of ecological systems. It may not even be the strictly economic efficiency of production once all the health treatment, law enforcement and research costs are factored in and once the government bailouts and insurance pay-outs are tallied up. (See chapter 9.)

Sources: David G. White, Shaohua Zhao, Robort Sudler, et al., "The Isolation of Antibiotic-Resistant Salmonella from Retail Ground Meats"; L. Clifford McDonald, Shannon Rossiter, Constance Mackinson, et al., "Quinupristin-Dalfopristin–Resistant *Enterococcus faecium* on Chicken and in Human Stool Specimens"; and Thomas Lund Srenson, Marianne Blom, Dominique L. Monnet, et al., "Transient Intestinal Carriage after Ingestion of Antibiotic-Resistant *Enterococcus faecium* from Chicken and Pork"; all in *New England Journal of Medicine* 345/16 (October 18, 2001): 1147–1166; Union of Concerned Scientists, cited in Marian Burros, "Poultry Industry Quietly Cuts Back on Antibiotic Use," *New York Times*, February 10, 2002, pp. A1, A23; U.S. Food and Drug Administration, cited in Philip J. Hilts, "Drug for Poultry Stirs Resistance Concerns," *New York Times*, October 30, 2001, p. D7; Andrew C. Revkin, "Virus is Killing Thousands of Salmon," *New York Times*, September 7, 2001, p. A10; Michael Pollan, "Power Steer," *New York Times Magazine*, March 31, 2002, p. 44.

And yet today's efficiency advocates do not want to hear the lessons of history. They are, by and large, progressives. They look forward to ever-greater human achievement, not backward to the ways of the past. Even without the history, though, they might take their cues from the plethora of well-known contemporary examples of efficiency gains leading to increased production and consumption and, for all we can tell, to increased environmental impact. More efficient aircraft have contributed to lower air fares and hence more air travel, the most energy-intensive form of transportation.[8] More efficient electronic circuitry has led to smaller computers and their worldwide proliferation, depositing heavy metals and other toxic substances in landfills everywhere. More efficient agriculture has led to more luxurious foods, and more groundwater drawdown. The list seems endless.

Efficiency claims, for all the history or lack of history, are indeed political claims. They may be dressed up in the language of science and technology and progress, and thus have an apolitical appearance. But appearing apolitical is a political act, a way of avoiding awkward trade-offs. It is a way of advancing a narrow agenda (increased return on investment, a new building, a changed curriculum) by appearing to advocate a broad agenda. And that broad agenda is palatable, indeed attractive, not because it represents the painstaking process of finding common ground among people of diverse interests and values, nor even because matters have been reduced to a common denominator such as money. Rather, it is attractive because everyone sees a gain. Efficiencies wash away the divisiveness so consensus can settle out. Environmentalists, industrialists, and politicians can fight tooth and nail about the value of a wetland or the importance of biodiversity. But, with efficiency, they can all come together: the environmentalist sees nature preserved when a housing developer agrees not to build on every acre. The developer sees lower costs because excavation and utility hookups can be consolidated when houses are clustered. Local officials see the same tax revenues with fewer government services.

It is easy to agree that the land should be protected, that climate change should be arrested, that pollution should be abated, that energy should be saved, that water should be cleaned. And it is easy to act to improve the environment if it appears that the efficiencies are just there for the taking, like hitherto undiscovered fruit waiting to be picked. It is quite another matter to spell out exactly where that fruit comes from, what is forfeited by consuming it now and at this rate. It is quite another matter to reveal what happens downstream, downwind, to reveal who benefits and who loses, and to do so over an ecologically significant period of time.

Efficiency claims are unavoidably ambiguous. And it is that very ambiguity that opens political space that is the source of efficiency's rhetorical power, its usefulness as a means of influence, of persuasion, of legitimization. An efficiency claim, a statement that my method is superior to yours, can only be established if I specify the ratio. For that matter, it can only be established if you and I agree on that ratio. Otherwise, all such claims are little more than assertions. My ratio makes sense to me; yours to you. Others may reduce the two ratios to a common denominator—money, say—but the values that underlie the choice of a ratio belong uniquely to each of us; they are incommensurate.

For too long in industrial societies, those values have centered on the immediate and expansionist. A policy that promotes efficiencies—roadway for transport, electric bulbs for street lighting, administrative structures for medical care and retailing, recycling for waste management, and concentrated animals for intensified farming—promotes increased personal and societal wealth in the here and now. It elevates monetary values as it depreciates values associated with the long term, with the security of ecological integrity and economic well-being.

Efficiency is suspect in the first instance because the ratio is rarely made explicit. In the second, it is suspect because ratios perceived are rarely ratios realized, because ratios proposed for all are only for some, because efficiency claims lead to the shading and distancing of costs, to deferral of impact in time and space. Efficiency is suspect because the benefits are readily highlighted, while costs are shaded and left for others to pick up.

A Partial Redemption

The technical and systemic ambiguities of efficiency ratios, their bias to the tangible and to near-term benefits, and their amenability to the prerogatives of the expert and the powerful might be sufficient grounds for dismissal. The term, so imprecise, so subject to political manipulation, is worthless, one might conclude. The concept may be a nice theoretical construct, a notion handy for promoting technical proficiency. But *in practice*, we see, it's a social construct, a rhetorical device to promote personal agendas, to achieve organizational advantage, to advance one group's interests over another's, and all, more often than not, irrespective of social and environmental costs.

This may be an unduly harsh judgment. First, the term is bound to be around for a long time. Second, popular concepts always suffer such fates. At a particular juncture in history, a new concept captures the public's fancy, it strikes a chord, it meets a need. But then it gets stretched and bent, often beyond recognition. It gets forced into every possible niche, whether it fits or not; witness calls a century ago for efficient devotion and now smart growth (efficient urban sprawl) (box 3.1). Conservation, a variant of efficiency dealing with natural resources, underwent such a fate, historian Samuel Hays writes: "At the first session of the National Conservation Congress in August 1909 delegates delivered speeches on the conservation of peace and friendship among nations, the conservation of the morals of youth, the conservation of children's lives, . . . the conservation of manhood, and the conservation of the Anglo-Saxon race!"[9] Concepts attuned to a sustainable society such as precaution, restraint, and respite may well suffer similar fates. This problem is not unique to efficiency. It is tempting to throw out such terms as soon as they get distorted.

But the challenge for analyst and practitioner alike is to set boundaries on the concept's usage, to continually refine the concept, to hone it for the needs of the day, especially those needs for which no other concept applies. This is the argument I have already made regarding sustainability (chapter 2). So here, a few words to suggest that efficiency is not beyond redemption, that it just needs harnessing, that correctives are possible.

Efficiency's original, modern application was the factory, which will probably remain its best application. But to the extent it is used for the policy goals set out in this book—namely, reversing the trends in environmental degradation and getting on a sustainable path—to the extent it becomes a *complementary principle to sufficiency*, it must be better specified.

Two-element ratios—cords per horsepower, miles per gallon, lumens per kilowatt, GDP/pollutant—are common in public discourse, yet are rarely adequate. From an environmental standpoint, from the perspective of complex adaptive systems, they are too narrow. From sustainability's long-term perspective, from society's need to live within the regenerative capacities of biophysical systems, they are mispecified. The sustainability advocate must demand ratios that, at a minimum, are explicit about scale—physical and temporal.

To say that an efficiency ratio is mispecified, that claimants should spell out their numerators and denominators more precisely, is not to suggest that there is one "right" ratio. As illustrated in the farming and corporate-merger examples and the various boxes of this chapter, there are better and worse specified ratios for a given purpose. But choosing the elements is ultimately a decision to emphasize some things and discount others. Take GDP per ton of pollutant, a popular ratio in the climate-change debate, especially in the United States. This ratio has an implicit "year" time frame—annual economic product per ton of carbon. This may be the convention, but it is a decidedly nonecological convention, one attuned, perhaps, to election cycles and investment decisions. A time frame with climate-change relevance, one that captures the huge time lags between cause (decades of fossil-fuel emissions) and effect (the climate instability imposed on future generations and, it appears, on some present generations), would be *century*. To choose the ratio GDP:pollutant:century is to force even the most ardent fossil-fuel advocate to question the long-term feasibility of "business as usual" with contemporary energy-use patterns.[10]

Regarding physical scale, GDP:pollutant has an implicit geopolitical scale of a single country, an absurd unit from an ecological perspective for an inherently global problem. If the leading greenhouse gas–emitting country chooses GDP:ton of carbon as its climate-change measure, rather than carbon:country:planet (that is, total global loading), it is elevating the value of economic product (goods, return on investment, jobs) for each unit of pollution, while neglecting that country's relative contribution to global climate change.

This country is in effect saying that all economic activity has environmental impacts (which is generally true) and that getting more bang (economic good) for the buck (environmental bad) is a good thing. It is hard to argue with such a position, certainly on its own terms with the designated numerator and denominator. It is absolutely true that the greater the ratio of good to bad, the better things are; better, that is, *when all else is equal*, of course. The other ratio—emissions per country per planet—suggests that all else is not equal. This ratio raises the possibility that one country's economic good may be another's environmental bad. The U.S. economy charges ahead getting ever more product for a unit of pollutant while the Maldives and Bangladesh slip below the ocean's waves. One country's efficiencies are another's undoing.

To espouse GDP:pollutant is to give credence and build legitimacy for a set of policies, including—in the case of the United States in the early twenty-first century—rules, regulations, and incentives to promote economic growth, conventionally defined, conventionally realized. To espouse pollutant:country:planet is to legitimize international comparison, it is to lay the groundwork for a distribution of climate-change responsibility and remedial action, and to do so on a global scale. For global warming, the scale must shift from the micro to the macro, from nation-state to global biosphere, and any efficiency ratio, however implied, must specify that scale.

Now consider farming. Ratios like bushels of wheat per acre are the standard basis of American agriculture's claim to being "the most productive in the world" (see box 4.6). But such ratios have an implied single-season temporal component—*x* bushels per acre per year—and an implied extrapolation into the future: if farmers can produce this much grain now, they will continue producing this much (if not more) in coming years.

An explicit time component of decades—or better, centuries—would challenge such simplistic notions. A long time frame in the ratio would force analysts to consider impacts on soil and water from current practices. If there is net soil loss, if water tables are dropping, and if persistent toxic substances are accumulating (all the norm in North America), a simple extrapolation (now an ecologically meaningful extrapolation) shows that this cannot continue. The analytic question, not to mention the policy goal, then shifts from maximizing yields per acre each year to optimizing yields over a long time—an entirely different enterprise from that which governs industrial agriculture today.

In both examples, those of climate-change mitigation and agricultural productivity, the simple addition of scale and temporal components to the ratios dramatically changes the very nature of the efficiency. Indeed, such changes challenge prevailing efficiency claims as well as the policies, rules, norms, and public and private investments that accompany such claims. Notably, the challenge stays within the very framework that efficiency boosters employ: a ratio of good stuff—transit, food—to unwanted stuff—petroleum burned, labor employed. This is a framework governed by the efficiency principle. The challenge merely posits a different ratio, which, a priori, is neither better nor worse than the prevailing ratios.

But when the sustainability goal is made explicit, when elements in those ratios incorporate long time frames and large geographic scales, the ratios can be useful devices (however rhetorical or political) for promoting the values of environmental protection and food security, say, rather than the values of labor mobility and industrial output. They can even be suggestive of principles like sufficiency, allowing, for example, restraint to rise in importance as specialization submerges. When efficiency ratios include the long term and the large scale they depreciate efficiency as a social organizing principle. Such ratios help put the genie back in the bottle where it belongs, back in the factory and engine room and, sometimes, the laboratory. At the same time they open intellectual and political space for social organizing principles more appropriate to the needs of the day, namely, environmental criticality.

5

Enough Work, Enough Consumption

The backward-bending supply curve for labor. Now there's a conversation starter. Or stopper, depending on the crowd.

It's a phrase that rolls off the tongue of those enamored of conventional neoclassical economics. Introductory courses devote a few lines and a graph to this oddity, dismissing the behavior as a quaint throwback to primitive times. For managers, it represents the bad attitudes of ill-trained workers: these are people who don't know how to work, how to be productive, how to be disciplined employees deserving a wage.

The idea is this. In earlier times, before people learned workplace discipline, workers would show up at the factory gate and labor until they earned what they needed, then leave. Or they would work a while and then saunter off to the alehouse, or go home and work there and maybe play with their children, then return to the factory. Of course, for the owners what that meant was idle plant and equipment. The owners could pay the workers more and, yes, they might work more; they would "supply" more of their labor for the higher wage, thus the upward-sloping portion of the supply curve. But at some point, no matter how high the wage, workers would offer *less* work; the supply curve bends backward. Contrary to received theory, not to mention the desires of the owners, the workers would still call it quits and go fishing when they had earned enough.

For factory owners and their investors this "irregular" behavior was, needless to say, unacceptable. Something had to be done, and on a massive scale. Library shelves are full of histories of England's Industrial Revolution, documenting the great wealth produced, the wrenching social transformations undergone, and the exploitation experienced by so many workers, including women and children. These histories also show the extent and severity of measures taken by land and factory owners, government officials, and religious leaders to create the "workforce" that made it all possible, to, in effect, straighten the supply curve for labor.

Straightening Work

Of all the official measures taken against "irregular" behavior, none was as momentous as enclosure. "To commercialize the land," writes historical economist Robert Heilbroner, "required nothing less than the uprooting of an entire feudal way of life. To make 'workers' out of the sheltered serfs and apprentices . . . required the creation of a frightened disoriented class called the proletariat." From the mid-1700s, the English Parliament passed some 4,000 Private Acts of Enclosure covering some 7,000,000 acres until the General Enclosure Act of 1845. "The English countryside [had] consisted in large part of peasant proprietors tilling their own lands, the yeoman, the pride of England, the largest body of independent, free, and prosperous citizens in the world," writes Heilbroner. With enclosure, the meadow, heath, moorland, and woodland that had been their commonly managed "open fields"—lands harvested, grazed, and left fallow as "insurance" or "buffer" against their own separate production—was now privately held and traded as a commodity. In one enclosure of 6,000 acres ten owners ended up with 81 percent of the land, the remainder divided among 116 people. Rents tripled. In another, in 1820, the Duchess of Sutherland dispossessed 15,000 tenants from 794,000 acres of land, replaced them with 131,000 sheep, and then rented each evicted family two acres of submarginal land. Even those who retained some land, the smallholders, could not support themselves and were forced to sell, further concentrating land ownership. By 1876 just 2,250 people owned half the agricultural land in England and Wales. "In village after village," writes social historian E. P. Thompson in *The Making of the English Working Class*, "enclosure destroyed the scratch-as-scratch-can subsistence economy of the poor—the cow or geese, fuel from the common, gleanings, and all the rest." The efficiency of enclosure was demonstrated by dramatically increased crop yields and higher land rents. At the same time, meadows were degraded and woodlands destroyed. "Enclosure," concludes Thompson, "was a plain enough case of class robbery, played according to fair rules of property and law laid down by a Parliament of property-owners and lawyers." Massive numbers of the dispossessed class with little means to support themselves became ripe pickings for agricultural and industrial employers. "It was a matter of policy to increase the dependence of cheap reserves of labour," writes Thompson. The government's enclosures were "endorsed as heartily by landowners as by manufacturers." The new laborers were ready to work long "regular" hours.[1]

Unofficial measures may have been equally consequential, setting the larger cultural context for a disciplined labor force. "Social improvers"—called "discipline propagandists" and "moralists" by E. P. Thompson—denigrated the dispossessed and others in the lower classes. "The most abandoned, and licentious wretches on Earth," one improver called them in 1745. "Such brutality and insolence, such debauchery and extravagance, such idleness, irreligion, cursing and swearing, and contempt of all rule and authority. . . . Our people are *drunk with the cup of liberty.*"[2]

So owners made sure there was little "liberty" on their large farms and in their factories where they divided the labor and supervised the laborers. Gone were the days when agrarians performed multiple skilled tasks, including those of the mind. There had been weavers, for example, "who taught themselves geometry . . . and were eager to discuss the differential calculus."[3] There had been miners who created their own libraries, providing "an enormous stimulus for debate and literary analysis."[4] And gone were the days when artisans put craftsmanship above mere payment. "The peasant, the rural labourer in the unenclosed village, even the urban artisan or apprentice," writes Thompson, "did not measure the return on labour exclusively in money-earnings, and they rebelled against the notion of week after week of disciplined labour."[5] Owners suppressed wages to prevent idleness. They installed bells and whistles and clocks in the factories. They added timesheets and time-keepers, hired informers, and imposed fines and physical punishments.[6] One factory owner wrote in his company code thus:

To the end that sloath and villany should be detected and the just and diligent rewarded, I have thought meet to create an account of time by a Monitor, and do order and it is hereby ordered and declared from 5 to 8 and from 7 to 10 is fifteen hours . . . [calculated] after all deductions for being at taverns, alehouses, coffee houses, breakfast, dinner, playing, sleeping, smoking, singing, reading of news history, quarelling, contention, disputes or anything foreign to my business, any way loytering.[7]

Outside the factory there was "a neverending chorus of complaint from all the Churches and most employers as to the idleness, profligacy, improvidence and thriftlessness of labour," writes Thompson.[8] Complained one clergyman in 1755, "The Churches and Streets [are] crowded with Numbers of Spectators" at weddings and funerals, "who in spight of the Miseries of their Starving Condition . . . make no Scruple of wasting the best Hours in the Day, for the sake of gazing." So also are wakes and holidays and the annual feasts of friendly societies, "wasting the day." So also is "that slothful spending the Morning in Bed."[9] Children, what is more, should be off the street and in schools and workhouses, gaining a "habit of industry," so that by the age of six or seven, they can be "habituated, not to say naturalized to Labour and Fatigue."[10]

It is not surprising, then, that the social improvers of the Industrial Revolution sought to curtail holidays, fairs, festivals and sports. In England, Saint Monday, otherwise known as Fuddling Day, was symptomatic of these "irregular" work habits. It was an unofficial day of rest taken on occasion by workers and so popular that some owners merely accommodated it. It was not until the nineteenth, even the twentieth century in some British industries, that the custom was stamped out.

In all, it turned out to be a monumental effort correcting such "irregular" working behavior, trying, as it were, to straighten out the supply curve for labor. "Wherever modern capitalism has begun its work of increasing the productivity of human labour by increasing its intensity," wrote Max Weber, "it has encountered the immensely stubborn resistance of . . . pre-capitalistic labour."[11] Eventually, though, as all the world knows, the straightening worked. "Economic labor was ground out of unemployed apprentices and dispossessed farm laborers," writes Heilbroner. It took the full coercive authority of the government and the moral authority of the Churches and the suffering of many. What had been an end in itself, says Heilbroner, "a natural way of life" where "economic life and social life were one and the same thing," became "a means to an end—the end being money and the things it buys."[12] Life divides between the economic and the social, the productive and the consumptive. And, we will see, the productive is denigrated as "labor," while the consumptive is celebrated as "freedom."

So workers did learn to supply the quantity of labor owners wanted, day in and day out. Over time, the new "discipline was indeed internalized," concludes Thompson:

> As the industrial revolution proceeds, wage incentives and expanding consumer drives—the palpable rewards for the productive consumption of time and the evidence of new "predictive" attitudes to the future—are evidently effective. By the 1830s and 1840s it was commonly observed that the English industrial worker was marked off from his fellow Irish worker, not by a greater capacity for hard work, but by his regularity, his methodical paying-out of energy, and perhaps also by a repression, not of enjoyments, but of the capacity to relax in the old, uninhibited ways.[13]

If "regularity" and the "repression of uninhibited ways" is the natural order of things, it is odd that so much concerted effort was needed to create such an order. It might just be that the backward-bending supply curve for labor, the propensity of "freemen" (those "drunk with Liberty") to design their own patterns of work, proved stubborn not because of ignorance and sloth. A couple of centuries of Herculean social engineering just might have been necessary because people have an innate tendency to work in a rhythm quite unlike that set by the shop foremen and timekeepers. It may be that people have a tendency to judge for themselves when a task should be taken up or rest is needed, that is, when they have done *enough work*. Maybe people just know that a "discipline of ends is no discipline at all," as agrarian and social critic Wendell Berry puts it, that "the end is preserved in the means,"[14] that real working is the source of satisfaction, not purchasing and consuming. "Goodness, wisdom, happiness, even physical comfort" do not come to a person from institutions, from external incentives, and certainly not from "leisure, some activity or some thing typically . . . provided by a salesman," writes Berry. Rather they come from "doing well what is in his power, and in being reconciled to what is not in his power. . . . The fundamental tasks of feeding and clothing and housing . . . were once done with consummate skill by ordinary people, and as that skill indisputably involved a high measure of pride, it can confidently be said to have produced a high measure of satisfaction."[15]

But worker satisfaction was far from the minds of the industrialists, economists, and nation builders. The lesson they drew was that humans indeed can perform as machines and timepieces dictate, that capital, driven by efficiency seeking, by "intensity of labour," by "productivity," was the ascendant logic, the logic right for progress. Workers just needed persuading and training: start early in life; put school-children in neat rows, segment their day with bells and compartmentalized lessons, teach them time management. Talk about good work; tell them they should specialize, be productive, perform as told, however meaningless those tasks may be. Such were the lessons over the past couple of centuries, lessons that may have been right for the times, for feeding a growing population, for overcoming seasonal constraints on production and transport, for relieving peasants of their drudgery and poverty, for creating the infrastructure of a great nation. They may have been right for democratizing, for creating that "system of perfect liberty," as Adam Smith called commercial capitalism in *The Wealth of Nations*,[16] for getting money into peoples' pockets and giving them choices, consumer choices, of course. All these were lessons whose effects persist today.

For those concerned about the integrity of families, communities, and ecosystems, about the sustainability of a global economy where supply curves of all sorts seem to extend farther and farther along the output dimension, a new lesson is in order. However dynamic a modern economy is, working and consuming more and more does not add up. "A society of undisciplined abundance," writes Berry, is "a society of waste." Training or acquiring job skills, as opposed to educating or learning or growing, let alone thriving, will "produce soldiers and factory workers and clerks," says Berry, but "it will never produce good farmers or good artists or good citizens or good parents."[17] It is reasonable to assume that "good persons" are what people want to be, not well-trained employees who spend more and more time on the job, who sacrifice all else about life—family and community, physical and mental health, the spiritual, the civic, the patriotic—to get ahead or just make ends meet. However much money people may be able to earn working more than, say, twenty or thirty hours a week, they know excess, they know when they have reached their sufficiency point. For wage earners consigned to drudge work, that sufficiency point may be ten or fifteen hours. For the self-employed, especially those whose work is their life's mission, that sufficiency point may be fifty or sixty hours a week. Whatever the number of hours, they, like their forebears, recognize a sufficiency point in labor supplied. And if it does not add up for the worker—because that person wants to be more a citizen than a work-and-spend consumer—it does not add up for the planet when all that "disciplined regularity," all that "productivity," just accelerates resource extraction and consuming and waste-sink filling. "A consumer is one who uses things up," says Berry, "a concept that is alien to the creation, as are the concepts of waste and disposability."[18]

Alternative concepts are needed. Here I posit a "working rationality" to parallel ecological rationality, all under the general social organizing principle of sufficiency. In a sustainable economy, individuals would seek enough work and policy would become oriented toward work choices, as opposed to consumer choices. It would be an economy that rejects the neat consumption-is-good/work-is-bad dichotomy (see below) and that allows individual consumption to follow work, not drive it. It would be an economy where individuals optimize between work and consumption, where choice is, in the first instance, made by individuals themselves in the context of their broader social commitments—family, neighborhood, nation. A *working rationality* would, in short, build in limits in work and, hence, limits in consumption. It becomes but one more step to make those limits congruent with ecological capacity. The case histories in coming chapters help set that congruence empirically and on a local scale. Here I show how, via time reckoning and self-determined work choice, a working rationality puts a brake on excess throughput of material and energy and how that brake is released when workers specialize, resource groups exceed a manageable scale, and sovereign consumers rule.

Work: Linking Consumption and Environment

So how does work link consumption to the throughput of material and energy? First, work, both wage and salaried, tends toward ever-increasing specialization via the division of labor, mechanization, and skill development. Specialization begets productivity gains, part of which translate into income gains, which investors and workers, as consumers, then spend. As income rises, spending increases, shifting from mostly so-called necessities to more so-called luxuries (or to necessities that were once luxuries). Second, productivity gains tend toward overall production gains. Although technically the efficiency of labor can improve in two ways—more output for a given input or less input for the same output—the tendency empirically is overwhelmingly the path of more output (chapter 4). The popular and political appeal of a growth economy—that is, growth in tangible and taxable things, not necessarily in well-being, let alone leisure—probably adequately explains this tendency toward more output, not less input. Greater worker productivity, more spending, and increased overall production results in greater overall resource use.[19] Work, conventionally construed, leads to more economic output, more income, and more spending, all of which translates into increased material throughput and hence increased ecological stress.

So how can the cycle of "more work/more throughput" be broken? How in the contemporary context can the supply curve for labor be re-bent, if not subordinated entirely? Until now I have used the term *work* primarily as employment, as, indeed, that economistic rendering, "supply of labor." But for present purposes—constructing a working rationality—an expanded conception is needed, one more sociological and psychological, one more grounded in everyday experience. So here, in the first instance, I use the term *work* to connote activities that are necessary for survival or reproductive success and that are generally burdensome, unpleasant, tedious, or lacking in any intrinsic satisfaction other than procuring necessities. Examples include dangerous hunts, long strenuous periods foraging for herbs and grubs, all-day mowing of fields, and monotonous operation of a machine. This is the mostly negative use of *work*, corresponding to toil and drudgery, but also the use that connotes necessity and hence "discipline" of a higher ethical plane than that concocted by the social improvers of the Industrial Revolution. I also use *work* to connote activities that, necessary or not, burdensome or not, satisfy the actor in some important way; they demand focused attention and acquired skills and result in a sense of competence, of "doing a job right." Examples include entrepreneurial experiments and investments, artistic expression, and childrearing. The challenge, then, is to identify patterns of work that avoid the productivity gains that become throughput gains and patterns that are likely to exhibit built-in sufficiency points and restraint.

Work locates limits to consumption and environmental impact in two ways. First, work is a key activity occurring at the interface of resource functioning (biological and geochemical processes) and human functioning (fishing and hunting, planting and irrigating, logging and transporting). This is where the levels and kinds of resource use are decided and where feedback from the biophysical system is registered (see chapter 2). Activity in the realms of policy and markets—legislating, adjudicating, administering, investing, producing, consuming—may function similarly, but decision making in these realms, especially in advanced industrial economies, is separated from primary resource-extraction and resource-use questions.[20]

Second, and possibly most significantly, it is in the rhythm of work that time sense is most noticeably expressed. The social organization of work largely determines the prevailing time sense in a society. In a captivating history of sugar, *Sweetness and Power*,[21] anthropologist Sydney Mintz shows in painstaking detail how sugar sweetened more than tea. It sweetened deals between industrialists and lawmakers to make possible, indeed imperative, work oriented to the factory clock. "The rise in the use of prepared foods, the increase in meals eaten out, and the decline of the meal itself as a ritual," writes Mintz reflecting on the long history of sugar, industrialization, and the nature of work,

have led in recent decades to different patterns of sucrose usage as well as to increases in the consumption of sugars overall. . . .

Alterations in the perception of time [by the British working class] . . . [set] the terms of work as if the machines demanded it, or as if daylight made it necessary, or as if the others in the work force fixed the tempo, or as if eating had to fit within a unit of time, rather than its being *the act of eating itself that determines how much time it should take.* . . .

How much time people actually have for different pursuits, how much time they believe they have, and the relationship between these are aspects of daily life shaped by externalities [to the individual] and, in particular in the modern world, by the reorganization of the workday. What seem visible to the worker, however, are the changed conditions of work. These new conditions shape in turn what is left of his time; yet how much time one "has" may be only fleetingly perceived as dependent, ultimately, on the work regime.[22]

The "work regime" of modern economies structures time and does so as mechanical time. It embodies a vision of the good life that cannot allow idleness, that cannot allow the act of eating, or working, or caring, or living, to determine "how much time it should take." Rather, the divisibility of tasks and the expansion of consumer goods provide the requisite measure of time, a measure that is inherently short term from an ecological point of view, that leans toward this year's output, even this quarter's earnings, more than to this generation's needs, let alone to that of the next and the next. With different conceptions of time, though, what I'll term "natural" time and task-based time, a different vision can arise, one more attuned to human need for association, meaning, and challenge as well as to ecosystem functioning, especially as sources of limits. It is from such conceptions that work and, hence, consumption and everyday connection to the material and social worlds become manifest. And it is in these expanded notions of time (beyond the mechanical) and work (beyond mere employment) that identity and satisfaction coincide with restrained consumption and can thus serve as essential building blocks for a working rationality and a sustainable economy.

Other Human Tides: Time Reckoning, Self-Direction, and a "Natural" Rhythm of Work

A few years after publishing his magisterial volume, *The Making of the English Working Class*, E. P. Thompson extended several key themes in a small article titled "Time, Work-Discipline, and Industrial Capitalism." Nearly buried in that article, in parentheses in fact, he asks whether there might be a " 'natural' human work-rhythm." He notes the work of fishers and farmers whose rhythm is dictated by tides and seasons. He describes how women working in factories in industrial England still cared for their children when they got home, still tended to their household duties and worked in the fields. "To this day," he notes, "despite school times and television times, the rhythms of women's work in the home are not wholly attuned to the measurement of the clock.... The mother of young children ... attends to other human tides." And in that attention, she undoubtedly would have sought a balance, a mix of the tedious (yet necessary) and the stimulating (and rewarding). Given a choice (and history reveals little, especially in the English Industrial Revolution), she would have said enough when any one (or combination) of the tasks became exhausting or overwhelming or boring. Thompson might have looked further, though, for "other human tides," even to men who, say, farm part time or repair house and vehicle or provision household meat by hunting and fishing. Their work, too, might be "irregular," alternating between "bouts of intense labour and of idleness."[23] They, too, might fall into a rhythm where enough work and too much work become self-evident, where feedback from sore feet and an aching back, from lapses in focused attention on the task, say enough.

So what would be a "natural" rhythm of work and productiveness when people have a high degree of autonomy and self-direction? How would such a rhythm build in limits? Although a large literature exists on work, it tends not to ask such questions, focusing instead on issues of workplace satisfaction and management-labor relations. The following, then, is an attempt to explore "other human tides," to ask what features of a natural rhythm of work would emerge when individuals or groups have work choices, when they can largely choose how to allocate their energies, their talents, and their time.

The first feature of a natural rhythm of work is *idiosyncratic regularity* (what the early industrialists derided as "irregularity").[24] Given a variety of work and productive opportunities, some of which are necessary to survival, some conducive to well-being, individuals tend to parcel their work time—their day, their week, their seasons—into regularized episodes of intense work followed by rest or social interaction.[25] One may begin the morning with physical activity (e.g., surveying, harvesting, building), stop to eat, resume the physical activity, then shift to mental pursuits (e.g., calculating, corresponding, planning). At some point, this individual turns to artistic endeavors (e.g., writing, gardening, painting, playing music). All of this may be interspersed with care of children and the elderly.

The regularity of this pattern should not be confused with the regularity imposed by mechanized routines—for example, on the assembly line. There the clock and the organization of wage labor compel standardized behavior among all workers. Some are hired only for physical work and others for mental work; the choice and distribution of work are externally imposed (chapter 3). Here, the pattern is established by the worker. The regularity derives from the need in one's productive pursuits for familiarity and predictability, on the one hand, and variety and challenge, on the other. Each individual's rhythm is particular, though. Some are inclined to lengthy periods of monotonous, familiar routines, others to continual exploration and experimentation. Given the choice, individuals will develop and maintain their own rhythms of work, their own combination of toil, expression, and nurturing. And they will be driven to do so because it is in such work that individuals achieve a sense of competency and self-worth. These people are not the individuals of the consumer economy (see below).

The second feature of a rhythm of work is built-in limits. Physical capacities are the most obvious source of limits. Exhaustion and occupational maladies such as carpal tunnel syndrome are extreme forms. Given a choice, individuals will readily shift from physically demanding work to rest or other forms of work long before debilitating fatigue sets in. Psychological limits may be less obvious but no less significant. Humans have a reservoir of directed attention that can be allocated to tasks but cannot be drawn down indefinitely without restoration. I can write for several hours, teach for a couple more, and attend a meeting or two. But if I don't go for a walk, rearrange my files, swing a hammer, or pull some weeds, I'm wasted. I'm irritable and intolerant. Colleagues and family members can provide empirical substantiation. One colleague, psychologist Raymond De Young, tells me that research indeed shows that effective restorative activities include walks, cleaning, and hobbies, as well as playing games, sports, and music. These are restorative to the extent that they

• Temporarily take the actor (physically or mentally) out of his or her overly demanding environment
• Provide a new environment (physical or mental) in which one can "lose oneself" and explore
• Offer the actor a degree of fascination (some challenge or stimulation but not so much as to further drain directed attention)

Sleep, even a full night's sleep, cannot by itself restore directed attention, especially when severely depleted.[26]

Regularly shifting from a demanding activity to a monotonous activity can be restorative and, hence, enhancing of both activities, heightening an individual's satisfaction and meaning. Notably, satisfaction and meaning not only come from the "higher" forms of work, the mental or artistic, say, but from the menial, too. Getting all my leaves raked before the first big storm is still a job well done. Most important for the purposes of this study, the two kinds of activity are self-limiting, physically and psychologically. Alternating between the two compels a self-directed individual to limit physically and mentally draining activities. This mode of work intersects with ecosystem functioning via time reckoning.

Time reckoning is the process by which we sense the passage of time. In preindustrial societies, time reckoning was predominantly nature driven and task based. The "time" to plant and to harvest and the "time" to have a child were dictated by season and physical maturity along with culturally evolved proscriptions. There was a time to work, a time to play, as someone once wrote and others sang. And the time it takes to create, to invent, to explore or to experiment was determined by the task, not by a task master with a clock. Anyone who has created a recipe, designed a landscape, or written a book knows how hard it is to answer the question, How long did it take? One may look for a clock-based answer because mechanistic time reckoning is dominant in contemporary society, but it makes little sense. Ask a parent how long it took to teach the child to be responsible. Ask professionals how long it takes to design a product, compose a song, build a winning coalition. Hours and days just do not capture the *quality* of the passage of time in such endeavors. One just does them. The time is up when the tasks are done.

Although clock-based time reckoning dominates contemporary thought and practice, it has by no means extinguished the preindustrial forms. Task-based time exists in the home, but also on the playground, along the trout stream, and in the meeting house. Most telling, perhaps, it persists in, of all places, automobile production—an industry that otherwise epitomizes Taylorist and Fordist approaches to work—and in various so-called hobbies (boxes 5.1 and 5.2). What is common to all is self-direction.

Social psychologist Melvin Kohn surveyed a wide-ranging set of studies on work, including longitudinal, psychological studies in the United States and other industrialized countries, and found that a research consensus exists on the conditions that promote well-being through work:

Of all the structural imperatives of the job, those that determine how much opportunity, even necessity, the worker has for exercising occupational *self-direction* [the use of initiative, thought, and independent judgment] are the most important for personality. . . . Exercising self-direction in work—doing work that is substantively complex, not being closely supervised, not working at routinized tasks—is conducive to favorable evaluations of self, an open and flexible orientation to others, and effective intellectual functioning.

In short, "people *thrive* in meeting occupational challenges"[27] and in pursuing purposeful work, not in purchasing that which is "provided by a salesman." They can certainly derive meaning from consumption, approach shopping as a challenge, as a modern form of hunting and gathering, say. But it is reasonable to assume that shopping, following fashion, or pursuing the latest and biggest car is nowhere near the same as the "thriving" of purposeful work. The purposes of good work are self-chosen, whereas the purposes of consuming are largely determined by others—commercial boosters in industry and government, even educators and environmentalists.[28]

Possibly the best evidence for the "thriving" of self-directed work and its associated natural rhythm, though, is negative, namely, the resistance to industrialization and the massive social engineering undertaken to overcome such resistance. In nonindustrial, unsupervised settings, it appears that humans do indeed perform just enough work to meet their needs, and they perform just enough wage work to meet some of their needs, leaving adequate time to meet other needs in other ways. That backward bend in the supply curve is quite appealing, given the choice.

Although it is easy to dismiss such work patterns as anomalous or primitive, it is at least equally logical to see them as suggestive of a perfectly natural tendency in work, namely, as an innate ability to recognize when enough is enough. The general case in which it occurs may not be when modernity meets traditionalism but whenever humans have considerable discretion over when, how much, and how they work. Preindustrial peoples are an obvious case. But the evidence presented

Box 5.1
A different time in the auto industry

For much of the twentieth century, the British car company Rover maintained considerable variation in the time cycles of its different operations—length of track, number of work stations, and number of operators per task, for instance—and a highly skilled, "lifetime" workforce oriented to community and family. It was quite "unlike other UK car firms," writes historian Richard Whipp, and certainly unlike American firms as it "did not follow the Fordist principles of centrally-directed, highly synchronized, machine-paced production." Instead, production was organized around workgroups and piece-work arrangements between groups. Members of these groups "learned to accommodate the irregular rhythms of market and inter-plant supply lines," writes Whipp. Moreover, "it was on the shop floor that the most intricate patterns of perceptions of time arose."

Unlike their American counterparts, workers in the UK auto industry retained a degree of craft skill and craft organization. "The key characteristic of piecework was the way management gave only general orders regarding tasks." The workers then took responsibility for carrying out these orders, setting the pace as they deemed appropriate. "Workers concentrated on issues related to their work stations or group's task responsibilities and payment: a concentration which produced a strictly localized perception of task-pace and regulation. . . . Track workers [for instance] were preoccupied with the base-rate payment per minute while trim workers were more interested in the rate per hour they could negotiate." In addition, "product and production engineers, far from working to rigid model policies prided themselves on their small, flexible, organic, design teams and their weekly, informal liaison with production staff." In short, there was considerable variation "in the time cycles of different operations" such that working time in the factory "could be punctuated by both technical and informal breaks in production."

For the plant, production could be flexible, adaptive to the high variability of the UK market. For the worker, doing even the most menial task entailed significant personal discretion and self-regulation. Together, a plurality of time reckoning modes existed, only one of which was set by the clock. "Time/work relationships," Whipp concludes after reviewing Rover's automobile production, British ceramics, and other industries, are "informed by both the subjective constructions of time and the plurality of time-reckoning modes which have continued to operate in industrial societies." Certainly people, workers and managers alike, order these modes by the clock, but so too do they order them by "the cyclical patterns of season, family and life-course, as well as the diverse perceptions derived from various social groupings inside and outside work." Even today, and even in the United States, some manufacturers attempt to capture the adaptiveness and self-determination of this work pattern with team-based production.

Sources: Richard Whipp, "'A Time to Every Purpose': An Essay on Time and Work," in Patrick Joyce, ed., *The Historical Meanings of Work* (Cambridge: Cambridge University Press, 1987) (quotes on 228, 230, 232, 233, 235); James Crowfoot, personal communication, 2004.

Box 5.2
Hot rodding, etc.—Cultures of work

Hot rodding may appear an odd place to gain insights into the nature of self-directed work. But in America in the 1950s and 1960s it had its own culture with its own beliefs and purposes, that is, its own myths. "The main myth of the culture," sociologist H. F. Moorhouse writes, "is of buying a junked Ford for a few dollars, of reclaiming various parts from it, and with these and some other standard and custom accessories reassembling, via a great deal of hard and skilled labour, a high performance vehicle." The hot rodder's project is a serious one, involving considerable theoretical and scientific understanding of the technology and great creativity in the design, all leading to a unique vehicle. It is not "an activity for the idle or for the spectator; it is not about triviality or passiveness or easy hedonism," says Moorhouse. In fact, participants in this culture stress the values of involvement, craftsmanship, learning by doing (and by failing), perseverance, progress by trial and error, and experimentation. There's no book learning here. What matters is "their absorption in the activity, the technical details of their car, their sweat, and dedication to their task."

Some of these attributes may be unique to hot rodding (the thrill of the drag race, for example). But Moorhouse asserts that many are common to a range of so-called leisure activities—angling, boating, gardening, cooking—all of which have uncertainty and risk, which demand skill, knowledge, the willingness to fail, and creativity, and which have an appeal beyond the actual outcome, and certainly beyond any monetary return. One might add computer networking, gaming, and hacking (there is an illicit side to hot rodding as well); hunting, bicycling (racing, mountaineering, commuting), woodworking (whether making bookshelves or Victorian reproductions, each cut is critical), model railroading, birdwatching, slam-dunk poetry, creative writing (whether freelance or amateur), community theater and orchestra, antiquing (collecting, restoring, showing), amateur science (which, in the nineteenth century, was the source of considerable discovery, Charles Darwin being one celebrated example). All of these activities entail challenge and complexity and, to varying degrees, social organization: even the model railroader who spends long hours in the basement laying track and arranging miniature buildings generally belongs to a club and travels to the conventions.

Here work is far from paid labor. It is a "multifaceted activity," says Moorhouse, done "as hobby, as relaxation, as fascination, as something *you really want to do* rather than being forced to do." But it is more than "hobby" or "pastime," those dismissive terms relegated to "leisure studies." It is "the special calling," writes sociologist Stanton Wheeler, "the investment in something for its own sake, the commitment, constrained only by the demands of work [employment] and family, to an activity that is its own reward." Real work is about "personally chosen projects," says Moorhouse, "about feeling *good* by working hard," irrespective of pay or even the end product itself. In farming, it is "a science of practice, an art," writes Wendell Berry, "for it grows not only out of factual knowledge but out of cultural tradition . . . a complex set of attitudes, a certain culturally evolved stance, in the face of the unexpected and the unknown. . . . It requires *style* in the highest and richest sense of that term . . . style as the signature of mastery, the efflorescence of long discipline."

Box 5.2
(continued)

> Proponents of "real work," of "style," those hot rod enthusiasts and model rail-roaders and model railroaders and agrarians like Berry who write and speak about their work, Moorhouse calls the cultural and moral entrepreneurs of unpaid time, people who provide "injunctions to strive, to create, to study, and achieve." We might label them the cultural and moral entrepreneurs of meaningful work, of deliberately and freely chosen "labors of love," of engagement over instrumentalism. These entrepreneurs, quite unlike their industrial predecessors, the "social improvers" and the "efficiency experts," people who were all too willing to separate workers from managers and labor from "real work," point everyday life away from the consumer economy and toward a "working economy."
>
> *Sources*: Wendell Berry, "Discipline and Hope," in *A Continuous Harmony: Essays Cultural and Agricultural* (New York: Harcourt Brace Jovanovich, 1972); reproduced in Berry, *Recollected Essays, 1965–1980*, 151–220 (New York: North Point Press, 1998), (quotes on 161, 174); H. F. Moorhouse, "The 'Work' Ethic and 'Leisure' Activity: The Hot Rod in Post-War America," in Patrick Joyce, ed., *The Historical Meanings of Work*, 237–257 (Cambridge: Cambridge University Press, 1987), (quotes on 244, 246, 247); Stanton Wheeler, "Double Lives," in Kai Erikson and Steven Peter Vallas, eds., *The Nature of Work: Sociological Perspectives*, 141–148 (New Haven: Yale University Press, 1990), (quote on 143).

here suggests that so is self-employment, or any productive activity with a degree of independence from outside forces, especially the coercive and manipulative.

In situations where individuals have a high level of autonomous choice, then—not just consumer choice, but producer or productive choice—the backward-bending supply curve is far from a sign of backwardness. Limiting one's work and hence productive output is perfectly rational. And this is so not just when the price of labor passes a threshold (the bend in the curve) but whenever the opportunity cost of the marginal work effort passes a threshold. If, for example, another hour of work means I jeopardize my health, risk a friendship, or neglect my children, less work makes perfectly good sense regardless of the proffered wage. Making such choices is perfectly logical, even natural when self-determination itself is taken as a high value. And "natural work" employs natural and task-based forms of time reckoning, which, unlike the mechanistic forms that can be repeatedly divided and accelerated, are governed by forces largely outside one's control, by physiology (sleep and waking, highs and lows through the day), cognition (capacity to function with a limited number of individuals), diurnal and seasonal cycles, and social interaction (cooperation and competition, consensus making and strategic gaming). These are all forces that establish immutable limits. No amount of tinkering can change that fact.

If self-limitation in self-managed work is natural, as much a part of human nature as choosing a mate and organizing for self-defense, then it follows that so is self-restraint in consumption and, hence, in resource use. Humans do not always want more. Goods may be good but more goods may not be better. Humans make trade-offs not just in their purchasing and investing but, given the opportunity, in their working, their producing, their productive being. Humans do not choose to consume more and more if the trade-off is between, on the one hand, unpleasant, meaningless, unrewarding yet monetarily compensated work and, on the other, pleasant, meaningful, and rewarding work, whether or not monetarily compensated. Simply put, if individuals have choices not just in what they buy or where they invest, but in the quantity and quality of work they perform, they are likely to minimize externally directed, routinized activities, those activities dependent on monetary compensation or, in the extreme, on coercion for their performance—for example, wage labor, contract hire, or paid employment. Instead they are likely to maximize internally satisfying work: self-employment, independent business, family farming, freelancing, consulting. One result is restraint in income-generating production and, hence, in the purchasing of goods—that is, in consumption. Recall that restraint is not self-abnegation. It is choosing less material use than what is possible in exchange for nonmaterial benefits; it involves opting for less material in the near term for more (or more secure) material in the far term.

The archetype for the work-and-consumption-restraining propensity may be the artist who works the day job only enough to make ends meet and then practices, performs, writes, and teaches the rest of the time because such art-related activities are the most rewarding. Close to artists might be independent scholars. In the business world, there are independent farmers, fishers, and loggers who often say that it is their love of the land or the sea and the associated way of life that keeps them from taking a more lucrative, wage-earning job. Entrepreneurs, store owner/operators, and publishers may also fit the mold. For them, a major motivation is to have one's own business, to be self-employed, to contribute directly to one's community. The desire to have one's own business may be as close to a universal yearning as any economic goal even in, or especially in, contemporary industrial societies.

In all these activities, from art to farming to self-employed business, individuals make money. And they undoubtedly prefer to make more money. But these occupations suggest that in the trade-off between burdensome work ("just a job") and rewarding productive activity ("making something happen"), many people do choose productive activity, however poorly compensated monetarily.

These propositions are admittedly provisional. Aside from the works cited here, there is to my knowledge no systematic research on the self-restraining components of work patterns. Labor studies focus on workers as employees and on the work environment provided by employers that either promotes or hinders worker satisfaction and, ultimately, company productivity and investors' return. By contrast, the historical and psychological approach taken here leads logically to the idea that work oriented to natural and task-based time reckoning is more likely to have built-in limits.[29] Such work is likely to be pursued naturally because self-direction in work is a demonstrated source of satisfaction and positive self-worth. In this way restraint constitutes itself at the individual level. At the level of organizations and the economy, though, three structural factors thwart such a working rationality. The first, specialization, is already familiar from the preceding chapters' discussion of efficiency but can now be elaborated in the context of work. The second, scale, brings work and consumption into the biophysical realm and, hence, connects the social and the ecological sides of sustainability. The third, the notion of the sovereign consumer, distorts people's sense of place in nature and society.

Specialization and Scale

Specialization is a driver in the unending cycle of goods-are-good-and-more-goods-are-better. With specialization, one can always produce ever more (or cheaper) goods.

From the perspective of the owner of a productive enterprise, specialization always makes sense—that is, the specialization of others, of the owner's employees, not necessarily of the owner himself or herself. Owners are often the quintessential generalists in part because their work, as organized, requires it and in part because they prefer it. They are, after all, the real self-directed workers thriving on occupational challenges. In early industrialization, owners—whether of factories or farms—did do everything. These "small masters" were "men who doffed their caps to no one and recognized no right in either squire or parson to question, or meddle with them," wrote a local English historian in 1884. If such a master "rose in the world high enough to employ a few of his neighbors, he did not therefore cease to labour with his own hands, but worked as hard or perhaps harder than anyone he employed. In speech and in dress he claimed no superiority."[30] Even as business shifted from a craft-based structure to a corporate structure, those at the top tended to have a broad range of skills and to exercise a broad range of tasks. The claim that specialization is a natural step in economic progress is thus suspect. If it is true for employed workers, it would have to be true for employers as well.[31]

From Adam Smith's time on, though, the specialization of workers by generalist owners has proceeded in both theory and practice. At the same time, a critique has developed of the alienating effects of industrialization, including specialization, on workers. E. P. Thompson sees the Industrial Revolution not so much as an expression of capitalist greed as "a technological differentiation between work and life."[32] Wendell Berry finds that specialization in the form of "new knowledge, political ideas, technological innovations, all are injected into society merely on the ground that to the specialists who produce them they appear to be good in themselves." A labor-saving device is presumed useful because it works, irrespective of the impact on people where it "lowers the quality of a product and makes obsolete a considerable number of human beings."[33]

But there has been little study of how specialization supports a production system dependent on satisfying consumers and on ever-increasing consumer spending, resulting in ever-greater use of material and energy. I offer three largely speculative propositions in that direction. The first is biological, the second deductive with respect to resource decision making, and the third historical with respect to craft-oriented work and ownership. Together they suggest how an economy organized around self-directed work might improve social welfare at the same time it puts brakes on ever-increasing consumption and throughput.

Specialization within and between groups, evolutionary biologist Matt Ridley argues, is a hallmark of human organization, having evolved from the earliest times, possibly 30,000, even 200,000 years ago. But "even if trade between groups came much later, at the brink of recorded history, its [specialization's] invention represents one of the very few moments in evolution when *Homo sapiens* stumbled on some competitive ecological advantage over other species that was truly unique. There is simply no other animal that exploits the law of comparative advantage between groups."[34] Some hunt and gather, others farm, and still others trade. In the end, the species outwits all others, controlling fire and flood, suppressing disease and pestilence, taming wild lands, all to expand its ecological niche.

Ridley may be right that specialization between groups defines much of what is human (at least from an evolutionary perspective). But like any evolutionary adaptation—biological or cultural—pushed to an extreme, specialization by individuals, groups, or classes can lead a species down a self-destructive path, especially when the environment changes. In this adaptation, positive feedback loops characterize the comparative advantage of the species: the more specialized a group becomes the more food it obtains; the more food the bigger the population; the bigger the population the more it can specialize. Yet positive feedback can overwhelm what would otherwise be self-correcting negative feedback only to a point (chapter 2). Space, resource constraints, and infighting can render the comparative advantage maladaptive. On the social side, slavery is the extreme example. Through history, slave catching, trading, and owning made economic (maybe cultural) sense. The more slaves one had the more wealth one could generate and the more slaves one could own. But slavery degrades the slaveholder along with the slave. Slave societies eventually lose their advantage as contradictions mount internally and condemnation builds externally. On the biophysical side, specialization divides the work of natural resource exploitation so as to contradict the inherently generalized, or integrative, operation of ecosystems, as well as to reduce the accountability of all actors. Box 5.3 employs "ideal-type" and rational-choice constructions and draws on systems theory to show how the social-biophysical dynamic can make specialization maladaptive. Box 5.4 shows how restraint in resource use via work is also governed by scale, especially the scale of human material activity relative to ecological capacity.

The Sovereign Consumer

Unchecked specialization and excessive scale of operation are thus two forces that thwart a working rationality. The view that the purpose of an economy is to serve consumers is a third.

The contemporary political economy that arose in England is epitomized in its modern form by the U.S. economy, one that is now being assimilated around the world. This is a political economy hailed as one that provides abundance for all, that promotes freedom of choice, that serves the consumer. In its early days, it was "a culture that seemed to offer everyone access to an unlimited supply of goods and that promised a lifetime of security, well-being, and happiness," writes William Leach, historian of the consumer society's formative years in the United States, 1890–1920. "Its hallmark was not 'the public be damned,'" as in the old industrialism of Dickens, but, with mass merchandising and distribution, "'the public be served.'" More than just good salesmanship and customer service, "from the 1890s on, American corporate business, in league with key institutions, began the transformation of American society into a society preoccupied with consumption, with comfort and bodily well-being, with luxury, spending, and acquisition, with more

Box 5.3
Loggers A and B: Whither specialization?

Sustainable resource practice requires high congruence between the functioning of the biophysical and social systems. Such congruence is most critical at the interface of the two systems, namely, where humans interact directly with the resource, where they cut the tree, plow the land, harvest the fish, draw the water. The organization of · work is a major determinant of that interaction. Consider two contrasting, stylized cases.

Loggers A and B each own sizeable tracts of timberland along with a sawmill and other equipment. Both are committed to long-term use of the resource. Logger A hires a specialist to handle each component of the operations from land surveys to marketing. He oversees all operations but doesn't actually carry them out.

Logger B, by contrast, does it all herself. She surveys the land, measures tree growth, monitors water quality and quantity, inspects soil conditions, marks and fells trees, hauls logs to the mill, and produces boards for shipment. She is not as good at any one of these tasks as the specialists logger A hires. But she is good enough to get the product to market and make a profit.

Logger A's workers perform the same tasks logger B does by herself and they get the same product to market. But, because A's workers have the most advanced skills, knowledge, and technology available, the tasks they perform add up to a more efficient overall operation. Logger A gets out big cuts and makes a sizeable profit.

From a sustainability perspective, the question is, how would the two firms compare over a long period of time, that is, a period of time that would afford a reasonable judgment on the ecological sustainability of the respective operations? Consider the harvest decision, a decision that inherently has high uncertainty as to long-term effects (except at the extremes—no cut or cut-out) and one that all timber owners must make on a periodic basis. It is a decision critical to short-term and long-term economic and ecological viability. And, in the end, it can be made by only one person or one body of people. What's more, it is a decision that involves the assessment and weighing of a multitude of factors such as standing volume, growth rates, soil conditions, water quality and quantity, harvesting techniques, and milling capacity. These factors can vary significantly from one location to another, some even from one tree to another and from one millhand to another. Assume adequate demand and, for both loggers A and B, a strong profit-making motive.

To make the harvest decision, logger A collects information and judgments from all his specialists. One specialist gives him growth rates for pines, another for alders; one for sandy soil, one for loamy; one predicts the climate fifty years from now, another estimates interest rates then; and so on. By whatever formal and cognitive means, logger A integrates this information and estimates maximum sustained yield.

Logger B gathers similar kinds of information but, due to the nature of her work, she necessarily does so in the course of her daily tasks. In such a pattern of work, she becomes highly aware of what the pines and the alders are doing. She may not accumulate as much hard data, but she does have considerable knowledge, a kind of knowledge that is gained through intimate experience with the resource and the machinery.

Box 5.3
(continued)

The primary difference between loggers A and B is in the *quality*, not quantity, of information and in the knowledge resulting from their two means of integration. One might assume that the quality of information is very high for logger A, both in the head of each specialist and in the aggregate. But the relevant information is that which the decision maker has, not the specialists, and this information is necessarily secondhand, filtered and reduced. On a strictly technical basis, that knowledge unavoidably has high variance. But all is not technical in an organizational and economic environment.

A specialist may be confident of the tolerance range for disturbance from logging, confident, that is, within one's own specialty. The soil scientist knows how much loss of vegetative cover can be sustained before nutrient cycling is disrupted, say. But if the loss of vegetative cover interacts with water quality neither the soil specialist nor the water specialist can, based on their respective specialties, predict the impact. By not incorporating the knowledge of all the other specialists, each specialist necessarily predicts a high tolerance range for disturbance. Each specialist recommends a harvest rate that, all else equal, that specialist's component (alder growth, loamy soil quality) can withstand. Aggregating each estimate of maximum sustainable disturbance therefore generates an upward bias when the possibility exists, indeed, the likelihood exists (due to the complexity of the systems) of positive interactive effects. If we add the familiar organizational dynamic of the collective action problem where individual interests override the collective interest and assume that higher harvests translate into higher wages, the upward bias is stronger still.

Logger A would be powerless to correct this bias in any systematic way because to do so would require specialized knowledge—precisely what he has hired, not acquired. He can play it cautiously by discounting the specialists' estimates and rejecting their calls for high harvest rates and higher wages. Not only would this strain the owner-worker relationship, but he would still have to pick a harvest level. He would be reduced to little more than educated guessing, what he could have done without hiring the specialists.

In sum, for logger A with hired specialists, a bias towards overharvesting would be structurally built in. A personal commitment to long-term resource use may ameliorate the situation, but would not fundamentally alter it. The knowledge inherent in a system of specialization contradicts the integrative knowledge inherent in the complexity and adaptiveness of a well-functioning ecosystem. More knowledge, and certainly more specialized knowledge, will not help. Specialists as employees within an organization or contract hires from outside are naturally more risk seeking with respect to the long-term capacity of the resource (say, the timberland) than the owner of that resource. Degradation means they find another job, transferring their specialized skills elsewhere. Degradation for the owner means finding a new forest or a new livelihood. The risk is thus far greater for the owner.

The ultimate effect of divided knowledge and divided risk is *divided accountability*. Specialists within an organization and specialized agents from without are not, and can not, be accountable in the same way as the owner. For Logger A, high variance esti-

Box 5.3
(continued)

---

mates from his specialists and low ecological integration means that more predictable, more tangible and more pressing factors weigh on his thinking, namely, the financial. Accountability necessarily leans toward the bottom line, toward short-term economic return, dependent as Logger A is on hired specialists.

Accountability for logger B has a greater likelihood of leaning toward ecosystem functioning. She, unlike A's specialists, is necessarily risk averse with respect to the resource as the owner/worker and is thus more likely than logger A to make cautious harvest decisions and ensure the long-term viability of the forest as a system. Her knowledge is more systems oriented, more cyclical and multiplicative, whereas logger A's is more linear and additive.

In short, the two loggers' knowledge is driven by the nature of their work. Logger A's specialization results in voluminous hard data but low integration; logger B's results in minimal hard data, but high integration. In all, logger B's resource decision is governed by a form of work and resulting knowledge system that is more congruent with the nature of biophysical systems than logger A's. Logger B is more likely to restrain her harvesting and meet her goal of long-term resource use, that is, approach sustainability, a goal logger A shares but will struggle to implement.

Generalist "owner-operators" tend to find congruence between ecosystem functioning and organizational functioning; they acquire the knowledge that lends itself to built-in limits. They restrain their resource use. Specialists can be highly profitable in the short term, maladaptive over the long term. They are unable to match uncertainty and divided knowledge and divided risk to restrain their resource use.

Box 5.4
Fishers and fishing: Where scale matters

Restraint in resource use is governed in part by the scale of human action—work—relative to ecological capacity. As with timbering (box 5.3), a key locus of interaction is direct resource use. Consider the stylized case of a fishery where several dozen fishers organize themselves so that no one takes an individually maximum catch and yet no one is excluded from fishing, either. In other words, they value equal access and assured catch more than maximum return on investment.

Each fisher works the fishery individually and restrains use for reasons of self-direction and generalization. But *allocation of the fishery among the fishers* in space and time is unavoidably a group function. The work of fishing, in short, is inherently both the individual harvesting and the collective management of the harvesting. (See chapter 7.)

The scale effect enters when the number of fishers increases. Assume the resource is abundant and able to support additional fishers. Overall effort—time on the water, numbers of fishers, and technologies applied—can readily expand. It does not necessarily follow, however, that the work of collective management can readily expand. A slight diversion to human evolution offers one explanation.

Box 5.4
(continued)

Humans have evolved to function in groups of roughly 20 families or 150 individuals. To interact effectively with others, people must process and store vast amounts of information, including information about facial and body features and a lifetime of behavioral traits and kinship ties. This information is critical to social interaction where reciprocity and reputation are essential, arguably defining characteristics of humans. But human brains are limited to acquiring such knowledge for only some 150 people. To have evolved greater social processing capacity would have been redundant in humans' hunter-gatherer stage. In fact, 150 is roughly the number of individuals in a typical hunter-gatherer band, the number of entries in an average address book, the size of an army company, and the maximum that employers prefer in managing a company. All others must be processed as "outsiders"; rudeness in the anonymity of big cities is illustrative.

From a sustainability perspective, the question is, under what conditions are there simultaneously scale limits in work and use limits in extraction and consumption? The common property literature suggests that exclusive, small-group use of an essential and well-defined resource is one such condition. Generalist work, not specialist, may be another (box 5.3). Yet another may be "occupational pluralism," the ability to shift from one form of work to another.

So in the stylized fishing case, if the fish stock is low this year, fishers who have occupational options, who, say, farm and teach, will shift to these alternative activities until the stocks recover. Doing so is strictly out of individual self-interest: fish catches are down, time to rebuild the barn, offer a new seminar. Such a choice also serves the broader collective interest by allowing fish stocks to recover. The very ability to shift work effort from one occupation to another helps tie the ecological and social systems together: negative ecological feedback (declining stocks require greater fishing effort) align with an appropriate human response (withdrawal from the resource). The rhythm of ecosystem dynamics coincides with the rhythm of work. The work response, though, depends critically on the ability of the participants to shift to other pursuits, that is, it depends on multiple and self-directed work, and on collective management at a scale that can accommodate such shifts. It does not depend, notably, on the government, except to ensure ownership rights. Nor does it depend on external incentives (for example, taxes and subsidies) and public education. Self-interest among generalist, multiple-working, self-directed "workers" is quite enough to ensure participation. At an appropriate scale, restrained resource use follows a working rationality.

Sources: Dan Janzen, personal communication, Ann Arbor, Michigan, February 25, 1998; Matt Ridley, *The Origins of Virtue: Human Instincts and the Evolution of Cooperation* (New York: Viking, 1998), 69–70.

goods this year than last, more next year than this," writes Leach. "American consumer capitalism produced a culture almost violently hostile to the past and to tradition, a future-oriented culture of desire that confused the good life with goods."[35]

That consumer society continued to evolve and solidify after World War II in the United States, where, writes historian Lizabeth Cohen, the satisfaction of "personal material wants" was seen as serving "the national interest, since economic recovery after a decade and a half of depression and war depended on a dynamic mass consumption economy." The consumer-led economy was "a strategy ... for reconstructing the nation's economy and reaffirming its democratic values through promoting the expansion of mass consumption." And then in recent decades consumerism has metamorphosed into a "Consumerized Republic, where self-interested individuals increasingly view government policies [and political campaigns] like other market transactions, judging them by how well served they feel personally." The GI Bill, changes in the income tax, restructuring of union-management collective bargaining, new residential and commercial development policies, all contributed to this consumer society as did ever more sophisticated strategies by marketers, advertisers, and political campaigners.[36] (see figure 5.1.)

Today, the very idea of a consumer society is enshrined in economics textbooks, has become a pillar of business education, and is reinforced daily by the media. In fact, the media is a chief purveyor as it fuels supposedly efficient and costless growth. It accepts outright a logic that associates economic "strength" with consumer spending, even excess spending. "Even as the stock market fell and unemployment rose," a front-page article in the American paper of record proclaimed in early 2001, "consumers continue to spend more than they earned, increasing their debt levels to buy new homes, cars, and other items." As a result, "the economy showed surprising resilience ... extending the longest American expansion on record." Borrowing money from the bank and resources from future generations, it seems, strengthens the economy; personal liability aggregates to become a social asset. The only worry is that these debt-ridden consumers won't do it long enough: "Economists and government officials remain concerned that consumers will rein in their spending in the coming months."[37]

A core belief of a consumer society is that producers respond to consumer demand by producing the goods the consumer wants and at a price the consumer will pay. If the consumer doesn't buy the product, producers don't make it. Governments do likewise: they intervene in the economy to serve the consumer. The government takes antitrust action against conglomerates because monopolists restrict production and raise prices, hurting the consumer. Conversely, if firms merge to capture efficiencies

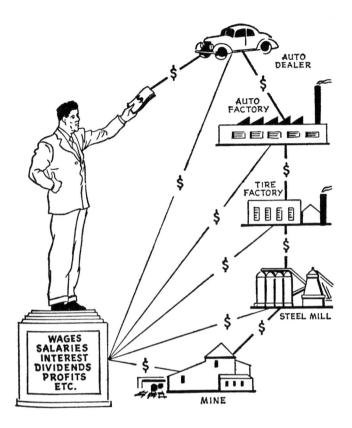

**AUTO
DEALER**

**AUTO
FACTORY**

**TIRE
FACTORY**

STEEL MILL

**WAGES
SALARIES
INTEREST
DIVIDENDS
PROFITS
ETC.**

MINE

Spending Creates Jobs and Prosperity

Figure 5.1
The sovereign consumer rules the economy. Reproduced from Robert R. Nathan, *Mobilizing for Abundance* (New York: Whittlesey House, McGraw-Hill, 1944), 81.

and offer consumers lower prices, the government supports economic concentration. If trade barriers prevent tropical fruits from reaching temperate shores or if they allow domestic producers to charge unrealistically high prices, the government lowers the barriers; not to do so is to restrict choice, to harm the consumer.

Proponents of this belief system, bankers, merchandisers, and others, "believed it was not the business of business to judge other people's desires," writes Leach. "Quite the opposite: Business succeeded (and people got jobs) only when business responded to desire, manipulated it, and extended its frontiers. Leach goes on to quote one prominent banker of the 1920s and 1930s: " 'The function of our economic organization is not to determine what the people *ought* to want, but to make the machinery as productive as possible of what they *do* want.' "[38]

As with any belief system, language matters. *Free trade, enfranchisement,* and *individual choice* were terms that had to be invented and promoted. So too was the very term *consumer,* uncommon before World War I, writes Leach, though it

began to compete for prominence with "citizen" and "worker" as well as with an earlier meaning of consumer developed by "consumers' leagues," which implied activism and not the passivity of the newer term. Related phrases or terms became popular, among them "consumer desires and wishes," "consumer appeal," "consumer sovereignty," "commodity flow," "the flow of satisfactions," and "sales resistance." This language expressed what had actually happened and, at the same time, ideologically explained it and gave it credence.[39]

Seventy-five years later two leaders of global finance could write that "in pursuit of higher living standards, we have created a new world of global markets and instant communication delivering gains in efficiency and competition that are beyond the powers of governments." Reacting to charges that globalization concentrates power among the wealthy few, they say that, quite the contrary, "the goal is not to disenfranchise the individual but to give individuals more power to control their destinies by lowering costs, broadening choices, delivering more capital and opening more markets." People are empowered, in other words, when manufacturers, financiers, and traders are allowed to serve their master (the sovereign consumer) by increasing consumer choice with more goods at low prices. What's more, these financiers insist, if "four billion people exist on less than $1,500 a year," producers, those ever-ready servants of the consumers, "can lift them from poverty and turn them into customers."[40] In this belief system, a world of consumers is an ideal world, one served by those with the capital, the expertise, and the vision to make it all happen. But consumers are *served*. Just as a sovereign king is entitled to privileges and perquisites, sovereign consumers are entitled to have their desires satisfied, to have ever more goods, and to do so all at low, low prices.[41]

Underlying this belief system is a logic integral to the operation of a modern industrial economy, one that is dynamic and organized to expand. The relevant discipline is, of course, economics. A century ago, the discipline departed from its "laissez-faire ideas of scarcity and self-denial," writes Leach, "in favor of the more appealing notions of [abundant] supply and prosperity."[42] No one had to be deprived, everyone could be "lifted from poverty." And for those already freed from the bonds of poverty, they too did not have to worry; abundance was for everyone, rich and poor. Frugality was a thing of the past; spending the thing of the future. Simon Patten, a founding member of the American Economics Association and professor at the then Wharton School of Economics, not to mention father of consumer theory, put it best nearly a century ago describing, indeed *prescribing*, a new culture:

We think of culture as the final product of civilization and not as one of its elements. Yet if we look at the facts, we find that culture is an index of activity, not of ancestral tradition and opinion. . . . Culture is the result of more satisfying combinations [of] consumption.

Consumer choice unifies a diverse nation and elevates the individual to high moral purpose, Patten argued. Thus, "all traditional restraints on consumption, all taboos against luxury" should be "eliminated."[43]

Now economics takes as axiomatic that an economy serves consumers: "Neo-classical economics sees the delivery of individual consumption as the main object of the economy system," writes economist Angus Deaton in *The Palgrave Dictionary of Economics*. In the modern world, "the flow of goods and services consumed by everyone constitutes the ultimate aim and end of economic life," Robert Heilbroner observes in *The Worldly Philosophers*.[44] In principle, that consumption need not always increase any more than production need always increase. Optimal economic activity, economic theory tells us, is generally not maximum activity: the output of a firm with fixed costs produces where marginal costs and revenues equate, not at full plant capacity; the macroeconomy with known interest and employment rates can grow too fast (risking inflation) or too slow (risking unemployment).[45] Enoughness is not an entirely alien concept, *in the discipline*. In *practice*, though, the allures of abundance and the ethics of material plenty have prevailed. If one's place in society and in natural systems once constituted "traditional restraints," they have indeed been cast aside. And new ones are few and far between. The political economy—firms and the institutions that support the economy—is nearly always one of maximum increase, of a never-ending "pursuit of higher living standards." It is "market demand for greater efficiencies and new products" that defines modern capitalism, writes political scientist Robert Gilpin in his lucid account of capitalism worldwide, *The Political Economy of International Relations*.[46] In all this, the idea of the sovereign consumer demanding ever more goods to meet an endlessly insatiable appetite is fundamental.

A Working Ethic for an Ecologically Constrained World

The sovereign consumer knows no bounds. The specialist can't integrate or be fully accountable. The oversized organization can't get the right feedback. These structural factors impede movement toward a working rationality; they make a sustainable economy hard to envision. So I conclude with a different vision of an economy, one with a different sense of purpose in material life. Here I wish to show that restraint has been and, arguably, continues to be, a perfectly sensible element in everyday practice, the practice of business, of enterprise, of, indeed, "real work." I pick up on the lessons of the Industrial Revolution and the contemporary findings of meaningful work as discussed. But I also bring in the ideals of nineteenth-century progress and populism, drawing on the masterful critique by historian and social critic Christopher Lasch in *The True and Only Heaven*.[47] Three strands of thought and practice can be discerned in the emergence of the progressive ideal and the corresponding submergence of the populist ideal. I call their proponents the rejectionists, the expansionists, and the producerists.

The first group, the *rejectionists*—possibly typified by the Luddites then and the Amish now—opposed much of the advances of science and technology. They valued self-reliance and community cohesion. They could adopt new technologies, but only selectively, only when the technologies did not disrupt existing social relations.

The second group, the *expansionists*, were just the opposite. Engineers and economists embraced scientific and technological advance. Boosters promoted cities and railroads and telegraphs, and just about any "new way of doing things." Public officials and the media extolled the virtues of an ever-increasing variety and quantity of goods. If innovation and, especially, efficiency seeking in the form of a division of labor, mechanization, labor mobility, and economies of scale came at the cost of worker dependence and alienation and an increasing concentration of economic power, the expansionists knew that the long-term benefits to individuals and to the nation (as a great power) far exceeded those costs. Continuous expansion was the essence of progress.[48]

The third group, the *producerists*, have largely faded from historical memory, eclipsed by expansionism. The producerists were a mostly unorganized collection of artisans, master craftspeople, small shop owners, and independent, yeoman farmers. Many were tinkers, inventors of the very technologies that excited the expansionists and helped propel the nation to greatness. The producerists were businesspeople, committed to making products, selling them, and earning a profit. They were also committed—some might say, fiercely committed—to the notion that political independence was inextricably intertwined with economic independence. Democracy depended on a populace that could produce for itself, not just in the aggregate, not just at the national level, but at the level of the individual, the household, and the immediate community. "Freedom could not flourish in a nation of hirelings," Lasch writes.[49] These small proprietors in the United States, England,

and France resisted the expansionists' label of working class, seeing themselves instead as *producers*, people who identified their enemy not as employers (they were self-employed, after all) but parasitic bankers, speculators, monopolists, and middlemen. Despite the ascendance of the expansionists through the nineteenth century, the producerist movement, if it can be called a movement, persisted until the turn of the century. They nearly epitomized "working rationality." "Even in the factory," Lasch writes, and as we saw in automobile production and other industries (box 5.1), "artisans often retained control of the rhythm and design of production; and it was their resistance to employers' attempts to introduce a more complicated division of labor and to replace skilled craftsmen with operatives, as much as the fight for higher wages and shorter hours, that shaped working-class radicalism right down to the end of the nineteenth century."[50] It was precisely at this time in the United States that expansionism achieved its ultimate conversion of everyday life: from producerism (the population was still overwhelmingly rural) to consumerism.

But producerism survived through the nineteenth century in part because the populace as a whole still believed that there was virtue in work, that making goods and services that were useful to others was a higher pursuit than merely accumulating wealth. Their vision of an industrial order (the producerists did not reject science and technology, let alone profit making) might be best captured by the notion of "a calling," an expression quite common not so long ago, but largely supplanted today by terms like *job* and *employment*. A calling not only guided people's choice of productive enterprise but embodied a sense of sufficiency via restraint. Traditionally, a calling had three elements, each of which suggests a source of limits in the nature of self-directed, producerist work.[51]

The first is *fit*. In a calling, individuals seek work that fits their skills and aptitudes. Some are meant to be poets, others road sweepers. This is absolutely contrary to the prevailing modern view that one "gets a job" to make as much money as possible and that the best jobs are those that pay the most. Pursuing jobs to maximize an income stream and consume freely has no limits. A calling, by contrast, is limited by the fit. From a progressive, liberal perspective, this would be, of course, a constraint on freedom. But free to do what? Earn and spend as much as possible. The liberal perspective accepts the nostrums of the turn-of-the-century boosters by assigning personal value and self-worth to consumption, not production, not to the deliberately and freely chosen pursuit (at least in the ideal) of one's calling.

The second element in a calling is *service* to one's community *through production*. Producers make items they deem useful to others. Notably, the producer makes this judgment, not, as in the belief system of the contemporary consumer economy, the sovereign consumer. In a calling, producers do not merely respond to demand. Automakers could not throw up their hands and exclaim, "but the consumers *demand* the gas guzzlers; we just produce them." Caveat emptor, let-the-buyer-beware, has no meaning in the context of a calling where the producer is responsible for the quality of the item, where the producer is accountable. In a calling, consumers are not sovereign, producers are, yet *in service to others*. As a result, pride of workmanship prevails over the techniques of salesmanship. Quality is preferred to quantity. This emphasis on service and quality and, in many contexts, direct, face-to-face contact, imposes limits on the producer largely unimaginable in today's large-scale, specialized, limited-liability corporate world. And these limits are not imposed from without, nor chosen by a company so as to be the "good corporate citizen." Rather, they arise as a rational means of operating over time in a community, of ensuring, as the producerists always argued, a livelihood for themselves, their community, and their successors.

The third element is, traditionally, service to God. A secular version might be service to the *long-term welfare* of present and future generations. Here, too, service is not to the whims and gullibilities of consumers, but to the producers' sense and, by extension, to the community's sense of what is right, what is truly good, not to what sells as a good.

The producerist ideal thus embodies a profound sense of meaning in work. It rejects the producer-consumer, work-leisure dichotomies of the consumer economy and the "discipline" of the clock and the supervisor. Instead it promotes the values of identity, economic independence, and citizenship through self-directed proprietorship. Inherent in such a vision is self-discipline, striving for purpose, and, not least, limits to ever-increasing material throughput. Lasch puts it this way:

Luxury for all: such was the noble dream of progress. Populists [producerists], on the other hand, regarded a competence, as they would have called it—a piece of earth, a small shop, a useful calling–as a more reasonable as well as a more worthy ambition. "Competence" had rich moral overtones; it referred to the livelihood conferred by property but also to the skills required to maintain it. The ideal of universal proprietorship embodied a humbler set of expectations than the ideal of universal consumption, universal access to a proliferating supply of goods. At the same time, it embodied a more strenuous and morally demanding definition of the good life. The progressive conception of history implied a society of supremely cultivated consumers; the populist [producerist] conception, a whole world of heroes.[52]

Global financiers may see a world of consumers, but those who understand "real work," who see intimate connections between work and citizenship and sustainability, see a world of citizens who work and thrive and contribute. These "heroes" are ennobled, not threatened, by limits. If Simon Patten, economist and founding father of consumer theory, could conclude a century ago that "all traditional restraints on consumption" should be "eliminated" and, in the intervening time, all restraints were eliminated, then it is now time, under global ecological constraint, to construct new "restraints," traditional or nontraditional. It is time for a wholly new emphasis, one that connects the limits of the planet to the limits of everyday practice. It is time for an ethic that celebrates not consumers as purchasers but workers as citizens, not unending expansion but working and living within immutable constraints. Consumption no longer unifies a nation and elevates the individual, as Patten and his successors see it, but, as practiced, undermine the bio-physical foundations on which nations and individuals rest.

The producerist ideal failed in the nineteenth century for many reasons, not the least of which was, as noted, the lure of expansionism. But it also might have failed because it lacked a *central organizing principle*. It was probably not enough for pro-ducers to argue that they wanted to keep their small shops and independent farms when progress increasingly meant bigger factories, bigger supply chains, and, finally, at the turn of the century with the development of consumer theory in economics, marketing in business schools, and demand stimulation in government, bigger con-sumer markets. "I'm figgering on biggering," the Once-ler exclaims in Dr. Seuss's children's classic, *The Lorax*. "And BIGGERING and BIGGERING and BIGGER-ING, turning MORE Truffula Trees into Thneeds which everyone, EVERYONE, *EVERYONE* needs!"[53] Expansion was the order of the day, the "natural order of things," the imperative of an efficiency-obsessed era, the raison d'être of a consumer economy.

Today, with the imperative to translate the self-evident limits of a single planet into the limits of everyday life, the organizing principle might be sufficiency. Such a translation is unlikely, arguably impossible, under the logic of a consumer economy where specialization, large-scale operation, and consumer demand prevail. It is possible, though, when work follows the rhythms of task and nature, when work is self-directed and generalist, and when work is more a calling than a job. It is possible under a logic of enough work and enough consumption.

II
Sufficiency on the Ground

6

The Pacific Lumber Company: The Evolution of an Idea

Timber harvesting in North America may seem an unlikely place to gain insights into the logic of sufficiency. Restraint was certainly an alien concept for those who sought their fortune supplying fuelwood and lumber to a rapidly industrializing nation. Beginning in Maine and the Maritime Provinces in the early nineteenth century, timber barons moved steadily westward, cutting as fast as they could, leaving little but charred stumps and slash piles in their wake. A major driver of this seemingly inexorable process was capital. Sawmills, railroads, and lumberyards had high fixed costs, leading lumbermen to compete intensely to "get the cut out" and pay down their debts. The cutting was as fast—indeed, as efficient—as possible and the results predictable, at least in hindsight.

But the process was not driven entirely by debt and low prices. A sense of noble purpose imbued timbering, a sense shared by operators large and small, efficient and wasteful, by everyone from the feller to the financier. Timber harvesting did not just supply the raw material for industry and housing. It made way for European civilization. Clearing the forests was the first step in taming the wilderness and settling a vast continent. To build a great nation, it was a necessary step. The forests were useful but at the same time they were a hindrance. Agriculture and manufacturing were the hallmarks of progress and, besides, everyone knew the forests were inexhaustible.

It is probably this last point—the perception of an endless supply of timber—that is most inconceivable to those of us beginning the twenty-first century. But as recently as the late nineteenth century, 100 years or so ago, it was the dominant belief, as common and natural a notion then as slavery once seemed before it and unending economic expansion on a finite planet seems to so many today.[1] The few who raised alarms about overharvesting and called for conservation were dismissed as naive doomsayers. But the great cutovers of the Northeast and Great Lakes regions were impossible to ignore, as was the natural limit to westward expansion imposed by the Pacific Ocean. Suddenly, it must have seemed to those living at the turn of the last century, conservation and preservation were in the air.

And yet, under the logic of capitalism and "manifest destiny" and, perhaps, just by habit, timber companies proceeded apace, as if the forests were indeed inexhaustible. Timbermen cut trees just as miners mined ore. Their tenure on a tract of land was a function of standing volume or extent of a mineral's vein and of consumer demand, transportation choices, and their own industry in getting the stuff out. That may have taken years or decades, but when the resource was gone, it was time to pull up stakes and move on. Farmers may settle in for the long term but industrialists, those who clear the forests for farmers and supply them their implements, were a different breed. Exploitation (in the nonpejorative sense) was their game, not cultivation. And, of course, on a vast continent, indeed in an unexplored world, there was always more timber and more minerals.

An Intellectual History

Albert Stanwood (A. S.) Murphy (1892–1963), born and raised in a lumber town in Wisconsin, straddled the two worlds of exploitation and cultivation. His family made its fortune as a major player in the forest cutovers of Maine and the Great Lakes regions. As a boy he worked in the woods and mills learning firsthand the timbering business—the business of getting the cut out. But coming of age at the turn of the century, he also must have heard the biting criticism of timber interests, of those rapacious operators rivaled only by the much-despised railroad barons. He must have heard about conservation and forest management and sustained yield. If he did, and his correspondence later in life suggests so, he got a chance to test those ideas as president of the Murphy family's last timber acquisition, The Pacific Lumber Company (TPL),[2] located in one of the most rugged and remote regions of the nation, Humboldt County in northern California, the heart of redwood country (see figure 6.1).

Working summers in the West in the early years of the twentieth century, A. S. Murphy no doubt climbed one hilltop after another and looked west, just as his grandfather, Simon Jones Murphy (1815–1905), had done. But the senior Murphy had started his timbering career in Maine and once that region was cut out, had moved to Michigan for the white pines of the Great Lakes states. From his vantage points, he could always see another forest. A. S. Murphy could only see the Pacific Ocean. The great cutover of North America that swept the continent from east to west, clearing the way for European settlement and enriching families such as the

Figure 6.1
Eel River. Notice the steep, rocky hillsides, which makes logging and passage in this region difficult, even today.

Murphys along the way, was coming to an end. A. S. Murphy was probably expected to continue the family tradition—cutting redwood as fast as technologies and markets allowed, banking the profits, and moving on when the stands ran out. His uncles and cousins after all were engaged in mining, manufacturing, and finance, even building and selling those newfangled horseless carriages.

But growing up in a timber town in Wisconsin and working in the woods, Murphy had gained a love for everything about the woods, including timbering. It is reasonable to assume that, in his early trips to Humboldt County and as he was being groomed in the 1920s and 1930s to assume the presidency of TPL, he asked himself if there might be a different way to run a timbering operation, to cut trees, mill lumber, and make a profit and yet not abandon the land when the forest was cleared. He would have known how the cut-out-and-get-out strategy had hurt the industry and the land in Maine and the Great Lakes and, among other things, how it alienated the public and sullied the names of timbering families like his. Derogatory terms like "timber tycoon" or "lumber baron" must have rankled for a family that had taken pride in settling the continent and generating wealth that multiplied throughout local and national economies.

A. S. Murphy's personal decision—whether to cut out or find a different way—paralleled a national policy debate. The grand assumption that forests were inexhaustible was, by the end of the nineteenth century, being discarded, in principle if not in practice. People had begun to realize that a resource as vast as North America's timber could actually disappear. And much was wasted. "During the period when our timber supply was thought unlimited," remarked a California forester in the 1920s, "fires were allowed to run at will"[3] and only the merchantable logs were taken, the rest left to rot. Such inefficiencies became unacceptable when wood was needed for fuel and construction. At the same time, the image of the forest as a foreboding place, or more benignly, as an obstacle to progress and the advancement of civilization, was changing. People like Henry David Thoreau (1817–1862) and John Muir (1838–1914) considered forests as places of pleasant recreation or spiritual uplift, a far cry from a "resource" to be mined. Policymakers such as Theodore Roosevelt and Gifford Pinchot, following public sentiment and industrial need, saw that something had to be done.

Timbering at the turn of the last century was thus at a historical juncture. The public was debating the need for preservation and conservation. Forestry, the scientific management of timber stands for long-term harvesting, was in its infancy. And timber companies were looking for new strategies. Most companies, it is probably fair to say, continued in the pattern they knew best—cutting as fast as technologies and markets permitted and abandoning land for new territories. Some concentrated on acquiring new land, others on intensifying production on their existing land. In part, A. S. Murphy pursued these strategies himself. But unlike his contemporaries in the softwood business, he appears to have rejected the premise of moving on when timberlands were cut out or other opportunities arose or, as his family had done in the East, of getting out of timbering entirely. For some combination of reasons—perhaps partly personal, partly hard-nosed business calculation, and partly public relations—he elected to stay put, to experiment with, indeed to *pioneer*, a business strategy premised on one tract of timber, one set of mills, and one company town. Also unlike many of his contemporaries, he and his followers talked to foresters, pumping them for information and ideas. The key figure in the redwood industry beginning in the 1920s was Emanuel Fritz (1886–1988), a professor of forestry at the University of California at Berkeley.

In short, by accepting the exhaustibility of forests, Murphy rejected unlimited expansion on a finite resource and intensification of production from that resource. He accepted the natural resource—the forest as it stood—as a given and based his policies on that fact. That departure from the norm of expansion and efficient extraction was not necessarily sustainable in its own right but, I argue shortly, was a valuable precursor. Confronting natural constraints—whether of limited forests or limited regenerative capacity of forests—is a first-order condition of sustainable practice. That one person and one company could do so in a business climate of intense competition, a climate where "the winners" were those who exploited the fastest and cheapest, those who could most efficiently convert natural capital to financial capital, is a testament to the brilliance of a businessman, a farsighted university forestry professor, and their followers.

The lesson in this case is not so much that TPL did everything right; certainly not in today's terms of environmental protection, holistic forestry, habitat preservation, species protection, watershed management, site-specific stewardship, and so forth. Rather, it is that TPL confronted natural constraints and still turned a profit. Indeed, TPL became an "exemplary timber company" as many routinely called it, the "shining light of the western timber industry,"[4] protecting forest and community alike. And it did so for the indefinite future, not for some calculated time period governed by technologies of extraction and discount rates in distant financial markets.

The story of The Pacific Lumber Company has been told in several ways. Company historians have waxed eloquently about its cutting-edge timbering and labor policies, tracing the sequence of owners and detailing changes in plant and equipment. Industrialists have admired its innovations in the woods and mills. Financial analysts have applauded the company's high capital-to-debt ratios, not to mention its ability to weather economic downturns and natural disasters like fire and flood. In other versions of the story, environmentalists have extolled the company's enlightened policies of selective logging and sustained yield as well as its civic-mindedness in setting aside some of the finest "cathedral" groves of redwoods. And, not least, public commentators have marveled at the social cohesion of the company town, Scotia.

In later versions of the Pacific Lumber story, critics focused on Houston financier Charles Hurwitz and his Maxxam Corporation's takeover of the company in 1985. The new owners doubled (some say tripled) the harvest rate and tapped employees' pension fund to pay off junk-bond debts. Protests, lawsuits, and legislative battles ensued, making for high drama, sensational press, and a tarnished image for Pacific Lumber. Nearly all of the company's former admirers were outraged. How could a decent company be ravaged like that, so hastily, so thoughtlessly, and merely because financiers had the money?

Much is to be learned from each of these takes on Pacific Lumber. In fact, I draw on and analyze portions of these accounts throughout this case study. But lessons for ecological and social sustainability are to be found in ideas that emerged within the company in the 1920s and 1930s, came to fruition in the 1950s and 1960s, and persisted until the 1985 takeover, possibly even after that. It was too early at this writing to tell if the new Pacific Lumber, "Maxxam/PL," with its 120-year "sustained yield plan" represented another step in the evolution of sustainable forestry or if it had simply embarked on the old strategy of cut-out-and-get-out. Rather than speculate about the company's future, I choose to concentrate on its past, particularly on the part that distinguished TPL from comparable firms.

This, then, is an effort to construct an intellectual history, an approach fraught with difficulty because A. S. Murphy and his successor son, Stanwood A. Murphy, left no memoirs and very little publicly available correspondence. From secondary sources—interviews with followers of the "Murphy philosophy," perusal of company histories and company documents, review of some of A. S. Murphy's correspondence between 1927 and 1944, and use of secondary material that did draw on extensive correspondence by Murphy—I trace the development of an idea, which I term *perpetual and profitable yield.*

On the face of it, the idea is simple, and yet even today so hard to grasp for those intellectually and economically ensconced in the efficiency principle and its promise of endless material plenty. The idea is that some resources can be used in perpetuity if certain conditions are met. One is that harvest rates are kept well below regenerative rates with a buffer, a cushion in company or public policy. Another is that mechanisms are instituted to put a brake on humans' natural propensity to want more and more from a resource. Such brakes would be most effective to the extent that they enhance another natural human propensity, namely, to limit immediate material gain in exchange for long-term goals such as economic security and benefits for descendants. To be protected from decimation, the resource need not be preserved or set aside as if in some pristine state of nature. It can be used profitably and in perpetuity.

If the *idea* of perpetual and profitable yield followed logically from Murphy's family history of timbering and the nation's history of clearing forests; the *practice*, we will see, was not at all self-evident then or now. Murphy, Fritz, and their followers were experimenting, following conventional business practices in some instances, unconventional ones in others, and throughout, subjecting themselves to criticism and pressure from many in the industry while winning the hearts and minds of those who lived the Murphy philosophy. Part of Murphy's success can be attributed to the fact that he inherited a strong company with a tremendously rich resource base as well as a company history of commitment to innovation and investment in its workers. A central feature was a long-term perspective on timber harvesting: "Although the Company takes pride in the hundred years that have passed," a TPL brochure quotes Murphy as saying, "our time is well occupied with what we have to do to produce an even more dynamic history in the hundred years ahead."[5] It is a perspective with antecedents in decisions of the company's first owners.

Enterprise for the Long Term
Pioneers and investors moved rapidly into northern California when Indian wars came to an end in the late 1860s. Some sought their fortunes in mining and timbering, others farming. Sawmills sprang up throughout the region, cutting redwood and Douglas fir near river and coastal shipping routes. For the remainder of the century, as mills consolidated and investment increased, the biggest challenge was transportation, both in getting timber out of the mountains and valleys and in shipping it along the West Coast, across the country and abroad.

In 1869, four silver miners from Nevada teamed up with mining, banking, and railroad interests in San Francisco to form The Pacific Lumber Company. According to an early company historian, Ben Shannon Allen, the four investors, "unlike some of their Nevada colleagues, were not plungers nor speculators. They had made their money in constructive enterprises. . . . These men were not planning for the coming year, not even for their generation. They planned in terms of perpetuity." Even discounting for the revisionism of a loyal company historian, that and other descriptions of the early years of the company suggest that TPL, from the beginning, intended to be in the business for a long time. By 1889 TPL had become the industry leader in redwood production, cutting such a large volume that investors from as far away as Michigan and Pennsylvania took notice.[6]

On a trip to Arizona, one of the Nevada owners found a buyer for the company, a well-known industrial and financial family from Detroit headed by octogenarian Simon Jones Murphy. The Murphy family not only had extensive lumbering experience in the East and Midwest but was known to be investing in the far West, having recently acquired citrus groves in southern California and timber holdings on the Russian River in northern California. Unlike the previous owners of TPL and other timber companies, the Murphy family's primary interest at the time was lumbering, not mining or railroading. The new owners were indeed eager to build up a major timber operation, intent on expanding production and sales. TPL already had its own rail lines, bridges, tunnels, and logging roads as well as the largest and most advanced mill on the Pacific Coast, mill A at Scotia, the company town on the Eel River, 25 miles south of Eureka and 265 miles north of San Francisco (see map 6.1 and figure 6.2). The Murphys now set about building an additional mill, mill B, carving out a 30-acre mill pond, and establishing three logging camps. To transport lumber inside the mill they hung an overhead monorail that, by the 1930s, had some 30 miles of track. The Murphys expanded the company's timber holdings, bringing the total to 65,000 acres by 1914.[7]

The Murphys' efforts to increase holdings went beyond the industry norm of holding no more land than could be profitably harvested—that is, profitable in time periods set by railroading, mining, and financial interests—after which most companies packed up machinery and moved to another site. The company's president explained TPL's expansion in a 1911 report to stockholders:

Your company, as we have all been aware, acquired a very large amount of timber, an amount very much in excess of timber ownership ordinarily back of an operation, and of course, out of all proportion to its production. . . . The argument has been used that we are overburdened with timber. It is our belief that while this is true from the standpoint of immediate profits in a large way which could be distributed, quite the reverse is true as to the ultimate outcome. . . . In addition to the almost certain market increase in the value of the stumpage which this Company holds, it is our opinion that the sale of a tract of timber like the Freshwater merely adds to our difficulties in obtaining a fair market price for our product as it would bring into the market still another competitor. It is also our opinion that instead of disposing of any of the present timber holdings of the Company (with the exception of iso-

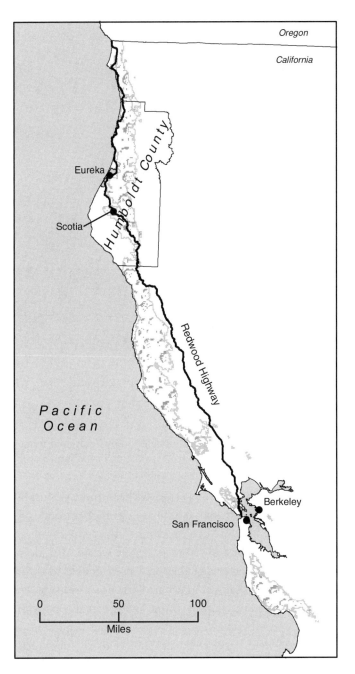

Map 6.1
The redwood region of northern California. The shaded area indicates the natural range of the redwood.

Figure 6.2
Mill A. First built in 1887, here running at or near capacity in 1998. By 2002 Maxxam/PL shut it and much of mill B down for lack of big, old-growth logs.

lated and scattered pieces), it would be altogether wise, if possible to buy additional timber adjacent to our present holdings where the same is likely to be available in the future operations of this Company, if the same can be obtained at reasonable prices.[8]

The president, in other words, had to convince his stockholders (mostly Murphy family members at that time) that deviating from the industry norm of cut-out-and-get-out actually made financial sense. Far from "overburdening" the company, large acquisitions would increase market control and hence prices. It would also allow timber harvesting for a very long time, something they had been unable to do in the Great Lakes region. Another company historian, Stan Parker, a transport and industrial affairs manager for the company, claimed in the 1980s that this position with regard to seemingly excessive timberland acquisitions was the beginning of TPL's continuous-yield or sustained-yield harvesting, the "object of all subsequent Pacific Lumber strategy."[9] Certainly TPL's land-acquisition strategy defied all previous practices. One reason may have been that at this time timbermen faced a new set of obstacles. Public opinion, preservationism, and government regulations, we'll soon see, joined with market volatility to force change. For some timbermen, change simply meant making one final profitable harvest, then getting out of the business entirely. For others it meant innovating, constructing an enterprise for the long term. The Murphys seemed well disposed to the long-term approach. As one business reporter enthused in the 1930s about this generation of redwood timbermen, "It is bred in them to take the long view of these amazing trees."[10]

So at the turn of the century, TPL led the industry as an innovator in extraction and milling technologies. Now it would innovate in *management*, especially with untried social and harvest policies. Its social policies, another indicator of its long-term orientation, were initially aimed at workers but, beginning in the 1920s, were extended beyond employees to the community and the public, notably tourists, preservationists, and government regulators. In so doing, the company's social activities—carried out in reaction to those novel external forces—drove other aspects of company policy including, we will see, its harvest practices.

Building a Timber Community

The Pacific Lumber Company's investment in the social side of timbering was often justified in terms of minimizing labor strife and ensuring a high-quality workforce. But over the years the social investment became integral to its management philosophy, one at once paternalistic, conservative, and future oriented. In congressional testimony shortly after the 1985 Maxxam takeover, A. S. Murphy's son, Stanwood A. Murphy, Jr., the last of the Murphys to lead the company, described that philosophy:

One of the key factors my family always felt in the company was the employees. My father always felt if you gave the employees a good rein, that they would give a good product. . . .

The company had a scholarship that was started out after my grandfather's death. Every employee's son had the privilege—or daughter—had the privilege to get a scholarship from the company if you qualified for college. It was very common in Pacific Lumber Co. that the fathers and sons—we were working side by side—it was a firm or common belief that when you got out of school, if you wanted to go work for Pacific Lumber, it was very, you know, likely that [if] your father worked for the company you could get a job there and you would have a job until you were 65 or whatever age you wished to retire at.

It has always been a pattern historically, and it has always been a family talent, too. The family believed the town of Scotia was vital to keeping a good crew, keeping good employees and quality employees also. The company has had a history of helping the community and at the same time the community has had a history of helping the company also.[11]

The origins of TPL's social policies predated the Murphys. According to company historian Allen, it was the town's growing population of women that converted the rough-and-tumble pioneer town into a settled, residential community:

These pioneer women of Scotia demanded all of the cultural amenities from which they had been all too long exiled. They found the men who planned Pacific [Lumber Company] entirely agreeable to their ambition for the education of their children and better living conditions for their entire families. These men were educated and quite aware that the primitive living conditions of a pioneer community were no longer either necessary or desirable. The school house was as much a necessity as the machine shop and quarters for classes were ready as soon as the workers moved into their jobs. Closely in the wake of the school came the church, the Sunday school and fraternal organizations.[12]

TPL continually invested in the town's amenities, which, by A. S. Murphy's time in the 1930s and 1940s, included a hotel, mercantile stores, garage, theater, churches, schools, laundry, and more than 300 homes. In the 1980s TPL was renting its two-bedroom houses for $70 a month. And if the occupants don't "take care of the lawn, the company does it for them," wrote one admirer in the business press. "The same with remodeling (to suit) and plumbing. There are no water or garbage fees, and electricity—produced by burning wood refuse at one of the town's two mills—runs about $15 a month."[13]

The company also operated a ranch for a time with cattle and sheep, as well as its own abattoir and refrigerating plant to provide food and commodities for the town.[14] The company store in the 1930s had separate departments featuring vegetables, meats, drugs, groceries, hardware, men's clothing, dry goods, and furniture. It was probably the largest store in the region, serving Scotia residents as well as those up and down the Eel River Valley. Prices were competitive with those of comparable stores in Eureka and Fortuna and generally lower than in stores in nearby small towns. The company extended credit to its employees but not "in a liberal manner," wrote historian Parker. "The company was much more anxious than the worker to avoid situations where he 'owed his soul to the company store.'"[15] In fact, the company store never had a reputation for gouging employees, which was common in company towns elsewhere. There were times when the store, butcher shop, and saloon were the only company activities making a profit.[16]

The company hospital in Scotia served residents throughout the valley. In the 1930s it was as modern as anything north of San Francisco and better equipped than hospitals at Eureka and Arcata. All employees were members of the hospital association. For a nominal fee of fifty cents per month, they had full coverage—all hospital, medical, and pharmaceutical bills, paid with no employee deductions.[17] A company theater operated by TPL was open to the public for movies and community events. A company hotel had up-to-date service and, some claimed, the "most refined dining room on the Redwood highway north of San Francisco."[18]

Murphy was convinced that such social amenities would help TPL secure a steady labor force and attract the loyal "family man." (See figure 6.3.) He remodeled the facilities extensively during his tenure, adding features like telephone service, television and natural gas, and recreational facilities, including a large gymnasium and indoor swimming pool. Hundreds of employees participated in a Scotia athletic program of swimming, basketball, table tennis, and other sports. The company's amenities were complemented by a rich natural environment, an ideal place, many observers and residents felt, for recreation and raising families. Every summer the company would dig out a swimming hole in the Eel River and erect diving boards. The Labor Day picnic would attract thousands. William Bertain, lifelong resident of Scotia and nearby Rio Dell and later a leader in a legal battle against Charles Hurwitz and other financiers of the 1985 takeover, expressed in the 1990s the meaning of Scotia to him and, as interviews confirmed, to so many others. Notably he saw an integral connection between the quality of life and the quality of the lumbering operation:

Figure 6.3
Residential street in the company town, Scotia. There was always a waiting list for employees eager to live here.

My dad called Scotia "home" from 1920 until he died in 1988. He lived in company housing from 1920 until 1946. I was the youngest of ten kids. I was born in Scotia, as were my nine older brothers and sisters. It was a great place to grow up. The school was good, good ball park, skating rink, swimming hole with three diving boards. Later, they built a gym with an Olympic-size pool. You could wander all over the town and the hills. And the company provided for the employees like no other company in the county ever did, like very few in the whole country. In the 1930s work was slow, but the company kept people on the job. They waived the rent, or at least lowered it. Scotia was practically insulated from the Depression. Then again in the early eighties, with the big timber recession, they cut people back to four days a week rather than lay anybody off. You didn't have to worry too much. You had job security—not just for yourself, but for your kids. At least that was the conception. In 1984, most kids graduating from high school had a reasonable expectation that they could work in Scotia until they retired at age sixty-five, and probably that their children and grand-children could work there too. That was because of the tremendous resource they had, and because of the philosophy of the company toward both the land and the people.[19]

Such reflections might be dismissed as nostalgic reminiscences or, with Bertain, posturing for effect on litigation. But they are consistent with numerous interviewees' accounts as well as media reports and sociological studies of the town. The continuous waiting list for company housing testifies to the fact that, in Humboldt County, one was considered lucky to work for *The* Pacific Lumber Company—"the best company in the world," as one forty-year employee called it—and lucky to live in a well-served company town and to be a member of its community. In fact, a forestry professor at nearby Humboldt State University viewed TPL as a social safety net for the region: no one would go hungry because one could always go to Scotia, push a broom, and get a meal. Scotia thus achieved an aura of community perfection in the region and, at times, with the help of the popular press, across the country. "Paradise with a Waiting List" was the title of one 1951 feature article in the *Saturday Evening Post.* A book about Scotia was titled *Life in the Peace Zone.*

Allen summed up the meaning to him of the company, the town, and the investment TPL made in them: "Both physically and spiritually, TPL is Scotia and Scotia is TPL."[20] What Allen might have added was that the third leg of the Pacific Lumber tripod, the forest, required its own form of investment, its own long-term orientation, one that began with timberland acquisition in the early years and culminated in perpetual and profitable yield in the 1960s and 1970s. A turning point came when TPL's board of directors chose young Albert Stanwood (A. S.) Murphy to be the company's next president.

A. S. Murphy: Maverick, Visionary

Following his teenage summers in the Scotia mills, A. S. Murphy at twenty became a miner in the Siskiyou Mountains and worked in the family's wholesale hay and grain business in Arizona. He joined the Navy in World War I and served on convoy ships in the Atlantic, returning in 1919 to become a clerk with A. F. Thane and Company in Palo Alto, California, export agents for Pacific Lumber. He worked in Scotia as a logger and in TPL's Chicago sales office. In 1925 he returned to Scotia as executive vice president of the company. He became president in 1931.[21]

By then he had witnessed plenty of boom and bust in the industry. TPL, like other firms in the area, had dramatically increased production in anticipation of improved rail service. Demand during the First World War and in the postwar boom of the 1920s assured profits for all in the industry. But the lumber industry took a nose-dive in the late twenties. TPL, for example, went from some $2.5 million in net profits in 1920 and $186,000 in 1925, to a *loss* of $320,000 in 1930. In the six-year period starting in 1929 and ending in 1934, TPL had a total loss of some $2.3 million. The company suspended dividends after 1926. Throughout the region, mills, including those of major producers, were closing or selling to competitors. Some could not withstand the combination of soft demand and loss of land to public parks. Hammond Redwood Lumber Company, for example, comparable to TPL in size, lost almost $8 million in the Depression, suspending production completely for awhile. On top of that, the entire industry was plagued by rapid employee turnover. TPL, known for being more stable than most, nevertheless had turnover rates of 320 percent in 1919, 290 percent in 1920, 253 percent in 1921, and 284 percent in 1922.[22]

In the heyday of East Coast and Great Lakes lumbering, volatility in the industry was expected and endured, certainly for the successful companies, the ones that could get the cut out fast and keep ahead of creditors. After all, once a tract was cut, everyone just moved on, building more sawmills and hiring more crew. Those who tried to settle at points along the way westward did indeed experience the boom and the bust, but for the captains of the industry—the investors, the managers, the shippers—production was experienced as continuous. On the West Coast, however, there was no more moving on, certainly not westward. Market forces would still inflict pain, but more and more, timber interests were cutting to get the railroad through or to sell the land to farmers or to acquire the capital to move into manufacturing and finance. That was the pattern of the Murphy family, which acquired great wealth in the process.

But A. S. Murphy seemed to have a different idea about timbering, an idea conditioned by emerging realities about forest use, including forestry—the deliberate management of timber stands. Part of that new reality was increasing national interest in conservation—conserving resources for the future. Notions like sustained yield were being bandied about and, although largely ignored or ridiculed by the timber industry, they were increasingly being explored and promoted by government policymakers, scientifically trained foresters, and a few timber companies. Emanuel Fritz, the Berkeley forestry professor, we'll see shortly, was a leading proponent.

But another part of the new reality, one constantly bemoaned, indeed reviled by the industry through the twentieth century, was the policy of setting aside groves of trees—that is, preserving them for posterity by permanently taking them out of timber production. Its proponents were always from afar, it seemed to Humboldters, mostly from the East Coast but in later years the San Francisco Bay Area. "John D. Rockefeller, Jr., has personally pledged $1,000,000 towards this cause," Murphy warned his mentor in Detroit of the movement's potential threat to the redwood timber industry.[23] In the early decades of redwood timbering, that threat was miniscule because few knew about the redwoods. "People of the populous Eastern portion of the United States had been told about redwoods, their girth, height and probable age," wrote two company historians, "but most of them dismissed stories about these great trees as typical California bragging." Few traveled to the remote redwood areas, accessible early in the century only by Pacific Coast "steamships over the treacherous bar to Humboldt Bay, or several days on stagecoaches over mountain roads." All that changed in 1915 with completion of the railroad from San Francisco to northern California. "Many of the fashionable and influential people from the Eastern States" could now "ride in the luxury of a Pullman sleeping car down the Eel River valley, and see the redwoods from the observation platform."[24] What they saw, as it turned out, were majestic groves—and majestic groves being cut down; magnificent trees—and magnificent piles of slash with charred stumps (see map 6.2).

Within a few years East Coast philanthropists and a few Bay Area people founded the Save-the-Redwoods League. TPL was their first target. A choice grove along the alluvial flats of the Eel River, the Dyerville Flat with, reportedly, the tallest tree in the world and some of the most scenic vistas, was about to be logged. There are indications that the Murphy family and other leaders at TPL actually supported the League's objectives, especially in later years and after the eventual acquisitions and set-asides were complete. But at the time, TPL leaders felt that, because the preserves would be for public use, the public, not TPL, should pay for TPL's withdrawal from production.

The funds were not immediately forthcoming, though. So in 1925, the year A. S. Murphy became executive vice president, TPL put a full logging crew to work

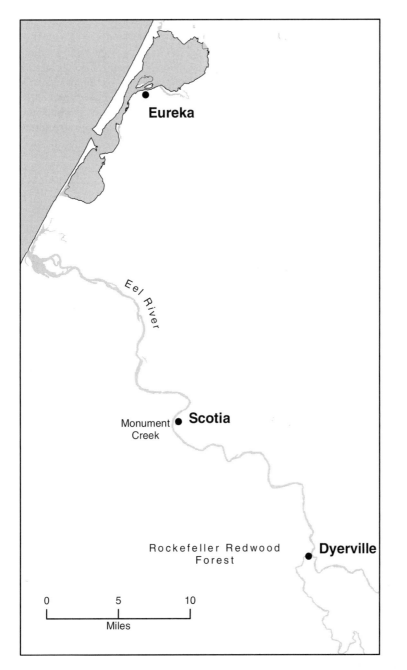

Map 6.2
Humboldt County, California. The Pacific Lumber Company's land extended from roughly Eureka to Dyerville. Many of the cathedral groves, mostly along the Eel River, were once TPL lands.

cutting trees at nearby South Fork and moving toward the Dyerville Flat. There was a "huge public uproar," wrote company historian Parker:

Lady conservationists chained themselves to trees. League officials brought a steady stream of potential donors to South Fork to see the havoc with their own eyes. Some particularly affluent potential donors came by their own private railway cars and had them parked so they could see it all from their own observation platforms. After a few weeks an injunction was issued preventing further logging there, and the shell-shocked loggers, who were unused to such attention, gratefully packed up their tools and went to other logging camps, decently hidden from public view.[25]

A few years later, TPL agreed to refrain from logging Dyerville Flat and a number of other groves until the League could raise the funds. TPL's cooperative approach was rewarded in future decades when the League and the more confrontational Sierra Club generally withheld criticism of TPL while lambasting others in the industry for wanton destruction and targeting other companies' lands for park acquisition.

A. S. Murphy entered this milieu of industry volatility and changing public attitudes with few guidelines. There was no timber company that had confronted the end of the frontier and worked out an alternative, no body of literature with extensive data and established prescriptions, no laws and regulations requiring timber-harvest plans. In part, he took his cue from his predecessors and past practices. But in the face of new challenges—in particular, the threat from preservationists—A. S. Murphy departed, especially with respect to harvest policy.

"He had been convinced during the Company's encounter with the conservationists [preservationists]," wrote Parker, "that it [TPL] would have to develop logging techniques that would leave the cutover areas in a more presentable condition than existing logging practices did. He was also convinced that Pacific, with its lands along the Redwood Highway, had a different problem from other redwood operators, and would have to find its own solution to that problem."[26] That problem was both aesthetic and political: how to appease the increasing numbers of visitors to redwood country who complained loudly to their elected representatives and gave generously to the Save-the-Redwoods League and the Sierra Club whenever they saw cutover lands.

One approach was reforestation. People could accept the commercial need for logging, but on their drive through the country they wanted to see greenery, not a desolate moonscape. A timber company might assuage travelers' concerns if they saw that cutover land was regrowing. For those concerned about the broader policy questions of timbering in North America, reforestation was effective in countering charges of cut-and-run: companies that replanted had obviously long-term commitments to the forest. So it was in the 1920s that TPL launched a program to collect seed, grow seedlings, and replant cutover lands. It cleared stumps south of Scotia along the Redwood Highway and planted several acres in redwood, cedar, spruce, Douglas fir, and white fir. The company's first "forester" was actually a horticulturist, hired in 1922 to start a nursery and study tree growth. The entire effort was abandoned in 1931, however, in part because redwood reproduced prolifically on its own, sprouting from stumps and roots, as well as reseeding naturally, and in part because "the whole nursery project was to improve the Company's public image, and that purpose had been served when the Save-the-Redwoods League began to function effectively and it became apparent that a good representative sample of the coast redwoods would be saved for posterity."[27] Reforestation was attempted at the same time another idea came to the attention of TPL's leadership: *selective logging*, a harvesting method that left enough trees standing to accomplish the objective of providing an acceptable view for Redwood Highway travelers and, as it turned out, transformed the company's operating time frame (see figure 6.4).[28]

Selective logging involved cutting only a percentage of trees, generally no more than 70 percent of the volume or 60 percent of the trees, leaving seed trees and others to continue to grow and repopulate the land.[29] The "residual" or "seed" trees would then be cut a half century or more later. One result was that hillsides remained green, or nearly so. To the uninitiated, the method might seem only a marginal change from past practices—cutting most but not all trees on a tract. In practice, however, it amounted to a radical departure from techniques developed and honed over a century of transcontinental logging. Selective logging was incompatible with the slack-line system, where everything in sight was cut or pulled down by cables to move logs by aerial cableways, after which the slash was burned. With selective logging, an entire pattern of harvesting—choosing fell trees, paying fellers by the board foot, yarding, safety measures, and so forth—would have to change. This was too much of a risk for most timber owners, however much the public complained about decimated forests.

But The Pacific Lumber Company was different. And A. S. Murphy was different, retaining perhaps an element of his family's pioneering spirit yet applying it in new ways and against hitherto unforeseen circumstances. Probably most significantly, Murphy's situation was different from that of his forefathers, radically different. None of them had to contend with public outrage, certainly not with well-organized, well-funded preservationists who, on their own, could buy up huge tracts of private land or convince governments to do it for them. And none of them

Figure 6.4
Selectively logged redwoods.

had to face the fact that the timber was exhaustible, that the march west had come to an end, that the rich mother lode of virgin timber, practically free for the taking in the past, was no more.

As Murphy was casting about for new ways of operating, the idea of selective logging was brewing in the emerging community of forestry scientists. But it had not been tested, certainly not in the redwoods. Emanuel Fritz, the University of California Forestry School professor, had conducted a study of second-growth redwood in Mendocino County just south of Humboldt, measuring growth on a plot that had been cut some fifty years earlier. Then, all trees were felled by axes and two-man saws ("misery whips") and the bucked logs hauled out by teams of oxen. Choppers only took the prime trees, leaving everything else—including young redwoods and sprouts—to grow. Harvesting, in effect, had been selective, but for entirely different reasons from those proposed in the 1920s and 1930s and subsequently.

Fritz cut a three-quarter-acre plot of sixty-five-year-old redwoods and found the quality of the lumber to be low. But he found that older trees left behind as immature had experienced rapid growth and produced a high percentage of top-quality lumber. Fritz concluded that second-growth timber was commercially viable and that selective cutting worked if only profitable trees are cut and unprofitable ones left standing, residual stands of immature trees are left to seed open areas, and residual trees are protected from injury during logging and burning slash. With such treatment, residual stands would show increased rates of growth—rates considered phenomenal in other forest regions of the country. Trees crowded in a virgin forest may grow less than 1 percent per year in volume, but they can and will grow from 3 percent to more than 10 percent per year, depending on their size, after they are "released from competition"—that is, when surrounding trees are removed. For trees 100 to 300 years old, wood added at the accelerated growth rate was free from knots. Fritz concluded that selective logging, cutting only profitable trees and leaving immature ones, "adds to the life of the logging operation, and it can go a long way toward making it perpetual."[30]

Perpetual. The very idea of continuous and profitable harvesting must have intrigued Murphy. Harvesting second growth, and doing so on a selective basis, may seem like an obvious approach today, but then it was not, especially in redwood country. Making the shift, just conceptually, was to have a profound effect on the industry. Until then, timbermen assumed second growth was worthless, the wood weak and lacking in tannin and other substances that made redwood rot resistant.

The early loggers interpreted the relative absence of young trees as evidence that the climate had changed, leaving only old trees and ensuring the redwoods' eventual extinction. "Nowhere is there any young growth," wrote an official of the U.S. Geological Survey in 1899. "With the clearing away of the present forests, the end of the species as a source of lumber will be at hand." In fact, because nearly all redwoods that the early pioneers encountered were several hundred years old, people assumed that "all second growth redwoods grow rapidly for a few years and then stop growing or grow so slowly as to take centuries to attain commercial size."[31]

With second growth dismissed, extending the life of a timber operation, as the Murphy's operation had done from the start and A. S. Murphy continued, meant acquiring more timberland—that is, more old-growth trees. Murphy, in fact, had become known as "the trader," acquiring timbered tracts wherever he could when the lumber industry picked up in the early 1930s. Instituting selective harvesting, originally done to mollify preservationists, had the unintended effect of making possible, indeed, *conceivable*, the cutting of second growth and thus *harvesting in perpetuity*. By leaving some trees to regrow and reseed, the key to longevity was not simply acquiring more old-growth trees, the staple strategy of the redwood industry for nearly a hundred years, nor was it to wait a thousand years for a new supply of old growth. If a long-enough time horizon was adopted, perpetual and profitable yield could begin now.

Perpetual and Profitable Yield

With selective logging and a shift from old growth to second-growth, something profoundly different was indeed possible. For the first time in Murphy family history, in some ways, in the industry's history, the nation's history, it was conceivable to harvest a forest, *the same forest*, in perpetuity. Treating forests "as a reproducible crop is a matter of great national importance," proclaimed one forester in the 1920s. "It marks a turning point in the history of the United States."[32] The emerging grand vision went beyond trees to entire communities, even economies. "Redwood land is not to repeat the story of decaying settlements and abandonment to barren, fire-swept wilderness," wrote an observer of the redwood industry in the 1920s. "The prosperous towns and villages of the present will continue to thrive with all the assurance of permanence that is vouchsafed to any community that is founded on the continuous production of the soil." Nor would there be a trade-off between preservation and production: "Groves of the great trees will delight the eye and stir the wonder and awe of the tourist and nature lover, while the forests as a whole will perpetually yield lumber and other wood products for the uses of a civilization that could scarcely endure without them."[33]

It was indeed a grand vision, worthy of bold newspaper headlines like "Timbermen Plant Trees" and "Reforestation to Feed Maws of Hungry Mills."[34] It was a vision that was entirely novel at the time, even radical, and yet, in hindsight, naive. Throughout the twentieth century, preservationists would force the trade-offs, and capitalists would compel ever-greater cuts. But at this point in history, people like Murphy and Fritz were on the front lines, traipsing through the woods, measuring and remeasuring, trying to figure out how to put such a vision into practice. Fritz knew that Murphy was "getting more and more interested" in perpetual yield, Fritz wrote the chief of a major timber company in 1947. With TPL's position in the redwood industry, including its propensity to innovate, TPL's interest "means a great deal," Fritz wrote. "We all realize it is not going to be easy to put a redwood operation on a continuous basis, but if any company can and will do it, it is the Pacific Lumber Company."[35] As Murphy gradually discovered, it was not easy because perpetual harvesting required taking fewer trees than what was possible and producing less lumber than what was considered efficient and technically feasible in the short term; indeed, it required operating at less than the most profitable harvest level. It required putting aside trees for the long term, bucking the trends of an entire industry for a century and a half.

In time, Murphy apparently also discovered that selective harvesting and using second growth were not enough. Such methods would go over well with the parks and gardens crowd, the "environmentalists," but by themselves they could not ensure yields and profits in perpetuity. The total cut, over time, could be no greater than regrowth. In fact, it had to be *less*, given the vagaries of that growth, the weather, the economy, and, not least, the politics. There had to be a buffer, a cushion against overexploitation. Appropriating the terminology of the day, Murphy called it "sustained yield." But unlike its current usages (and there are many), he would not pursue *maximum* sustained yield, but, one might say, *conservative* sustained yield, a policy that deliberately kept harvest levels below what all actors—investors, managers, salespeople, workers, and consumers—would have preferred. But first he had to try selective harvesting, to see if, in practice, it was at all feasible. Abandoning tried-and-true methods—aerial cableways and logging rail lines—was, as noted, risky.

The opportunity came in 1935 when lumber sales increased rapidly and existing operations were unable to meet demand. TPL opened a logging operation just across the Eel River from Scotia itself, which became known as the Monument Creek

logging show. At the time, loggers in the Northwest were experimenting with tractors, or "cats" as they were called after the Caterpillar Tractor Company. For
decades, loggers had rigged up steam donkey engines and an aerial system "of long
cables that snaked the logs down to the railroad or river, smashing smaller trees
right and left and destroying" nearly everything in their path. The "cats," by contrast, could "scoot up steep slopes like mechanical rabbits, hitch on to one end of
the log . . . by means of derrick and cable, lift it slightly off the ground, then tear
down the slope to the loading places,"[36] maneuvering all the while around obstructions, including standing trees. TPL purchased a few tractors for the Monument
Creek operation, marked trees to retain for future growth, and, indeed, found that
usable trees could be selected and removed, leaving others to grow. There were problems, but the experiment was successful enough for the company to adopt selective
logging for its subsequent old-growth logging operations.

Selective harvesting and sustained yield thus emerged as central management principles, converting TPL's timber operation from *profitable mining* (harvesting efficiently until the timber ran out) to *perpetual and profitable yield* (harvesting for the
indefinite future). The principles were straightforward, at least in retrospect. Their
implementation was a different matter, however, requiring new techniques in the
woods and new practices in the offices and boardrooms. Management of the forest
required strategic commitments, organizational mechanisms to bind interested
parties and encourage restraint in harvesting when more is always tempting, when
more is, by conventional measures, economically rational. *Management* and *self-
management* had to go hand-in-hand.

Perpetual and profitable yield policies, by this reconstruction of events and
ideas, came about almost inadvertently, as by-products of trying to cut, process,
and add value from old-growth redwood, and all without being shut down by
preservationists and government regulators. That is the least charitable interpreta-
tion of what otherwise would be seen as enlightened timber management. But I
lean this way to make the hard case: a timber owner or, for that matter, any extrac-
tor of a potentially renewable resource need not convert to environmentally correct
or politically correct positions to move in a sustainable direction. One need not
forsake self-interest or profit making or even capitalism to chart a new path, one
that depends less on frontier exploitation and more on settled regeneration. A. S.
Murphy's genius was not that he anticipated the future (the goal of sustainability,
say), but rather that he dealt with the present and did so in novel ways. His
correspondence over several decades suggests that the idea of perpetual and profitable yield evolved gradually. In discussing timber acquisition he argued for "pro-
longing" and "extending" the life of the timber operation, always implying that

there would still be an end to that operation, that there still would be a cut-out date. In time, though, he employed "forever" and "perpetuity," suggesting the grander vision.

The context of Murphy's timbering was radically different from his predecessors and so were his methods. Rather than continuing the old methods until the timber was all cut out or until someone discovered new forests or more efficient ways of using existing forests (e.g., intensification), Murphy made his own radical departure from the industry norm. The methods themselves "brought about a change in our concept of the forest, a change in our attitude on conservation," said one TPL executive in a speech to Humboldt County residents in 1960. The leaders at TPL came to the "realization that the day was not too far distant when the old growth virgin forest would be no more, a realization that the life of the invested dollar which controls the economy of our County was endangered if certain practices were continued, a grim realization that our children would never have the opportunity of viewing the forest or deriving any of its benefits if policies continued."[37]

Interviews with people in and out of the company and perusal of company histories and industry reports reveal that Murphy and his followers took heat from many quarters, especially from other members of the industry, for TPL's departure from industry norms. At industry association meetings, in the clubhouses and the halls of the state legislature, many looked askance at what were considered Murphy's deviant practices, especially if those practices made others in the industry look bad. Nevertheless, from roughly the 1950s until the 1985 takeover, TPL stayed its course, weathering criticism for being stuck in the ways of the past, for missing opportunities for more efficient timbering—for being "wedded to old methods" and lacking an "intensity of effort," as one senior Maxxam/PL executive put it in the 1980s. And it was criticized, not least, for "forgoing revenues" by limiting the harvest.

Forgoing revenues. As we'll see, TPL could have made more money using conventional industry practices. But was its path to perpetual yield financially sound? The answer from the business press was a resounding yes. TPL "so cherishes its wealth, and has become so wedded to a pattern of success," wrote one regional magazine in 1976, "that it is becoming a virtually classical case study in how to not plunge with your bankroll." Its stock in the 1970s sold at seventeen-times-per-share earnings, the same magazine reported, a rate double to triple that of major corporations in the country.[38] In its day-to-day management, TPL was simultaneously conservative and adventurous: conservative with respect to industry and stockholder expectations, adventurous with respect to employee conditions, public relations, and harvesting methods. It must have been ironic for players in the industry to preach efficient, financially optimal harvesting and then witness a firm cut less than it could have, less than "optimal," invest more than it needed to, and eschew debt like few businesses anywhere and, as a result, have profit margins like this and hear observers everywhere say it "did things right"—and "right" not just for the workers and the forests, but for investors.

One anomaly remains, however. A. S. Murphy was an "expansionist," according to Parker, a businessman who had to be "frugal" during the Depression years but, by nature, was a "trader." Having weathered lean years and challenges from preservation and union movements and, as a result, "achieved the complete support of the Detroit group of stockholders," A. S. Murphy "envisioned . . . the Company's greatest need [to be] more forest land and a larger timber base."[39] On the face of it, he was like any other businessman bent on capturing market share or maximizing investors' return or simply pursuing growth as the overriding goal of business enterprise. But the motives are in the details. Two acquisitions in particular reveal that, for Murphy, a man keenly aware of the history of logging in North America, growth was a means to a larger goal, namely, perpetual yield, at least as it was understood in his day.[40]

In 1950 a nearby lumber company, Dolbeer & Carson, was for sale. A closely held, financially sound company with a history even longer than TPL's, it had extensive redwood timberlands and a working sawmill. Murphy bought the company and associated assets for $4.3 million, confident that TPL could now produce "enough new growth each year to equal the amount of logs harvested,"[41] Parker recorded. But tellingly, Murphy sold the sawmill. Then, again, in 1958, another major company, Holmes Eureka, was put up for sale, Murphy negotiated, acquired the entire company, land and mill, and, in 1962, sold the mill.

If Murphy was merely expanding, growing the company to be bigger and bigger, to produce more and more, he would have kept the sawmills, both of which were well equipped and ideally located on the Humboldt Bay waterfront. But his "sustained-yield concept was based on optimum consumption of logs by [the existing mills at] the Scotia plant," Parker contended.[42] In other words, the number of logs produced in a lumbering operation normally varies, a function of the amount of standing timber, harvesting techniques, workforce, transportation, and consumer demand. At any given time, milling capacity is a constant and thus sets an upper limit on the number of logs produced and processed. But plant expansion or acquisition can make that upper limit variable as well. If the goal is to produce more and more lumber, one follows the *efficiency principle*, manipulating all variables for optimum output. If the goal, however, is sustained yield, a different principle is needed, one that accommodates the fact that the timber base cannot continually chase an expanding plant. The *sufficiency principle* implies that more logs cannot translate into perpetual yield unless the available logs, over time, equal or *exceed* plant capacity.

When A. S. Murphy took the helm at TPL, he was handed two of the biggest and best-equipped mills in the business. They could be improved at the margin, but for the most part their capacity was set and there was no room on the Scotia flat for another. What's more, TPL's timber harvest was fully accommodated by its two mills. The only constraint was in transportation and sale of finished lumber. If Murphy were to run the Scotia mills at full capacity (to do otherwise would have been extremely difficult from an organizational and managerial perspective; see below), he eventually would cut out the company's holdings. The combination of standing timber and growth rates was not enough to sustain the operation. More timber and more milling capacity would not change that fact. It would increase production, but *not the sustainability of that production*. One of the variables had to be a constant. Because labor, transportation, sales, and, to some extent in his time, timberland, were inherently variable, the only factor that could be fixed was the plant, in particular, mill capacity.

Murphy apparently knew these dynamics well. To produce more, one could never have enough land and equipment. To produce sustainably, by contrast, one could have *too much* plant or *not enough* timber or both. Sufficiency did not preclude expansion, it only established the *purpose* of that expansion. And it compelled the establishment of limits in the organization of production at the most amenable locus. In this case, it was mill capacity. In other cases and other resource industries it might be elsewhere in the production process, in the technologies of extraction or points of sale, say.

But Murphy's genius was in recognizing and accepting the natural limits of the forest, its extent and its regrowth capacity, and translating those factors into organizational limits. By acquiring the Dolbeer & Carson and Holmes Eureka properties and dispensing with the sawmills, he committed TPL to perpetual yield. He discovered a "capacity commitment," as pioneering an achievement for his day as those of explorers before him. He enacted *self-management* under *ecological constraint*.

It is not hard to imagine that company managers and stockholders were incredulous to learn that Murphy was selling two well-equipped, ideally located mills. The desirability of the Dolbeer & Carson mill was soon confirmed when a group of

Portland, Oregon, investors seeking entry into the redwood industry paid $1.8 million for it. Had Murphy combined that mill with the Holmes Eureka mill and its 130,000-board-foot production capacity he could have increased TPL's overall production capacity by a third, given that, at the time, mills A and B at Scotia had a maximum capacity of some 600,000 board feet a day.[43]

But Murphy had other things in mind, notably to be the first to make a valid claim to sustained yield. Historian Parker stated that that claim could only be made in the early 1960s, following several more timberland purchases, and he might have added, *no significant increase in mill capacity*. That idea, limiting capacity, we will see, may have come from Berkeley professor Fritz. "Continuous operation can be approached now," Fritz exhorted one redwood company owner, "only by a combination of reforestation and the extension of the old growth by reducing the mill capacity." But, Fritz went on, "if the company wants to continue operating on its present large scale, there is nothing that you can do now to bring about permanence."[44]

Selective harvesting, taking second-growth trees, and maintaining a sufficiently large timberland-to-mill-capacity ratio added up to one overarching operational principle in TPL's timber harvesting strategy: *restraint*. "The Company . . . has had many years of practice in restraining itself from over-harvesting its timber resource, limiting itself to a harvest equivalent to the amount of growth," concluded Parker and a colleague, articulating what by the 1980s had become gospel among TPL timber managers. "It has been exercising this restraint for several decades, reducing production in some cases even in times of good markets of its products, which is most unusual in this industry whose sales are largely cyclical." Combining land acquisitions and restrained harvesting, "The Pacific Lumber Company achieved sustained yield logging . . . the most important long-term goal of [the] Company."[45]

If TPL indeed was "restraining itself from overharvesting," that should have become apparent on the ground, at least some time after 1960. Standing timber should have been constant or, if the policy were truly conservative, as observers in and out of TPL thought it to be, increasing. But assessing timber volumes is notoriously difficult even today with sophisticated computer-modeling techniques and satellite imagery. Redwood may be especially difficult to measure because so much of it grows in remote regions, accessible only when a tractor clears a path along steep hillsides. And some of it grows remarkably fast and some of the biggest trees are blown down in storms or uprooted in floods. Even in the mid-1980s, "the biggest problem which exists [for timber managers] is lack of sufficient data for which to make yield projections," wrote one forestry consultant to Maxxam/PL.[46] TPL did conduct a timber "cruise," an inventory of standing timber, in 1956 but did not make it public. In general, timber firms are loath to reveal the information they do have, in part for strategic reasons within the industry and in part for tax-collection purposes, a nontrivial concern in California, where standing timber, not harvested logs, was taxed. As it turned out, it took several decades and the trauma of the Maxxam Corporation's takeover of 1985 to confirm that, indeed, TPL was cutting well below the industry norm, even below what many considered sustainable. A consultant in the late 1980s for the newly merged company cited, among other forms of evidence, several annual reports from the Murphy era. One, a 1981 letter to stockholders signed by the board chair and the president of the company, read:

Management has evolved a long-term philosophy for the prudent management of the Company's valuable timber resources which we believe is unique in the forest products industry. As a result of adhering to this philosophy, despite short-term variations in industry or national economic conditions, management believes it has succeeded in providing Company stockholders with very satisfactory current returns and at the same time has contributed to the very significant increase in the value of the Company's timber resources.[47]

"Satisfactory current returns." In other words, you, the stockholder, could have gotten a higher short-term gain elsewhere with your investment but we feel this is "enough." Over the long term, the truly long term—that is, decades, maybe even centuries—you and your descendants cannot do better.

The consultant concluded that such statements, along with analysis of timber inventory, are "indicative of curtailed production levels while the timber resource became larger which directly implies harvest at below sustained-yield levels at the expense of current revenues."[48] According to a 1986 report, "Company lands are stocked with all the timber TPL's mills can saw on a continuous-yield basis. There is a good supply of old growth—which on California's North Coast means very large trees. But a long history of selective logging has also ensured abundant second-growth timber."[49]

From the standpoint of maximizing shareholder value and efficient use of the resource, the company's strategy all those years was ludicrous. First of all, Murphy's policies were simply too rigid. "With an exclusive reliance on selective harvesting," argued then executive vice president John Campbell and soon-to-be president of Maxxam/PL, "all of the old-growth trees would eventually become 'residuals' scattered in small stands over a wide area. This would not only make them increasingly vulnerable to wind damage, but also more expensive to harvest because of their wide dispersal. Moreover, when they were harvested, the damage to tender new growth between the residual trees could be excessive."[50] A variety of management techniques should be employed including clear-cutting, Campbell argued, each chosen to fit the specific conditions of each site. A dynamic, growing company must always be on the lookout for opportunities, ready to change on a moment's notice. TPL just did the same thing year after year, "running on a very even keel," observed an industry trade journal,[51] prompting one financial analyst to conclude in 1976: "I'm not impressed by a company which moves THAT slow."[52]

Even more ludicrous from this standpoint, however, was curtailing production at the expense of current revenues. A leading forestry consulting firm found in the mid-1980s that Pacific Lumber could cut much more than it was. Long-run sustained-yield harvest levels could be 216 million board feet per year, some 58 percent above the pre-1985 harvest levels.[53]

Possibly the most ludicrous feature of TPL's policies, not just from an industry standpoint but from the conventional policy and business perspective, a perspective that presumes the broader economy exists to serve consumer demand (chapter 5), was TPL's marketing strategy. "Conventional marketing strategy," TPL's leaders wrote to stockholders in their 1980 annual report,

attempts to stimulate demand for a product, increase its volume of sales through greater market share and increase profits through economies of scale which result from a higher volume of production. Conventional marketing strategy also prescribes market research and new product development to keep pace with changing consumer preferences.

In contrast, the Company's strategy for marketing its redwood lumber is unique. Because of the *limitation on lumber production* which results from its continuous yield policy, the Company is *unable to increase its volume of sales in response to consumer demand.*[54]

Sorry, TPL *can't respond to consumer demand*. Its production limits, tied to natural limits, set sales volume, not salespeople, not consumers. Quite a statement from a company that "cherishes its wealth," that is "wedded to success," from a company owned by a family that built an empire from Maine to Michigan to California. As further evidence, when offers came the company's way to export second-growth logs, TPL refused. The price may be right, but export would thwart perpetual yield, one long-time employee observed in an interview in 1997.

Curtailed production. Forfeiture of current revenues. Selective harvesting. Nonresponsiveness to consumers. These just did not fit the industry norm where, to survive, businesses constantly had to seek efficiencies, grow either outward or inward, maximize near-term revenue, and, above all, please consumers. But from the perspective of a company that emphasized quality in all aspects of its operations, one that valued and invested in both social stability and resource regeneration, one that put long-term economic security and sustained yield above immediate return on investment and consumer demand, the "Murphy philosophy" made perfectly good sense. And those who lived it—those who worked in the woods or in the mill, played on the company's ball field, swam in its pool, or hunted on its land—they knew it made sense. Restrained harvest ensured revenues—and jobs and company amenities—for one's lifetime and probably for that of one's descendants. All the talk among industry analysts about "curtailed production" and "under-harvesting" and "overcapitalized assets" did not change that fact. Restrained harvesting, from this perspective, was rational, *socially*, *ecologically*, and even *economically* rational, if one counted first and foremost those who most depended on the resource. In the late 1980s, however, those who counted most in American business were not the resource-dependent communities, but shareholders, especially shareholders guided by corporate-takeover artists.

Throughout the 1980s in the United States, financiers, so-called corporate raiders, targeted "undervalued" publicly traded companies. They would obtain a majority of a company's shares, often through the use of high-risk "junk bonds," then use the company's assets to pay off their debts. Houston financier Charles Hurwitz paid $840 million for Pacific Lumber Company, of which $770 million was debt acquired through Drexel, Burnham, Lambert of Beverly Hills, California, and other financial houses. As owner of the "new" Pacific Lumber, Maxxam/PL, one of Hurwitz's first moves was to take $50 million from the "oversubscribed" $90 million employee pension fund to help pay his takeover debts. He also enlarged the workforce by 25 percent, dropped the forty-hour week, put mills A and B on ten-hour shifts for five days, and added an eight-hour shift on Saturday. And he bought another mill. Maxxam/PL abandoned selective logging and adopted clear-cutting. By some accounts the harvest rate doubled, others said it tripled. Much of the new cutting was old growth. Many employees and residents of the region applauded the changes, while others opposed them, taking their case to Sacramento and Washington, D.C., as well as to the courts. This part of the Pacific Lumber story has been amply told elsewhere.[55] What needs explication, however, are the implications of the takeover for management and self-management, for sustainability in a world governed by efficiency principles like capital mobility and resource intensification.

Maxxam Corporation's takeover polarized the Pacific Lumber Company community and much of the debate over sustainable forestry as well. With regard to harvest policy, according to one view, Pacific Lumber came under the control of a disreputable financier who knew or cared little about timber or timber-based communities and their environments. By stepping up the harvest dramatically, increasing mill capacity, and going after the biggest, highest-value trees, he converted a "model timber company" into a company no better, perhaps worse, than all the rest. Pacific Lumber was cutting out. From the opposite view, Pacific Lumber was only catching up on its harvest rate, making up for lost time and lost revenue, and actually continuing the pioneering efforts of earlier owners, striving for truly sustained yield. By planning for the very long term, at least 120 years (see below), and on a large scale, watershed and greater, and by incorporating a suite of values–timber, wildlife, watershed, recreation–Pacific Lumber was embarking on a sustained yield program far more thorough and more sophisticated than anything the Murphys and their followers could have imagined.

Resolution of these two competing views is unlikely for years, maybe decades. But two conjectural points are worth raising in light of the company's evolution of the idea of perpetual and profitable yield. First a counterfactual. If the Murphy era had persisted and a corporate takeover craze in the United States had not occurred, indications are that the "old PL" under the Murphy philosophy eventually would have cut out all the old growth. From the earliest days of the company, that always was the intention and no evidence exists to suggest otherwise. Even the Sierra Club acknowledged as much in 1988.[56] The "old" Pacific Lumber might simply have done so over a longer period of time than the "new" Pacific Lumber chose to do, converting to young growth gradually. But the endpoint, say 50 or 100 years hence, would have been roughly the same as that projected by Maxxam/PL. That leads to the second point.

Maxxam/PL's Sustained-Yield Plan, submitted to the California Department of Forestry in 1996, is notable for two features, aside from its extensive provisions for habitat protection and species preservation. One is the time frame–120 years. According to company officials, specifying a time frame, especially one that long, is unprecedented in the timber industry.[57] It appears that this time frame would not be eclipsed by discount rates derived from financial markets or excessive consumer demand. Models used to calculate the planned-for harvest levels build in two key constraints. One is a maximum harvest increase or decrease, *between decades*, of 8 percent. The other is that harvests in each period must always be *less than* the estimated *long-term sustained yield* (LTSY). In other words, however valuable monetarily the trees may become in future years, however much consumers crave redwood siding and redwood decks, however high "current revenues" could be, the harvest rate cannot respond in lockstep. More demand and higher prices will not push harvests beyond the estimated level of LTSY. In effect, then, the baseline harvest policy is, indeed, the old PL's restrained harvest.

Although these features of TPL's sustained-yield plan may not seem like much, certainly not to Maxxam/PL's critics, the company's harvest *plan*, its stated policy endorsed by the state of California, is not cut-out-and-get-out. Nor is it necessarily a strategy of growing inward—that is, intensification. To be sure, the plan calls for a full range of "silvicultural prescriptions," 170 in all, which no doubt include fertilization, pesticide applications, reduction of tree-species diversity (which actually began decades previously when slash burns eliminated many "whitewood" species—fir, pine, hemlock, and spruce, for instance—and allowed almost total recolonization by redwoods), and genetic manipulation. But a key premise of the harvest model is that there is a *single* LTSY for the 120-year period, implying that no amount of intensification would increase yields.

These conjectures may be unduly optimistic with regard to the future of sustainable forestry at Pacific Lumber. But their significance lies less in their interpretative and predictive accuracy than in their testament to the power of an idea—what I have termed perpetual and profitable yield. With its 120-year plan, Maxxam/PL may be primarily reacting to public opinion and the threat of ever more government interference. As this account has hopefully demonstrated, though, from the early days of the Nevada owners to the Murphy era, the bulk of Pacific Lumber's history regarding sustained yield has been just that: timberland acquisition to compensate for public set-asides, reforestation to appease tourists, selective harvesting to satisfy conservationists. If getting on a sustainable path, whether for a firm or an entire economy, means key actors must be first converted to the wisdom of environmental protection and the multiple goals of sustainability, then our society is indeed in trouble. But if, as I argue in different ways throughout this book, it means we understand the conditions under which actors lean toward restrained, long-term resource use, whether out of self-interest or altruism or some combination of the two, then there is hope. If key actors choose restraint over mobility and intensification so as to enhance their public image or head off a political movement or get a tax break or avoid unpleasant decisions or ensure a high quality of life with economic security for self and immediate others and, as a by-product, a natural resource can regenerate indefinitely and succeeding generations can profit from that resource, so be it.

Understanding the enabling conditions is key, though. For A. S. Murphy and The Pacific Lumber Company, many of the conditions were set by the redwood industry, by state and federal regulators, by a public concerned about conservation and preservation, and by an emerging profession, so-called scientific forest management or, simply, forestry. In the redwood belt of Northern California, forestry was virtually synonymous with one man, Emanuel Fritz, "Mr. Redwood."

Emanuel Fritz and the Quest for Permanence

The idea of perpetual and profitable yield certainly did not originate with A. S. Murphy and The Pacific Lumber Company. As noted, Murphy's family history and the tenor of the times regarding timber practices meant that the idea was emanating from many sources. In fact, by midcentury everyone was talking "sustained yield," although few timber owners could make a credible claim to having put it into practice. And no one could argue that the timber industry as a whole was structured for anything but rapid exploitation of the resource. For this larger "institutional" side of the story, we must return to Emanuel Fritz, the Berkeley forestry professor who first demonstrated that second-growth redwood was biologically and economically viable. Here we find that, although the principle of restraint can be found in the operations of one company, sufficiency as a broader social principle necessarily required involving the entire industry as well as the regulatory structure in which it operated. The story of how Fritz came to this conclusion thus becomes the necessary complement to that of A. S. Murphy and his followers at Pacific Lumber Company, paralleling and contributing to TPL's experiences yet extending beyond the management of one stand of timber and the self-management of one operation to the management of the whole industry. In part, it is a story about erecting barriers to entry, about insulating the existing redwood operators from competition, with the unavoidable implications of market-controlling firms capturing monopoly rents. But it also is a story about resisting federal regulators, zealous preservationists, and, possibly most importantly, outside business concerns, those transient opportunists who would come only for the wealth of the standing resource and leave when it was gone—in short, latter-day frontier miners.

The fact that Fritz mostly failed at the larger social transformation only attests to the inertia of then-contemporary principles for resource management, grounded as they were in the premises of frontier exploitation and efficient extraction. As he told one redwood company owner in 1946,

Your company, like all others in the United States, considered lumbering as a liquidation business. The timberland was regarded as a mine and, when completely cut over, was either abandoned or sold off for other uses. Such a policy was understandable when there was a surplus of timber and an operation could be moved to another state or county. Obviously, this is no longer possible.[58]

What *was* possible was movement toward perpetual and profitable yield on several fronts, including harvest method and regrowth. In this, Fritz largely succeeded. That he and the industry could not effect change on the broader social front is nevertheless instructive. Insights derived from attempting to manage and self-manage at the collective level—at the level of the industry and of society's larger institutions—suggest how, in timber and other natural resource arenas, the transformation to sustainability might be achieved. I take up those broader lessons soon.

The Advocate   Fritz was a prolific writer, not just of technical reports and journal articles, but of correspondence with company officials, foresters, and the public. His voluminous life's work collected at the Bancroft Library at the University of California at Berkeley provides rich documentation of the changes of an industry through the first half of the twentieth century and, not least, one man's attempt to influence those changes. These materials reveal an evolution of thought, a growing realization that the challenge of perpetual and profitable yield was not primarily technical or managerial. Rather, through tireless efforts to organize the industry and lobby government officials, he discovered that the biggest challenge was "getting industry to become aware of their responsibilities,"[59] as he put it; it was changing industry structure, identifying key institutional principles, and enacting them collectively.

Fritz committed his professional life to one overarching goal in timbering: "permanence," not just "conserving" virgin stands to make them last longer as one might do with a vein of ore or a pool of petroleum, but deliberately managing forests for use into the indefinite future. He spoke of permanent forests and, in deference to timbermen's primary interest, perpetual income. His "laboratory" was redwood country, in particular, privately held timberlands of California's Mendocino, Humboldt, and Del Norte counties. Key players were large, well-established companies, "operators" he called them, of which Pacific Lumber was a leader. Central to his mission were three ideas that, at the time, were not only novel but were considered by the softwood industry to be radical and wholly unnecessary. He advocated that timber companies convert from old-growth to second-growth cutting; shift from slack-line clear-cutting to selective harvesting; and, perhaps most difficult for a profit-making firm in a competitive environment, limit output.

Fritz became known as "Mr. Redwood" not just because he knew the tree's biology so well, but because he knew the redwood industry so well, working closely with it and championing private forestry and foresters. He was "no swivel-chair advisor," wrote a business reporter in 1937. "More than half his time is spent knocking around over the rugged roads to the lumber camps talking conservation and forestry engineering with gang bosses."[60]

In 1936 Fritz organized the Redwood Region Logging Conference (RRLC) under the auspices of the California Redwood Association (CRA) and served as secretary-manager on its board of directors until 1958. Although the conference emphasized logging techniques and issues, timbermen's major concern, Fritz saw it as "an important factor in bringing forestry to the logger." He found that at meetings loggers argued about forestry "like foresters in a SAF [Society of American Foresters] meeting." Those discussions were crucial opportunities, Fritz realized, to advance the ideas of forestry and permanence with those who do the work on the ground. He urged redwood operators to attend other softwood conferences as well to learn more about forestry. "The Douglas fir and pine people are so deeply involved now in growing a new forest that the discussions are strictly down to earth," he wrote the logging manager for TPL in 1948. He urged TPL participation in a Western Forestry and Conservation Association meeting in British Columbia: "Forestry is still rather new in the redwood region. . . . I feel rather strongly that the leading redwood companies should be represented. May I suggest therefore that you give consideration to sending a representative from your company?"[61]

In 1934, when the timber industry was subject to a Depression-era federal Lumber Code Authority, Fritz became consulting forester to the California Redwood Association, a trade group of major timber companies based in Eureka. "It is up to us [foresters] to keep the operators constantly alert to what they are up against, not only as to public criticism, but as to the business aspects of a diminishing supply, an increase in stumpage values, and therefore the opportunities in continuous production through timber growing."[62] When the government controls were lifted, Fritz designed a CRA program to forestall further federal involvement in private forestry, modeling the program's forest-practices code on the federal controls, which emphasized "the conservation and sustained production of forest resources" and the importance of leaving "some portion of merchantable timber (usually the less mature trees) as a basis for growth and the next timber crop."[63] He told industry leaders that if they eliminated destructive logging practices, the government's primary justification for controls, and if they complied voluntarily, they were more likely to head off new federal intervention. One means of "sustained production" in the redwood forests was selective cutting, Fritz argued, and to that end he instituted a grassroots education program, convening conservation conferences and working to improve public relations for lumbermen, companies, and associations. He continually sought to improve the public image of the redwood industry, urging operators to abandon the slack-line system, which, to the public, appeared as destructive as fires. He taught logging crews about forest protection and insisted that government officials base their reports on actual observations in the woods, not on information obtained in distant bureaus. He wanted the public and the government, especially those inclined to intervene in the affairs of private companies, to see the improvements private foresters and their companies were making.

In 1943, Fritz became a consultant for the California Forestry Study Committee, visiting forests throughout the state, talking to practicing foresters and lumbermen. He wrote the committee's report, *The Forest Situation in California*, and drafted several of the legislative bills that became the state's first forest-practices code. Among its provisions were requirements that forestlands be left in a productive condition—that is, productive of continued timber growth—and that at least four residual trees ("seed trees") per acre remain after logging, in short, that some kind of selective logging be practiced. That "outstanding requirement," as Fritz described it, effectively institutionalized selective logging. Even so, he urged timber operators to exceed the code's requirements by leaving more than four seed trees and instructing chopping bosses to prevent damage to the remaining trees from sideswiping equipment and slash burning.[64]

From research to organizing, Fritz was above all an advocate, a promoter of ideas. He was convinced that redwood operators, contrary to conventional wisdom in his time, could do more than cut trees. They could grow them, too. They could have redwood forests and timber and profits forever—perpetual and profitable yield. And they could do it now. Always the optimist, he expected results in his lifetime: "Don't get gray over the future of the redwoods," he wrote a U.S. Forest Service official in 1937. "It looks good to me. I am more than pleased with the progress already made. And I can see a lot more ahead."[65] And a dozen years later: "I expect to see forestry [permanence] in the redwoods improve so steadily that before I am unable to climb over those rough hills it can be pointed to as one of the best in the United States. That's the goal I have set for myself and I think I am going to see it before I have to be helped into my boots."[66] At the same time, he was a realist: "If the present system of liquidation is continued," he warned in 1949, "operations would cease or be severely curtailed in thirty years." All along he knew the problem was not primarily biological: "There is a human problem there [in the industry] that is far more important and more difficult to solve than the saving of trees."[67]

The Murphys may have pioneered as timber tycoons across the continent, but Fritz was a pioneer of a different sort. Like A. S. Murphy, he came of age when conservation proponents like Theodore Roosevelt and Gifford Pinchot were decrying the decimation of the nation's forests and when the new discipline, "forestry," was just developing. Patterned after the German school of natural resource management, forestry at universities such as Yale, Cornell, and Michigan made land restoration the primary task—that is, healing the vast cutover lands of the Northeast and Great Lakes regions. Forestry schools and those promoting forestry as an approach to land management concentrated on reforestation—reseeding, replanting, and regrowing. But in the far West there still were large tracts of uncut timberland. A few people in the profession, like Fritz, entertained the idea that forestry need not *follow* logging, that extant forests could be managed for perpetual yield. To be sure, old growth, including 1,000-year-old trees in the case of redwoods, would disappear eventually. But *forests*, assemblages of growing trees, some fast-growing seedlings, some mature with tight, clear grain, would be permanent. No longer would it be necessary for timber companies to level a region and then wait for regrowth as Eastern states were forced to do. Regrowth could occur simultaneously with harvesting.

This idea—simple and straightforward as it may seem in the early twenty-first century—was, then, a radical departure from standard practices. These practices were premised on the assumption of unlimited supplies or eventual regrowth or both, and were associated with a noble way of life: timbering, clearing the way for civilization, supplying a growing nation with fuel and building material. That life was not planting and tending, not farming. The idea of simultaneously cutting and growing, what Fritz put under the term *forestry*, was, in the early twentieth century, "looked upon as a crusade of idealists and academicians," Fritz wrote in a 1948 memo to the CRA. "At that time it was considered foolish to think of ever being out of virgin timber."[68]

And to hard-nosed timbermen, forestry was an equally "foolish" idea. It took many forms through the twentieth century, from cautious, low-impact, selective logging to intensive, high-input monocultures. But initially, even in redwood country, it was reforestation and then selective logging. And, yet, larger forces made conversion of the timber industry from cut-out-and-get-out to forest permanence difficult. Uppermost in the minds of operators was the federal government.

The Feds   Like A. S. Murphy, Fritz was a deeply conservative man, committed to private enterprise and opposed to government involvement in timber management and ownership. "I have always felt that if forestry is engaged in on purely business grounds," he wrote redwood owners in 1947, "no one outside the industry would have grounds for criticism, while the operator would enjoy the advantage of better realizations and then, possibly, permanence."[69]

If private owners were best suited to creating permanence in timbering, they would have to counter the threat of government intervention as it came from two directions. One, well-known to TPL, was the parks movement, private citizens, many wealthy and politically well connected, goading state and federal authorities to set aside scenic groves, thus taking private land out of production and reducing targeted companies' holdings. Some of these set-asides Fritz supported because he, too, valued such groves; he was a longtime member of both the Save-the-Redwoods League and the Sierra Club. But he also supported set-asides because he saw important public relations value for the industry. The other source of threat, probably less known to the general public, was a concerted attempt by the federal government to extend its regulation to private timberlands. "If a man farms his land to the waste of the soil or the trees," declared President Franklin D. Roosevelt in 1938, "he destroys not only his own assets but the Nation's assets." Warning that no citizen had an inherent right "to do with his land what he wants—to cultivate it well—or badly; to conserve his timber by cutting only the annual increment thereof—or to strip it clean," the need for government control is clear: "The day has gone by when it could be claimed that Government has no interest in such ill-considered practices and no right through representative methods to stop them." Roosevelt's Chief Forester, F. A. Silcox, then drew the implications for private timber owners:

Nowhere has private initiative succeeded, of itself, in establishing forest management on a sustained yield basis generally, with its added security to labor and industry through an uninterrupted succession of forest crops. Instead, public regulation in some form has invariably been necessary. With a crop that matures as slowly as trees do, perhaps the time has come when we, too, should exercise a margin of sovereignty over private forest lands.[70]

Such statements caused an uproar among timber owners, especially in the West. A 1938 editorial in the trade magazine *West Coast Lumberman* summed up their views:

The lumber industry of the west for years has borne the shock of government blunders, been shaken from time to time by such things as unfair reciprocal trade treaties, lack of adequate tariff protection, etc., and now comes the chief Forester branding the lumbermen as despoilers. Under such a barrage, is it any wonder that the product itself at times seems to get into disrepute and that potential builders look upon it with suspicion and turn to competitive materials? Is it surprising they feel that an industry so iniquitous as the lumber business, cannot possibly produce a clean, worthwhile product? Is it any wonder that lumber projects are difficult to finance? Under such conditions is it to be wondered at that the industry at times lags? And who suffers most? First of all the men in the camps and the mills. Then the thousands of employees in allied industries, such as railroads, steamship lines, foundries, machine shops, stores, etc. Whenever the lumber industry is prostrate general business in the west is also flat. This is just as true today as it was fifty years ago.

Such statements as those found in Forester Silcox's report also do great harm to the cause of real forestry in the west.[71]

Fritz shared the timbermen's feelings, referring in a private note to "the ill will on the part of the socialistic fringe in the U.S. Forest Service and those who are hell-bent for federal regulation."[72] But he did not hesitate to use the threat of federal regulation to goad the redwood industry into adopting selective logging, eliminating waste, and coordinating themselves to lobby the California legislature.

The "Invaders"   The redwood industry, with the help of people like Fritz, largely succeeded in repulsing government interventions. And companies like TPL mostly succeeded in implementing selective logging and shifting from old growth to second growth. But by the late 1940s, to the surprise of nearly everyone in the industry, including Fritz, other forces made conversion by the industry from cut-out-and-get-out to permanence even more intractable. The redwood industry, Fritz saw, was threatened by excessive mobility in cutting and investing.

"In the Redwood region the situation has changed drastically and significantly," Fritz warned in a 1946 memo to CRA members. "We used to think we have a 75 to 100 year supply of redwood. The catch always has been in the phrase 'at present rates of production,'"[73] rates expected to prevail through the Great Depression and World War II and beyond. A forest survey released in 1944 "shook the industry to its foundations," wrote a scholar of the redwood industry in 1952. The reason: "In only a quarter of a century, [the redwood industry] had logged about one-half of its crop with no more redwood timber immediately available."[74] At the same time, the postwar boom brought dramatically increased consumer demand and higher prices, which, with dwindling supplies elsewhere, encouraged new entrants into the redwood industry. Some were local men trying to get a start in the business. Derided by old-time operators for their "popgun mills," they often failed but paved the way for outside operators. The small, so-called fly-by-night operators worked on contract and were "interested only in a 'quick clean-up,'" Fritz contended. With no property holdings and therefore no incentive to practice selective harvesting, but instead an incentive to harvest as fast and as efficiently as their contracts allowed— and then some—"they have no interest in future use of the land," Fritz warned. If they proliferate

they would slash the young stuff wastefully and disturb the market structure for old growth. Fires will be inevitable and they will get into adjoining properties not belonging to them.

The federal Forest Service is making much capital of the current premature cutting of second growth. The small operator can't afford to pay what the second growth is worth to the present operating old-growth owners. The net result is trouble, headaches and public condemnation.[75]

The other outsiders were an even bigger threat—large, well-financed timber concerns who had cut out their lands in Oregon and Washington and were now, midcentury, buying up rich tracts elsewhere and often liquidating them. Fritz urged the well-established redwood companies to hold on to their land and resist the temptation to sell, even seemingly useless cutover lands and second-growth tracts. To minimize such depredations, he advocated that they buy up small tracts and consolidate their holdings wherever possible and almost regardless of merchantable timber. "I believe it would have been much better to have existing mills supplied with enough reserves to eventually go on a permanent basis on present production schedules than to have additional mills," he wrote. "But that is hardly possible now. To achieve permanence, tag ends of timber must be picked up, the production of some mills must be gradually stepped down to prolong their life, and cut-over lands must be put to work."[76]

Although Fritz did not frame the issue as one of excess mobility and absentee ownership, his admonitions to established redwood operators implied that *permanent* residential ownership was necessary for *permanent* forests and *permanent* harvesting. To achieve such permanence, established companies would have to coordinate themselves, in effect creating barriers to entry, a risky proposition when antitrust sentiments were still strong in the country. Established redwood operators like TPL may be doing things right, but these newcomers, fly-by-night contract loggers and big-time investors, were coming in for a killing, many making good business decisions to be sure, getting the most for each investment dollar, but thwarting the ability of the redwood industry as a whole to "achieve permanence." Between 1940 and 1948, the number of mills in the region increased from a half dozen to 214; production increased 30 to 40 percent.[77]

This "invasion," as Fritz termed it, led him to an even bolder proposition. First, production volumes had to align with the timber base: "Based on present plant capacity and average output, the chances for permanent production are very slim except in a very few instances." Second, these established timbermen, rugged, no-nonsense businessmen accustomed to getting the cut out, would have to think the unthinkable. They would have to actually *reduce their output*: "If present output is reduced and if a complete selective cutting and protection plan is set up, the chances [of resisting these invaders] are good."[78]

Those were two big "ifs," accomplished for a couple of decades by TPL perhaps, but by few, if any, others. The second "if"—selective cutting and protection—was, to varying degrees, facilitated by the industry's abandoning of the slackline system in favor of "cats." Later, the California Forest Practices Act and changes in the tax code helped. But the first "if"—reducing output—was quite another matter, yet probably the most important at midcentury and, arguably, today. "The fact that current output may have to be decreased is of serious business consequence," Fritz acknowledged. "The benefits of permanent production must be carefully weighed against this handicap."[79] A "handicap," that is, as measured against the so-called "efficient" producers, those who please their investors by getting a quick, "optimal" harvest off a tract of land and, then, when all is cut, make an "optimal" investment in a new tract of land, only to do it all over again. Sufficiency in throughput—in this case, reducing production to align with forest and plant capacity—was an alien concept whether at the level of the firm or at the level of a region and its industry. Efficient use, whether optimal harvesting or simple liquidation for maximum return on investment or intensified production was, and still is, the norm.

Resisting outsiders, reducing output, and bringing plant capacity "in line with the growth capacity of the land," as Fritz put it,[80] highlighted what may have been forestry's biggest failing and what Fritz began to sense as far back as the Depression years. Forestry did not help the industry when it focused on stand management and harvest method, ignoring or sidestepping timber owners' overriding concern: profitability. "[Not] the Forest Service, nor the University, nor any other forester," Fritz wrote, "has yet been able to give substantial proof that the arguments for the forestry idea are sound from a business sense." And, now, in midcentury, just as the proof was developing for one firm, maybe others, the established industry was coming under attack, infiltrated by "invaders" with capital to burn. Advocates like Fritz labored for a half century to get *permanence* or *perpetual* or *sustained* into the landowners' vocabulary, but *profitable* was always on their lips. And, short of complete governmental appropriation of the resource, it had to be. To achieve perpetual and profitable yield, the biological and organizational imperatives had to go hand in hand; forests must replenish themselves, companies must pay for themselves. New *operational principles* were needed—restraint via buffering, say, sufficiency in both harvest and profitability. But such ideas were not adequately articulated nor could they compete at the time with such seemingly all-powerful efficiency notions as optimal harvesting, maximum sustained yield, and fully utilized capital.

In short, the best of company practices, as TPL eventually discovered after going public in 1975, could be overwhelmed by structural conditions of an industry, including capital mobility and absentee ownership. As for Fritz, he succeeded with individual companies like TPL, convincing them that second growth was viable and selective logging feasible. And he succeeded in shaping state legislation, preempting federal control and encouraging selective logging and regrowth. But at the larger level—that is, the institutional setting where mobile capital and absentee ownership are revered elements of a "free" market—Fritz failed, as did the redwood industry and, for that matter, society as a whole. The country, indeed the entire political economy, was still operating as if resources were inexhaustible or substitutes could be found or, later in the twentieth-century, as if resource extraction could be unendingly intensified.

Still a Possibility

Emanuel Fritz and A. S. Murphy shared the dream of a permanent redwood timber industry. Fritz's controversial ideas of second growth, selective harvesting, and restrained output were only realized on a limited basis, meaning that, at the level of the redwood landscape, the larger goal—"permanence" or sustainability—was still a distant prospect at his death in 1988 and at the beginning of the twenty-first century. In retrospect, his greatest hurdle was not biological or technical, but a question of human organization—management and self-management for long-term use. TPL got closest, implementing, however imperfectly, selective harvesting, sustained yield, and limited mill capacity. Through the 1960s and 1970s TPL could make a credible claim to "sustained yield," even "sustainable forestry," at least as the terms were understood in those days. But it became a different company, first when, after A. S. Murphy died in 1963 and his son, Stanwood, died in 1980, the "bean counters" took over from the visionaries, as one former executive put it, and then when it went public in the mid-1970s and, finally and more dramatically, when it was bought by a distant investment house, a group of high-powered, clever folks who apparently loved the game of high finance. Pacific Lumber did not just subject itself to the shenanigans of technically sophisticated but ethically challenged financiers. (At least two participants in the takeover did jail time for insider trading and Hurwitz, in addition to the suits filed by Bertain, was sued by federal regulators seeking damages of $250 million for his role in the failure of a highly leveraged savings and loan company. This failure cost taxpayers $1.6 billion.[81]) Beyond the ethical issues, Pacific Lumber exposed itself to the imperatives of interest rates and investor expectations. Permanence, let alone restrained harvest, were indeed alien concepts for the people from Houston, Beverly Hills, and Wall Street.

But the redwood industry as a whole failed too, and well before the corporate takeover craze of the 1980s. It was unable to tackle the thorny issue of industry structure—that is, structure for permanence as opposed to structure for frontier appropriation. The CRA was effective at marketing redwood products and even at influencing the state's forest regulations. But it could not stabilize the industry. It could not make an argument for protecting existing operators without being self-serving, if not in violation of antitrust law.[82] Nobody, not even A. S. Murphy or Emanuel Fritz, could articulate a principle that rose above production and its mantras of efficient extraction and maximum return on investment. Conservation and sustained yield and permanence all sounded fine and, in fact, these have long been the buzzwords of public and academic foresters, even the timber industry. A different principle was needed, one that captures the ideas propounded by Murphy and Fritz regarding restrained harvest and limited output, a principle that not only says there can be too much cutting (a widely articulated notion since the days of the early conservationists and preservationists), but one that says there can be too much short-term gain, too much mobility of capital and equipment, too much efficiency in product and not enough efficiency in regrowth, too much return for those who depend not a wit on the forest or its regenerative capacities.

Sufficiency as I have articulated it in these pages—or something close to it—was needed to counter the charges that TPL and the redwood industry were mired in the past, that they needed radically new methods and new ownerships, that they needed and could get far better returns on those huge "underutilized" assets, those massive "inventories" of high-value "fiber."

From Itinerancy to Settlement: Precursors to Sustainability

A single case, however rich in social-biophysical interactions, cannot be the basis of a theory, including a theory of sustainability. It can, however, raise questions, suggest propositions, and contribute hypotheses. Most important for the normative purposes of this book it can show what is possible; it can offer lessons for sufficiency in practice. I next explore several.

It's the Rates
On the face of it, the important story in The Pacific Lumber Company case is the company's choice of selective logging over clear-cutting. In the public's mind, clear-

cutting is synonymous with the timber industry's notoriously destructive, cut-and-run practices. And it is aesthetically offensive. One need only stroll through a recent cutover to see how thoroughly the landscape is rearranged, how everything but the scrawniest bush is leveled, how the soil, once a blanket of life-giving organisms, nutrients, and water, has been opened like a fresh wound to the sun and rain. Prepare yourself, a forester told me as we approached a clear-cut in the redwoods, it isn't pretty.

So much of the political debate of this century regarding forests has centered on the relative merits of harvesting methods: Should a tract be cut and, if so, how? If that debate was resolved for the public lands of the Pacific Northwest, it was a yes to cutting public forests and, by all means, clear-cut, open the land to sunlight, "release" those Douglas fir seedlings and, by whatever means necessary, suppress the spruce and hemlock, which would otherwise become the dominant trees.

In redwood country, though, where nearly all land has been held privately, aesthetics was the public's primary concern. The sheer magnificence of 1,000-year-old, 300-foot trees occupying a narrow, fog-enshrouded strip along the Pacific Coast captured the public's imagination. From industry's perspective, it was the view from the highway that drove public policy. Yes, produce the siding and decking boards, homeowners and developers seemed to say, but preserve our view as we drive up the Redwood Highway on vacation. In Douglas fir country, production trumped parks. In redwood country, it was the other way around.

But for the purpose of gaining insight into how society can use resources sustainably, the tug-and-pull of production and preservation is less important than harvest rate. The real story is not in the size of cuts or in the silvicultural prescription, but in the rates. And in midcentury redwood country it is how one industry tried to achieve "permanence," how one company in particular tried to implement, "on the ground," in the woods and mills, perpetual and profitable yield.

A. S. Murphy, with his son, Stanwood Albert Murphy, and others, devised an approach, indeed, a philosophy, for building a resource-dependent economic enterprise, one that was profitable and yet did not depend on uprooting machinery and workers when the critical resource was exhausted. TPL did not presage the sustainability goals articulated in the 1980s and 1990s. Rather, and this may be more telling in the end, by pioneering as *settlers*, not as *miners*, by choosing harvesting for the *long-term*, TPL leaders were compelled to develop measures both ecological and social that serve as important precursors to sustainable resource practice. Those measures were in part procedural—on-the-ground practices. But they were institutional, too; they expressed principles of organization that were necessarily long term, necessarily social and ecological, which I put under the term *sufficiency*. Consequently, the lessons for sustainability are more fundamental than harvest method and habitat protection, the current preoccupations of timber companies sensitive to public opinion.

Harvest rate is an issue the industry to this day continues to dodge, preferring to act as if more timber can always be found somewhere, in some distant land where the technical know-how, the capital, and the transport options have been lacking, where "the public," local landowners, and government officials are all too happy to pick up some revenues. The industry did accept one kind of limit, though. When cut-out-and-get-out was eventually abandoned by the industry (at least in the industry's public rhetoric and with respect to domestic operations), it implicitly acknowledged the finiteness of North American forests. But this was an external limit; the absence of virgin forests puts an obvious end to frontier expansion. An internal limit is different, still unthinkable in mainstream industry: one can always expand by *intensifying*, by getting more lumber, more fiber from an acre of timberland, by planting monocultures and genetically modified "supertrees," by fertilizing and weeding, the hallmarks of "efficient" modern timbering.

A. S. Murphy, by contrast, accepted both limits, external and internal, limits not just of the continent's forested landscape, but of his one piece of that landscape. He practiced industrial forestry as a business enterprise, but he departed from industry norms when he needed mechanisms to limit harvesting to a level the forest appeared able to withstand.

And he not only managed, he self-managed. It is precisely this restraint, this sense of sufficiency—experienced by nearly all actors in the enterprise—that distinguishes The Pacific Lumber Company. And it is restraint such as this that has been notably absent not only in the timber industry but in so many self-proclaimed sustainability projects. In this sense, then, Murphy, Fritz, and their followers as well as the community as a whole were far ahead of their time.[83]

As precursors to sustainable practice, their strategies embody a goal, perpetual and profitable yield; they generate broad principles of decision making; and they establish procedures for implementation. As the preceding history and, as we'll see, Murphy's correspondence and reconstructed "memoirs" reveal, these goals, principles, and procedures, which together might be termed a management regime or an "institution," evolved over many years through trial and error. Although they originated from the confluence of personal, organizational, cultural, and ecological factors, not deductive reasoning as presented in the preceding chapters of this book, they are consistent with the findings there. Indeed, the deductive and inductive methods are complementary, one from conceptual development and the other from practice, both addressing the same analytic question: How can human behavior be organized given immutable ecological constraint and humans' twin desires for material wealth now and material security into the future?

A Settlement Strategy: Keeping Players at Bay
Pioneering in the nineteenth- and early twentieth-century timber industry was *itinerant*. It depended on moving into frontier territory with resistance from resident peoples neutralized, extracting the marketable components of the resource, and then moving on, leaving what remained to those who would farm, build factories, or establish parks. As argued in chapter 2, and as Emanuel Fritz himself said, this is mining, and it continues today in various guises.

The Pacific Lumber case suggests that a different brand of pioneering was possible, one that depended less on continuous exploitation of new lands and more on continuous use of the same land. This kind of pioneering still required innovation and hard work, commonly called "industry." And there was no reason to believe that it could not still be industrial in the sense of high capital investment and technological innovation. But could a more settled pattern of resource extraction turn a profit, let alone compete with all those who continued the lucrative, cut-out-and-get-out practices? Could it do so year after year, generation after generation?

In some ways, A. S. Murphy was the perfect person to test such a proposition. Through inheritance he was handed a large, timber-rich piece of property in one of the remotest areas of the nation. He had his family wealth backing him and, maybe more important, his family reputation. If he tried something different, even something radically different such as putting down roots for long-term resource use, few would probably object or even notice, especially if profits continued to accrue. He also came into the business at a time when the use of natural resources was questioned by many. By the end of the century it was clear the forests were not endless. Some argued for preserving remaining stands, others for more rational extraction.

A. S. Murphy came of age as the resource debate intensified, leading to the preservationist parks movement and the utilitarian conservation movement. Having grown up in the Great Lakes region in one of the leading timber families of the time, Murphy must have gained an appreciation for the logic of capital and its interaction with consumer demand and employment. He must have known that such a logic created seemingly inexorable forces that drive timber exploitation beyond sustainable levels. In time he may well have reasoned that countering this logic would require a logic of its own, a logic that provided a shield against such forces while still attracting investors to the company and workers to its mills and buyers to its products, a logic that aimed not at a specific cut-out date but at the indefinite future. It would have to be a logic that put decision making in the hands of timbering folks, not distant capitalists or consumers or preservationists. None of these distant actors knew or cared about the timber industry per se. Murphy did. He was, above all, a businessman who wanted to stay in business, especially the timber business. But unlike virtually everyone else in the business, including those in his own family, he seemed to understand that, to stay in business, he had to cut timber not by constantly moving on but by staying put. He seems to have reasoned that if he was to succeed in timbering, he would have to be a different kind of pioneer, one who confronted not just untamed wilderness, but insatiable investors, consumers, and preservationists. A different logic was needed to keep such players at bay yet still allow participation in the market, a logic that would lead to profits but would build in a buffer against the well-known pressures that compelled timbermen to harvest as much as possible and as fast as possible and that then forced them to get out and move on.

In short, to pursue perpetual and profitable yield, he would need a logic that put the limits of the resource above the demands of the investor, consumer, and employee. It would have to build in restraint—that is, an institutional commitment to use the resource at levels below what is possible in the short term as a means of ensuring timber supply for the long term. With a resource that regenerates, a timber owner could be less a miner and more a farmer, less an itinerant and more a settler.

Such a logic required a strategy, a set of principles and procedures that would make sense to key actors. For Murphy in his time, the sources of that strategy were many: the silviculture of eightieth- and nineteenth-century Europe adopted and modified by the emerging forestry profession in the United States; governmental promotion of conservation in early twentieth-century America; and, more indigenous and practical, the minds of innovators such as the Murphys and Emanuel Fritz who, in their professional lives, faced the exigencies of redwood timbering. Murphy's settlement strategy evolved over decades as he wrestled with the logic of capital, new technologies, volatile lumber prices, wage and employment demands, the parks movement, and, most notably, a perceptibly limited supply of timber. That strategy can be distilled into three concepts—buffering the harvest, the indefinite future, and self-management.

Buffering the Harvest   Today, everyone in the timber industry is committed to some notion of sustained yield. Debate continues over method, of course, whether selective or clear-cut harvesting is best, whether an intact forest is necessary to sustain harvests or monoculture plantations can substitute. The question that is routinely skirted, however, is whether an acre of timberland can generate ever more board feet (or "fiber"), whether the forest (or the plantation) has a limit, an upper bound on the volume of wood that can be appropriated over the long term.

In the 1990s members of the timber industry, academe, and advocacy groups conducted a major collaborative study of "sustainable forestry." Their report had all the buzzwords—forest scarcity, sustainable forest, forest resilience, dynamic balance, ecosystem management, ecoculture, forest stewardship, cooperative management, adaptive learning, accelerated innovation, natural capital, and green finance. Limits, however, are never raised. Instead, in the compilation of case studies, one chapter after another is written as if the "traditional industry objective" of "increasing the rate of raw resource output" can go on at the same time the values of habitat, watershed, genetic diversity, agriculture, and climate regulation are maintained.[84] Similarly, a private initiative by the U.S. wood and paper products industry calls for reforestation, minimization of visual impacts, prudent use of forest chemicals, and the protection of water quality, wildlife, and historic sites.[85] Its *number one* goal, however, is "to increase growth and timber quality of all forests, so that the volume and quality of domestic timber resources available are adequate to meet public needs now and in the future."[86] These studies, as laudable as they are for raising critical issues and attempting to organize the industry, in no way acknowledge a forest's ultimate capacity. Limits is an alien concept.

A. S. Murphy eschewed limits, too, but with respect to value added or technologies of harvesting and milling, not the forest itself. A researcher in American studies in the late 1970s and early 1980s, Merline Williams, reconstructed Murphy's words from his voluminous correspondence, materials that disappeared with the 1985 takeover. She put his views about limits this way:

The redwood industry was obviously restricted by climate and geography, and its finite limits demanded our immediate attention. I followed Pacific Lumber's tradition of respect for our natural resource. . . . It had not always been so. For the pioneer settlers of Humboldt county, the redwood trees posed a problem. Their tools and techniques were inadequate for profitable cutting, and often these enormous trees, which grew right down to the shoreline, were seen as standing in the way of other industry. And they seemed limitless. Every early description talked of eternal forests and a perpetual timber source. And at their contemporary rate of harvest, that may have been accurate. But by the late 1880s technology and experience led to profitable cutting, and soon after, people began estimating how long the redwood would last. Some experts said fifty years; others predicted one hundred; all agreed there would be an end. The acres and acres of redwood stumps in the counties surrounding San Francisco provided a dramatic visual reminder of the finite limits of the redwood forests.[87]

As Fritz and other foresters would insist and Murphy apparently accepted, perpetual yield was possible only within limits, the limits of regeneration, growth, and, not least, managers' ability to implement the method. The challenge at the time was not to squeeze out ever more board feet but to find a way to cut profitably and to do so for generation after generation, in perpetuity. Not knowing what the capacity of the forest was (systematic measurement of volume and growth really only began in the 1950s) but knowing the harvest rate had to be much less than the industry norm, a norm governed by the cut-out-and-get-out philosophy, Murphy logically had to implement a very conservative harvest regime—that is, cutting *well below* the estimated growth rate. Some observers attribute the resulting harvest level at TPL to sheer ignorance: nobody knew how much timber was on TPL lands so they just cut as much as they wanted. Because the stuff sprouted and grew like crabgrass, this view has it, TPL managers were just lucky, and, ever sensitive to public opinion, they labeled it sustained yield, or conservation. Others attributed the conservative harvest rate to the leaders' old-fashioned ways, their stubbornness or inability to consider new methods of maximizing value. A more compelling explanation is that at TPL a very different logic was at work with respect to the crucial decision of harvest rate, a logic that deliberately built in a *buffer* against overharvesting.

By midcentury, maybe earlier, the industry as a whole had abandoned frontier extraction. If timber owners cut out it was mostly to get out of the business. Some eyed public lands to make up the difference. Those who stayed with their private lands chose to either manipulate the land and the trees to "increase raw resource output" or, in rare cases like TPL, to work within the limits of the forest's regenerative capacity. The difference can be interpreted as two competing logics, each entirely sensible on its own terms, but fundamentally opposed. One is grounded in economic rationality with its efficiency precepts, clearly the dominant logic in the contemporary political economy (chapter 3); the other is grounded in ecological rationality (chapter 2). Both can be profitable, at least in the near term, but the economic requires continuous external inputs, whereas the ecological is likely to be self-sustaining. The difference is not so much in the degree of human appropriation of the resource but in the applied worldview of material use. The Pacific Lumber case reveals that difference through the choice of restrained, buffered harvest.

Harvesting based on *economic rationality* is cutting trees according to a combination of economic and biological factors, adjusting continually for market conditions to maximize value—that is, financial value—to the firm. For example, if this year's mature trees were a product of luxurious growth a century ago, it makes no sense to cut only a few trees just because this year's growth was low due to, say, a drought. Similarly, if this year's prices for timber are high, it makes sense to cut more trees now, bank the additional revenues, and reduce the cut in succeeding years. Silviculturists and forest economists can come up with many more scenarios. But their expertise is not necessary to see that the rationality of adjustable harvest rates is straightforward. It is economically rational because the factor mix is constantly adjusted at the margin to maximize profits or return on investment or market share.

Harvesting based on *ecological rationality*, by contrast, is cutting no more trees in the long term than regrow in the long term. This too is straightforward, especially when, as we will see, the "long term" is the indefinite future. It is ecologically rational because the crucial decision—harvest rate—is made primarily in response to signals from the forest ecosystem (however imperfect) and only secondarily in response to signals from investors and consumers. And because those signals are "fuzzy," because there is high variability and complex interactions among a multitude of factors in the biophysical and social systems and therefore unavoidable limits on predictability, a cautious, risk-averse approach to harvest levels is appropriate, indeed, rational.

The two approaches differ not in the reasonableness of their prescriptions, but in their purpose and their implementation. They differ in particular in their ability to allow decision makers to capture efficiencies on the one hand and to build in restraint and resist pressure for increases on the other. The strength of the economically rational approach is its ability to capture efficiencies by adjusting to marginal changes in a host of factors that influence a forest enterprise. But it is that same adjustability that is its weakness when long-term regenerative capacity of the forest ecosystem is at stake. Advocates of an adjustable policy intend for the adjustments to be made only with respect to sound economic and biological criteria. And they intend the adjustment to go *both ways*. One year the harvest rates are increased, another year they are decreased. On balance, the rates over time are held within sustainable bounds. Intentions are one thing, actual practice quite another.

As Murphy seemed to know from family history, national history, and his own experience, and as Fritz witnessed throughout the industry, harvest rates tend to ratchet up. If there is a good reason to increase the harvest just a bit this year, that same reason, or another, will exist next year. Rarely do advocates of increased rates push for decreased rates when their rationale for increased rates disappears. They push for a slightly greater cut, just this year, of course, when times are tough or when opportunities are too great to pass up. They argue that an increased harvest would do no harm because there are plenty of trees, a surplus in fact, and, besides, with replanting and natural regrowth, plenty remain to grow into equally lush forests for future generations. A group of workers might argue for higher wages to keep up with inflation, pushing for an increased cut to give themselves a pay increase without diminishing company profits. If inflation drops, they are unlikely to then ask to reduce the cut and, with it, their wages. Similarly, a sales manager might build up a clientele by guaranteeing a minimum volume of lumber each year. That salesperson will be rewarded if the volume increases, but not if it decreases. Even if that salesperson knows that not all salespeople can increase their volume indefinitely, there is no incentive to unilaterally cut back. It is the classic collective-action problem where it is individually (and economically) rational not to cooperate with others (in this case, to restrain sales volume) yet collectively suboptimal, even destructive (because the company overharvests). The entire collectivity of salespeople within the firm pursues individually rational strategies but, in the aggregate, drives the firm from boom to bust. Perhaps most significantly, logging managers, those "bosses" in the field who get the cut out and feed the mills, are "likely to have very little interest in the land itself once the profitable logs [are removed]," wrote Emanuel Fritz. "It has often been said, for lumbering as a whole, that the logging boss is the weak link in the permanent production chain."[88]

Workers, salespeople, and logging bosses only represent the internal pressures on timber owners for increasing the harvest rates. External pressures come from a capitalist economic system. High fixed costs must be paid by continually competing on price, volume, or innovation, all of which encourages, even compels, ever-increasing resource use. That "vicious circle" of undercapitalization, debt, overproduction, low prices, and accelerating destruction of the forests in the nineteenth-century Midwest that historian Cronon wrote about pertained across the continent.[89] And Murphy knew it. The pressures were ubiquitous and, although some realized huge profits, many suffered boom and bust. Murphy undoubtedly witnessed and heard plenty of stories of boom and bust and, as his correspondence suggests, vowed never to repeat it in his family's last timber operation. "The experience of my grandfather and my father was not wasted on me," Murphy wrote, as reconstructed by Williams. "I determined to find a way to prolong the life of our last forest."[90]

Adjustable harvest rates, then, may be efficient in the short term, but they are vulnerable to upward ratcheting in the long term, which clearly cannot be sustained. The flexibility of adjustability is also the flexibility of slipperiness. Managers cannot be simultaneously flexible in response to market signals and inflexible regarding the time horizon and the propensity to continually increase the cut. Murphy's principle of buffered harvest obviated the adjustability and, hence, the potential slide into overharvesting by instituting a seemingly rigid, inflexible, and certainly inefficient (biologically and economically inefficient) harvest policy.

Put differently, from the perspective of complex adaptive systems (chapter 2), not all production factors are commensurate. Workers are not machines and ecosystems are not markets. Efficiency-driven economic rationality, by contrast, seeks commensurability everywhere: each factor should be adjustable, and every one tradable against another. Mobility in all respects—land, labor, and capital—is the norm, the goal, the vision. The greater the adjustability at the margin, the greater the realizable value. There are no limits beyond humans' ingenuity in finding new ways to adjust and mix factors. There is *never enough* and *never too much*.

For some reason, A. S. Murphy saw the world differently. Maybe it was because of his upbringing in a company logging town, maybe his socialization into the "family code," including company policies that commit resources to workers and community, however "old fashioned" and paternalistic those policies may seem to us today. From interviews and numerous secondary sources, it appears that TPL did not treat workers as expendable commodities. Unlike many in the industry, the company did not release workers when they were injured or too old to perform optimally. Instead TPL hired for a lifetime and moved workers to less strenuous positions as their physical abilities declined. Nor did the company compel single-minded specialization. Company policy was to encourage workers to develop new skills, to be versatile, to be able to move from one position to another. To be sure, the company's narrow objective was to have a skilled and loyal workforce. But the practice was contrary to the prevailing industry norm of hiring and firing to maximize worker output, accepting high turnover as a cost of business. Workers at TPL, in short, were not treated as machines. They required investment as workers and, again, contrary to the industry norm, as a social community. Scotia is the concrete manifestation.

Proponents of economic rationality in timber management might concede the *human* limitations to their logic, but insist that factor mobility and exchangeability be applied to the *material* inputs. Financing a timber operation, like any business, is, after all, a constant game of securing capital at favorable rates and with minimal conditions. Any given capital source—an individual or an institutional investor, say—is irrelevant aside from the rates and terms each offers. If one source dries up, the firm shifts to another. Mobility in capital flows ensures efficient allocation. From this view, a forest just provides another material input into a larger economic process.

But from an ecologically rational point of view, a forest is *unlike* all other material inputs. Trees adapted to one region are no more mobile than the soil in which they grow or the hydrologic and nutrient cycles in which they are embedded. Ecosystems are uniquely constituted, and no amount of human manipulation will change that fact. Translating this biophysical imperative into social organization means that the forest as a material input engenders *dependency*—the dependency of workers, managers, the broader community, and, to a lesser extent, investors and consumers; it's a dependency on the unending productiveness of that one portion of forest. When one source, one "factor input" is critical, indeed irreplaceable, management policies are necessarily *risk averse*. Financial capital comes and goes but a forest is a unique input, as essential to a company's perpetual yield as heart and lungs are to an organism's respiration and circulation.

A risk-averse approach to the harvest rate means that harvests are not continuously adjusted, nor, as we will see shortly, are they pushed up against a theoretical maximum. Rather, because the capacity of all ecosystems is highly variable, the harvest is kept well below the estimated "sustained yield," a term that generally denotes measurable and recent growth rates of the relevant commercial tree species. In short, a *buffer* must be built in. Whatever growth rates are today and whatever is conceivable as a corresponding harvest rate—that is, the maximum rate—one must cut less. Restrained harvest is not just "conservative," a term commonly applied to TPL's harvest policy as if "liberal" or "dynamic" or, indeed, "growing" is the preferred alternative. Restrained harvest is risk averse with respect to the critical biophysical underpinnings of the entire operation. The immutable constraint of the forest's regeneration translates into a harvest rate that accepts high variability and low predictability—that is, a *buffered harvest rate*. From the perspective of either systems theory or physiological metaphor (for instance, vital organs), buffered harvests are perfectly sensible, indeed, ecologically rational. From an efficiency, short-term value-maximizing perspective, they make no sense; "curtailed production" and "underharvesting" forfeit benefits and are therefore inefficient and economically irrational. A critical difference is time frame.

The Indefinite Future   A. S. Murphy appears to have been deeply conscious of the past and inclined to look to the future, the far future. As a manager he could also appreciate the importance of role, of an actor's immediate interests, dependencies, and reference points in making critical decisions such as harvest method and harvest rate. He seems to have learned that if one was going to depend on a fixed and finite resource—some 150,000 acres of prime redwood timberland in this case—one could not rely on good intentions or professed ideals when the temptation, indeed the logic, for a big harvest, for a quick return on investment, for paying off debts immediately was pervasive and compelling. The construction of time (chapter 5) was one means of ensuring a buffered harvest.

Within the timber industry and within forestry science the terms *sustained yield*, *maximum sustained yield*, *continuous yield*, and *perpetual yield* are used variously. Here I create a semantic distinction between maximum sustained yield (MSY) and perpetual yield (PY) to connote a difference in time framing: a difference between a finite period of time, however long that may be, and the indefinite future. The significance of this distinction lies not in the conceptualization per se, but in its implications for actual practice—that is, the tendency, on the one hand, to use resources as mere factor inputs for maximum gain over some period of time and, on the other, to use renewable natural resources as essential underpinnings to production and community development, and to do so in perpetuity. In MSY the goal is to maximize board feet or fiber per acre in a given year, decade, or other specified period of time. The yield is sustained for that long. MSY logically compels resource users to push all inputs in the production process, including the resource, to their limits. Efficient use means no productive capacity goes wasted. Of course there are risks, but they are built into the maximization calculus.

Maximization certainly makes sense when the risks are to factors of production that can be replaced, when a machine can be overhauled, a worker rehabilitated, or an investor found elsewhere. But when a factor is an integral part of a functioning, complex system, in this case trees in a forest ecosystem, that system cannot be replaced. Trees, as discussed, are uniquely constituted as elements in an open, complex, adaptive system, not as substitutable elements in a closed, mechanical system. In a timber operation, pushing the limit on trees cut, harvesting at the maximum conceivable (or calculable) rate, effectively singles out one component of the system, that tree species, reduces its variance (all trees are cut at the same age, for example), and makes the entire system brittle, vulnerable to disturbance, and more likely to flip into a degraded state (chapter 2). In a forest, the risks of unpredictable and irreversible ecological change occur when soil is eroded, nutrient cycles broken, or associated species lost.

To jeopardize an ecosystem is to jeopardize production itself. Maximization, pushing the limits in the short term, makes no sense, certainly not ecological sense, and not even economic sense over the long term. A qualitative difference or discontinuity in the production function therefore exists precisely where, in the mix of factor inputs, ecosystem-dependent resources enter production. A production policy that does not account for this discontinuity is unlikely to lead to long-term, eco-logically grounded resource use. It's not ecologically rational and it's unlikely to be sustainable.

A half century ago, well before "ecosystem management" and theories of complex systems were well developed, Emanuel Fritz, ever sensitive to the "business end" of forestry, conveyed a similar point to redwood leaders. He chastised them for con-centrating on milling operations—getting more board for the log—to the neglect of the land and trees. "Lumbering is a *basic* industry," he wrote, adding that the raw material of lumbering is

derived from the soil and it is replenishable. If the raw material—trees—continues to be regarded as exhaustible there must come a time when the operation must cease. . . . The [redwood industry's effective] policy of liquidation has caused attention to be centered on the mill, whereas the mill actually should be regarded only as an intermediate conversion plant. The real value is in the timberland as the real and sole producer.[91]

The real producer is the land. A humbling thought for producers of lumber and paper, for the masters of industrial timbering who see no contradiction between ever-"increasing resource output" and "sustainable forestry." The maximization goal serves such masters by compelling logging bosses, timberland managers, and foresters to push the resource, to treat timberland like any other factor of production.

The maximization goal reduces forests to interchangeable factors in part because it sets the time frame in a way the perpetual supply goal does not. Consider the ratio of board feet per acre, which would be maximized under MSY. The time period is not specified in the ratio but acts implicitly as a second denominator, set by the firm's harvest rate, the extent of its holdings, regrowth, and the economy's interest rates.[92] As a firm's decision making attaches more to short-term decisions—for example, shareholder returns, debt payments, wage rates, shipping schedules—the implicit time period shrinks. To be sure, the ratio increases, and so meets the maxi-mization goal. But harvest rotations ineluctably shorten: trees are cut at earlier ages, growth is stimulated with thinning and fertilizing. Not only does the time period shrink, but it becomes *finite.* The finiteness of a time period, any time period, engen-ders an end game among decision makers, especially distant investors looking for the best return on their investment or managers looking for the best pay for their skills. As game theory shows so clearly, with an end game—a finite and predictable number of plays (or business cycles, harvest cycles, annual reports, or quarterly earn-ings)—participants seek an optimal return before the game is up. They can avoid specifying a number of years by choosing a discount rate, but the effect is functionally the same. It is still a finite time period with an end.

The critical managerial questions then become: What factors tend to get associated with the harvest decision, what are their implicit time frames, and how can a focal point be constructed that encourages sustained use? A forester can tell us that 150 years is biologically correct because that is when growth rates peak, but everyone knows that for a given watershed, even for a given tree, the peak is highly variable depending on climate, soil, and light. Moreover, growth and regeneration are not the only factors entering the calculation of the production ratio. Financing, wages, and many others, all of which have much shorter time periods, enter the calculation. They can easily override the forester's time period if the decision making resides not with the forester but elsewhere. These factors, in effect, conspire to bring the original number of years down to a lower number of years. What starts as biological time framing, becomes financial time framing. And, once again, should these factors change, no one is likely to ask to lengthen the time period. If interest rates improve, financiers will not ask for less volume. If wages increase, workers will not demand lower harvests, certainly not with a risk that lower wages would accompany such harvests. Finite time periods ratchet down, not up. And they are especially prone to do so when there is no countervailing principle.

A. S. Murphy and Emanuel Fritz did provide a countervailing principle, though, what they called the "indefinite future" or "in perpetuity." Harvesting should be *forever*, not for ten years or twenty, not even for a century or two. Indefinite may not fit a conventional scientific framework for resource use, nor a management regime that must be scientifically and economically defensible, amenable to calculations of maximum harvesting using biological growth rates and economic discount rates. But it may very well fit a sustainability framework, a framework that is acutely sensitive to the risk of harvesting too much. It may very well be the most defensible ecologically and organizationally, especially in the everyday context of managerial decision making. In fact, it may be the only designation of the future that, in practice, does not degenerate into finite and ever-shorter time periods.

Indefinite may be fuzzy from a scientific management perspective. But it is no fuzzier, no less useful for the purpose at hand (reversing the trends in environmental degradation and getting on a sustainable path) than that routinely employed in contexts outside of natural resource extraction where high-order values are at stake. These contexts may include framing a constitution, investing in children and grandchildren, preserving precious works of art, adopting a religion, endowing an academic chair, promoting national and cultural symbols, and defending territorial boundaries. Who would argue that these should be carried out for just a year or a decade or even a century? Who would argue that their future should be discounted according to a rate set by narrowly financial, notoriously short-term "investors," by arbitrageurs, money managers, day traders, and speculators? Constitutions are written and territories defended for *forever*, or at least for as long as one (and one's descendants) can imagine.

Framing time as the indefinite future leads to an operational rule that is grounded first and foremost in the resource and the specific ecosystem that sustains that resource: cut only what grows—or less. It is a rule that aims right at the intersection of the biophysical and social systems. Signals of potential ecological decline—disease outbreak, slowed tree growth or premature death, diminished populations of associated species, shifts in soil nutrients—portend production decline, they become negative feedback in the social system, perceived threats to the buffer. Because the buffer cannot be manipulated (to do so would be to pursue MSY) but must be maintained, even nurtured, and because the buffer is inherently fuzzy, such signals compel harvest reductions, regardless of sales opportunities. A spike in demand, say, can translate into big profits, but such an opportunity only exists for the time frame implicit in the demand spike—a few years, perhaps, as occurred in lumber sales in the immediate post–World War II period. The indefinite-future principle erases or, at least, subordinates such considerations. The unavoidable "long-termness," the indefiniteness of ecosystem functioning confers primacy on the ecological buffer, not the market opportunity. "Because of the limitation on lumber production which results from its continuous yield policy," as TPL's leaders wrote to stockholders in their *1980 Annual Report*, "the Company is unable to increase its volume of sales in response to consumer demand."[93]

Operationally, then, time framing as indefinite future becomes a first principle, whereas organizational response to commodity and financial markets is a second principle. The indefinite future guides the resource user in the periodic choice of a harvest level and simultaneously provides a means of resistance, a reason, an excuse, indeed, a way of saying *enough*, when other forces would compel managers to shorten the time frame and increase resource use, when stakeholders have trouble reconciling the twin desires of benefits now and benefits in the future. Not only is the resource likely to be sustained, but so is the economic enterprise, the firm, and the dependent community. Indefinite future and the operational rules that follow thus approach a necessary condition for sustainable practice and, in the aggregate, a sustainable economy.

Self-Management   Because A. S. Murphy lived and worked in a social milieu that revered economic efficiency and depreciated social and ecological capital, implementation of his conservative, buffered-harvest strategy created its own special management demands. To begin with, Murphy needed new kinds of information. It was no longer enough to survey a hillside, eye up the standing timber, and then set the company fellers and gyppo loggers loose, cutting until the tract was cut over. The company had to know some basic facts: standing timber in merchantable board feet, and growth rates. Although in principle this information should be readily obtained, in practice it is not, due to extreme variability from rainfall, fire, floods, earthquakes, slides, and, not least, public opinion and the ease with which private timberlands can be converted to public parks. For the redwood industry as a whole, "No one yet knows exactly how much growth can be expected," wrote Fritz in 1949. He, if anyone, ought to know growth rates in the redwoods, but he explained that "although growth studies have been made, their results have not been checked by actual field experience. It will be a long time before they can be so checked."[94] And even if they are checked, natural events remain notoriously difficult to predict even today with far more sophisticated techniques. As with any business, every decision entails risks; the question is, what risks and for whom?

If Murphy had embraced economic efficiency with respect to all factors of production and hence pursued MSY, he would have needed only to calculate an optimal rate of extraction given expected prices, interest rates, and available timber. These, too, are difficult to measure but the risks are straightforward. In a maximization strategy, if one either overestimates and cuts too quickly (and, say, can't sell the excess lumber at a profit) or underestimates and cuts too slowly (and misses potential sales), one forgoes monetary income. This forfeiture may translate into lower wages and dividends and a competitive disadvantage in the industry. In a buffered perpetual-yield strategy, underharvesting (harvesting below the industry norm, even below "safe" levels) also results in forgone income, but it has the benefit of giving the resource growing room. Variability in features that determine the long-term capacity of the resource—water retention and soil structure, for instance—will be more easily accommodated the lower the harvest rate. The lower rate, in effect, extends the fallow; it adds cushion where ecological variability and risk of overshoot are real. It is a kind of respite, an ecologically rational measure, intuitively obvious for those who face directly the uncertainties of complex systems (chapter 2).

Maximum harvesting, by contrast, threatens the buffer and leaves nothing but monetary gain, an economically rational measure to be sure, sensible for those who pursue maximum financial gain and for whom mining is not an issue because there is always another forest, always another source of fiber, always another enterprise in which to invest one's capital. In a mining strategy the risk in "underharvesting" is diminished monetary income, nothing else. Investing is all about taking risks—with money, and often with other people's money. In a settlement strategy, the risk in "underharvesting" is still diminished income, but for the settler that apparent loss is compensated by enhanced resource quality and the possibility of future income from that resource. The miner expects to always have another resource to turn to when the present one is exhausted and is thus risk seeking with respect to both financial and natural capital. The settler, by contrast, has no alternative resource and is thus logically risk averse, conservative both financially and ecologically.

However Murphy came to accept diminished monetary income and buffered harvesting, it is clear he departed from the industry norm—the norm then and, arguably, now. Nobody harvested less than was technically and economically possible. No one amassed a fortune exercising restraint. By the time he took the reins at TPL, Murphy knew the timber industry well enough to see that it was precisely the buffer that investors, sales agents, millworkers, tax collectors, and anyone else with a financial interest in the company would go after. Each of these players—in contemporary parlance, "stakeholders"—had incentives for a higher cut, for risk seeking with respect to the resource. To ensure yields in perpetuity, however, Murphy knew that although these players, in their personal and professional lives, may share the dual desire for short-term gain and long-term security, he had to keep them at bay; only he and those fully committed to his settlement strategy could provide the counterforce. Only he and his followers were likely to vigorously promote the long-term view, to forgo high yields today for an unending, yet moderate supply tomorrow. Only he and his followers had the overriding incentive and the decision authority to exercise the restraint, even if the others understood its rationality. Promoting the long-term view vis-à-vis moderate, buffered-harvest rates was never easy. It was more than "managing the resource."

Commands from the top are not enough to maintain a resource buffer. Tactics must be invented that make it difficult for those in the leader's network of critical relations—investment, labor, sales, government, activism—to pursue their demands for more and more. It requires mechanisms that make it easy, or possible, for a manager to assure those who can accept moderate returns in the near term that they will receive adequate, "satisfactory" returns in the far term. Recall from chapters 1 and 2 that the "enoughness" employed in this book is a sense of sufficiency that is tightly coupled with future security for oneself and others, not a purist's notion of what is fair or what appears biophysically possible, let alone economically optimal.

A. S. Murphy employed several tactics in this component of his settlement strategy. Possibly the most obvious was controlling information. Interviews with those who worked for TPL in the Murphy era suggest that, although everyone from the mill janitor to the board of directors knew the harvest rates were well below industry norms, only a few people within the firm actually knew the volume of standing timber. According to one respondent, the results of the timber cruise done in 1956 were never revealed. Only Murphy and a few others had the estimates and they kept them well guarded. Other interviewees claimed the numbers were known more widely, especially among board members. Either way, it appears that Murphy kept people guessing about the company's total merchantable timber. Of course, everyone in the industry did the same, trying to keep competitors and tax collectors off balance.

But Murphy had an additional incentive. If TPL stakeholders did not know how much timber stood on those lands, they could not pin him down on an "appropriate" rate of harvest. They would simply have to accept his choice of harvest rate, an acceptance made more palatable when coupled with TPL's steady return for investors and, for workers, secure employment, generous housing, ready permission to hunt and fish on company land, and other benefits that far exceeded the industry norm. The case reveals that TPL's management had to deliberately educate its stakeholders, especially, perhaps, its stockholders, to show them that what appeared to be "excessive" timberland and only "satisfactory" returns were necessary for TPL's "unique" position in the industry, cutting selectively and on a sustained-yield basis.

A second mechanism for implementing a buffered harvest rate was securing a high timberland-to-mill-capacity ratio. As discussed, Murphy's penchant for timber acquisitions at the same time he rejected increased mill capacity can best be explained as a means of promoting perpetual yield. But now it can be further interpreted as a tactic, as a means of committing the entire operation to the reality, indeed the necessity, of cutting less than possible. If the mills were running at full capacity and if TPL could hold to its long-standing policy of never selling logs to other mills (a policy abandoned by the Maxxam owners), Murphy virtually guaranteed a conservative harvest. This was a commitment in a strategic and managerial sense. Murphy's decision not to expand mill capacity commensurate with timberland expansion constrained his own decisions in the future and those of everyone else in TPL. This *capacity commitment*, probably more than anything, more than public pronouncements, more than strategic plans, more than company-government agreements, is the essence of *self-management.*

Buffering the harvest, cutting less than what was possible, "curtailing production" and "forfeiting revenue," far from being a policy born of backwardness, stubbornness, ignorance, or greed, was a skillful manipulation of very human tendencies, namely, the desire to always want more and yet to have something in the future too. Controlling information and maintaining a high land-to-mill ratio simultaneously addressed these tendencies, countering the individual's desire for more and an entire society's obsession with value maximizing and efficiency seeking, and it did so by reinforcing the desire for future gains and keeping harvest levels safely within regenerative capacity. It was risk averse with respect to people and place, to stakeholders and forest. More generally, to be ecologically rational, a company's imperative is not just to grow as a company, which TPL certainly did throughout its history. It is to grow the right things, adjust technologies, promote worker skills, and develop new markets, yet always be sensitive to and accepting of immutable constraints. The ecologically rational manager doesn't escape constraints but finds ways to build them into organizational structure.

Timbering in the late nineteenth and early twentieth centuries meant getting the cut out. Managers were rewarded for volume and for innovations that increased that volume. To implement a settlement strategy at The Pacific Lumber Company, A. S. Murphy had to tame such practices saying, in effect, yes, keep harvesting, keep seeking efficiencies, but don't take too much timber, leave some for the future. Today, such a go-slow policy may seem self-evidently wise, especially for those of us deeply concerned about environmental trends, but then it was downright absurd. No one in the industry was cutting less than they could.

To actually implement such an absurd demand on management—optimize production *and* regrowth; produce, but *not too much*—Murphy, with the help of Fritz and others, launched an experiment to find a different way. His strategy had elements that, when operationalized, became managerial expressions of ecological rationality, falling primarily within the logic of sufficiency and only secondarily within the logic of efficiency. In TPL's complex web of decisions, its extracting, processing, shipping, marketing, wholesaling, retailing, and consuming, the most critical decision—the annual harvest rate—was deliberately retained and influenced by those who knew the resource intimately and who depended most on it. Those at company headquarters in San Francisco and in sales offices across the country necessarily responded to market signals; the incentives were for increasing sales and the risk was that assets would not bring their maximum return. Those who resided in Humboldt County, by contrast, responded to a host of values. Some were market oriented such as timber prices and wage rates, but others, personal and community oriented such as long-term economic security, self-sustaining community, and a way of life that allows for abundant recreation and vibrant family life. "Those of us who live in Humboldt County," said William Bertain in congressional testimony, "refer to our region as 'God's country.' That regard is, in no small part, due to the natural beauty and resources of our area."[95] If the company overharvested, the risk was not merely a forgone marginal return on assets—it was livelihood, job security, and community for themselves and their descendants.

A. S. Murphy pushed his forest-management practices after witnessing through his own family history one cutover after another, from Maine to Michigan to his home state, Wisconsin. After arriving on the West Coast, he could see the same scenario playing out all around him. He could hear the excuses for overharvesting, for abusing the land, and for destroying the streams and estuaries. He could witness the same denial: these forests will never be exhausted. From a broad historical and ecological perspective, though, all were living on borrowed time, exploiting centuries of forest growth, investing little in its regeneration, and presumably content to move on or move out of timber once the natural capital, the forests, were spent.

A. S. Murphy was all business, but for him business was defined first and foremost by the residents of Humboldt County—the managers, the workers, the community members—not by sales representatives in Chicago, and certainly not by financial wizards in New York or Houston. He saw TPL's critical transition in agricultural terms—the cultural terms of a community committed to and bound by one place, and the natural terms of the resource that community depended on. "We had reached a point where profit could align itself with conservation," as researcher Williams reconstructed Murphy's views from his private correspondence. "Gradually we came to realize the agricultural nature of our enterprise and to view each year's trees as a crop to harvest. Our goal was 'steady-state growth,' a balance between board feet cut and board feet grown. It had become essential to find ways to cut within the limit of the forest, to respect the natural resource."[96]

"Essential," that is, for those committed to one place, one forest, and one community, and all for the indefinite future. All others could cut as markets dictated and investment opportunities arose. But TPL was different. And TPL management rarely missed a chance to proclaim it so. To the stockholders, many of whom were TPL workers and retirees, management told them the company may not return as much on the invested dollar as other companies, as much as the typical investor might expect, especially with the size of TPL's assets. But—and this was the hardest message of all, harder than any a pitch a salesperson would have to make selling a product, harder than any a conventional CEO would have to make promoting a company to investors—this was a company that did things right precisely *because* it achieved "steady state." This company was still in business and promised to be in business beyond anyone's lifetime *because* it balanced "board feet cut and board feet grown." And it did so by balancing actors' simultaneous desire for gains now and gains in the distant future.

In short, TPL management philosophy combined "enough" return now with "enough" return for the future. That combination was not just "good enough" but "the best," *sufficient* in the highest sense of the word.

In the end, though, efficiency, expressed as capital mobility, maximum harvests, and maximum "shareholder value," won out. The predations of external capital cut through what barriers Murphy could erect around his company and what norms Fritz could effect in the redwood industry. Their failings are perfectly understandable when the external institutional environment—capital markets, antitrust laws, and an overwhelming norm of efficiency-driven economic growth—was so conducive to itinerancy, so hostile to settlement. It didn't have to be, of course. For insight into the possibility of sustainable practice supported by a larger institutional environment, including the state, we cross the continent to a tiny island in the Atlantic, just off the coast of Maine.

7

Monhegan Lobstering: Self-Management Meets Co-Management

One day in November 1995, lobster fishers from the tiny island of Monhegan looked out over the surrounding ocean. To the south they spotted five boats with fishers setting traps in Monhegan's traditional lobstering grounds, just outside the legally designated two-mile boundary. The Monhegan lobster season was closed and all Monhegan boats were tied up in the harbor. The fishermen on these five boats were outsiders, lobster catchers, it turned out, from the mainland harbor of Friendship some twenty miles from Monhegan. Soon to be dubbed the "Friendship Five," they had come to harvest one of the richest lobster bottoms of the entire Maine coast. And they came legally, with licenses.

As the Friendship Five set traps, they kept a close eye on boat movements in Monhegan harbor. In fact, they kept one boat anchored at all times just outside the harbor and spent the nights in their boats, all to monitor Monheganers' boat movements and to guard their traps. The Friendship fishermen knew as well as anyone that, license or no license, on bottom traditionally held as territory by lobster catchers from a local harbor, the "law of the knife" prevailed. Defenders of territory would first tie a knot in an intruder's trap line as an "unwelcome" mat. If the violator persisted, someone would cut the lines, making retrieval of the trap nearly impossible. It's not legal but it's a tradition that has mostly worked for more than a century.

For several days that November, the Monhegan fishermen stayed in their harbor, watching the Friendship fishermen setting and hauling traps. Finally, some could not wait any longer. Several Monhegan fishermen took their boats out and circled a Friendship boat. "Things can get dangerous out here," one Monhegan fisherman yelled. The Friendship fishermen kept hauling traps, but from this point on the possibility of violence was real. And everyone knew it—the Monhegan and Friendship lobster fishers, other residents of Monhegan, state officials, and even the U.S. Coast Guard. In short order, state officials learned that both sides were not only exchanging threats but some boats were carrying guns.

Two years later, Monhegan and Friendship fishers left their boats and traps at home and headed for Augusta, Maine's state capital. There, with other fishers, marine officials, concerned citizens, and a pack of lobbyists and lawyers, they plied the halls of the legislature. The Monheganers were asking for the impossible in fishery management, a law reserving the lobstering grounds around their island exclusively for themselves. The Friendship Five and their supporters were challenging every claim, objecting to every provision. They called the proposed law closed access, an exclusive, elitist, discriminatory, unconstitutional measure that would spell the end of public waters for public use. But for Monheganers, it was not a fishing issue but a community issue. They, fishermen and fisherwomen, sternmen and sternwomen, store owners, gardeners, caretakers, carpenters, and many others, were at risk of losing their way of life. An incursion from mainland fishermen, legal as it was, represented more than a slice into Monhegan lobster fishers' total catch. It was the beginning of the end of year-round residency and a blow to the vitality of a community dependent not just on a rich natural resource but, given the precariousness of their island lives, on each other.

As in any true community, there are differences among its residents, and conflicts. But on this issue, there was unanimity. With fishing laws and regulations written as they were, the threat of becoming a summer vacation spot, catering to wealthy folks "from away" and fishing, if at all, on crowded waters where the most aggressive always did best, was real. Along the Maine coast only 14 islands still had year-round residency, down from some 300 a century ago. Monhegan, everyone guessed, was next. It all hinged on the Monheganers' ability to impose strict limits on fishing, limits that they and their predecessors had long imposed not just on others, but on themselves. With the help of sympathetic mainlanders, summer residents, lobbyists, and researchers, they were to show that the house bill, LD 2021, was not a marine version of a land grab. Rather, it was a logical extension of nearly a century of restrained resource use, of practices that set Monhegan apart from other lobstering regions and other fisheries that could not manage ever-increasing fishing pressure. It was conservation, to be sure, but conservation built on a recognition that a given fishery can be overharvested, that it can be reduced to irregular and miniscule catches of puny lobsters, and that the only way to prevent such an outcome is to restrain resource use, to ask how much is enough for the long haul, not how much is the most possible for today's haul.

"Real Fishing"

The Monhegan case centers in part on the present, the fragility of island life with pressures from mainland lobster fishers, visitors, and investors. Greater fishing and higher real estate prices all conspire against those who deem residential ownership and place to be important. But the Monhegan case also derives from the past, from a century of fishing and an evolving system of largely self-regulating fishery management, an evolution, a series of experiments, that continues to this day. The self-managing, self-limiting aspects of that evolution and its conjunction with state management are the focus of this case history. It has three major developments: a self-imposed half-year closed season formalized in a 1907 state law; a self-imposed limit on the number of traps per lobster fisher instituted in the 1970s; and, most recently, an unprecedented, state-sanctioned limited-access fishing regime for the island. The context is nearly two centuries of ever-increasing pressure on the lobster fishery along the Eastern seaboard of the U.S. and Canada and the threat, realized in many places, of depletion and loss of livelihood.

Depletion: A Constant Threat

Not until the twentieth century, even late twentieth century, was depletion a real possibility in North Atlantic fisheries. Migratory fish such as cod, halibut, and tuna may have been threatened locally but were, over their range, plentiful. "When I visited [Monhegan] island 30 years ago," wrote one summer resident in 1998, "one could easily catch 40 pound cod and 100 pound halibut."[1] Until recent decades, fishing technology—sail power, hook and line, and lack of refrigeration—made it nearly impossible to put a dent in such populations. Lobsters may have been different, though. Being mostly sedentary (at least in their adult stage) and harvested close inshore, they could always be caught with simple techniques. In the early years of European settlement, gaffs, nets, and even a gloved hand were enough to fill a crate. English settlers in the early 1600s reported that they gaffed fifty lobsters within an hour at the mouth of the Kennebec River. Later, a variety of easily constructed traps with rotting fish parts as bait could attract great numbers of lobsters daily. As a result, local and regional instances of depletion were recorded as far back as the early 1800s.[2]

Increased demand in major metropolitan areas along the Eastern seaboard and, concomitantly, increased numbers of lobster fishers, drove lobster depletion. Lobster canning, the first means of overcoming lobsters' high perishability, also played a part. Live shipment soon followed and continues to this day. Fishing pressure in the

southern regions—New Jersey, New York, and the lower New England states—
decimated those lobstering grounds to the point that, even today, most have never
recovered. In what was likely the first systematic study of lobster fisheries, a 1887
federal investigation found an overall decrease in lobsters up and down the East
Coast: "The weight of the evidence collected . . . leads to the conclusion that there
has been a decrease in the abundance of lobsters within comparatively recent years,"
wrote George Brown Goode of the Smithsonian Institution, the lead author, "and
in some localities this decrease has certainly been great enough to entirely change
the standing of the fishery and render its pursuit unprofitable to the fishermen. . . .
The decrease has been most marked in those regions which have been fished the
longest, and especially in the shallow water areas near the coast, which are easy of
access and which have been subjected to incessant drains."[3] Cape Cod, for example,
had one of the richest lobster grounds, but fishermen came from other states and
sold to the profitable New York and Boston markets. As early as 1812, residents
of Provincetown at the tip of the cape "realized the danger of exhausting the grounds
around their town, and succeeded in having a protective law passed by the State
legislature."[4] But it was not enough. The lobstering grounds were exhausted.

The pressure just moved up the coast, slowed only by increasingly difficult
weather and distance from the metropolitan markets. The story of one lobster-rich
inlet on the coast of Maine illustrates the vulnerability of local lobster fisheries, even
in relatively remote locations in the nineteenth century:

The basin opened directly into the sea, and was large enough to afford a remunerative fishery
to several lobstermen. Two years' time was sufficient to reduce the supply of lobsters to such
an extent that fishing became unprofitable. After an interval of about five years they [the lob-
sters] became again abundant, and the supply was once more exhausted. Had this inlet not
been so situated that it readily received accessions [migrant lobsters] from without, it is prob-
able that it would have required a much longer time to become replenished.[5]

It is not hard to imagine that stories like these, many based on the experiences
of fishermen, dealers, and canners, circulated among fishermen as well as biologists
and regulators. Depletion was always real for those who sought to make a living
off lobsters. And for those who sought to make a *steady* living, not just a boom
every five years when stocks replenished, it is not hard to imagine fishermen and
others cooking up schemes to ensure a reliable, year-in-and-year-out supply. One
strategy, as illustrated in that Maine inlet, was to find a rich spot, fish it out, and
then move on. This might have been an economically rational strategy in the early
years of lobstering. But even in the late 1800s, demand far exceeded supply as the
1887 federal study documented, and the numbers of willing fishermen exceeded the

number of accessible lobstering grounds. So as the rich lobstering grounds near the biggest markets were fished out, fishermen migrated up the coast, northward and eastward. The migrations continued right through the twentieth century, not just of lobster fishers but of gear and boat technologies, each putting new pressures, ecological and social, on the fisheries. In 1920, Maine's Department of Sea and Shore Fisheries declared that "it is no exaggeration to say that in practically every known natural region of the North Atlantic Coast the lobster fishery is either depleted or in a state of decline."[6]

Claims and counterclaims of imminent depletion continue to this day. Biologists estimate population levels and reproductive rates and predict imminent collapse. If they had done so at the last turn of the century, they would have been right. The 1920s and 1930s were indeed a "bust." Harvest levels were one-eighth that of the 1990s. Water temperature and predation probably played a role. But so did harvesting practices. Lobstermen then took everything they hauled. The big ones fetched high prices. The little ones, the "shorts," they "smashed up . . . every day . . . and used for bait" or to feed the chickens or fertilize the garden.[7] And the females with eggs they stripped and sold along with all the rest.[8]

For roughly the first hundred years of European lobster fishing, then, people knew that the lobster fishery as a whole included the very real possibility of depletion, especially locally. The cases may vary and claims of depletion or abundance may be challenged. But the historical record shows that, through its natural range—that is, from the Carolinas in the United States to Newfoundland in Canada—the so-called Maine lobster was depleted significantly. No one setting traps on a piece of bottom anywhere could assume that their prey would always come back, certainly not within time spans that would support a family or community continuously and certainly not if fishermen continued to enter the fishery, let alone if technologies continued to make harvesting ever more efficient. On a continent long known for its vast and abundant resources, indeed, for its *inexhaustible* resources, it is easy to assume that at first lobstermen likewise perceived inexhaustible lobster supplies, just as others perceived inexhaustible cod and halibut stocks into the 1980s. But the evidence cited here suggests that for nearly two centuries, lobstermen realized their dependence on this resource was tenuous, not just because of the dangers on the water or in handling gear. Those are givens in the business. Rather, their livelihood was tenuous because its foundation—ever-renewing lobsters—could not be taken for granted. This knowledge was, I surmise, as much a part of their historical sense and the human capital they brought to the fishing grounds as any other detail of fishing—tending traps, watching the weather, selling catch.

With the possibility of depletion a long-standing and integral part of Maine lob-stermen's knowledge base, it is no surprise that people experimented to prevent depletion. In fact, a gleaning of Maine Sea and Seashore Commission files from the mid-twentieth century suggests that a primary means of dealing with the threat of depletion for government and dealers was to "enhance" the resource, to build hatch-eries and "develop markets." But the fishermen themselves did their share of exper-imenting and it is this part of the coevolution of the lobster fishery and of lobster fishing practices that the Monhegan case best illustrates. Closed seasons, trap limits, and limited access exemplify one harbor's attempts to ensure a steady livelihood, for themselves and for their descendants (see map 7.1).

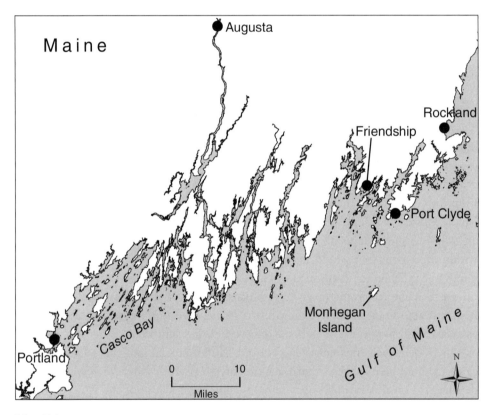

Map 7.1
Midcoast Maine.

Closed: Back in Six Months

Of all the measures taken by Monhegan lobster fishers to protect their resource, none is as significant as the closed season. Put into law in 1907, the practice probably dates to the 1890s, maybe much earlier. An 1899 report of the U.S. Commission of Fish and Fisheries indicated that Monhegan lobstering took place from about January 1 to about May 15 and that that season was rigidly self-enforced.[9] Although the start and close dates have varied over the years, the closed season on Monhegan has always been for roughly six months out of the year, beginning the end of June when lobsters begin to molt, or "shed," and mate, and then finishing the end of December. This means that not only are the lobsters given a reprieve from fishing pressure during their critical growth and reproductive stages but, for the lobster fishers, much of the fishing occurs during some of the coldest and roughest times of the year, from January through June, when blizzards and gale-force winds are not uncommon. The hardships of winter fishing are offset, however, by the fact that the lobsters are hard-shelled and abundant, especially around Monhegan Island, where resident lobsters, many believe, are joined by inshore lobsters migrating offshore during the cold weather.

The origins of the closed time may have started with the simple and unavoidable practices of lobstering itself. At some time, fishermen need to take their traps out of the water to dry and kill the woodworm that destroys the traditional traps made of oak or spruce and the barnacles and other sedentary organisms that clog all traps, wood or wire. Lobster catchers also need to occasionally take out their boats for painting and repairs. "When I was a youngster," one dealer recalled in 1945, "the lobstermen took their traps in to dry in the summer, took time off to paint their boats, and acted as though they had time to help their neighbor."[10] But times were changing.

Since each harbor's lobster catchers mostly shared the same bottom and everyone had to tend traps at some point, it would make sense either to stagger the maintenance and repair time among the lobster fishers or to do it all at the same time. Either way, it would be critical that no fisher would gain an advantage while others were performing necessary operations on equipment. In some harbors, staggering maintenance might have made sense, especially if competition locally or with other harbors was not high. In other cases, weather conditions might have been compelling enough reason to sit out a period at the same time. Summer is the best time for drying, painting, and repair work. The biology and economics of the lobster would also weigh on the side of a summer closed time. When lobsters shed and mate in the summer, they tend to hide in the muddy bottom, among beds of kelp grass, or under ledges, making them difficult to lure into traps. When the lobsters are caught, dealers and others consider them inferior because their new shells make them easily damaged. If weather and biology would sway a harbor of lobster fishers to fish hard in the spring and fall and take a break in the summer, others might actually choose the winter for fishing when the supply of lobsters to markets is lowest and thus the price the highest. Waiting until the lobsters harden and fill out their shell with greater quantities of meat and selling when prices are up would make sense if others in the harbor would agree. Evidently, Monheganers could make such an agreement among themselves when mainland harbor groups could not. The difference may be the greater competition between neighboring harbors on the mainland and the threat of encroachment should bottom be left unfished. Islanders, being more isolated, were insulated from such pressures, especially a century ago. Monhegan lobster catchers apparently realized this cycling of fishing effort and price early in the development of the midcoast fishery and capitalized on it by fishing when others were ashore repairing traps and staying warm, and, not insignificantly, when the price of lobsters was rising.

From an ecological perspective, the closed season allows the lobsters to molt, grow, and reproduce. Today, conservation biologists routinely prescribe closed zones or closed periods to ensure the survival of critical species. Spatially, *respite* from harvesting pressure can be achieved with protected reserves amidst harvested regions. Temporally, it can be achieved though closed seasons, especially seasons that correspond to periods of reproduction. The fact that Monhegan's closed season fits this relatively modern prescription of ecologists is probably fortuitous. And yet anthropologists and historians have shown that humans across cultures have long recognized the value of avoiding harvests during reproductive periods of prey and gathered plants. It is not hard to imagine that, even if the economic rationale for a closed season was paramount for the early Monheganers, the biological rationale contributed to their decision. Intuitively, those who depend directly on natural resources know not to eat the seed corn and not to harm the brood stock. "We give 'em the other half a year to grow," said one Monhegan fisher. "You don't see farmers killing all their chicks. You might say lobsters are our chicks."[11] Thus the sources of knowledge may have been different—modern science versus traditional practice— but the outcomes similar. In this management regime, respite was an implicit principle.

Once the Monhegan lobster fishers instituted a closed season and then procured reinforcement with state legislation in 1907, the biological and economic success of a closed season became clear. Monhegan lobster fishers enjoyed successive years of substantial harvests, largely avoiding drastic swings in catch. They may not have had the huge bounties of some regions, but then they did not suffer the crashes typical of those fisheries either. As the evidence for success mounted, the biological justification for closed seasons has become prominent among lobster catchers and observers. As we will soon see, at the end of the twentieth century, Monhegan's closed season and its conservationist effects became a prime justification for reserving Monhegan waters for Monhegan fishers. Legal scholars among others could argue that this apparent "restraint on trade" in the form of limited access among Maine lobster fishers could be justified on the basis of resource conservation, even of making "efficient" use of the resource. And fishers didn't have to worry about losing their fishing rights by not using the resource. Usufruct in common law held—and, in many situations, still holds in the United States—that if a person does not use a designated resource, the right to that resource reverts to the state or to those who do use the resource. A fallow is antithetical to conventional resource practice as promoted by governments worldwide. Not to use a resource is deemed a waste of that resource, an inefficiency. It is to the credit of those who sought closed times on islands like Monhegan and to those who have supported them over the ensuing decades, that long-term resource practice could flourish when respite was instituted. As with any apparent inefficiency, these proponents no doubt were challenged. In 1938, for example, Monhegan "municipal officers" (not necessarily representing fishermen) petitioned the state Commissioner of Sea and Seashore Fisheries to shorten the closed season by two months. In 1943, a Monhegan hotel owner proposed a year-round lobstering season, arguing that summer residents would be better served and that elderly lobster catchers would be better able to earn a living. Both efforts failed, but they suggest the pressure proponents of respite experienced.[12]

Unlike governmental measures pushed by lobster fishers and dealers up and down the coast to protect their interests, Monhegan's 1907 law was not enforcement of quotas or gear types or any other "infringement" on the resident fishers' business. And it was not legal exclusion of non-Monheganers. Legally, any Mainer with a lobstering license could still fish in Monhegan waters. Rather, although the documentation is skimpy, the primary purpose of the 1907 law appears to be external sanction, a formal means of allowing resident fishermen to *impose on themselves* a highly restrictive harvesting practice, a legal sanction, in other words, to exercise restraint.

These are the functional arguments for a closed season. They establish the rationale for current practices and hence create a part of these fishers' ecological rationality. Historical arguments complete the picture, though, adding a sense of the strategic and managerial. Respite acquires meaning, then, not just as "time off," a "break," but as a deliberate means of meeting critical life-supporting objectives, one of which is long-term resource use.

Every lobster fisher may agree that some kind of closed period makes sense for lobster fisher and resource alike, whether several months out of the year or a string of weekends. Coordinating the downtime is the problem. It is easy to appeal to the fisheries chief, but with limited patrol capacity and numerous lobster catchers scattered throughout the state's inlets and islands, setting and pulling traps every day, a state-enforced close time was nearly impossible. In fact the industry was moving in the opposite direction. What had traditionally been an eight-month season for many fishers was, by the turn of the century, giving way to year-round lobstering.[13] Not everyone liked the trend, though. Mainers are famously independent and self-reliant, the quintessential self-directed, pluralist workers: "The [early] inhabitants of coastal Maine farmed and gardened, hunted, fished for halibut and cod, collected oysters and crabs, dug clams, cut trees for lumber and fuel," writes a contemporary observer of those times. They "went lobstering mainly in the spring and fall, usually tending no more than a few dozen traps near shore in rowboats or small sailing craft. They made their own gear. They didn't owe anybody anything."[14] Only when fishing pressure increased, when fishers *did* owe something to the local bank or a loan shark or when they simply wanted to make more money, only then did lobster fishers begin to specialize and, eventually, fish year-round.

For some reason, Monheganers bucked the trend. And so here, at a scale smaller than the state, a closed season was possible. Here, lobster fishers who otherwise coordinated the use of an identifiable and defensible piece of ocean bottom among themselves would only have to go one step further and agree to refrain from fishing for a period of time. The historical record, as noted, is inadequate for assessing the actual conditions and decisions. But it appears that the Monheganers themselves imposed some kind of close period well before they went to Augusta in 1907, probably as a hedge against the trend toward year-round fishing. Being relatively isolated fifteen miles off the coast, they may have been able to hold on to their pluralist working rhythms and, hence, seasonal lobstering a bit longer than their mainland counterparts. And once the pressures reached their tiny rock in the sea, they may have been able to experiment incrementally with a designated closed season, beginning with a few days or weeks and expanding to months. In so doing, they would have been able to resist the mainland trends and simultaneously experience the advantages of a closed time for themselves, for their gear, and, quite possibly, for the fishery. The fact that in the same year that the Maine legislature passed Monhegan's six-month closed season it conferred similar protection on a half dozen other communities suggests that Monheganers' self-limitation was not an aberration.[15]

Many fishing communities were looking for ways to avoid the boom and bust of frontier exploitation and the intensification of fishing practice. They wanted a secure income year after year even if that meant forsaking the bonanzas they could find moving from place to place, fishing year-round. Six months of fishing, it seems, was sufficient. Respite—six months away from fishing, working at other things—was a rational strategy for long-term economic security. The lobster fishers, through seasonal closure, were simply moving one step away from frontier exploitation and economic intensification, moving toward a congruence of economic and social needs, on the one hand, and limited capacity of the resource on the other. They were shifting from short-term revenue maximization to long-term economic security and, in so doing, limiting their predation on a bottom feeder. But respite required boundaries, too. Just as Pacific Lumber managers accepted the finiteness of redwoods, these fishers would fish only from a given piece of bottom, only in a territory, a delineated zone of water. If they overfished that territory one year, they paid the price the next; there was no moving on.

Limited harvest in a defended zone, then, meant that lobster fishers would forgo the boom harvest but increase the chance of a steady or, at least, a dependable harvest, enough for a living. "Enough," or sufficiency, was not maximum sustained yield, which was to become so popular among economically oriented fisheries managers later in the twentieth century. Fishermen could not estimate with precision the number of lobsters supportable by their territory. In fact, any observant fisherman with some years of experience knew that, with the multitude of factors impinging on this line of work—weather, oceanic circulation, markets, competitors, predation, disease, biological growth, and reproduction—no one could estimate in any meaningful way an upper bound on lobster take. No one could confidently push fishing efforts up against that bound and expect to maximize return on investment year after year. Since roughly the middle of the nineteenth century, sufficiency for lobster fishers meant that boom times on the lobstering grounds were over. Enough was what one could harvest reliably and make a living from, year after year. It was more than the piddly catches lobstermen were taking out of unregulated, depleted regions to the south. But it was considerably less than what early European lobster catchers found when they first arrived on these near-virgin waters. Now enough was what could be caught given the technology, the demand, and, not least, the costs of maintaining the self-constructed territorial management regime.

Wire Traps, Social Traps

The closed season, once instituted on Monhegan, has been remarkably durable. The lobster catchers have changed the actual start and close dates over the years, but the rhythm of six-months-on, six-months-off has been stable. Of course, as with any dynamic resource-exploitation regime subject to internal and external forces, this was not always enough to ensure a livelihood. Fishing pressure, expressed as a combination of numbers of fishers and of numbers and quality of gear, could still build beyond a biologically sustainable level in a closed season. Limiting fishers legally was always out of the question. Maine waters have always been open to all licensed Maine fishers and federal waters to all federally licensed fishers. And beyond a nation's territorial boundaries, the high seas have always been open to everyone. No upstart bunch of lobster catchers on a tiny rock in the Atlantic, or anywhere else for that matter, was going to upset that age-old tradition. Thus, unlimited entry of individuals into a fishery has always been held sacrosanct, a tenet of efficient resource exploitation to ensure both livelihood for citizens and revenue for the state. Unlimited use of equipment, however, is a different matter. Certain kinds of equipment and some levels of use confer unfair competitive advantages on some fishers while excluding or leaving behind others. Electronic devices such as sounders, which display the ocean floor in different colors for rock, sand, and mud, and plotters which pinpoint one's location, enhance a lobster fisher's search for prime bottom, but they are expensive. And occasionally equipment is associated with depletion. Restrictions, even for the archetypal fisherman, the fiercely independent Mainer, are acceptable if applied uniformly.

For lobstering, the critical equipment are boats and traps. Boats are mostly immune to restriction, because they are innately limited by what can be handled in shallow, wave-swept, near-shore waters. The biggest technological change was from sail to gasoline and now diesel power, though boats have remained largely the same ever since. (However, many are faster and have greater ranges, an issue that forced the state to consider a formal, limited-access regime for Monhegan, as we will soon see.) But traps or, more generally, lobster-catching devices—including gaffs, nets, and trawls—can expand indefinitely in type and number. The state of Maine long ago banned all but the trap for lobstering. One reason given in recent years is that traps do little harm to the bottom, unlike bottom-scouring trawlers. Numbers of traps, however, have been a different, and much more contentious, issue (see figure 7.1).

The problem of an increasing total number of traps in the water and of increasing numbers on a per–lobster fisher basis was recognized at least as far back as the

Figure 7.1
Lobster traps drying. For six months a year, while nearly all other lobster catchers are busy setting traps, Monheganers have their traps on land.

1880s. The impetus for increasing the number of traps was "competition, rivalry, and the supposed decrease in abundance of lobsters," wrote Goode in his 1887 report.[16] One observer from Boston, possibly a dealer, put the problem this way in a speech to the American Fish-Cultural Association more than a century ago:

In looking for a reasonable solution to this problem [of supply not meeting demand], an inquiry concerning the means taken to provide the supply now, as compared with those taken in former years, might properly be prefaced by a statement of the fact that not as many lobsters are consumed now as formerly. A few years ago fifty or sixty traps per man were considered a good number, while at the present time from seventy-five to ninety are used, and even with this addition it requires twice the number of men to catch the same amount of lobsters. These facts seem to show the danger of depletion in our efforts to keep up the supply, even if size and quality are disregarded.[17]

If the danger was widely recognized, little if anything was done about trap numbers for nearly a century. Only in the 1960s did statewide limits appear to have the support of the industry. By this time, lobster fishers were setting more than 250 traps each, some 300 to 400 traps, and tending them with high-powered boats and hydraulic haulers. Some of the large operators, known derisively as "hogs" or more respectfully as "highliners," were, especially in the crowded Casco Bay region around Portland, running from 1,000 to 2,500 traps.[18] In 1964 Maine fishers set out an estimated 1 million traps, quadruple the number in 1952. By the end of the century they were tending some 2.6 million.[19]

The fishing community on Swan Island "downeast" of Monhegan felt that a proposed legislated limit of 275 traps per fisher would be a good thing because, among other things, it would help lobster fishers avoid overworking themselves. "We are all excited about the 275 trap bill and really hope it will pass," wrote one longtime fisherman in 1965, adding that

We had a meeting and voted with 38 present. The votes was 37 yes and 1 no. Most fishermen can see that we have been overdoing the whole thing. I have talked with many fishermen and they are getting tired of working themselves to death. That's what it amounts to. I believe in two years or less we will be catching the same amount of lobsters. The law if passed will be hard to enforce. But with a stiff penalty of a year without license and a fine one would think it over before trying to pull anything. And with the help of every fisherman I think we all can start living again.[20]

"Living" presumably would be running enough traps to "earn a living," to work the bottom effectively, but not so much as to "work oneself to death," to constantly chase after more and more lobsters, setting more and more traps. A sufficient number of traps for this lobster fisher at this time with his equipment was about 275 traps per boat. Unfortunately statewide enforcement was indeed a problem then and continues to be to this day.

But others have felt that a lack of professionalism and greed were the real issues. This was a theme Monhegan fishermen, old-timers and young captains alike, expressed often in interviews. Being professional, or as many put it, being a "real fisherman," meant that a lobster fisher going for a big haul did not crowd out others. He did not place his traps near or, as they put it, right *on top* of others' traps. Hard work was respected, but not aggressive methods that hurt others. Lobster fishers who accumulated large numbers of traps were "hogging" the bottom. A lobster fisher with excess traps could not possibly tend all those traps effectively. He could "cover a lot of bottom" and prevent others from using that bottom, but he couldn't haul them frequently enough to prevent cannibalism among the lobsters, let alone return undersized and oversized lobsters and other creatures safely to the water. And covering the bottom forced everyone to spend time untangling gear. Hogging the bottom was thus not professional. It was an unduly competitive practice that generates animosity and can lead to trap wars, which is destructive for everyone but the trap manufacturers. In one incident in 1962, resentful lobster fishers cut about a thousand traps in Casco Bay. "Somebody felt that these big operators were hogging too much of the lobster bottom of the area," said one fisherman. A week later some 200 traps were cut in nearby South Freeport.[21]

According to a seventh-generation Monhegan lobsterman with more than forty years fishing experience, through the 1960s and 1970s the problems of hogging were building on Monhegan as well. One lobster fisher was pushing 1,000 traps. And everyone knew what was happening elsewhere along the coast, where crowding and blanketing the bottom with traps were leading to the cutting and destroying of traps and, occasionally, violence. Not waiting for the state to set a limit, the Monheganers met in the fishhouse, a large, nondescript structure at the waterfront where gear is repaired. There, in 1975, they eventually agreed to a 600-trap limit, the first community in Maine to do so. The seventh-generation veteran had been setting some 800 traps himself at the time but saw the problems coming and supported the local, collectively imposed limit. He emphasized that, as it turned out, he lost no income cutting back to 600 traps. Now, few Monheganers fish more than 500 traps. For them, it just is not worth the effort on the water—it is not real fishing, nor is it "living." And the possibility of being branded a hog is not worth the strains it creates within the local fishing community (see figure 7.2).

Elsewhere, though, hogging was becoming the norm, and the industry as a whole, along with the resource, suffered. A mainland Boothbay Harbor fisherman described the situation this way in 1965:

I have been a commercial lobsterman for 55 years. I have raised four children. I own my own home. I have had lots of sickness but I owe no one and I have never had to have more than 250 traps.

The one thing that ails the lobster business today is greediness. We have in this region close to 200 fishermen and about 20 of them are monopolizing the bottom. Some of them have 800 traps and with the help of a hired hand it takes them two to three days to haul that amount. They are in such a hurry they have no respect for the other fellows' gear and dump their[s] right back on top of him and when they haul again they cut his warps [ropes]. I had one warp last summer with eight knots in it. Some times I'd think I was on the third tier down. If we had a limited number of traps there would be a little more elbow room and we all would have an equal chance.[22]

Hogs in a hurry make big bucks in the short term, but they bring everyone down over the long term. From this view, trap limits are eminently sensible. For others, so-called hogging is really just honest hard work. The proposed legislation to limit traps to 250 "would be unconstitutional insofar as it would limit the free enterprise of a small businessman and is the opposite basis of our democratic society," wrote one lobster catcher in 1965. He added:

Figure 7.2
Fishhouse, Monhegan Island. The fishhouse is the center of equipment-maintenance activity as well as collective decision making among boat captains.

It has taken me six years to build my lobster business to its present point and this legislation would make the past six years of hardship all for nothing. I could not support my wife and three pre-school age sons on the income derived from 250 traps. . . . Hard work and industriousness should be rewarded and not legislated against. We lobstermen have had a hard time finding the lobsters this year but, again, hard work paid off and I came out ahead. . . . I do not believe that the cutting down of my string of traps to 250 would make any significant difference in the overall catch of the other lobstermen.[23]

It wouldn't make any difference in catch because he works hard and others do not. Those who work hard should earn their just rewards. They are, after all, merely exercising their constitutional right of access to a public resource.

The problem of increasing traps arose in part because every harbor, it seemed, had at least one such hard worker, one ambitious lobster fisher who simply enjoyed the hard work (and the extra income) or needed to pay bills. One need not impugn such fishers with greed or monopoly power or a selfish disregard for others to understand the phenomenon. It arguably occurs in all occupations where a few have the inclination and skills to get ahead. Rather, the problem here, as elsewhere, stems from the difficulties of collective action and escalation within a group. As a collective-action problem, at some point in the self-development of a fishery by a harbor of fishers, it makes sense for a given lobster fisher to set one additional trap. The cost of doing so in equipment and time is negligible, but the benefit in catch can be significant. After all, that one extra trap may end up on a rich spot that yields above-average hauls. But even average hauls may be worth the extra trap. If the increase in one fisher's traps stopped there, one can imagine little problem for anyone. But if that one additional trap made sense, then yet another trap would make sense, too. And so it goes. But not only for the one lobster fisher. Others would get wind of the benefits of additional traps and would increase theirs. What starts as an individually rational, incremental increase in gear becomes a collectively irrational increase in overall fishing effort. Escalation becomes the name of the game. Crowding, gear entanglement, and conflict follow.

Such a collective-action problem can partly explain how, once trap limits were introduced, cutting back on trap numbers did not hurt most lobster fishers. By increasing traps, the lobster fishers were neither catching more lobsters nor making more money. In fact, at some point in the escalation, they would have been increasing their costs of operation with little additional benefits. Escalation among users sharing a common resource is a social trap. They all recognize the problem and the essential irrationality of it all, but they cannot get out—unless, of course, they can all agree on a limit. At the scale of statewide lobstering, that has been impossible until very late in the game when enough political support could be garnered for the state to impose a 1,200-trap limit. This limit was set so high that many lobstermen seem to dismiss it as meaningless except for extreme cases of hogging. Even then enforcement remains a problem. At a smaller scale, however, a scale where interested parties, especially direct users, can sit down face to face, work out a limit for themselves, and then be confident that self-monitoring and self-enforcement within the group are feasible, agreement is likely. This is what happened on Monhegan in the fishhouse in the 1970s. And it has stood up for some three decades.

For the Monhegan lobster fishers to impose a 600-trap limit on themselves is a form of restraint. It is restraint in the sense of escape: escape from their own potential entrapment in an irrational game of gear escalation. The collective agreement capped each individual's possibility of ever-increasing material gain—lobsters and revenues—and did so in exchange for the nonmaterial benefit of knowing one did not have to play that game, of knowing that hogs in a hurry would not be the norm, that overharvesting would be unlikely. This is the difference between "real fishing" and "hogging."

Real fishing, that veteran, seventh-generation Monhegan lobsterman explained in an interview, is best illustrated by the change in fishing practice after the season first opens. Initially, when all the boats go out on "Trap Day," usually January 1, the catches are large. The lobsters have had a six-month reprieve, they have grown into their new hard shells, and they are hungry. Anyone can fill a lobster car in no time by just getting the traps in the water and hauling. This is probably akin to what the early European settlers found when they arrived: an abundant frontier resource just waiting to be exploited. Fishing was more like gathering in virgin territory. It took little skill, just some effort. But, then, on Monhegan, after a few weeks of such bonanzas, the catches diminish. This, explains the veteran lobsterman with emphasis, is when the *real fishing* begins. This is when knowledge of bottom conditions is crucial, as well as the lobsters' movement patterns, the currents and temperatures, and a host of other factors. A longtime lobster fisher picks up signals from the flow of water, from patterns of catches along a string of traps. "It's something you have a feeling for," a veteran lobsterman from another harbor says. "When you start hauling in the spring, where you set your traps, when you move 'em, where you move 'em—you have to know your bottom and what's going on down there."[24] It is knowing without seeing, knowing by doing—and doing and doing and learning from those who have been doing it a long time. One does not acquire such knowledge overnight, let alone from formal instruction or books. It is acquired from years, even decades of being on the water, living and making a living from fishing and from the know-how passed down from one generation to the next. It is acquired by paying close attention, which a person in a hurry is unlikely to do.

"Hogs" typify people in a hurry. They set the most traps possible and cover the most ocean bottom possible as a means of maximizing catch. Part of hogging is just plain hard work, hauling traps and delivering to dealers as fast as boat and equipment allow. But part of it is gaining control over other lobster fishers and their use of traps and bottom. It is, in effect, a reversion to frontier resource exploitation. In its time, it probably made sense for the individual as well as for the development of the larger community. Day-to-day survival and rapid growth in industry were the orders of the day. But today it is a short-term harvesting strategy. Hogs are well known for treating the business as a get-rich-quick scheme. They may work extremely hard but their plan is to move on to something else, even early retirement, once they have built their nest egg. "They act like crazymen over a few lobsters and a few dollars," one longtime lobster fisher wrote around 1945. "These very men to whom I refer, fish in the harbor and rivers for lobsters in the early shedding season. They paint their boats while afloat or tide work and then they are on the move."[25] Hogs seem to be most prevalent when prices are high and where the resource is abundant or where, through intimidation, they can corner much of the bottom and the market for themselves and their followers.

From a long-term sustainability perspective, what is significant about hogging is that there is never enough. One can always put out more traps, if not to catch more lobsters, to at least secure more bottom for oneself and to increase the chances of coming upon that bonanza haul. A fixed work day doesn't limit the number of traps, only the tending of traps. More traps are always better. And if for some reason 1,000 or 1,500 or 2,000 traps are overtaxing, the hog can effectively expand by bringing other lobster catchers under his control. This pattern of hogging is well documented.[26] For hogs, social capital is built only to expand and maintain one's hold on the frontier resource. It is not to ensure continuity over the generations, let alone to build the larger community on which lobster catchers depend (see below). It is going for the bonanza now and leaving the regulating, and the future, to others.

"Real fishing," by contrast, unavoidably asks how much is enough, how many traps one can tend properly, how many hours one can safely spend on the water. For the veteran lobster fisher on Monhegan who was pushing 800 traps, it seems to have been more like 600. That was enough to make a decent income (roughly the same income, after an adjustment period, he emphasized). Another Monhegan lobsterman, a much younger captain, found after more than a dozen years of fishing that 500 to 550 traps is just right, below Monhegan's collectively imposed limit of

600. His explanation is that, to do it right, to really *fish*, to tend the traps in a manner that respects both the resource and his fellow lobster catchers, he couldn't handle any more. His choice of tending fewer traps than what is possible exemplifies *restrained resource use at the individual level.* Restraint here is a matter of calculated self-interest, to be sure. But it is also restraint as a matter of collective choice to limit harvesting, to deter hogging. And it is restraint as a matter of work, of a particular, culturally mediated conception of what real fishing is, of being professional. This "working rationality" is fishing with purpose, a purpose that extends beyond short-term, maximum gain for oneself to the larger group, to his competitors and his community, and to the resource. The younger fisherman was quick to point out in an interview that his conception of "real fishing" came from his mentors, the old-timers for whom he served as sternman and apprentice and who continue to advise him (solicited or not). When he began his own operation as captain, they not only passed boats and gear to him (often at a deep discount or even free), but passed on the principles of operating as a fishing community on a tiny island with a mostly fixed amount of lobster bottom. Key among those principles is the idea, however expressed, that, yes, there can be too many traps individually and collectively, too much pressure on the resource, too much risk to people's health and future livelihood as well as to the community as a whole. In this study, I call that idea sufficiency.[27]

The issue of trap limits thus signifies the opportunity, indeed the necessity, of resource users translating biophysical limits into daily practice. Whether people call it "real fishing" or "working rationality" or "sufficiency," the practices and principles of this lobstering case suggest that the likelihood of success is greatest where the users themselves devise the means of translation. It is here where experiential knowledge and mentoring constitute the critical social capital necessary for interacting with the natural capital. The dynamics of the two forms of capital are highly complex, as are the systems from which they derive. The inherently limited predictability of the two (Who is next to be the "hog"? When will the ocean currents shift?) renders mechanistic forms of regulation such as maximum sustained yield and total allowable catch highly problematic. Translation of external regulation into user practice is subject to such tremendous variability, not the least of which is the strategic gaming people engage in when external authorities issue edicts and offer rewards and punishments. Self-imposed and self-enforced methods where restraint (e.g., trap limits) and respite (e.g., seasonal limits) are built in, have a greater chance of tempering individual's striving for more, of converting hogging to real fishing so as to ensure enough, enough for now and for the future.

Crustaceans and People: Communities with Limits

Trap limits can arguably be seen as strictly a fishing issue. Only the lobster catchers enter the fishhouse and only they can collectively agree on gear limits, while members of the larger community—families, store owners, public servants—are removed. The effect on the nonfishing members of limiting traps is minimal and indirect. By contrast, the seasonal limit has a significant impact on the functioning of the island's larger fishing and residential communities, imposing a biennial rhythm on everyone's work and daily life. The historical record is too scant, however, to assess this community impact. But the "limited-access" regime formalized in 1998 legislation, we will see, is recent and can be provisionally assessed for impact beyond the resource and the direct users. Its significance locally is succinctly captured in statements made repeatedly by Monheganers in interviews regarding the threat of outsiders, in this case, the Friendship Five, fishing Monhegan waters. This is not a fishing issue, they told me. It's a community issue. A few additional lobster catchers, especially ones from outside the fishing and residential community of the island, jeopardize the viability of Monhegan as a self-sustaining, year-round, permanent community. The significance of limited access thus goes beyond Monhegan or even Maine lobstering to suggest that *residential rights and responsibilities* to fisheries are a necessary condition for sustainable practice. Owner operators directly dependent on a local resource are more likely to restrain their use and institute respite—individually and collectively—than highly specialized, highly mobile operators, "hogs," those whose signature mode is fish out and get out, leave the regulating to others. Lobster catchers from nearby Matinicus Island know residential rights and responsibilities, too. "By tradition you must own a home here in order to fish," they wrote the fisheries commissioner in 1997. "You won't find that rule in any book of law but it is just as binding and it maintains order and the survival of lobstering in this area." Without residency, "Matinicus will not survive as a year-round community."[28]

Thus, the third major development on Monhegan in the evolution of self-limiting behavior is limited access with residential ownership. It extends the scale from the immediate, direct users, the lobster fishers, to the larger social network of relations in which ocean habitat and lobster fishers are embedded.

That day in November 1995 when Monheganers spotted five boats just outside the island's legally designated two-mile boundary was a wake-up call. The Monhegan lobster season was closed, but now what had always been "their bottom" was being fished by non-Monheganers. The Friendship Five came legally, with licenses, but they knew as well as anyone that, license or no license, on bottom traditionally held as territory by lobster catchers from a local harbor, they were throwing down the proverbial gauntlet. They were challenging Monheganers and state officials alike to decide whether such self-limitation and, as the Friendship fishers saw it, such exclusion, would persist.

The three-mile arc to the south of the island where the Friendship fishermen had placed some of their traps was, like all state water, technically open year round but, also like much of state lobstering grounds, restricted by tradition. Monheganers had traditionally fished to the south two miles out in accordance with the 1907 law, but also three miles out in state waters and, from there, ten miles or more out into federal waters. A lone boat from another harbor would occasionally set traps there but soon find their line tied or gear missing. The furthest reaches of the area may have been fuzzy, but few lobster catchers ventured that far from the mainland anyway. Mainlanders may fish around the north side of the island up to the two-mile line, but rarely would they steam the extra miles to get to the south side. The Monhegan lobster fishers applied the closed season to their entire, regularly fished region, not just the two-mile zone designated in the 1907 law. They defended the entire area year-round as "Monhegan bottom," regardless of political jurisdiction. For decades this practice had worked, defending Monhegan bottom for Monhegan lobster fishers who lived on Monhegan. The Friendship Five's incursion was yet another instance of ever-increasing fishing pressure throughout the Maine lobster fishery, exacerbated in part by changes in boat technology.

Until roughly the 1980s, nearly all lobster boats were fairly small as oceangoing boats go, generally no bigger than thirty or thirty-five feet. Constructed of wood and powered by gasoline, they could sail at only about ten knots. They were well suited to near-shore fishing, able to maneuver around rocky outcroppings and reefs. But in rough seas they would be thrashed about by the waves, making it impossible to handle traps. This drawback actually gave Monhegan lobster fishers an advantage over mainland fishers. When lobsters migrated offshore and into deeper waters in the late fall and winter, they would congregate around areas like Monhegan, tempting lobster catchers throughout the region to set traps out there and hope for calm water. But rough seas were less of a problem for Monhegan lobster fishers since the harbor was always close at hand should a storm come up. And the harbor was only big enough for the safe moorage of some dozen or so boats. In a storm, mainlanders would thus have a long, dangerous trip home.

Recently, however, the islander advantage has mostly disappeared. Large fiber-glass boats have become popular among many mainland lobster fishers. At forty feet in length or more and diesel powered, they can steam at twenty-five knots and handle well in all but the roughest seas. One result is that when harvests decline in late fall near the mainland harbors, lobster fishers can indeed follow the lobsters out to deeper waters. In some places such fishing presents little problem, because the area is large and the number of fishers who actually go far offshore is still small. But around Monhegan it was a problem. During the closed season, many of the lobsters caught by traveling mainlanders would not be available at all to Monhegan lobster fishers once the Monhegan season opened. Lobsters do not move about much in the winter. And during Monhegan's open season, lobster fishers' movements would quickly lead to a competitive race to see who could catch the most lobsters from what is essentially a fixed number on the Monhegan bottom at a given time. As it turned out, after a year of steady fishing past the two-mile boundary by Friendship fishermen, that bottom was fished out.

The Friendship move into Monhegan water was unprecedented for its boldness. This was not a matter of one lobsterman setting a couple of traps a few feet into another's territory to test the boundaries or, more commonly, to sneak a few big hauls. In recent years with advanced sounding devices, a mainlander would set a legal trap with a buoy just outside the Monhegan line then extend a trawl line of ten or more traps without buoys—and thus invisible to passing patrol boats and Monhegan lobster catchers—into Monhegan water. At night they could pinpoint the traps with their location devices and use a grappling iron to snag the float line and haul in the unmarked traps. If they were caught, the marine patrol would fine them severely. If the warden just found the traps and could not prove who had set them, they would confiscate the traps, declare them state property, and sell them at auction. The risk was often worth it, it seemed, because every year the marine patrol would catch hundreds of illegal traps in Monhegan waters. Pulling in a line of such traps reveals the reason mainlanders went to such lengths and took such risks. The first trap, on or outside the line, would typically have just one or two lobsters in it. The traps just inside the line might have four or five lobsters each. Those well into Monhegan waters would have ten or twelve lobsters in each trap. The difference between heavily fished bottom with traps littered as far as the eye can see, on the one hand, and Monhegan bottom, on the other, was stark, as were the profits. It is little wonder some would try other means of getting access to Monhegan water.

But Friendship's move was different. It was widely seen as a flagrant, coordinated attempt to capture a significant piece of rich lobster bottom, a direct challenge to an entire harbor's exclusive use of bottom, of territory that had been successfully defended for as long as anyone could remember. It was a planned, highly visible effort by five fishermen to fish and fish hard for an extended period of time. The full extent of the threat to Monhegan fishing did not become apparent, however, for nearly a year.

For several days that November in 1995, the Monhegan fishers stayed in their harbor, watching the Friendship fishermen haul lobsters off "their bottom." Although well-known for aggressively defending their traditional territory, the Monhegan fishers may have been deterred by the fact that two of them were, at the time, defending themselves in court on charges of violating others' traps. (They were later found not guilty.) When those Monhegan fishermen did go out and one yelled, "Things can get dangerous out here," the threat was clear.

Throughout Maine, "lobster wars" had broken out periodically, especially in crowded areas to the southwest near Portland. Many of the traditional territories centering on mainland harbors were breaking down from the ever-increasing fishing pressure of more fishers and more traps.[29] But some of the perimeter-defended territories around islands appeared to have escaped such developments, at least until faster boats and the unintended effects of new regulations made them, too, vulnerable. Monhegan, despite its long tradition of tight self-management and territorial defense, could not be immune forever. Many inside and outside the Monhegan community felt that the Friendship move meant that Monhegan was next in line, a premonition buttressed by the fact that the Friendship move was carefully planned, highly visible, and entirely legal.

Confrontations between mainland and Monhegan lobster fishers had been going on for years, but they had never escalated to the point of an outright "trap war," nor had they involved state authorities in anything but routine marine patrols and occasional seizure of traps. In December, state marine officials, fearing an escalation and a trap war, proposed a temporary solution. They asked that Monhegan fishers have exclusive use zero to two miles from the island, share with the Friendship fishermen the two- to three-mile arc at the southern end of the island, and then, because everything outside three miles was federal water, both groups would fish further out as they pleased. The two sides accepted this "gentlemen's agreement" and tensions lowered. But even after Monheganers commenced fishing, state officials heard reports that both sides were cutting traps. The "hate and discontent," as fish wardens referred to it, continued until the Friendship fishers finally withdrew in March 1996 due to low catches.

That 1996 January-to-June lobstering season on Monhegan was like no other in the island's or, for that matter, the state's lobstering history. Economically, the outsiders' hauling was a threat to Monheganers because they were competing for what is mostly a fixed pool of legal lobsters. Socially, the "Friendship incursion" was a threat because, as the Monheganers saw it, five more boats was roughly a 50 percent increase in fishing pressure on Monhegan bottom. That bottom had, for a century, shown itself capable of supporting a dozen or so fishermen, all of whom lived on the island, fished out of the one harbor, met at the fishhouse, and worked out differences among themselves with measures such as the closed season, trap limits, and, we will see, apprenticeships for newcomers. A 50 percent increase in fishing pressure from individuals who, at best, were only accountable to their own mainland communities and to state authorities, was seen by Monheganers as a threat to the quantity and the quality of their accustomed catch. It was also a threat to the fishhouse rules they had worked out among themselves over so many years. As a result, Monheganers—lobster fishers, their families, store owners, the schoolteacher, and others—saw their very livelihood at stake. The issue was not just fishing competition, but a threat to their community and way of life, especially the year-round viability of the island (see figure 7.3). "The winter community and the fishing community are so interwoven that you cannot separate the two," said longtime resident Alice Boynton.

Without a healthy winter fishery, people would be forced to move inshore for work since you cannot commute from Monhegan Island. The fragile balance unravels, many holes are formed. Gaps are created as winter homes and residents are replaced with summer rentals and transients. We start to lose our fire department, town officials, school board. Jobs such as these do not interest summer residents. It doesn't take too many vacancies in a community of 70 or so to destroy the infrastructure. It is this destruction of the community which we see happening by opening up the fishing territory to everyone who wishes to use it. The delicate network unravels. We know the community will fall apart, we can only conjecture that the lobster population will follow—and for what reason? So the mess created inshore can spread to a carefully managed area. Ruining this community will not solve the inshore problems, it will just add to them.[30]

What is "community" in a place like Monhegan? Why was there such interdependency among residents and between fishing and other aspects of the economy? Everyone has a different answer. But few people know such communities as well as the owner of the general store, the focal point of daily life. Sally MacVane is one such person. She puts community this way:

My parents began going to Monhegan in the 1920's and in the 1960's built a summer home. As a result, my children spent their growing up years on the island. Today three of my four

Figure 7.3
Mainstreet, Monhegan Island.

children live year round on Monhegan. My two sons are lobstermen as is my son-in-law. I also have four grandchildren who have the good fortune to be growing up on the island. From 1979 to 1986 I lived on Monhegan year round as an owner of the general store. Like most small stores of this type in Maine we were, especially in the winter, the hub of the community. Our customers could "charge" year round and I was in a perfect position to see those balances go up and down. From the end of August until shortly after Trap Day in January we "carried" much of the fishing community financially.

Monhegan fishermen are not rolling in money or lobsters. Almost without exception the people who live on Monhegan must work in some capacity during the tourist season. From running a small business to changing beds at one of the inns or doing some carpentry or picking up trash—it is necessary to find some other work in order to make ends meet . . . and still they run out of money. Island living is also expensive and when times are hard they do not have the option to seek work elsewhere off of the island. And for women, unlike mainland living, there is zero opportunity to bring in that necessary second income.[31]

Community on Monhegan means that key members not only live on the island year round but are tied in some way to the fishing. The owner of a specialty store who came to Monhegan in the early 1970s surveyed residents in the late 1990s and found that all those who had ever fished out of the harbor had lived on the island, without exception. Men then living on the island but not lobstering had all "gone sternman"—that is, worked as an assistant to a boat captain. And a good many of the women had either been sternwomen or were active participants in lobstering—bagging bait, painting buoys, monitoring the CB (citizens-band) radio, carrying traps.[32] "Lobstering truly IS their life and their livelihood," says store owner MacVane. But

it is also the livelihood of the entire community. What it is like to live on Monhegan year round is difficult to explain. Perhaps only another island person can truly understand it. It is a community in the truest sense of the word. *It is insular.* This is not to say that it is "special"—but it is a different life—even different than Port Clyde where I now live, which is also a fishing village. Monhegan's short season makes for some pretty intense fishing. If you don't make it financially in January or February—there is a good chance that you *won't* make it before the season ends. It is for this reason that Monhegan set their own reduced trap limit, long before it became a popular concept in Maine. They knew they had to protect their resource. I might also add that from my own observation the number of Monhegan boats has rarely exceeded 12 or 13. And for good reason. More boats mean more traps and this means more lobsters will be taken.[33]

In short, the Friendship threat was serious, not just to the margin of a few lobster fishers' incomes, but to the very identity and livelihood of the year-round community. And everyone knew from the severity of the threat and the history of lobster wars in Maine that the situation would lead to trouble if someone didn't step in. That unenviable task fell to the Maine Department of Marine Resources, the DMR.

For many years, the primary role of the DMR was to promote the industry. A review of department files from the 1950s and 1960s (then called the Sea and Seashore Commission) shows that much of what DMR officials did was respond to requests from lobster fishers and dealers for assistance. The DMR would help them sell more lobsters and get better prices. To do this, the department conducted research, launched larval seeding programs, and explored myriad ways of promoting the product. In recent decades, however, the emphasis has changed from promotion to protection. This means protecting the lobster industry from the fate suffered by virtually all other fisheries in the area—collapse.

In general, the DMR's approach to protecting its fishing industries has been like that of other fishery agencies, state, federal, and, to the extent they exist, international. "Managing the fishery" has meant developing mathematical population models of recruitment and growth and prescribing limits on fishing pressure via "total allowable catch." Quotas are then assigned and sometimes traded like commodities. A game of counterstrategy follows whereby boat captains and fishing corporations intensify their fleets—bigger boats, more powerful engines, and more sophisticated equipment, all in the name of "efficient" harvesting. "With the help of new technology," one lobsterman wrote in the late twentieth century, "wire traps, lorans, big diesel engines, fiberglass [boats], and synthetic ropes, we as an industry have become a very efficient catching machine."[34] As with efficiency measures in general (chapter 4), in only a few instances have these governmental measures actually reduced pressure and fostered a healthy fishery. Critiques of this approach are voluminous.[35]

With respect to lobstering, the Maine DMR has pursued the population-quota approach to some extent. But it has simultaneously developed an alternative approach, one based on the recognition that much of lobstering has been self-regulating and, from both an economic and a biological perspective, successful. Despite predictions of collapse from the population modelers, predictions made regularly for more than a century,[36] the lobster fisheries have been extremely productive. The 1990s set record harvests. In 2000 the fishery yielded 56.7 million pounds, triple the catch of the mid-1980s.[37] There are several reasons for the apparent success of self-management. The lobster itself is relatively sedentary, breeds prolifically, and cannot resist climbing into a trap for a hunk of rotting fish carcass. The collapse of other fisheries, most notably that of cod and haddock, has reduced predation since many of those bottom fish feed on lobster larva and baby lobsters. In addition, lobster harvesting practices are all near shore and employ simple means—traps. Finally, self-monitoring is relatively easy since boats and buoys are highly visible and recognizable. The challenge for state officials has been to reinforce such practices without sacrificing the larger statewide goals of public access to public resources now and in the future. Some observers have termed the evolving approach "co-management."[38]

Part of the DMR's trouble on Monhegan stemmed from the state's attempts to institute a formal comanagement scheme for lobstering. In 1996, the Maine legislature passed legislation that attempted to encourage and, in some respects, mimic the local, self-management institutions of lobster fishers by devolving decision making to a lower level and dividing the state's lobstering region into seven lobster-management zones, each of which included both island and mainland harbors. Councils of lobstermen elected by lobstermen themselves would represent a zone and have the authority to set more restrictive rules on themselves than the state would. When the seven zones were created by law and then implemented through DMR rules and regulations, it was widely assumed that the restriction of registrants to their registered zone would not only limit lobster fishers to a zone, but would deter them from fishing away from their residence. Monhegan fishers would fish Monhegan waters, Friendship fishers Friendship waters (see map 7.2).

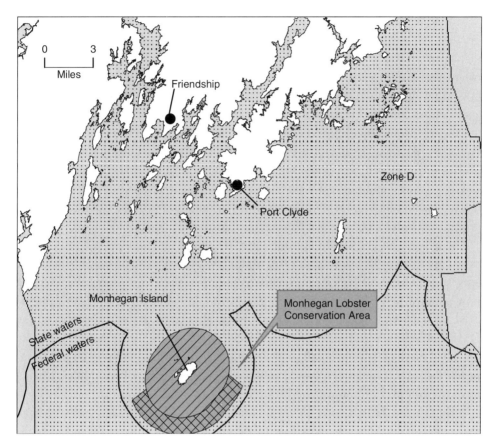

Map 7.2
Monhegan Island. Within Maine's Zone D, the hatched dark-shaded area is the Monhegan Conservation Area, restricted to certified Monhegan lobster catchers. The double-hatched portion at the southern end of the conservation area was fished by lobstermen from Friendship.

Monhegan was in zone D along with the Friendship harbor and others. But because Monhegan had a six-month season and a history of effective self-management, the DMR considered Monhegan a "subzone." For Monheganers this meant they could carry on as usual, largely managing their affairs themselves yet, as always, in accordance with state requirements for licensing, trap tags, double-gauge measurements, escape vents, and daytime fishing. For other fishermen, including the five from Friendship, the coastal management zone meant Monhegan was now part of "their territory," zone D. For the first time in memory, mainlanders presumably reasoned, they could steam out to the rich lobster grounds around Monhegan, set traps, and not fear reprisal. They now had state sanction. The new state management regime appeared to override traditional means of territorial defense by giving state assurances of open fishing in each zone.

The Monhegan-Friendship episode upset the state's attempts to reinforce traditional practices by its usual monitoring and, now, by the coastal management zones. State enforcement officials found themselves in the awkward position of protecting non-Monheganers' right to fish Monhegan waters, knowing that such fishing threatened an otherwise successfully managed piece of bottom. By ensuring access, the DMR's efforts, in effect, opened up one local, traditionally fished and traditionally defended piece of bottom to all who desired to fish there (from zone D) and compelled the state to intervene should traditional means—tying off trap lines, cutting traps, or gun play on the water—be attempted.

Although the 1996 season closed in June with no overt conflicts and although tensions had abated, everyone knew the drama was far from over. Friendship fishermen made it clear that after lobstering in their home waters that spring and, likely, fishing for tuna in the summer, they would be back to Monhegan in late summer or early fall. The DMR scrambled to prevent violence locally and to save the coastal management zone system statewide. The first result was to propose a new set of rules designed specifically for Monhegan. The rules would

• Create a Monhegan Island Conservation Area, a two-mile area around most of the island with an extension to three miles at the southern end
• Require lobster fishers to register to fish in the area, open, as always, to any Maine lobster license holder
• Establish a trap limit of 600 traps per person and per boat
• Keep the closed season the same as current law, June 25–January 1
• Require that a person who fishes the Monhegan season cannot fish in other state waters when the Monhegan season is closed
• Require lobster fishers registered in the Monhegan zone to use a Monhegan trap tag

• Create a Trap Limit Advisory Committee consisting of three Monhegan lobster fishers, one lobster fisher who is not a Monhegan resident, and one member appointed by the Commissioner to advise the Commissioner of Marine Resources on the Monhegan program[39]

The proposed rules would formalize what the two groups had informally worked out to get through the 1996 season. Notably, however, the rules apparently would also codify Monheganers' exclusive use of a piece of lobstering bottom, a rich piece of territory that would otherwise be a public resource open to all duly licensed members of the Maine public. After all, everyone presumed, no one from the mainland would regularly steam out fifteen or more miles to set and haul traps, let alone forgo fishing elsewhere.

Before implementing the rules, the DMR held a public hearing, packing a room with some seventy lobster fishers from the mainland and fifteen Monhegan fishermen and women. Predictably, the mainlanders vehemently opposed the proposed area, charging that it would amount to an expansion of Monhegan's ocean bottom already made exclusive by its legislated closed season. No, said the Monheganers, this was an allocation issue, a question of who can use a public resource and whether some get special treatment, namely, state protection to fish others' waters. Special treatment? replied the mainlanders. Who is getting special treatment here? You Monheganers, of course! It is simply not fair that so few lobster catchers have exclusive use of such a large piece of rich lobstering bottom, when everyone else in Maine has to fight tooth and nail to set a trap on productive bottom.

For DMR officials, this debate was no-win. They were determined to frame the issue narrowly, as a case of traditional defense of territory and of the state's commitment to sound conservation practices, which the Monheganers had exercised for decades. The DMR commissioner stressed that with these rules any license holder could fish in the designated Monhegan zone if they complied with Monhegan's rules, including the legal six-month season and the traditional trap limit of 600. No one was being excluded.

No one doubted, however, that the intended thrust of the new rules was to discourage, indeed, virtually prevent non-Monhegan residents from fishing Monhegan waters. The DMR wanted to preserve one of the last, well-functioning harbors with a rich, well-managed lobster fishery. But it could not go so far as to prohibit licensed Maine lobster fishers from fishing in a portion of state waters. If a Friendship lobster fisher wanted to fish in Monhegan waters and complied with Monhegan conventions, that was his or her legal prerogative. As noted, though, at the time, DMR officials and Monheganers were confident these new rules would deter future moves into Monhegan waters, largely because of point 5. Lobster fishers from the mainland would not give up their rights to fish other state waters during Monhegan's closed season just to get access to six months of Monhegan lobstering. That is, if a mainland lobster fisher registered for the Monhegan Conservation Area, and lobstered there from January 1 to June 25, that lobster fisher could not lobster anywhere else in Maine waters. Such a restriction would only make sense for local Monhegan lobster fishers, all of whom kept their traps dry for those six months anyway.

Virtually all other lobster fishers in Maine were now fishing year-round, except for the occasional part-timer—often a college student with a rowboat and a few traps making some summer money. Full-time fishers could ill afford to fish part of the year when competition for bottom was so intense, loan payments on boats and gear had to be made, and other expenses were incurred year-round. Everyone assumed the Friendship fishermen were no different. They would steam twenty miles out to Monhegan waters when their own catches were low along the mainland. But they certainly would not come out for only six months of lobstering and then forgo lobstering the rest of the year, especially in their home territory.

Despite vehement opposition from mainlanders, on November 25, 1997, the DMR did put the new rules into effect.[40] Only Monheganers registered in the newly designated Monhegan Conservation Area for the 1997 season. In so doing, they effectively conceded their traditional bottom beyond three miles where, indeed, Friendship fishermen returned to fish in the fall. By winter, however, the Friendship fishermen were mostly fishing back in their home territory around Friendship, keeping enough gear around Monhegan, but still three miles beyond the island, to, as was the traditional practice, hold bottom. Restricted to the new two- and three-mile area, Monheganers fished the 1997 season without incident but continued to protest to state authorities. The new rules were designed to create disincentives for all but resident Monheganers, and the first year of implementation, the 1997 season ending June 25, led everyone to believe it had worked. Full-time, year-round lobster fishers would never forgo their lobstering in all state waters just to get six months on Monhegan water. Only Monheganers would do that. And all along, the Friendship fishermen indicated they only wanted access to outlying bottom, certainly not bottom right up to the island itself.

Everyone was shocked, therefore, when, on September 1, 1997, three months before the 1998 season was to begin, the Friendship Five did sign up for the Monhegan Conservation Area. They wanted, as they said repeatedly, to "join" Monhegan—that is, to fish there during the open season and abide by the local rules.

DMR officials were aghast. They knew several of the Friendship Five were highly successful fishermen, "highliners," hard-driving, hard-working lobster fishers skilled both on the water and in the fishhouse, among the top producers in their community and widely respected. But they did not anticipate these fishermen's determination to take over a century-old fishery. Their registration for Monhegan lobstering and, consequently, their forfeiture of lobstering at home during Monhegan's closed season, proved to state officials that they were no longer after outlying bottom only. They wanted access to *all* of Monhegan bottom.

As DMR officials and others saw it, the Friendship Five were using state rules to otherwise do what highliners are so good at—earn high incomes by constantly shifting their lobster operations from one spot to another. They would look for rich bottom and defend what they found with lots of traps, securing the cooperation of other fishers who benefit from them or fear them. Traditionally the highliner may test others' territories and back off if they are well defended. But now the Friendship fishers were leaving the testing and defending to the state marine patrol.

Tradition has had it that groups of lobster catchers, "lobster gangs," earn a territory by fishing it regularly and defending it vigorously. Tradition also has had it that no self-respecting, independent, freedom-loving Mainers would bring the government into their affairs unless absolutely necessary. But, as DMR officials saw it, this is precisely what the Friendship fishermen were doing. By signing up for all of Monhegan territory, the five compelled the state to ensure their right to fish there. It was the law. They weren't muscling out a weak gang of lobster catchers, folks who didn't know how to fish or how to defend territory. They were using the threat of state coercion to upset a well-managed, biologically rich lobster fishery, a fishery that had supported a tiny island and its residents for over a century. In private, some fishermen from Friendship and other mainland harbors condemned the move as a "land grab." At the same time they resented the fact that a small group of fishers, the Monheganers, had monopolized a rich fishery for so many years. Their fathers and grandfathers had always complained about the situation out there on that island. Until now, though, no one had done anything about it. If the Friendship fishers were adjusting territorial boundaries in the traditional way, some reasoned, at least they were doing it, making the attempt, regrettably with state sanction. The Friendship Five deserved their support, at least publicly, and, as it turned out, many of these supporters wrote letters and testified when the issue finally went to the state legislature.

Soon after the Friendship Five signed up for the Monhegan subzone, several DMR officials arranged a private meeting in Friendship with the instigators. Do you understand what you're doing? the officials asked repeatedly. Do you understand we could have a bloodbath out there? You're crossing traditional fishing lines that haven't been crossed in a hundred years. And you're expecting us to back you up!

In one of the great ironies of the entire Monhegan-Friendship episode, the Friendship fishermen replied by citing state law and the DMR's own regulations: it's our right to fish Maine water, and since we've accepted the conditions of the zone with the closed season and trap limit, all we want to do is fish. If there's a problem around Monhegan it's that too few boats are working such a large area.

One warden was exasperated with their apparent lack of concern. Even if that was true, he answered, even if the area could support five more fishermen, it could not support an unlimited number. With the law as it is—open public access to all of Maine's public waters for all licensed Mainers—and the newly created Monhegan Conservation Area as it is now constituted, there is nothing stopping dozens of mainlanders from coming out and doing what you're trying to do.

That's not our business, replied a Friendship fisherman. We face that kind of thing every day on the mainland. It's about time Monheganers did, too. And it's up to you guys to enforce the rules you set up.

Until this time, throughout the state of Maine, state officials had always been in the position of trying to impress fishers with the importance of fishing laws and regulations. The lobster catchers would respond with arguments about the importance of traditional practice. Here, the DMR officials found themselves lecturing fishermen about tradition: tradition has it that you should not be doing this. This is not right. This is not how lobster catchers in the state of Maine acquire territory, sidling up to the government for protection and comfort. The roles had completely reversed. The DMR officials and likely everyone else concluded without a doubt that the Friendship Five were bent on taking over the entire Monhegan bottom. In the words of one official, they were determined to fish all of Monhegan, dismantling the islanders' system in the process. And they had no compunctions about doing so, whatever the consequences for Monhegan fishermen and women, island residents, and, for that matter, the resource.

Such was the dilemma of state officials. The intentions and sentiments were clear on all sides. No longer could they let "tradition" settle things. In lobster wars competing gangs can lose thousands of traps and then, after it is all over, much like territorial contests of power between nations, the two sides return to the status quo ante with no change in boundaries or leadership. But if state officials could not leave the matter to tradition, neither could they leave it to the agency's rule-making process. The DMR can promulgate rules regarding lobster size and fishing gear, but those rules must apply to everyone. It can restrict access to a piece of bottom, but it must restrict everyone's access. No one gets special treatment. And certainly no one can be excluded while others are included. To do anything that smacks of favorable treatment for a few would require a change in the law, if not in the entire normative structure in which modern fishing and natural resource use exists in the United States. If some segment of the population was to be excluded, that exclusion would have to be based on a principle that overrides free and open access by all members of the public to public resources.

As it turned out, that principle was couched as conservation and preservation—conserving a resource and preserving a community. Underlying those notions was the idea that, because the ecological and social system that sustains a segment of the population is constrained, "too much" is indeed possible. Too much short-term extraction and too much strain on community relations would jeopardize both the resource and the community. The intersection of the biophysical system and the social system is precisely where the brakes must be applied. In this situation, the best evidence of the ability to apply brakes is in the Monhegan fishery itself, the self-managed, self-restrained activities of resident lobster fishers and resident islanders. To extend that managerial intersection to distant lobster fishers, to people who come and go, foraging optimally for the largest, short-term net return on effort, is to break the bonds that make sufficiency possible, that make restraint rational and profitable.

The tension rose even higher when it was revealed that the newcomers, the Friendship fishermen, were lobstering in non-Monhegan state waters at the time they registered for the Monhegan Conservation Area on September 1, 1997. Monhegan fishers cried foul. "The intent of the conservation zone, as the lobster advisory board said, was for anyone wishing to fish in it to pay the penalty up front by not having traps in the water after June," argued Monhegan's lead spokesman and longtime lobsterman, Doug Boynton.[41] In other words, Monhegan fishers saw this as further confirmation that the Friendship fishermen were registering only to make a quick haul in the winter season of December 1997–June 1998 around Monhegan and then, when harvests diminished, move on, just as they had done when they first set traps near the island in 1995 and 1996. Their overall strategy, Monheganers' reasoned, was to enter these lobster-rich waters, make big hauls and big bucks for a few months, or a few years even, and then withdraw. They were known for "muscling their way" into other's territories, either to extend their own territories or to, in effect, poach until harvests declined. This was just a more flagrant, more ambitious instance. There would be risks, to be sure, but no "penalties."

In fact, the "penalty" Boynton alluded to was multifaceted, a critical element in the Monheganers' success for over a century. It involved a commitment among Monheganers to a set of highly restrictive lobstering practices that applied not just for a season or two, but for years and decades and, for that matter, for *generations* of lobster fishers. The time frame was the very long term, or probably more accurate, the indefinite future (chapters 2 and 6). In general, a commitment is worthless if it does not entail some cost, some sacrifice. Monhegan lobster fishers had long made that sacrifice, forgoing income by lobstering only six months a year. A week or two or a month longer on the water would have been profitable and may have been "sustainable" economically and ecologically. But all these years they kept to the six-month season because they knew it worked. They knew it worked not in a scientific sense (nobody knows that) but in an experiential sense. They probably all suspected that six and a half months or seven or eight months would have also worked. More time on the water each year may have been possible, but the level of harvesting experienced over decades—that is, at six months a year—had been enough. It was *sufficient* in the sense of providing a secure income over the long term for this self-contained group of fishers, for their descendants, and for new-comers who are gradually assimilated after demonstrating their fit in the community. Some increase in fishing was too much fishing. Pushing toward that increase was not worth the risk, the risk of repeating the boom-and-bust cycles other lobster fishers have experienced since the early nineteenth century in the southern range of *Homarus americana*. And it was sufficient in the sense that it was *best*, not a compromise solution but, given the range of values, time frames, and risks, the best that one could achieve even if, in a given year, a greater harvest was possible. In any given season, as lobster catchers young and old explained in interviews, there's at least one "gung ho" lobster fisher who wants more, whether to pay debts, to send a child to school on the mainland, or to maintain a habit. But since 1907 and likely well before, six months had become the focal point for the length of the season and, all else equal, for the size of the total harvest. Six months was recognizable in part because of its tradition but in part because everyone knew it worked. It was the ready-made answer to the question, how much is enough harvesting around this tiny island. As is often the case with the sufficiency question, no one could answer the question precisely; it can't be expressed in days of fishing or in tons of lobsters caught. Complex systems do not allow for such predictive accuracy. The six-month season provided a convenient and ready-made answer bound up in both tradition and law that recognized the varying needs of each fisher. At the same time, it incorporated ultimate limits, limits that had been exceeded time and again elsewhere for at least a couple of centuries. That excess was well known to all and, presumably, a background condition for discussions in the Monhegan fishhouse about how much is enough and how much is too much.

"Trap Day," a seemingly minor piece of Monhegan's overall resource-use pattern, illustrates the penalty resident Monheganers often imposed on themselves, the restraint they exercised as a group. The season officially begins January 1, but if gale-force winds are blowing or one fisher is ill or a boat's mooring has been damaged, they all wait. "It is interesting and business-like to see the men working together in every detail," wrote one resident in 1963. "The boats come in to the wharf, the helpers pass down the traps; when loaded they take off to set and other boats take their places and so on until the last trap is off the wharf and in the water. . . . It is almost an invariable rule, that if one man is sick or has an accident, the others will wait a reasonable time until he is ready to go."[42]

Such restraint may appear minor—only a day or two out of a six-month season—but its effects are nontrivial, especially socially. To collectively agree not to fish is to make a commitment to each other. Commitments are just words unless they incur real costs, "penalties." Not to fish is a form of commitment because every day missed is income lost. Everyone still must finish the season by sundown on June 25. Deciding collectively when to start is to annually visit the possibility of self-imposed limitation, of restraint above and beyond that which is legally mandated. To delay the season's opening conveys a sense of being in the business together when otherwise each fisher is an independent operator striving for a large and secure income. Having a flexible, self-designated start date still allows for individual initiative and competition with each other on the water. But it helps create a level playing field; it prevents anyone with a bigger boat or greater risk-seeking propensity from gaining an unfair advantage by being the first to go out. A flexible start date thus reduces the inequities in access to capital and technology that are otherwise so common in fisheries everywhere. Conversely, a start date that is only legally mandated, one that is not collectively decided by the resource users themselves, is not just *a*social but *anti*social. It forces everyone to go out at the same time, regardless of weather or readiness. Here, restraint makes no sense individually. There is never enough, just the most possible.

Monhegan lobster fishers also paid the "penalty," made the sacrifice Boynton referred to, by working and living on one tiny island, in one community that was tight—sometimes too tight, some would say—and where employment alternatives were few and far between. Fishing "effort" for them was not just a matter of getting the gear right and putting in the hours on the water. It was investing in the island fishing community as a whole, training those who might become full-time lobster fishers, penalizing those who violated the norms, meeting for long hours in the fish-house to decide on procedures, and, occasionally, lobbying legislators, giving inter-views, and hosting visitors. If, by contrast, Friendship fishers would need only sign their name to a form, remove their traps only when ordered by the state, and set foot on the island only to fuel up, they would not be making the commitment. Since they had not paid the "penalty" in the months leading up to the 1998 season (and a December 1, 1997, start date), there was no reason to believe they would in the future.

And yet the Friendship fishermen were playing a different game, trapped as it were in a different way of earning a living. Hailing out of a mainland harbor, they were accustomed to fighting for every square foot of bottom they could get their traps onto. And they were accustomed to searching for rich lobster spots, fishing them until the return on effort made it unprofitable, then moving on to the next spot. They weren't being greedy nor did they enjoy preying on others' good for-tunes. They operated in a frontier mode, one more like a gold rush than clearing the land for crops or selectively cutting trees for perpetual yields. With intense pres-sure along the mainland lobstering grounds, the Friendship Five had little choice. They, like the Monheganers, could not restrict access legally and, unlike the Mon-heganers, the traditional territorial means were weak. They could still make a decent living but it was not by investing in the building of their own community of fishers and certainly not by forgoing catch via seasonal or trap limits. Rather, the only strat-egy open to them was optimal foraging, frontier exploitation. From this perspec-tive, Monhegan was just another frontier, one widely perceived as rich, even *unduly* rich given the few fishers who exploited it. To share in that bounty was only fair, many mainlanders reasoned, and if the fishery should be depleted it would always recover, in which case they and others could come back. If Monheganers could not continue the "easy life," as one Friendship fisherman put it, a life propped up by rich artists and tourists from away, they could move to the mainland like everyone else. From there, they too could steam out to the Monhegan Conservation Area now and then and haul traps. It may not be an ideal existence, the Friendship fish-ermen seemed to be saying, but it had worked for thousands of lobster catchers to this point and it is better than the alternative—a job at Wal-Mart.

A Rock and a Hard Place

With the new Monhegan start date (December 1), fast approaching, the DMR's attempt to ensure harvest and implement a novel "co-management" regime was in jeopardy. More than rules and regulations was at stake. On the island, people were comparing notes on the shooting range of different rifles. Similar discussions and preparations were rumored to be taking place in Friendship. Accusations flew back and forth over the CB radios and in the press. Lodged between warring factions within their own jurisdiction, understaffed, and likely to be caught in the crossfire, figuratively and literally, the DMR was between the proverbial rock and a hard place.

DMR officials made plans for a continuous presence in Monhegan waters. They prepared new moorings in the harbor for their patrol boats, scheduled wardens for around-the-clock patrolling, made special arrangements with medical staff on the mainland, and alerted the Coast Guard. To sustain such measures with the necessary manpower and funding for any length of time was doubtful, however. With 2,500 miles of shoreline and 90 fishing harbors, the entire state had only 45 marine patrol officers. The entire year's budget for overtime would be spent in a month. If a long-term, continuous presence became necessary, the DMR simply did not have the wherewithal. The logistics of keeping two groups of lobster catchers, people seething with "hate and discontent" and who would likely be armed, separate on open water, day and night, setting thousands of traps all within two or three miles of a rocky, windswept island, were horrendous. A fish warden's worst nightmare was taking shape very quickly.

In early October the DMR commissioner bought some time by getting the Monhegan lobster fishers to agree to delay their 1998 season start date (now scheduled for December 1, 1997). The commissioner and governor, as well as many legislators and other observers, were known to be sympathetic to Monhegan's case. In many ways, Monhegan was a showcase, a place where the resource was rich and disputes were rare. It was a place that somehow managed to manage itself, demanding relatively little of state services. The assigned DMR official, in fact, was known for having little to do, compared to his counterparts assigned to mainland harbors.

But for all their sympathy and apparent authority to write and rewrite the rules, DMR officials could not protect Monhegan fishers from outsiders. The issue now was entry—that is, unlimited versus limited entry. And no one in the executive branch of the state government had the authority to restrict the entry of duly licensed Mainers on Maine water. The commissioner could, say, close off an area to fishing to allow populations to recover. But the commissioner could not close off an area to some fishers and open it to others. Only the legislature could handle such a revolutionary idea. The principle of full public access to public resources has been sacrosanct since the nation's founding, if not before. Even if some legislators were willing to tackle such a thorny issue, getting a bill through the process could take months. The procedure begins with legislative council, then entails committee hearings and deliberations, readings and votes by both houses of the legislature, and finally signing by the governor, followed by a ninety-day waiting period to become law. With the next legislative session starting in January 1998, the lobstering season could well be over by the time a bill wound its way through. Monheganers' willingness to delay the season until the legislature considered their case could thus put at risk the entire season and, if deliberations did not go their way, future seasons of exclusive, self-regulated use. The agreed-on delay in the opening of the season put pressure on everyone to find a solution.

So in October 1997, Monhegan lobster fishers were sitting at home wondering when, if ever, they would begin the year's lobstering. The end date of the season, June 25, was fixed. Even four or five months on the water meant that, at best, they could meet their expenses. "It will be a huge sacrifice," complained Doug Boynton, the veteran lobsterman and now spokesman for the Monheganers. "We will basically be giving up our profits for the season. I'd much rather go fishing in January than go lobbying in January. I think fishing builds character. I don't know about lobbying."[43] By contrast, a veteran Friendship lobsterman, Donald Simmons, predicted little sacrifice for the Monheganers, especially compared to the conditions he experiences daily in the mainland harbors: "The way a lot of us feel is that if somebody is allowed to fish, they should be allowed to go where they want. There's plenty of lobsters out on Monhegan. They could catch lobsters all year round out there if they wanted to. Every town would like to have it that easy."[44] Of course, to Monhegan lobster fishers, nothing about their life, on or off the water, was "that easy."

For the interim, then, the DMR commissioner, Robin Alden, tried to get the parties to work out their differences between themselves, at least enough to ward off hostilities and, maybe, commence fishing. But the acrimony between the two sides precluded direct talks. So the commissioner appointed an independent mediator to facilitate negotiations between the two sides. The mediator's task was to get an agreement that prevented violence and that, ideally, allowed everyone to catch and sell lobsters, at least until the legislature convened. Both parties agreed to participate. Commissioner Alden also agreed to close the season entirely until the legislature could take up the issue.

The mediator was from a private conflict-resolution center in Portland. He had handled a variety of public disputes in Maine and New England and came to the DMR highly recommended. The first session took place on November 17, 1997, at a motor inn in Rockland. At the table were all thirteen active Monhegan lobster fishers, the five Friendship fishermen, several DMR officials, and two state legislators, one of whom represented both Monhegan and Friendship.

After a briefing from DMR officials, the mediator met with everyone in the same room. He soon separated the two parties and moved back and forth between them soliciting information and exploring interests. By one Monhegan fisher's account, he was "all business," "hammering" on each side to get an agreement. By other accounts he served as a gentle persuader. Whatever his style, that first day accomplished little in the way of movement toward agreement, not an unusual outcome in the early mediation stage of a protracted, intense dispute. The mediator kept the parties in the rooms from 9 a.m. to 10 p.m. that day and then resumed at 7:30 a.m. the next day. Late in the afternoon of the second day he informed the state officials that the parties were intransigent. Monheganers would concede none of their traditional bottom and the Friendship Five would accept nothing less than full access to all Monhegan waters. The mediator could not see how to reconcile their differences.

DMR officials conferred. A newcomer on the staff, a warden for Friendship with only three years experience, spoke up. He said that if they would give him a half hour with the Friendship fishermen, he thought he could get an agreement. At an impasse and lacking any other ideas, the senior officials agreed. Another warden joined him. The newcomer had only a few years experience but in many ways epitomized the ideal marine patrol officer. Unlike a street police officer who approaches the job as a search for violations and the need to write up tickets, the fish warden must develop a personal relationship with every single fisherman and fisherwoman in the district. The good ones know all the lobster fishers on a first-name basis and can readily identify each one's boat, buoy (by the color pattern), and pickup truck. When the wind is blowing and all the lobster fishers congregate in a coffeehouse or bar, the effective warden joins them, plays cards, and asks about the spouse and kids.

Above all, wardens must have credibility. They build it in part by the personal relations, but also by enforcing the law fairly. They need to convince everyone that their job is not to penalize but to create a level playing field for the honest fisherman, as one senior official put it, and for that they need everyone's cooperation. If someone is cheating, the warden needs to know. There are just too few wardens and too little equipment to directly monitor all the goings-on. Fishermen and fisherwomen are the real eyes and ears of state enforcement. But it is well known that they will cooperate only to the extent they see that it is in their own interest and only if they are convinced the warden does not have a hidden agenda and is not playing favorites. If someone makes a minor violation, the warden must know when to look the other way to preserve the relationship and ensure a supply of information on more consequential violations. Credibility thus comes through the daily activity of enforcing state laws and regulations, activity based on intimate knowledge of the fishers' livelihood and the mutual respect that can develop over years of practice.

The newcomer in the mediation session had, in his short tenure in Friendship, built such credibility. A woodcutter for a dozen years, he had come from inland Maine and knew little about fishing. But he did know how to listen. All indications were that he was well respected by the fishing community in Friendship. Alone with the Friendship Five and one other warden in a meeting room at the motel, he told them that if they didn't come to an agreement, the matter would go to the legislature, where they wouldn't be treated so well. You may have your differences with the DMR, he argued, but at least officials there understand fishing and the issues involved in a dispute. Legislators don't necessarily. And they can't just talk it through and work out an agreement that accommodates everyone's needs. They write laws and then turn them over to others—such as DMR officials—to implement. But the legislating is out of the DMR's hands. The legislature is alien territory for most fishermen, he explained. If you want to avoid going that route, now's the time to make concessions. But if you do have to go there, you need to look good, you need to curry their favor, and that begins here. Either way, you can't come across as the obstructionists. The Monhegan folks have already begun to line up public support. You have to do it, too, starting here.

Within a half hour, the Friendship Five agreed to fish only in the three-mile zone south of the island and stay out of the two-mile zone around the rest of the island. Everyone congratulated the newcomer fish warden. Agreement was now at hand.

Or so it seemed. When the state officials and mediator took the concession to the Monheganers, they balked. After saying all day that the Friendship fishermen had to stay out of the Monheganers' legally mandated two-mile zone, the Monheganers now backtracked. A series of private discussions ensued. Late that evening, DMR officials told the Monheganers that if they don't accept this concession it will be they who come across as the obstructionists, not the Friendship fishermen. If the issue does go to the legislature, the Monhegan image will be tarnished. As one official put it, you now have the power to "prevent a bloodbath" and to look good before the legislature, should that come to pass. And you know you can deal with us wardens up to a point. If you let this opportunity go, there's little else we can do for you, on the water or in the legislature. The Monheganers conceded but were clearly unsettled, fearing that they were making a terrible mistake, setting a precedent with Friendship presence that may ultimately doom their community. They insisted that the agreement only be a temporary measure and that, should the issue go to the legislature, nothing in the agreement would prejudice the legislative outcome. They also insisted that no Friendship fisherman could be "grandfathered" into future fishing around the island on the basis of their previous fishing there.

At 11 p.m. that day, after some thirty hours of negotiations, the mediator announced an agreement. The twelve fishermen and one fisherwoman from Monhegan and five fishermen from Friendship agreed to a December 1, 1997, start date. The Monheganers would set their traps only within two miles of the island, the area designated since the 1907 law regarding the closed season but an area considerably smaller than what Monheganers had traditionally fished and defended. The five Friendship fishermen agreed to lobster in the remaining two- to three-mile arc of the Monhegan Conservation Area to the south of the island. They agreed to so share Monhegan waters through June 25, 1998, the official close date.

With the agreement, the entire complexion of the dispute changed. To this point, the dispute had been local, just a difference between two harbors. Each side believed firmly that it was right, that, once officials and the public understood the situation, its position would prevail. They probably believed that taking a hard line and occasionally issuing threats would eventually force the other side to back down. And both sides probably felt they had enough support and the means to influence the DMR. Their local warden and the commissioner herself would eventually see the rightness of their cause and do what's necessary to settle it favorably. They knew many of the state officials personally and generally felt comfortable with them and trusted them. But now the measure was going to the legislature, out of the hands of both the fishing groups and the DMR officials. Now legislators from throughout Maine would deliberate, and not just as a local dispute but as a larger question of public resource policy. As it turned out, this was a turning point not just for two harbors and their tiny dispute but, quite likely, for fishery management throughout Maine, and possibly beyond.

When December 1, 1997, the newly designated start day for lobstering on Monhegan, arrived, high winds and rough, choppy seas made it dangerous to go out, especially for the smaller boats. The Monhegan lobster fishers, as was the custom, met and agreed to postpone Trap Day so that all Monhegan fishermen, regardless of boat size, could start together. The Friendship fishermen did set sail, but with water crossing their decks, they only stayed out about two hours. In that time, they set some 50 to 100 traps in the two- to three-mile area of the Monhegan Conservation Area, as agreed. Monheganers started several days later. Both groups continued fishing through the 1998 season, interrupted frequently by trips to Augusta to lobby for and against LD 2021, the bill written to decide once and for all who could and who could not fish Monhegan waters. The politicking began in earnest.

Immediately after the fishermen and fisherwoman signed the mediated agreement and legislation was imminent, Peter Boehmer, editor of the self-published *New Monhegan Press* and a companion online service, sent out an "SOS" to his readers. Recipients included past residents, summer residents, and short-term visitors, all individuals who, by virtue of their subscriptions, had a personal attachment to the island. Letters poured into the Marine Resources Committee from all over Maine and other states. And both sides sought professional political advice. Residents on the island passed the hat. By one account, Monheganers hired the state's best political consulting firm; the Friendship Five hired the second best.

From Lobstering to Lobbying
Legislative hearings began in late January 1998. Several legislators in the Monhegan and Friendship areas submitted bills, but the DMR took responsibility for consolidating them into one piece of legislation, which became known as LD 2021 on the house side of the Maine legislature. The bill's main features were provisions to restrict lobster harvesting to Monhegan fishers and to limit entry to the fishery via an apprenticeship program administered by Monhegan fishers. The baseline number and identity of lobster fishers would be precisely those who were registered with the DMR in 1996 for the Monhegan Conservation Area and who actually fished in the area during the 1997 open season, namely, fourteen residents of Monhegan Island. Fourteen would also become the maximum number of lobster fishers for the future. Newcomers would become one of the fourteen only (1) by completing a two-year apprenticeship with a minimum of 150 days on the water with one of the existing fourteen registered fishers, and (2) after one of the existing fourteen leaves the Monhegan program. Such entrants would be admitted according to the chronological order in which they completed the apprenticeship program. One of the practical effects of the bill would be to accord existing fishers the authority to decide who becomes a Monhegan lobster fisher. They would hire the sternmen and sternwomen and process the apprenticeship paperwork. Such authority would thus formalize what the Monhegan fishers had been doing for a long time. This legislation "establishes, finally and formally, a specific lobster conservation zone around Monhegan

Island," said the acting commissioner of the DMR, Penn Estabrook. It "is simply reflective of the current practices on the island, but formally adopts them through legislation."[45] At the same time, it would directly contradict what the state had been officially doing for an even longer time: guaranteeing all licensed Mainers access to all Maine lobster bottom. Some observers thus saw the bill as an attempt to close off a public resource, reserving use to an exclusive, privileged few. Others saw it as simply preserving a valuable resource, one that had been protected and nurtured by generations of fishing folk. Still others, especially those who had been wrestling with the larger policy issues and trying to maintain the ideals of public use of public waters, on the one hand, and local, self-management on the other, thought the choice was not so clear. The former commissioner, Robin Alden, elaborated:

[Monhegan] is far closer to working in concert with the resource around it than most places on the coast. There is some objective data and plenty of common wisdom to support this conservation result. In a fishery as critical to the state's coastal economy, the state should not squander the opportunity to learn from this.

As commissioner, I had to evaluate what was right in this situation. With the history of conflict, this is not a situation where there is any clear right and wrong if you examine the bitter history between the island and the mainland towns. At the same time, I did investigate and become convinced that the island's winter fishery is not the bonanza some suppose it to be, nor [are] the fishermen exceptionally well off. Friendship and Cushing [a nearby fishing village] fishermen likewise are excellent fishermen, competitive on the mainland terms they have been living with. It comes down to a simple matter: Monhegan has evolved as a fishery and a community because of the state protection it has had for over 90 years. That cannot survive if they must fish unprotected with fishermen competing on mainland terms.[46]

Among fishers, views on the bill varied with location. Islanders and mainlanders tended to differ, as did those from either western harbors or eastern harbors. East of Monhegan where fishing pressure is least and fishermen often move their traps freely to follow lobster movements, testimony was the most opposed, especially from the mainlanders. "This is state water, everyone should be able to fish it," said Harvey Crawley, president of the Downeast Lobster Association. "That is why you pay for a state license in the first place. There is no reason why fourteen fishermen should own that much territory in the Gulf of Maine. If all the other islands come up with the same idea for private fishing, what will happen to the mainland lobsterman? They will have to move farther and farther into federal waters just to make a living."[47] Keith Simmons, one of the Friendship Five, agreed: "I don't think the Atlantic Ocean belongs to anybody, and a lobster doesn't belong to anybody until it's in your trap."[48]

The larger issue was the very nature of lobstering in the late twentieth century. The Friendship Five, commissioner Alden noted, were "excellent fishermen, competitive on the mainland terms." The great variability in the fishery due to bio-physical conditions (water temperature, nutrients, food sources, predator-prey rela-tions) and human conditions (technologies, entrants, market dynamics) has required successful fishermen to do more than hold bottom. Fishing on "mainland terms" means they can never be content with a few favorite spots. They must constantly explore underwater conditions—substrate (rocky, sandy, or vegetative, for example), topography (ledges, flat bottom), ocean currents—and set traps in unlikely places. Going far from one's home harbor is one means of exploring, not necessarily to relocate but to find alternative ground when one's own is yielding poor harvests. And the Friendship Five were indeed good at it, says a fellow Friendship lobster-man who was not one of the five: "I know some of the five from Friendship have fished for lobsters in federal waters for years and have found lobster bottom that no one has ever fished before." In fact, Monhegan fishers were pursuing this strat-egy to some extent themselves in federal waters, a fact not lost on mainland fishers. "If Monhegan's conservation zone is working for them [the Monheganers]," asked the same fisherman, "why do they have to come into federal waters and fish also?" He added:

I strongly feel they shouldn't. I have fished my lobster traps with the five Friendship fisher-men inside and outside federal waters and know what these five fishermen have given up [by registering for the Monhegan Conservation Area]. . . . Now, Monhegan fishermen have set their traps out in these [federal] waters before their season opened in their own zone. Again, I feel that this issue is not right. If they, the Monhegan fishermen, want their own conserva-tion zone to remain untouched by outsiders, they in turn should be made to stay inside of their designated boundaries.[49]

Unlike many of his mainland compatriots, this fisherman was not rejecting the idea of exclusive zones. He was objecting to a double standard: some get exclusive ter-ritory (traditionally, a common practice, but now proposed as law) along with the opportunity to fish elsewhere, while others have no exclusive territory, thus com-peting everywhere they go. If exclusion is necessary, it should go both ways. That is, if a group of fishers can exclude others from their bottom, those fishers in turn should be excluded from all other bottom. In effect, the remaining fishers who are left to constantly scramble for good bottom, who must fish on "mainland terms," should not have to compete with those who have their own pot of gold or, at least, as in the Monhegan case, a steady and reliable supply of lobsters. This argument, understandably opposed by many Monheganers, eventually found its way into the final legislation. To get exclusive use of the two- and three-mile zone around their island, Monhegan fishers had to forfeit lobstering rights in all other state and federal waters. They could exclude others, but they themselves must be excluded. They can close the gates, but in the process they pen themselves in.

Monheganers answered the charge of exclusiveness by pointing out that most of the current lobster fishers on the island, the so-called "Monhegan" lobstermen and lobsterwomen, had come from off island—from other islands, from the mainland, and even from out of state. But each worked his or her way up through the ranks, apprenticing with an experienced captain, working odd jobs around the island, and eventually buying or borrowing enough gear to go out on one's own. Apprenticeship, they argued, is the key to their success, not exclusion. The purpose of the conservation areas created several years back by the legislature and enacted by the DMR was "to reflect more closely the traditional practices which have been so successful," a Monhegan lobsterman wrote early in the lobbying effort. But "these rules did not include our apprenticeship program because DMR didn't feel it had the authority to implement it. This loophole is being used by another harbor to move into the conservation zone, defying common-law practices respected throughout Maine. The proposed law would turn common law into State law."[50] In other words, traditional practices have proved inadequate when fishing pressure builds and the state is reduced to fixing one problem at a time with a hodgepodge of rules and regulations. In each locality, traditional practices, including apprenticeship, have been part of a larger social whole that has evolved over decades. Apprenticeship, however informal, has been an important way to control entry, and not just the number of entrants but the kind of entrants. "The apprenticeship provision is how Monhegan has regulated both the amount of entry into fishing around the island and the quality of that entry," Commissioner Alden noted, pointing out that

there is a lot of subtlety to the issue surrounding lobster trap reductions and entry control. Monhegan has both formal and informal controls on scale of operations, entry, and fishing practices. Monhegan's trap limit and season have insulated them from all legal competition from those fishing more than 600 traps. The island fishermen's informal apprenticeship and consensus approach to such things as when to set traps has protected them from having to invest in vessels that can [be] set regardless of the weather.[51]

The newest of the fishing captains on Monhegan described his introduction to Monhegan and the importance to him of apprenticing:

I first came to Monhegan Island eight years ago while on summer break from the University of Maine. I originally came to the island to do carpentry work to put myself through college. The following spring I got a job sterning and shortly thereafter I got a job as a deckhand on an island groundfish boat. It was at that point in my life that I decided that the sea and the life style it represented was in my blood. . . . I soon decided that there was no better place to spend the winter than on the island working on a lobsterboat.

I spent five full seasons working as a sternman. While I could of [have] gone off earlier on my own I chose not to. I am glad that I made this decision. I feel more prepared to fish on my own because I learned from people who had come up through the ranks like I had done. I learned what works and quickly what doesn't.

Part of the apprenticeship program is to prepare a person for going out on his own. Seamanship, boat and gear maintenance, knowledge of the local waters are but a few of the many things one learns as a sternman. On Monhegan being in our apprenticeship program also develops trust with your fellow fisherman. The trust, however, as I have learned, is a two-way street. Not only do your fellow fishermen learn to trust you, you learn to trust them. . . .

As the newest captain in the Monhegan fleet, I feel that I am proof that the apprenticeship program on the island works today as it has for generations. I was not born on Monhegan and in fact I grew up in another fishing community. I came to the island as an outsider and now consider myself to be part of the community. I am now on the Board of Assessors for the island, our equivalent of a town council.

I, like a few other captains, do not own property there. All but one or two lobstermen started fishing on the island before they owned property there. Monhegan's informal apprenticeship program has allowed access to Monhegan's harbor for generations.

I was told from the beginning of my tenure on the island that in order to fish here you had to do your time in the stern. I equate this to being an apprentice in any trade be it a baker or a welder. In order to be successful, you need the proper training—lobstering is no different.[52]

"Doing time," getting properly trained, and building trust are some practical effects of apprenticing. But it all occurs within an institutional setting designed in large part by the fishers themselves and in part by the state. "Apprenticeship is not just about catching lobsters," says Monhegan lobsterman Doug Boynton.

It's also about building trust and cooperation among lobstermen who are going to work the same area, and also to help DMR [make sure] that the laws are obeyed. Our investments and our economic future is dependent on cooperation and good management of the area. If this could be taught from a book it would. But it can only be taught through an apprenticeship program. This is why most harbors have some system for outsiders to gain acceptance.

On Monhegan Island, our apprenticeship program teaches an attitude about the lobster resource: not greed or short term gain, rather a system to ensure a plentiful resource for future generations. Outsiders find it hard to believe that we buy lobsters in the off-season when they are plentiful a few hundred feet from home. You have to live it for awhile to understand.[53]

That intergenerational "attitude" is reinforced by fishing and residing with those who have a long Monhegan history. On my visit to Monhegan in 1998 I spoke for a couple of hours with one such gentleman in his seventies, the one who distinguished "real fishing" from "hogging." As we sat and talked next to his garage overlooking the harbor and the open ocean, his teenage grandson busied himself with the propane-gas equipment that the two distributed around the island. Earlier that year, the boy's father gave evidence of this family history in legislative testimony: "I live on Monhegan because my family has always lived here, for six generations." His great-great-grandfather was a lightkeeper and great-grandfather built many of the houses on the island. And his great grandfather on his grandmother's side was from Friendship, "and had the first lobster license in the state of Maine, which is 1A, which he passed on to me after 70 years of lobstering."[54]

And he will no doubt pass number 1A on to his son or daughter. I can imagine that when that descendant presents his or her license for renewal or when a warden asks to see it, eyebrows are raised. Officials routinely see license numbers in the thousands, sometimes hundreds, but rarely single digits. Official and fisher alike cannot help but be struck by the time frame, the history, the intergenerational knowledge embodied in such a license number.

On Monhegan, apprenticeship is closely linked to residency. Once a person has "gone sternman" for a few years and lived side by side on this tiny rock fifteen miles out in the ocean, in season and off, and worked other jobs there, everyone knows—the potential entrant as well as the other fishers—whether the person fits. They know whether he or she has the requisite skills and knowledge and whether the individual is inclined toward "real fishing" or toward hogging bottom. They know whether the newcomer leans toward highlining or can exercise restraint. And they know whether the individual can function within the collective. Apprentices are scrutinized by the community of fishers and the island community as a whole. Those who do not learn the rules and abide by them, who put their self-interest above the group interest, are ousted. They are fired as sternmen or refused gear when they try to fish independently or simply denied advice and help. Similar to the guildlike structures of modern professions (law, medicine, and academe, for instance), full acceptance (making partner, becoming a surgeon, getting tenured) is a long time in coming. There are many tests, many hurdles, many checks and balances.

The result is not exclusiveness, if that term implies access by birthright, family name, or wealth. But it is not open access either, if that term implies unfettered choice in a free and open society and the right to exploit public resources as one sees fit. Joining a group is not an individual choice when training, trust, cooperation, and restraint are necessary for economic and physical survival. The *right* to fish is balanced by the *responsibility* to fish right, to make a living in a way that does not deny others their chance to make a living now and in the future. Not just anyone can or should be able to practice law or perform surgery. The risks in those professions are well known. It is only now in the waning decades of frontier exploitation and a nascent transition to sustainable resource use that the risks in fishing and other natural resource occupations are becoming clear. Some of the risks are immediate and visible to resource users. A storm comes up on a fisher handling twenty miles offshore and the engine fails. Other risks are diffuse or distanced or simply harder to grasp. A big haul today translates into a miniscule catch tomorrow. Harvesting the largest or tastiest individuals changes the age structure of the population and upsets its productive and reproductive cycles. Tearing up bottom with a trawl destroys essential habitat. In all these scenarios, the most fundamental risk is to the resource itself. When, for so long, resource abundance and technological advance have been premises of social progress, complete openness probably made sense. It certainly was logical for rapid and efficient exploitation of a frontier resource. Now, fishery managers in Maine and elsewhere are realizing that a resource can be depleted, sometimes permanently. Individual lives can be wrecked, communities can be destroyed. An emerging understanding is that self-management—that is, control of fishing effort by those who fish, those who depend most directly on the resource—is necessary to minimize that risk.

The proposed legislation did represent exclusion in a literal sense. Not anyone could fish that piece of bottom. But it was never the case that literally anyone could. From the early nineteenth century the state restricted fishing in Maine waters to Mainers. Other U.S. citizens and certainly Canadians and other nationalities have been excluded. And, for that matter, Canada, Norway, Japan, and a host of other countries have excluded Americans from their inshore fisheries. Wherever fisheries have been under pressure and institutional mechanisms—traditional or governmental—have evolved, residency has mattered, and not just at the national or provincial level. The state of Maine long ago gave local residents preference on licenses to dig clams in their coastal and island communities, and coastal towns have controlled their local alewife fisheries.[55]

So, from this view, *selectivity* was the real issue in the Monhegan case. It is less about excluding and more about including—that is, carefully including those who can support and maintain the community of fishers. Part of that effort is sustaining the resource, working to restrain harvests (closed season, trap limits) even when everyone could use a bit more income. And part is sustaining the community, the community of fishers and the community of island residents who depend directly or indirectly on fishing. Yes, others are excluded from Monhegan waters, but selectivity is about fishers managing fishers.

In Augusta after some two months of lobbying, a series of legislative hearings, and considerable press coverage statewide, LD 2021 was given emergency status and, once out of committee, promptly passed by a 29 to 1 vote in the State Senate and by a 132 to 14 vote in the House. On Friday, February 27, 1998, the governor signed the legislation before a mostly pleased group of Monhegan fishers.

The legislature as a whole accepted the argument that the island community was, indeed, threatened. It recognized that its survival depends intimately on the survival of fishing, and that opening traditional bottom to nonislanders would destroy that fishing. Legislators opted for exclusive—or "selective"—use because the value of year-round, resource-dependent island communities outweighed whatever value otherwise inhered in providing all fishers with open access to all Maine waters, a situation that hardly ever existed in the first place due to traditional practices. For many, this was not an usurpation of local tradition, but a reinforcement of that tradition.[56]

Postscript   By June 25, 1998, the close date for Monhegan's 1998 season, only two Friendship lobster fishers remained, the rest having returned to their home territory. When the new legislation was put in place, all five Friendship lobster fishers asked the DMR to withdraw their registration from the Monhegan area. As of November 1998, there were no new entrants into the Monhegan fishery.

On December 1, 1998, a howling wind kept the Monhegan boats in the harbor. December 2 was the same, but the next day winds abated and thirteen captains with assorted sternmen and sternwomen began setting traps around the island, much as their predecessors had done for over a century. Only this time, by state law they could not venture more than two miles beyond the island except on the south side, where they could set traps three miles out but no more. And now mainland boats were setting traps not just on the north side of the island, but all around, just outside the official Monhegan zone. Not a few strayed into the Monhegan zone. In fact, the marine patrol captured 120 traps in one day, illegally set in Monhegan water. The jockeying for prized lobster bottom goes on. Monheganers may enforce the new zone by traditional means, tying off trap lines and cutting traps, but now with the new legislation, the marine patrol has an added incentive, if not staff and resources, to ensure Monheganers' right to fish their zone and nothing else.

As of fall 2003, the system is working for the Monheganers, says lobster fishing authority James Acheson. But it has come with a price. The "hate and discontent" continued well after the incident with the Friendship Five, only now it is directed at Monheganers by mainland fishers as a whole. One Monhegan lobsterman's boat was sunk while docked in Port Clyde. His brother was beaten on another occasion. One of the legislators who represented both Monhegan and Friendship lost reelection, and everyone knew why. Another did not bother to run. DMR officials dislike the arrangement because they are obligated to monitor the boundaries. With traps littering the waters all around Monhegan, it is nearly an impossible job. On the more positive side, Swan's Island fishers have created a subzone of their own and imposed a 350-trap limit on themselves. And local, small-boat groundfishers are proposing a similar system of zones as cod and haddock populations recover. The Monhegan case may be exceptional but, says Acheson, it may well serve as the model for fisheries management, too.[57]

From the Fishhouse to the Statehouse: A Sense of Sufficiency

Supporters lauded the new legislation for upholding tradition, preserving a rural community, and promoting conservation. But the terms *tradition*, *preservation*, and *conservation* can be misleading. The Monhegan case was not a matter of holding on to the past, of saving quaint practices in the face of advancing progress. If there was a tradition to be upheld it was the tradition of continuously experimenting with new methods of self-management—that is, of resource users' self-conscious decisions to impose on themselves harvest limits. If this was "tradition," then moderns have a lot to learn from those who, with neither sophisticated scientific knowledge nor the coercive authority of the state, came face to face with resource limits and adapted, that is, *adapted to the limits*. It may be a defining characteristic of modernization, of "progressive" resource extraction, that human cleverness is largely applied to *escaping limits*, to displacing costs, to shading and distancing, to optimal foraging as if there was always a resource frontier. Maybe "traditionalists" knew intuitively that an endless supply of virgin resources has never existed. Or, more humbly, maybe they knew they were not going to be the pioneers who find them. Or, more heroically, maybe they did not care. What they really cared about was providing for the long-term economic security of themselves, their families, and their communities. Maybe they reasoned that if economic security could be had at this scale it would necessarily aggregate into economic security at the national, even international, level. Regardless, those who sought a different path from fish-out-and-get-out were pioneers of their own sort, much as were A. S. Murphy and Emanuel Fritz and their followers in the redwoods. But unlike the redwood case, here the state instituted enabling conditions. The Monhegan case was pioneering for *self-management* and for *co-management* with state authority.

The essence of such tradition, if we are to call it that, is putting the resource first or, more precisely, according primacy to users' interaction with the resource rather than to the designs and desires of absentee owners, efficiency-oriented managers, distanced investors, ill-informed regulators, and price-sensitive consumers. Informally, tradition in the Monhegan case has meant that users themselves control use (through seasonal and trap limits) and entry (through apprenticing). Formally, tradition has meant that the state reinforce such practices through laws and regulations, rule making that limits or outright prohibits the most technologically efficient means of harvesting (general bans on bottom trawls, underwater diving, and all other means besides the trap), and owner-operator laws requiring all Maine fishers to do their own fishing. That kind of tradition can be fiercely defended by a Mainer. "The people who call the law that bans the catching of lobsters by any other means than the conventional trap a backward piece of legislation may be right," wrote one local newspaper editorialist in the 1960s. "The traps are inefficient they say, and obsolete. They may be right. But the meaningful truth of the matter is that the conventional trap, inefficient and cumbersome though it may be, hard life though it may represent, catches just about all the lobsters that crawl just as soon as they are big enough."[58] But that's not all they catch. "Crabs, sea urchins, whelks, starfish, sculpins, sea fleas and a ravenous horde of other freeloaders drop in at all hours of the day and night to help themselves," writes a *Smithsonian* magazine editor.[59] Scientific study has shown that 94 percent of lobsters that enter traps just walk right back out after sampling the bait. The lobster trap may be the most inefficient device in fisheries today. And lobster catchers know it. "It's a very primitive trap we use," remarked one lobsterman. Rather than a cause for concern, though, rather than raising the progressive's tireless red flag of "inefficiency," lobster catchers see a connection between the "traditional" on the one hand, and limited harvests and long-term security on the other. "We're traditional in a lot of ways," the lobsterman continues. "As long as we keep using traps, we'll never catch them all. . . . I think that's going to save us in the long run."[60] Traps, it seems that Mainers—fishers and lawmakers—have discovered over time, create a tradition all right, a tradition of sufficient technology, of built-in restraint.

As for preserving a rural community, the new legislation did that. But it did so not by appropriating funds for development projects, not by subsidizing employers and bailing out failed businesses, and not by attracting foreign investment. Rather it "preserved the community" by providing the larger institutional context in which community members could, individually and collectively, sustain themselves. *High government* was important here because it enabled *low governance* to operate. The analytic and prescriptive task for analyst and policymaker is not so much identifying which institutions are most important—local or state. And it certainly is not to presume that the state is the most important, the prevalent approach, one that privileges state authority, expert knowledge, and the necessity of major financial backing. Rather, the task is to understand how a series of overlapping institutional arrangements reinforce each other. Sustainable practice, this case suggests, begins with the resource, the lobsters, and with the users, the fishers. From here we see how each user's practice shapes and is shaped by the users' self-devised norms and rules of fishing, which in turn are nested in the larger community of permanent, year-round island residents. All are then nested in the institutions of the state—the subnational (states or provinces), national, even international.

The Monhegan case suggests that true conservation requires a combination of things: intimate knowledge of the resource, dependency on that resource, and the space—physical, social, and temporal—to experiment with technologies and self-limiting mechanisms. Those in a hurry rarely have such a combination. They are too busy hauling traps and capturing bottom, too specialized in some piece of the biophysical equation or in some component of the regulatory machinery. They themselves are not pluralists in their work and certainly not dependent for their income on any one resource. When a septuagenarian lobsterman tells me he's just an old fisherman who doesn't know anything, he's right in only one sense: he doesn't know how much he knows. He doesn't know that the rhetorical line so-called experts have fed fishers like himself, let alone the media and the public, is logically deficient. He doesn't know that when it comes to long-term sustainable resource use, environmentalists and resource managers have been looking in the wrong places.

Laboratories, legislatures, and lecture halls, not to mention the deep pockets of governments and foundations, may build hospitals and dams, get us to the moon, and defeat foreign enemies. They certainly spur efficient resource extraction. But they are intrinsically ill-equipped to handle what is otherwise such a prosaic, mundane task as organizing and managing for long-term resource use. At best, they (the present author included) can help others discover that old-timers like this lobsterman, as well as lumbermen like A. S. Murphy, foresters like Emanuel Fritz, and fish wardens like those in Maine's DMR, know what elements of tradition and conservation go hand in hand on the ground and on the water. Those others would include people without direct experience, especially those enamored of the promises of scientific and technological progress, those who ardently believe that net gains and political neutrality follow from the application of efficiency principles. Experiential, long-term intimate knowledge is thus one condition for sustainable practice, an element of ecological rationality most likely to be acquired by those who make their living in direct contact with the resource. Embedding that knowledge and its practice in larger institutional structures—communities and the state—is a second condition. Together these are the knowledge and institutional conditions that can put a society on a sustainable path. Rights to access—I call this "selective permeability"—and ownership are two more. All these are governed by principles that embody limits, that say enough when the opportunities for increase are ever-present.

Like a Cell: Selective Permeability

With lobstering up and down the Maine coast "busting out at the seams," as the chief of the Maine marine patrol put it, limiting traps, restricting gear types, and setting closed seasons was not enough, especially on a statewide basis.[61] Exclusion, anathema to those who believe public resources should be freely available to all members of the public, we have seen, was also needed. With fisheries of all sorts collapsing around the world, managers and policymakers as well as fishers themselves have come to realize that open access cannot work. When boats and gear are increasingly efficient and consumer demand strong, allowing anyone to fish anywhere means that overharvesting is virtually inevitable. Limiting access has increasingly become the watchword, in principle if not in practice.[62]

Exclusion implies territorial defense of some sort. Just as wolves, crows, and nations set up and defend territory, fishers, farmers, and loggers tend to carve out a piece of the resource for their exclusive use. It all seems perfectly natural. What this case reveals, however, is that a precondition for such "natural" exclusion and defense is restraint and respite, a precondition, that is, when long-term, secure resource use is the goal. The beneficiaries of exclusion cannot consume nature's bounty, only sustain it. Excluding others requires controlling the value of entry, setting a sufficient level of gain from the resource, not a maximum level. The six-month season, 600-trap limit, and residential apprenticing were all means of doing less; not doing less as a matter of sacrifice or high moral principle, but doing less than what was possible, less than the contemporary industry norm. Such self-limiting measures go beyond physical boundaries to questions of time, technology, and livelihood in work and community. They blend the need to make a living season to season and across generations with particular day-to-day practices. Most significantly, they render short-term maximum gain, "efficient" exploitation of the resource as measured in tons per year or revenue per investment dollar, secondary, not primary. Although few in Maine lobstering would use terms like *restraint* (recall though, that Pacific Lumber officials did use that term) or *sufficiency*, it is clear that Monhegan's social practices with their biophysical effects were not driven by efficiency principles. Practitioners, policymakers, and analysts may speak in efficiency terms, but this case suggests that, under certain conditions—namely, ecological and social threat—the long-term time frame puts sufficiency above efficiency as the dominant principle of social organization.

Still, there is a politics of exclusion. Special treatment for a select few is a touchy issue in a society like the United States that prides itself on mobility and free and open access. And it becomes a touchy issue for those who would extend that pride around the world. Opposition to LD 2021 is a case in point. In the context of long-term resource use, though, exclusion may not be entirely antithetical to the democratic precepts of openness and equal access. In fact, exclusion has a long history in the European settlement of North America, where private property and political jurisdictions were laid out very early on. Even in the heyday of frontier exploitation, fences and state lines established what land can be tilled, whose cattle can be grazed, and who has a say in public disputes. Some people were in, some were out. Some got good land or nice ocean bottom, some did not. Formal and informal means of boundary setting have been long practiced wherever there was the slightest possibility of competition for a resource. Only Mainers fish Maine waters, not New Yorkers and not Canadians or Japanese.

Monhegan may represent, therefore, only a special case of exclusion, which I have termed *selectivity*. In lobstering, traditional practice was the first institutional mechanism to deal with resource competition a century or more ago. Territorial defense was the marine equivalent of fencing. But with rising numbers of fishers, ever more efficient boats and gear, and simply the mobility of participants geographically and in and out of the industry, these means of exclusion proved inadequate. Territorial defense intensified in some places, restrained harvesting emerged in others. In extreme cases, harbor gang leaders became warlords constantly jockeying for more and better territory, threatening others by whatever means necessary, legal and extralegal. In other cases the state experimented with formal measures, backed up by its coercive authority.

But the issue on Monhegan as elsewhere has never really been one of complete exclusion. Much as the body's cells protect their interior organelles at the same time that they exchange gases and nutrients with their environment, boundaries are never rigid or impassable. And just as humans and other animals benefit genetically from migration and crossbreeding, resource communities benefit from the movements of seed and prey and new participants. Boundaries are necessary but they must be permeable. What is more, for a resource as wild as the lobster and for individuals as mobile as the typical fisher, they must be *selectively permeable*.

The most direct means of being selective is apprenticing, an age-old practice, which, as noted, continues to be prevalent in a variety of occupations—the trades, medicine, law, and academe, for example. Apprenticing may contradict the efficiency experts' ideal of complete factor mobility, but that ideal may never have applied beyond the factory and frontier (chapters 3, 4, and 5). The Monhegan case suggests that selectivity via apprenticing may be a necessary condition with contemporary pressures. Those who came from away and stayed on Monhegan were, in the first instance, self-selecting. They would do their time and undergo the apprenticing, experiencing firsthand the closed season and trap limits. After months and years on the boats, working their way into the fishhouse, they would learn that they would not get rich here, but nor would they get trapped into an endless pattern of highlining and hogging. If they stayed, they would do so knowing that these local measures slowed and controlled for entry into the fishery, that they were selective— self-selective and other-selective. Put in terms of ecological rationality, they are the measures that create the intersection between the social system (the fishhouse, the larger harbor community, and the state government) and the biophysical system (the immediate ocean bottom and the larger Gulf of Maine and North Atlantic oceanic ecosystem). They facilitate feedback between the two.

The Monhegan case reveals how traditional practice controlled the mobility of users in and out of the fishery and how, with increasing pressure, state authority has been increasingly necessary to reinforce that control. Of course, the rhetoric of state action and the hegemony of the efficiency principle are such that state actors cannot publicly oppose efficiency lest they be charged with standing in the way of progress. Instead, in Maine the state emphasized "conservation," "community," and "heritage," even "developing the resource" (by conserving it) when justifying Monhegan's exclusive zone. The state's acts of limitation are best interpreted, though, as a check on mobility, as a boundary on the application of the efficiency principle and thus restraint expressed at the governmental level. A government always needs more revenues and always during the current fiscal year. Here the state of Maine could probably always gain revenue by increasing the access of all fishers to all Maine waters and by allowing large operators—irrespective of ownership—to enter the industry. But Maine has refrained from doing so. Instead, it has repeatedly reinforced self-determined work (only owner-operators are eligible for a commercial fishing license) and local economies. "Elsewhere in the country, in the world, fishing is becoming a corporate venture with fishermen as serfs," a Bangor, Maine, newspaper editorialized on the eve of LD 2021's passage. Those "serfs," those hirelings attached to the resource by no more than a wage or a contract, are employed to extract as much as possible from the sea. Fortunately for lobsters and lobster catchers and the communities that depend on them, that world of hirelings is still anathema in Maine, "the last stronghold of the individual owner-operator," says the Maine editorialist.[63]

How Much Is Enough?

Lobstering is one of the few remaining fisheries in North America, perhaps in the world, in which the resource is abundant and, it appears, self-reproducing. Fishers can earn a decent but not luxurious living and pass on their gear and know-how to their children and others. And lobstering is one of the few kinds of fishing that can still be carried out by small operators or private businesspeople who are their own boss—self-determining individuals who do a little of everything (chapter 5). Some succeed by being brutally efficient, getting every last lobster off a piece of bottom and fending off interlopers. Others succeed by being adaptive, adjusting to climatic and biological shifts right along with the social and economic shifts. Maybe both— the "hogs" and the "adapters," the frontiersmen and the settlers, are needed, or can be accommodated, in a sustainable system. Maybe the two are comparable to what ecologists call the "r-strategists" (the pioneering, fast-growing, quick-to-colonize species) and the "k-strategists" (the settled, low-maintenance, long-living species). But this case suggests that the ecological, nonhuman analogy is imperfect, especially with respect to the goal of long-term sustainable resource use. The frontiersmen hogs may get their bonanzas, becoming the envy of newcomers and the subject of media accounts, but it is the adaptive settlers who enable the resource and the livelihood to endure. It is the settlers who invest in the social system as much as their boat and equipment, who forgo the bonanzas, who carve out a pattern of work with rewards beyond this season's sales.

Lobstering is also one of the few fisheries for which external restriction, constraint, has been less important than internal restriction, restraint. The coincidence with a thriving fishery is more than accidental. Restraint involves deliberately using less of a resource than is possible in the short term in exchange for tangible and intangible benefits in the long term (chapter 1). It is a resource strategy that rejects the lure of material bonanzas in exchange for other, generally less material benefits such as long-term economic security, kinship support, and community integrity. One doesn't "game" restraint, as one games constraint (e.g., tax evasion). And lofty principles such as conservation or sustainability are not needed to enact behaviors and build institutions that are, indeed, conserving and contribute to a sustainable development path. Nevertheless, the evolved, limited-access regime of this case reveals that higher principles can be invoked to make the choice of restraint easier and, importantly, to resist external, destructive forces. From the

Monheganers' perspective, one of the external forces was "fishing pressure," that combination of people and gear caught in an escalating game of getting ahead or of keeping up, a game in which all too many actually fall further behind. The critical evidence proffered on behalf of Monhegan before the Marine Resources Committee of the Maine legislature was its history of restraint. At the close of the twentieth century, it could be framed as conservationist or simply farsighted, even "sustainable." It could be argued then that what Monhegan was doing is good for the state, good for other fishers as a model of resource management, good for other lobster grounds as a source of spawn. But the reality was that Monheganers for at least a century saw the frontier closing all around them and consistently chose a different path, one that depended less on "efficient production," less on fish-out-and-move-on, and more on diversified work, more on restrain-our-fishing-and-institute-our-procedures.

It is tempting to idealize this case. For those of us who struggle to envision a sustainable society, this is about as close as one might get to a contemporary example in an industrialized country. Here is a community whose economy is grounded in a renewable resource and whose members have deliberately chosen a low-impact way of life, both on the water and on the land. Monhegan's rejection of the private automobile on the island and its low level of electricity use contrasts greatly with American society as a whole and even with other islands, especially the tourist spots.

But one has to be careful about putting this tiny community up on a pedestal. Monheganers remain vulnerable to larger forces outside their community. And within their community, it is never a given that the choices they make today—be it expanding their fishing season or building a power generator—will not undermine their fragile existence tomorrow. To claim that this island is "sustainable" is not only inaccurate but does injustice to the concept: sustainability is a process, a vector with direction and magnitude, not an endpoint. What can be claimed and what can serve as a model is this community's ability to be both reflective and willing to forgo temptations.

Although conjectural, it is reasonable to assume that a century ago fishermen and their families had to think long and hard about the implications of denying themselves lucrative lobstering for half the year. They may have had alternatives then such as longlining for groundfish or farming or logging. But they must have also known that fishing, like farming and logging, is highly variable and highly unpredictable. What Monheganers probably could not have foreseen is that their efforts established a reflective tradition of sorts, a self-conscious, self-examining pattern of collective behavior that has been passed from generation to generation and from old-timer to newcomer, a pattern applied not just to the resource but to everyday life. What distinguishes Monhegan is not the rich lobstering grounds per se (there were even richer ones all throughout the lobsters' natural range), let alone the solar panels on the rooftops or the quaint, movie-set village ambiance. Rather, it is a practice that embodies a habit of asking how much is enough and how much is too much, and doing so not just as individual choice but as collective choice.

Did the actors back then see "sufficiency" in their lives? Certainly not with the terminology I have introduced in this study. But the historical and contemporary evidence suggests that many fishers, Monheganers included, were seeking more than a bonanza. They knew that lobsters could be fished out; it had happened all along the Eastern seaboard of the United States, a wave of depletion rolling up the coast beginning in the southern range of the species where human populations were densest and moving northward. The threat to fishers who desired a more stable source of income and were willing to forgo the bonanzas was real. If they didn't "get their act together," a phrase common among these self-reliant, residential islanders, they too would be looking for new lines of work. They too could forsake the independence and satisfaction of self-employment and "get a job," as so many were doing in the latter part of the nineteenth century and into the twentieth. They too could become yet another "worker," an employee, fighting for the right to organize and the right to claim a piece of the wealth others owned. Or they could stake their claim, organize themselves, occasionally solicit help from the state as in 1907 and 1998, apply principles of sufficiency—restrain their resource use, build respite into their annual rhythm of work—and resist incursions.

Put this way, the choice was clear. But it is crucial to stress that it is a choice few others have made in the United States and other industrialized countries. The bonanza has been too tempting, too alluring in its easy money and illusions of wealth and consumer satisfaction. The real wealth, stories like Monhegan and Pacific Lumber tell us, is not in bonanzas, not in efficient exploitation of natural and social capital with depletion presumed unavoidable, a negligible or correctable "externality." The real wealth is in achieving congruence between social and biophysical systems, ensuring their long-term functioning and reproduction. It is in constantly conducting small experiments, experiments that, if they fail, do not threaten calamity and, if they impose burdens, those burdens are not exported to others. More precisely, from a systems perspective and with a long-term orientation it is the intersection of the two systems that is critical. This intersection establishes the difference between inherently short-term, frontiersman, and economistic strategies on the one hand, and long-term sustainable strategies on the other. It is in these experiments and ongoing practices, the "work" of fishing, one might say, that the exchange of information, the feedback, the "knowing" in all the ways that one can truly know the people and the resources exists. It is through such "ecological rationality" that wealth is created, material (biophysical and monetary) and human (personal and social). This is true wealth. It comes from application to task, coordination of effort, finding a place, securing a livelihood. It comes from, indeed, pursuing a calling. It cannot be purchased. There is no consumer logic here, only a logic of "real work" (chapter 5).

To ask how much is enough is to invite a calculation, an estimate of the numbers or pounds of lobsters a fishery can support. From a conventional fisheries-management perspective, one grounded in quantitative modeling and economic calculation, this question implies a notion of maximum yield and leads to figures for a total allowable catch. By contrast, self-management regimes that have evolved over many years with the resource and under the influence of external institutions of governance and markets do not ask the question of how much is enough. Instead, they seem to ask *how much is too much* and then keep well within that upper bound. And they seem to employ *indirect limits* on resource use. Monhegan's six-month season did not maximize catch; it made fishing effort constant (six months of fishing, no more) while catch and, hence, income varied. If a member of the fishing community wanted steady income year after year, or increasing income, that fisher would make up the shortfall with extra work during the closed season, doing odd jobs or serving tourists, not fishing more, not demanding more and more of the resource. Because history has shown that, over time, six months of lobstering can be sustained, the rhythm of fishing follows the rhythm of the natural resource, not the other way around.

This case suggests that fishery management—that is, the management by fishers and others of human fishing effort, self-management—is successful when indirect means are employed for controlling effort, and when those means are developed over time by the fishers themselves. External means of limiting catch through population measurement and external enforcement are much less likely to endure. From a scientific management perspective, one might assume that if only the fishers had the data, or better data, they would adopt something like total allowable catch. But lobstermen in Maine and fishers elsewhere probably have as good a set of scientific data as can be had for a fishery. And, from experience, they put little faith in such data. In part, this is an epistemological issue. What fishers know from spending hours a day, day in and day out, year after year and generation after generation can never be matched, let alone surpassed, by scientific study. Certainly, scientific study can complement the knowledge system of the fishers. Lobster biologist Robert Steneck, for example, has shown that Monhegan has a significantly greater density of lobsters per square mile than elsewhere along the maine coast. He could not say, though, whether five more fishers would destroy the Monhegan fishery. Steneck's work may have been politically useful in making the case that Monhegan waters are special, both for the Monhegan fishery and for many others in Maine. But as he himself admitted, his data cannot inform managers about how much is enough. At best, he can point to a fishery like Monhegan and conclude that it is *not too much* and point to the fishery around, say, Portland, and conclude that it is *probably too much*. But such conclusions are no better than hunches, and certainly no better than what every experienced lobsterman and lobsterwoman knows. In fact, it sometimes appears that what scientific study does is confirm or legitimize what the fishers already know. The day may come when fisheries managers assume that the requisite knowledge already exists, or, at least, that such knowledge has developed in places where scientific management, technological marvels, big capital investments, and state coercion have not run roughshod over resource users and their self-management systems. Fisheries managers' task would then be to translate the requisite knowledge for those still immersed in notions of optimal foraging and frontier resource exploitation. Epistemological primacy resides with those who experience the resource and its great variability over long periods of time. This is a radical notion within the logic of efficiency and under the goal of rapid economic expansion, but it is perfectly sensible within the logic of sufficiency and under the goal of sustainability, especially for those who live with and depend on such resources.

One fisherman told me that autumn is his favorite time on Monhegan. The weather is pleasant, the tourists are gone, and there's not a lot of work to do except to get the boat and gear ready for the upcoming fishing season. One can imagine an efficiency expert's objections: lobstering needs a longer season, starting in, say, October or even September. Boats, equipment, and manpower are sitting idle. With shedding complete and mainland lobsters migrating offshore in the fall, many toward islands like Monhegan, the lobsters are there for the taking. Yes, declares the efficiency expert, the longer season would be an unambiguous efficiency gain. One can also imagine that a few would-be "hogs" or just young fishers starting out and trying to pay off debts would support such a change. But the strength of the Monhegan fishing and residential communities suggests that a proposal for an expanded season would quickly sink. Just as "real fishing" begins on the water after the first few weeks of easy catches, "real living" for Monheganers begins on land when the tourists leave and the weather is still warm and the days are still long. *Restraint in harvesting translates into respite in livelihood.* These values cannot be captured in an equation, let alone a bottom-line dollar figure. A large enough component of the community knows this, and interviews, testimony, and written accounts suggest they would defend it to the utmost. Restraint in resource use and respite in livelihood make sense for a host of reasons—personal, family, community, and resource biology. That "working rationality," that logic of sufficiency, is probably more stark on Monhegan than elsewhere, in large part because the direct ties to the resource make it so.

But the point should be generalizable. Seeking sufficiency can be empowering. It can free up time and energy that otherwise would be dissipated by the "work-and-spend treadmill," by the pursuit of ever greater efficiencies at work and ever more "goods" at leisure. It can motivate the larger truth that the work-leisure dichotomy and never-ending efficiency seeking contradict basic individual and social capacities, not to mention ecological constraints (chapter 5). Livelihood, by contrast, builds in restraint and respite in recognition of these capacities and constraints. Indeed, it is the acceptance of limits, not the perpetual and ultimately futile attempt to escape them, that is enlivening and often empowering. For all the challenges of surviving in the modern world on a tiny rock in the Gulf of Maine, dependent on one resource and tourism, Monheganers seem to grasp this truth. At risk of romanticizing their otherwise difficult lives, they seem to know that doing less than is possible in one realm (the material) enables them to do more than is otherwise imaginable in other realms (family and community life). That such an understanding dovetails with restraint in resource use is more than coincidental. It is precisely in such interactions that essential feedback from the biophysical system reaches the social system. That intersection is more than the transmission of information, as critical as negative ecological feedback is. It is also the capacity of individuals and collectivities to organize their lives and livelihoods in ways that respect a fixed, renewable, but ultimately exhaustible resource.

More Than an Island: Security in Limits

It is tempting to dismiss the apparent sustainability of Monhegan fishing and community life as an artifact of island life. Islanders are isolated and insulated. They have to do things differently. They cannot, as one Monheganer after another said, just hop in the pickup and get another job down the road when things get rough. If the island is to be their primary basis of economic and social life, they do have to be adaptive. They have to weather downturns with new sources of income or by doing without. On the mainland, by contrast, there are always alternatives. One can always push the limits of a job or a neighborhood or a resource and, if it fails, move on. On an island, one is stuck.

But if island life is different from mainland life, the important question from the sustainability perspective is whether it is merely an anomaly or potentially a model. In searching for insights into the behaviors and institutions necessary for long-term resource use (a major purpose of this book), I have developed this case study on the assumption that island life just might be more than a quaint throwback, more than an existence inordinately constrained by geography, transportation, and communications. If this assumption is reasonable, then what distinguishes island life for individuals and communities is *limits*, perhaps an intense sense of limits. "By definition, life on an island is all about limits," say two longtime residents of Monhegan:

> The awareness that the resources around you are limited is intrinsic; it creates an attitude, a way of life that is unique to island communities. An island community feels its parameters in everything it does. There are limits to the space you have to move around in, limits to the resources, limited job opportunities. Being aware of limits, we must always conserve water, we limit the numbers of vehicles on the road, we vigilantly recycle our trash. We limit development to a small area of the island to preserve the forest that covers the rest.
>
> Recognizing our limits also translates into a respect for each other's piece of the economic "pie." We all share the limited economic opportunities on the island. This creates an unspoken but very real ethic of cooperation that tempers competition, because we all have a vested interest in each family being able to make a living. Conservation is at the very core of island values—and a way of daily life.[64]

Put differently, go to an island like Monhegan and you will find that limited resources and limited ability to externalize costs stare you in the face day in and day out. To act rationally you must find ways to survive by living *within* those limits, not by escaping them. With practice and discipline you can even thrive. You can find meaning through the challenges of individual action ("work") and social interaction ("teamwork"), all within the constraints offered by nature and human nature. You can be, in short, ecologically rational when all the world, it seems, is only economically rational, if that.

So how is it that ecological rationality is so straightforward to islanders, so alien to financiers, government leaders, academics, and journalists? Resource dependence is an obvious difference. And yet, from a global ecological perspective, the denizens of New York, Tokyo, and Geneva are no less resource dependent than those of Monhegan. As global ecological constraint tightens, even those best able to buy their way out of resource limits, to externalize the costs of their consumption, will feel the impacts. No one escapes climate change or freshwater shortage or persistent, bioaccumulative, endocrine-disrupting substances. As ecological constraints intensify, as all the environmental adages take root around shacks and mansions alike (what goes around comes around; no "away" to throw the trash; it's all connected; we're all downstream) even the comfortable will find we're all on one island, planet earth.

Economist Kenneth Boulding called it spaceship earth, a ship floating in space completely dependent on a complex web of biophysical life-support systems. This is an island of life where people are acutely aware of limits in their everyday life, limits to what they can draw from nature, and limits to what can be demanded of individuals and collectivities. If such an island, the planet, is to have "an economy," it must be one grounded in long-term ecological and social interaction, not in frontier exploitation, not in maximum income or GDP, and certainly not in displacing true ecological costs and perpetuating ever-increasing throughput. It must be governed by principles like restraint and respite.

Back on Monhegan, on the waters around the island, downeast, in and about the Maritime provinces, and in many other lobster fishing areas, restraint and respite are no mere abstractions. They are concrete, daily occurrences. Come to Monhegan in the summer, prime tourist season, order that longed-for lobster dinner, and tell yourself: this one pound "bug" came from elsewhere. As tempting as it may be for fisher and visitor alike, no one on Monhegan catches lobsters in the summer. Boats are moored; traps are set on high land to bake in the sun. Fishing captains are turning bedsheets or serving you that lobster "from away." But they aren't fishing. This is respite, not a fanciful ideal, but a reality.

And then next time, come to Monhegan before June 25 or after December 1 (and bundle up good). Watch a lobster boat (binoculars will help) as the helmsman and sternwoman pull in their traps. Watch them prop a trap on the boat's starboard rail, open it, and lift out lobsters. Imagine all the effort the two fishers put into setting that trap and luring those lobsters in. And then watch the two fishers proceed to throw back four or five, six or seven, even eight or nine of every ten lobsters caught. Yes, they do so by law—the double-gauge limits on size require it of lobster catchers and dealers alike. But they also do it by convention—the V-notch on egg-bearing females is entirely voluntary (see figure 7.4).

But it wasn't always that way. Before the big crash of lobsters in the early twentieth century, few lobster catchers returned lobsters, even if gravid or undersize, let alone oversize. Instead they would sell them to a local restaurant, try to pass them off on a dealer, take them home for dinner, or smash them up and use them for bait

Figure 7.4
Lobsterman tosses back a healthy lobster.

or fertilizer in the garden or feed for the chickens. For decades, though, as easy as it would be, virtually no one has done this, on Monhegan or anywhere else in Maine. A set of norms has evolved to govern practice, norms that say excess is possible, that restraint and respite not only make sense for others, but for oneself and one's kin. One can imagine that the early proponents, whether fishers or "fishcrats," were scoffed at: Nobody will throw back lobsters! People are too selfish. They're short-sighted. All they think about is money! Get rich and get out! Much of the evidence cited here suggests this was the prevailing attitude. But the proponents persisted. And now norms like restraint and respite, however they are labeled ("conservation," "preservation," "wise use," "saving the chicks") are, indeed, "normal," practiced day in and day out in the coves and inlets, and even a dozen miles out to sea.

On the surface, what was at stake over the years on Monhegan and elsewhere was fishing pressure, excess effort for a limited resource. But more fundamentally, the issue has been knowledge and the relations between natural and human systems. It was not so long ago in fisheries management that "traditional" means of man-agement were scoffed at, derided as primitive, backward, unscientific, and ultimately ineffectual. Today, scientific study both biological and social is uncovering some of the inherent wisdom and, indeed, effectiveness (if not efficiency) of the traditional means. After all, it is only at the close of the twentieth century that officials have dared experiment with closed access. The fishermen have been doing it "traditionally" for a century. The language of "fishcrats" and lawmakers has changed dramatically. Many of the quotes above indicate not just a grudging acceptance of traditional means but almost a reverential deference to such means. This is probably most pronounced in certain academic circles (not the fishery modelers and resource economists, but the social and systems analysts), a sentiment increasingly picked up by policymakers and enforcement officials. When the chief of the marine patrol in 1997 warns the Friendship Five that if century-old, traditional management systems are allowed to erode it will lead "to the demise of the fishing industry," he is elevating traditional means of self-regulation from obscurity and derision to a level on a par with the formal means, those grounded in law, economics, and population biology. When the seventh-generation Monhegan lobsterman states that he doesn't know anything about the fishery, that he doesn't have data or scientific proof of its health, he reveals two things. First, for most of his life the knowledge he has had about the fishery has been routinely dismissed by people with fancy credentials and official titles, people who have made decisions that profoundly affect his ability to make a living from the sea and yet who themselves are not grounded in the work and livelihood of the sea. Scientific knowledge has reigned supreme throughout the last couple centuries, along with economic analysis and legal prescription. He has been a beneficiary, but also a victim. Second, he is out of touch with the dramatic changes in attitudes (the "sea change") among many credentialed and titled people, including many who make critical resource-management decisions. It is probably no exaggeration to say that the twenty-first century will see an even greater change as certain ideas ascend, ideas like community and ecological integrity, and, dare I say, ecological rationality, self-determined work, and sufficiency through restraint and respite. This will be the first century in which people in all walks of life will be forced to come to grips with ecological constraint, just as this senior fisherman and his ancestors have done and his descendants are now doing. This will be the first century in which planet earth will look an awful lot like an isolated island where limits stare you in the face. Far from "knowing nothing," those who interact with the resource day in and day out, for years, decades, and even centuries, and from one generation to the next, are precisely the ones with the knowledge that informs us all, that tells us not just how to manage resources, but how to manage our relations with resources, how to ask how much is too much.

8
Toronto Island: Resisting Automobility

Imagine a large, North American metropolitan city with a typical set of urban problems: crime, drugs, traffic congestion, sprawl, pollution. Imagine further a middle-to lower-middle-class neighborhood there. You walk up to one house after another and the doors are all unlocked, whether or not the occupants are at home. Walk down the street (there are no sidewalks) and you pass others on foot and on bicycles; some are pushing strollers or carts loaded with groceries. Occasionally you step aside to let a motorized vehicle—a service van or maintenance truck or, less often, a car—pass by. Having come to this neighborhood from the center of the city, it takes awhile to realize how remarkably quiet it is, even with people all about, including children. In fact, the children are playing in the street and you feel a little unsure whether they are unduly impeding your movement or if you are unduly interrupting their games.

For those of us who know urban life in North America, such a neighborhood is truly imaginary—or, perhaps for seniors, a distant memory. But it exists today in Toronto, the fourth-largest metropolitan area in all of North America and the capital of Ontario, Canada's most populous province. This neighborhood exists in part because of a peculiar geographic feature—it rests on two tiny islands a half mile offshore in Lake Ontario. Longtime residents and city historians know that geography explains only part of this scene, however. The other part is the relative absence of cars. That absence was not a simple consequence of being a tiny island, though. Connecting the island to the mainland via bridge or tunnel has long been straightforward technically and, in fact, city planners have tried—again and again throughout the twentieth century. Rather, the reason is that residents have consistently rejected the development schemes of others, electing—sometimes fighting in court and on the streets—to retain their community as a community, one mostly devoid of automobiles. They have deliberately and self-consciously limited automobile access in their attempt to carve out a different kind of neighborhood.

Today, most residents who live there, people who have never locked their doors and who don't think twice about sending their children out in the street to play, know at least intuitively that a consequence of limited auto access is a high quality of urban life. One observer, Sally Gibson, wrote a doctoral dissertation and book on the history of the Toronto Islands. For the early history of these islands—their residential life and parkland recreation—I draw extensively on her work and a follow-up interview, as well as on numerous official documents and news accounts. I also conducted interviews on the island with a half dozen or so residents, including one who has lived all her sixty-some years there.

The portrait is admittedly biased, favorable to the life and the choices of those who live there. But it is a bias that is more than ideological. It derives from a theoretical orientation that looks for and tends to see value in sufficiency—in this case, to see value in the "too muchness" of contemporary open-access automobility in North American cities and in the "just rightness" of having a few cars and a few service vehicles in one's residential neighborhood.

Certainly the unique history of the Toronto Islands cannot be replicated elsewhere. But the fact that a sufficient level of automobile access can be deliberately chosen by a community can serve as a model—at least at scales such as this. The motivations for sufficient mobility may vary from place to place, community to community. But the conclusion may well be the same: for a host of reasons, some "quality of life," some economic, some ecological, a city can have too many cars, too much parking, too much exclusion of pedestrians and bicyclists and wheelchair users, and too little spontaneous conversation and unstructured play.

Much of the issue of automobile use on Toronto Island centers on the question of access—who can drive to and from the islands and, especially, how many can drive. In the automobile culture, the answer to this question is straightforward: anyone can drive a vehicle of one's choosing and do so whenever and wherever one likes and for whatever purpose one has. Maximum mobility is the ideal. Certainly, commercial vehicles require a separate license and a curfew may limit driving times. One lane may be closed for repairs or reversed to facilitate rush hour traffic. But these are the exceptions. The rule, indeed the principle, in auto culture is that public roadways are for any member of the public with a vehicle and a license to use any time and for any purpose. If external costs are created in such private consumption of public space, laws need passing, fines imposed. But mobility, automobility, is sacrosanct, beyond questioning, beyond anything but marginal tinkering. In automobilia, to even ask the question of auto access is strange except under extreme circumstances.

In the 1950s, as almost everywhere else in North America and much of Europe, the desire for auto access was intense. And a common destination was parks, especially parks with amenities—picnic tables, beaches, and rides. Toronto officials, like others, added a proviso: a city park should not just be open to "the public" in the same way that a theater or restaurant is open, but it should be open to as many people as possible. The utilitarian notion of the greatest good for the greatest number meant that all citizens should have access—and equal access. Wealthy summer visitors on the Toronto Islands with their well-appointed "cottages" (many of which would be termed mansions anywhere else) should not get preferential treatment. And the year-round folks, those commoners in ramshackle tents and huts at the two ends of the islands, people who were effectively squatting on public property (albeit with city leases), certainly had no inherent right to their cheap housing, especially with the public subsidy they enjoyed with ferry service to the mainland.

Residency versus recreation. Daily living versus amenity. This, we will see, is how the conflict over the Toronto Islands played out midcentury. At century's end, it was economic stagnation versus economic stimulus; a "business-friendly" environment versus a park, a small-time airport, and some houses. At the center of it all, though, was the automobile, a technology supremely designed for private mobility, private consumption, and private access. But at issue was not just the technology, but the culture of the automobile, the worship of mobility and speed and convenience. Automobility is not just about transport, but about a community's very conception of access and amenity, indeed, of the "good life."

This chapter is thus about a peculiar cultural form, automobility. Embedded in a larger culture, one wedded to expansion and speed and efficiency, it elevates one value (private mobility) at the same time it depreciates others (community, health, climate stability). As a sustainability analyst and member of such a culture, to take on automobility is, admittedly, a bit daunting. The automobile, with its associated industries, is so pervasive, so dominant that, for most of us thoroughly immersed in its culture, it is, like efficiency, the water in which we swim. We can't see automobility as a cultural form, let alone question its benefits.

So as something of a disclaimer, I must add a personal note before proceeding. I was born in the heyday of the automobile and expanding automobility, the 1950s. I now live just down the road from three of the world's largest automakers. My salary, real estate value, and a lot more is intimately tied to that industry. In my daily professional and personal life I am surrounded by environmentally concerned individuals, yet when the subject of automobiles comes up, few talk about anything but better pollution control and more efficient engines. Even fewer have deliberately experimented with restrained auto use and restricted mobility; few have chosen to own only one car, say, or choose their residence on the basis of proximity to work. To open the question of restrained use and restricted mobility is to challenge underlying assumptions at many levels of social life—personal, family, community, and nation. It is thus with a bit of trepidation that I tackle this topic; automobility and, in particular, the *level* of auto use, is not like timbering and fishing where, as the analyst in the ivory tower, I can maintain some distance. I may work in an ivory tower (a contentious point I elect not to engage here), but I also live in a community, or collection of communities, personal and professional. The communities I know operate for the most part as if there is not a problem of automobility. Intellectually, everyone is well aware of the automobile's impacts but in practice, its use, including its ever-increasing use, is taken as given: retailers require parking to bring in customers, as do employers to attract good employees. In fact, all groups—businesses, customers, employers, employees, students, citizens—feel they not only need parking, but they are entitled to it. Talk to me about economic development or biodiversity or climate change or social justice. But don't talk to me about parking—or driving or road building. Those things, here in automobilia, are off limits, as taboo as questioning parental authority in most cultures.

I do take some comfort, though, in the fact that the cases in this chapter and in so much of the "sustainable transportation" literature represent more than utopian visions of a car-free society. These cases are conscious attempts to put the car in its place, to assess a full range of costs and benefits, to elevate the values of physical, psychological, and social space. They are, in short, collective attempts to decide how much auto use is enough and, certainly, how much is too much. If nothing else, the purpose of this chapter is to show that, even with the automobile, arguably the most environmentally significant technology of the twentieth century, and, likely, the twenty-first, a technology that, in its production and use, epitomizes efficiency-led progress amidst resource plenty, even here, sufficiency is possible.[1]

The Birth of an Auto-restricted Neighborhood

The Toronto Islands were originally a series of continuously shifting sandbars carried westward from the mouth of the Don River by Lake Ontario currents. By the early 1800s the longest of these bars extended nearly nine kilometers, forming a natural harbor between the lake and the mainland, just across from Toronto. Depending on the water level, the sandy spit of land was either a peninsula or a string of islands. First-nations peoples had long established campsites on this land, using them, according to early European reports, to take advantage of the fresh air and to hunt and fish. Recent observers say the islands were places of healing.

In the early 1800s European settlers built a carriage path to the western tip of the peninsula. Pioneer families traveled out in the summer, some to fish, others just to relax. In the 1850s severe storms eroded the eastern portion of the peninsula, requiring frequent repairs to small gaps until finally, in 1858, an island formed when a storm completely separated the peninsula from the mainland. One break, the so-called Eastern Gap, has since become a major shipping route into Toronto Harbour. Other gaps separated the former peninsula into a series of islands, the easternmost being Ward's Island, named after David Ward, a local fisherman who had settled there about 1830. The western end became known as Hanlan's Point, after the Hanlan family, which settled nearby in 1862. The major island in between became known as Centre Island. Here, from the 1890s to the 1930s, Manitou Road became the islands' commercial strip, "a sweet, raffish thoroughfare that looked like a stage-set from *high noon*," wrote former resident Alexander Ross in 1965. "It had an incredible hotel . . . a sloppy old firehall and an assortment of fly-blown general stores."[2] The west side of Centre Island became a resort destination for Toronto citizens; the first summer-cottage community was built here. By the 1890s there were three hotels and a summer recreation centre. In 1880 the city decided to build Island Park, transforming over 200 acres of marsh, sand, and water into a proper city park. With ferry service from the mainland, it soon offered picnicking, boating, and hiking, all with a panoramic view of the harbor and downtown Toronto on one side and Lake Ontario on the other. (See map 8.1.)

A Community Emerges

When the federal government transferred the islands to the City of Toronto in 1867, the city divided the land into lots, allowing cottages, amusement facilities, and resort hotels to be built. By the late 1800s, many of Toronto's wealthiest families had built Victorian summer homes on Hanlan's Point and along Lake Shore Avenue, east from Manitou Road all the way to Ward's Island. The islands were never strictly a preserve for the rich, however. From its earliest days, visitors from all walks of life came for fresh air and recreation. In the 1880s, a few people pitched tents to camp overnight, and by the summer of 1888 there were upward of 100 tents ranging from the simplest eight-foot by six-foot outfit to large, family-sized "marquee" abodes with carpets, curtains, and furniture. Most of these were on Hanlan's Point, which had the best ferry service. Island life was still quite primitive, though, with no indoor plumbing, no city-supplied running water, and, on Hanlan's Point, only one store.

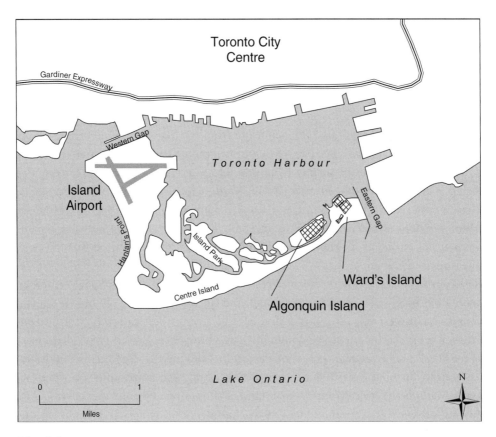

Toronto City
Centre

Gardiner Expressway

Western Gap

Toronto Harbour

Eastern Gap

Island
Airport

Hanlan's Point

Island Park

Ward's Island

Centre Island

Algonquin Island

Lake Ontario

N

0   1

Miles

Map 8.1
Toronto Islands

By the mid-1880s there were some fifty summer residences, and when the city park officially opened in 1888, the island "had been transformed into a complete village," writes historian Gibson, with a summer population, including cottagers and tenters at both Hanlan's Point and Centre Island, reaching about 1,000. Ward's Island, still quite remote, grew more slowly.

At the turn of the century, the total island community had some 2,000 summer residents and about a hundred year-round residents. They built a church, a one-room schoolhouse (open May to October), several general stores (open only in the summer), along with hotels, bathing beaches, and boating clubs. And the city provided ferry service to the mainland—at least when the bay wasn't frozen over. In 1906 the city ran water lines to the islands, alleviating the hardship of pumping fresh water from wells.

Throughout these early years, Ward's Island, bordering the Eastern Gap and lacking direct ferry service, was always a remote point. Most visitors were content to leave the marshy land and sandy beaches there to the few fishers, hunters, and residents such as the Wards. At the turn of the century there were probably no more than a dozen tenters on Ward's, served in 1906 by one small general store and a city water main with taps at the campsites. Even with the store, Ward's Islanders then, as now, had to get the bulk of their provisions on the mainland. The 1920s were the heyday of Ward's Island camping, with some 1,000 registered each summer. This period also saw the beginning of wooden roofs and even wooden walls in some "tents." Although the city of Toronto originally opposed permanent structures on the islands (with the exception of the well-appointed cottages along Lakeshore Drive, which generated significant lease rent and taxes for the city), it gradually gave in through the late 1920s and the 1930s. By 1937, there were 130 cottages and only 32 campsites. In that same year, the city converted many of the leases from seasonal licenses of occupation to yearly leases. One effect of this transition was to create two classes of summer residents—the "permanents," those who came back to the same cottage summer after summer, and the "transients," those who only pitched a tent. The "permanents" were arguably the forerunners of those who would defend island residences—cottage or tent—from demolition and repeated attempts to open the islands to the automobile. The newly created leaseholders, some 190 at this time, formed an association to deal with "the usual matters of dogs (prohibit them), cyclists (curtail them), rats (eliminate them) and sanitation (improve it)." It also set a precedent for future residents by taking a stand "against the use of leases in this community for money-making purposes."[3] This would be a residential neighborhood, not a commercial development, they in effect said. Possibly their most significant move, however, was building a clubhouse, a permanent structure that could accommodate concerts, dances, church services, and meetings. It soon became the center of social life and organization on Ward's Island.

The islands were nearly deserted during World War II but with a housing crisis following the war, the permanent population grew rapidly, from a few hundred to several thousand. Most of the newcomers were young and with little means; many were poor immigrants from Europe. But together they became "another generation of the enduring non-conformists who have always populated the Island," writes Gibson.[4] Algonquin Island, next to Ward's, grew from some 50 cottages at the end of the war to 89, with a substantial winter community. Ward's Island increased its winter residences from 4 in 1946 to 37 in 1948. The local school had 68 pupils in 1946. That increased to 256 in 1950 and 534 in 1954. The Red Cross renovated an old lodge as a convalescent home with a new library, a radio, and a record player. More stores on the Main Drag stayed open year round and "more and more trucks rumbled and skidded around Island streets during the off-season delivering coal, milk, bread, groceries and goodies from Eaton's and Simpsons to the thirteen hundred or so winter residents."[5] The Manitou Hotel continued to be a gathering place for card playing, beer drinking, and dancing. In 1950 a 1,700-seat theatre opened, bringing current movies to the islands. The pastor at the island church, St. Andrew's-by-the-Lake, added a Parish Hall, open year-round not only for church activities but for girl guides, boy scouts, and other island groups. Summers were the high points for many, "the happiest period of my life," wrote former resident Ross. "There were bicycle rides to the yacht club, willow trees overhanging the canals, girls who sometimes missed the last water-taxi to the mainland. And island children, who, despite their parents' slum incomes, grew up beautifully in a sane and lovely environment."[6]

So by the 1950s, the Toronto Islands were a vibrant community, growing not only with new buildings and ever-expanded year-round residency (638 houses and some 2,500 permanent residents in 1955[7]), but also developing a sense of neighborhood identity. Islanders, everyone knew, were different. They relied very little on the city except for basic services such as water, electricity, fire protection, and ferry service. They otherwise prided themselves on doing without when necessary, trekking through snow and across ice to get to work, and creating their own forms of recreation. Life could be harsh, relative to other Toronto neighborhoods. "But they had each other," wrote Ross in 1965. "They had the Island, and they'd developed a unique and, to me, admirable style of life."[8] In interview, residents expressed how the ride to the mainland marked a transition in one's daily life, from home and neighborhood to city and work. And some just liked the ferry ride itself: "The tugs that I ride on are neat, trim, seaworthy vessels," wrote one Ward's Island woman in 1957,

and even though we are crashing our way through thick ice, it would be ridiculous to think that there is any element of danger. In fact, coming over to the city on one of these boats is a wonderful way to start the day. The stillness of the early morning is broken by the sound of the waves and perhaps the cry of a bird. Then there is something exhilarating just being on the water with the open sky overhead. One hates to approach the city with its canopy of smoke. And coming home to the island, what a contrast to city traffic, where you are crowded like a sardine in a street car or plodding along bumper-to-bumper in a car like so many links in a sausage chain. When the bay is frozen over and the tug has to fight its way through the ice it is like a miniature trip in the Arctic circle. Where else could one have such a trip, so close to the heart of a big city?[9]

The 1950s brought another change, though, not only in Toronto but across North America. Coming out of the successes of the war years, the can-do, publicly minded spirit of those times, this was the start of the grand public works projects that would transform city after city with "urban renewal" and "slum clearance," with new parks, and, possibly most significantly, with major roadways. In Toronto, a prime target for such "progress" was the Toronto Islands, city land only partially developed as a city park and, unfortunately for those with grand schemes, leased to an odd collection of summer-cottage owners, mostly quite well-to-do, and year-round residents, mostly a ragtag bunch of deviants who, these postwar boosters would have it, had no right to occupy city land. They all had city leases, some of which came due yearly, others that were to expire in 1968.

Maximum Use: Serve the "Many," Not the "Few"

In this time of postwar boom and resulting housing shortage, most residents, especially the year-round ones, were happy to have a place to live. They took whatever the city gave them and made do when necessary with icebound ferries, crowded bus rides across the islands to get into the city for work and supplies, floods, and even hurricanes. Still, they envied the services other city residents enjoyed. And, after all, they too were city residents, taxpayers, and voters, just living in a city neighborhood with special needs.

So in 1947 the four island residents' councils banded together as the Inter-Island Council (IIC) to press their demands at City Hall for improved services. To their surprise, what they got back were not objections but challenges, challenges to their way of life, to their very residency on the islands. Throughout the late 1940s and most of the 1950s the city drafted one plan after another to redo the islands. The city planning board, for example, proposed creating warehouses, dockyards, and wildlife sanctuaries there. It recommended eliminating all existing houses and replacing them with apartments and hotels. Since Hanlan Point had already been converted to a small airport, it proposed building a tunnel under the Western Gap, what was now only some 100 meters wide. With the tunnel and passage through (or under) the airport, a cross-island highway with parking for 5,000 cars could be constructed. By one estimate, parking under this plan would require between 60 and 70 acres and roadway some 40 acres, this out of a total of 570 acres of available parkland.[10]

The IIC responded to the new city plans for the islands with a plan of its own. Not surprisingly, that plan rejected tunnels, highways, and parking, suggesting instead that the city improve "the existing assets of the Island—its parkland, its beaches, its lagoons and, of course, its existing residential communities."[11] One resident said that a tunnel would destroy the attractions for the people now living on the island, provide all the problems of motor transport, and "do it for the people with cars, who don't want to use the island anyway." An island businessman of twenty-nine years countered, saying that facilities at the island were "degenerating" and only proper use of motor transport could see them improved. The roadway would be "screened," and there would be only one main thoroughfare. And, besides, he stated, 100 percent of island merchants were behind the tunnel proposal.[12]

The city did not formally respond or move on its own plans, but it raised the issue of residential leases. The city made no decisions at this point, though it did entertain the possibility of allowing all leases to expire, thus ejecting all residents from the islands. "From this time on, the sword of Damocles dangled over Islanders' heads," writes Gibson.[13]

The city's Official Plan of 1949 had a section on the islands, including a provision to raise the level of the islands and build a highway, though not to eliminate housing. The plan's provisions for the islands were never implemented, however, the city turning instead to the federal agency, the Toronto Harbour Commission, to come up with a solution, one that, not incidentally, might bring federal funds. In 1951 the commission issued a joint proposal with the city planning board establishing as an overriding goal "the maximum use of this natural asset for the largest number of the citizens, to serve the 'many' not the 'few.' "[14] Islanders were among the "few"; visitors, including motorists, would be among the "many." Initially, the joint proposal included a tunnel for automobile access. Although it explicitly called for the expulsion of residents, when "the tunnel idea was permanently laid to rest," writes Gibson,

the seductive phrase ["serve the 'many' not the 'few' "] came to mean turfing out Island residents. If this plan were implemented, the Island would be straightened out, tarted up and overbuilt. Winding lagoons were dangerous and hard to maintain—straighten them or fill them in. Unkempt cottages with no indoor plumbing were an affront to postwar suburban man—tear them down. Narrow, carless streets were antiquated and outrageous—widen and pave them or obliterate them altogether. Big cars, big developments and big, but significantly unspecified costs were all signs of progress.[15]

Proponents indeed defended the joint plan as a means of serving the many and maximizing use. What is more, they argued, the islands should be a self-sustaining recreation center without subsidies for ferry service and other amenities. Opposition from islanders and mainlanders alike was so strong, though, that the developers backed off, at least temporarily. They might have known that city government itself was about to be reorganized, modernized for the larger mission great cities would assume in the postwar era. A new governmental body, the Metropolitan Toronto Council, or "Metro," was formed; among its responsibilities was the islands. Its first chair, Frederick Gardiner, took office in April 1953. Like his contemporary in New York, Robert Moses, he favored large-scale, highly visible public works projects such as expressways, water treatment plants, housing projects, and, not least, public parks. Within four months of assuming office and after publicly assuring islanders that residency would be retained on the islands, bulldozers began rolling down island paths. When leases came due, Gardiner announced, the houses would be demolished, a statement that prompted many owners to turn in their leases before expiration. Those with houses along Lakeshore Drive, many elegant mansions, would be compensated, but residents of Ward's and Algonquin islands, many of them with only simple cottages, would not. In an era of "slum clearance" and "urban renewal," demolition of substandard housing was deemed in the public interest.

In 1956, Gardiner's parks commissioner T. W. (Tommy) Thompson announced Metro's $14.5 million plan for the islands. It would have three huge picnic areas, a spring garden, and a children's wonderland; a regatta course; a bridge or tunnel; and a four-lane road with 50 acres of parking for 7,500 automobiles. All this, Thompson explained, because a "large number of people want and expect a development on the Island that will allow the greatest variety of use." And for that, easy access was essential because "people resist the use of certain park areas when there are not convenient places to buy refreshments and to enjoy some type of entertainment." Ferries could provide some of that access because they "have an aesthetic value," but, he stressed, "this is an age when the majority of people expect to be able to drive an automobile to within a relatively short distance of the picnic table and beach, and to deny this privilege is to purposely restrict the use of any park area." And for those worried that the automobile will destroy the "insular characteristics of the area," Thompson explained that the roadway

would give access to the parking facilities only, and under no circumstances would automobiles be allowed beyond these areas. . . . Random crossing of the roads by pedestrians would not be allowed and no sidewalks adjacent to the pavement would be built. Because public transportation facilities are an important consideration, bus stations would be provided for the safe loading and unloading of passengers.[16]

Not everyone shared the autocentric vision, though. One planner imagined islands with a special charm, not unlike a famous car-free city in Italy:

It may seem preposterous to compare a distinctly unglamourous place like Toronto Island with storied Venice with its historic and artistic treasures. However, an analysis of the charm of Venice shows that this charm persists also in the many parts of that city which are little more than slums; it derives from the feeling of ease and leisure of an environment which is free from vehicular traffic.

"Pedestrian Island" has become the term for such areas, even where they are not actually islands, but merely areas free from traffic. The creation of such "islands" is being attempted all over the world. . . .

As the automobile becomes more and more ubiquitous, the demand for such "islands" will increase and the uniqueness of Toronto Island will become more and more an attraction. By sheer good luck Toronto got free and on a large scale what others are trying to create at great cost. It would be folly to destroy it.[17]

But destroy it they did—or tried. By January 1957, the city bulldozed and burned 125 buildings, including many on the once-lively Main Drag. As residential owners and visitors alike disappeared, so did businesses. The school population dropped, forcing ten of the school's seventeen classrooms to close. By September 1960, some 20 stores, a number of hotels, and 261 houses—a third of all island buildings—were bulldozed and burned. In their place, Metro added extensive new picnic grounds, a petting zoo, a cement mall with fountains, and flower gardens. "It was a *neighborhood*, something that may be going out of style," former resident Ross lamented. "And now it's been replaced by a lot of municipal potted plants."[18] In the end, 260 houses were left standing, all on Ward's and Algonquin islands. Proposals for an amusement park on Ward's and a golf course on Algonquin were put forth.

One of Metro's plans called for a tunnel (estimated to cost between $5 million and $8 million) and 11,810 parking places on the islands. "I believe it would be an advantage to have Sunday drivers tour the length of the island," said one Metro planning board member.[19] Indeed, editorialized the *Toronto Star* in 1960, Toronto Island is a "neglected asset" because

it is too hard to get to. . . . Unlike Montreal and Detroit, Toronto has pursued the short-sighted and selfish policy of keeping it as a special preserve for those who have the income to maintain a summer cottage there, or the leisure to put up with slow ferry schedules. Each time the suggestion of auto access to the island is made, there are outcries that the automobile will destroy the pristine beauty of the park. But the experience of Montreal and Detroit has proven exactly the opposite. It simply makes that pristine beauty accessible to a great many more people, without harming it.[20]

A public resource, in other words, is a private reserve unless everyone has access. And there is no better way to provide access, midcentury or now, than with the automobile. "Those sentimentalists who fear motor cars will spoil Toronto's Island are not being realistic," continues the *Star*; "those who want it kept for the few and not for the many are not being democratic. Toronto Island will never be the playground envisioned by the pioneers who acquired it for the city 100 years ago until it is tied to the mainland by a bridge or tunnel."[21] Metro Chairman Gardiner put it succinctly: "A road on the Island will do it no more harm than the road to Belle Isle in Detroit." Historian Gibson, from the vantage point of the 1980s and apparently a holdover antidemocratic sentimentalist, saw the matter differently: auto access would provide "Toronto with an interesting new model of civic grandeur based on the car capital of the Western world."[22]

But the promoters of grand public works could not anticipate two trends of the 1960s. Student activism and a sense that one actually could "fight city hall" emerged, fueled in part by worldwide protests and, locally, by mainland residents' success in stopping a major expressway from cutting through some of the city's most treasured neighborhoods. Detroit was not their model city, nor were sprawling, car-dependent suburbs. Islanders formed a new political association to lobby government and engage Metro in a contest of public images. They led garden tours for government officials, journalists, and the public and urged residents to spruce up their places with renovations and new paint. In the press they portrayed the residential islands as unique and colorful, a "living community." Metro and newspapers sympathetic to Metro's views countered these idyllic images by portraying the two residential islands as run-down slums occupied by social misfits feeding off the trough of public largesse. The residents' unwillingness to move off city land showed that they were far from good citizens: only selfish and greedy people such of these would deny others access to the city's "jewel across the bay." At one point city officials spread rumors about a possible typhoid epidemic coming from the islands and their shoddy plumbing. For a time in this contest of "charming" versus "squalid" it appeared squalid was winning. But a housing shortage across Canada helped the islanders somewhat, making public officials look foolish bulldozing perfectly serviceable houses within city limits.

For many, rest and relaxation, not residing, was the real good and, once again, access the real issue. "Here, right on Toronto's aquatic doorstep, is a delightfully picturesque little archipelago, a unique and naturally beautiful spot for recreation, refreshment and rest," wrote one engineering partner in a local architectural and engineering firm in 1973. "Yet relatively few people ever use it for a reason that in an age of super technology and massive expenditures for public purposes is simply impossible to accept—the reason that it's hard to reach." His firm found that a tunnel would be "a more efficient means of access to the islands" than the ferries, ensuring that "the Islands are fully used, not just on a few weekends of summer, as at present, but every day throughout the year." The tunnel would cost between $75 million and $100 million, but that may "not be excessive," he wrote,

given cost-sharing by three levels of government, the contribution made to the employment and economy of that area, the kind of traffic that could thereby eventually be generated to the Islands, their enhanced appeal to tourists, the prospectively substantial annual returns to the municipality through tolls and, most importantly, the immeasurable dividends of refreshment that would accrue to countless Toronto citizens for generations to come.[23]

More efficient access, more visitors, more traffic, more government revenues, and, somehow, the "delightfully picturesque little archipelago" will remain a "naturally beautiful spot." And others will foot the bill. Residents, who actually did live there year round and pay taxes and ferry fares year round, did not buy it. Nor did those who might pick up the tab.

Citizen protest, the need for housing, and the exorbitant cost combined to slow and eventually halt the demolitions and keep the tunnel from being built. A new mayor in the 1970s was sympathetic to the islanders' cause, and the city council included many people dedicated to preserving established neighborhoods. On November 21, 1973, the city council voted 17 to 2 in favor of preserving the island community. But Metro was adamant: the residences would go and public parkland would span all the islands. (As late as the 1990s, Metro still described the Toronto Islands as parkland, the sole purpose of the city's transfer to Metro in 1956, with no mention of residential communities.) And then, after two years of court cases, provincial mediation between Metro and the city, and citizen rallies, the Ontario provincial government passed legislation on December 18, 1981, preventing any further demolition of homes. Islanders obtained 99-year leases. (See figure 8.1.)

For the first time in decades, islanders could take a deep breath, secure in the knowledge that bulldozers would no longer roll down their lanes. Little did anyone anticipate that other vehicles would now threaten their hard-won residency and way of life. Some of these vehicles would merely carry more visitors. Others had wings and would carry people in a rush, people who, as one consultant put it, valued their time more than their money. For business executives and high-level public officials, time was scarce and money abundant. Getting to the heart of Toronto's commercial center in the most expeditious manner possible was now the name of the game—for executives, for public officials, and, of course, for building contractors. An airport runway extension and a little bridge or tunnel, a so-called fixed link spanning the 120-meter Western Gap, is all it would take to enable an eight-minute drive from airport to city center. Access. That is all they needed—access, not to the islands,

Figure 8.1
Algonquin Island residential street; Toronto city center in background. Photo courtesy Jennifer Clapp.

but to Canada's commercial heart. From that, mobility and time saving and economic stimulus and jobs would follow.

No longer was the goal public access, clean air, and natural beauty for the many, but, in the 1980s and 1990s, saving and stimulating, efficient use of time and space for those who spur the economy, those few who have the smarts and the capital to make things happen, to make Toronto's economy "take off." This was now the goal, or so a vocal and powerful coalition of developers and government officials had it. Residents, once again, would have none of it.

From Automobility to Jetmobility: A Slippery Slope

So just as peace and stability seemed well in hand on the islands, trouble was brewing across the harbor. The 1980s brought a building boom to the harborfront. In a matter of a few years hotels, condominiums, and exclusive shops sprung up. Much of the development was haphazard and, by some views, destructive of the very character of the waterfront. A public outcry led then-mayor David Crombie to create a Royal Commission on the Waterfront. Among the commissioners' recommendations was that there should be "no fixed link" from the waterfront to the islands. In particular, they recommended against a bridge or tunnel across the Western Gap, a link "that would destroy a healthy balance of existing uses."[24] This position reaffirmed city positions taken as far back as 1937, when Mayor Sam McBride blocked a federal attempt to build a bridge. The city acted on the Royal Commission's recommendations by reaching a three-way governmental under-standing in 1983, the so-called Tripartite Agreement, among the city, the federal government, and the Toronto Harbour Commission (a federal agency soon to be renamed the Toronto Port Authority). This agreement prohibited a fixed link (bridge or tunnel), any lengthening of the runways, and jet traffic. The integrity of the islands—the parkland and the residential neighborhoods—was assured. Or so it seemed.

"Existing uses" was precisely the problem for those who saw "Great City" status in a full-service city airport. In executive suites and, apparently, selected newsrooms and consultants' offices, in Toronto and as far away as London and Stockholm, plans were afoot for the tiny airport at Hanlan's Point. A "mutual support and consultation group" known as the Conference of City Centre Airports had suc-ceeded in developing several city airports in Europe, increasing passenger ridership as much as tenfold. "The only one that didn't move was Toronto," said one con-sultant to the group. "We always thought [this] was a great tragedy because the benefits to (European) business communities are well recognized. . . . Toronto has a textbook example of a perfect city airport," said another consultant, because "it's almost in the middle of the business community," just eight minutes from the ter-minal to the city's business core. And "once (the bridge is) there, it will be like a snowball rolling and the regional airlines will become interested at that point." In fact, the airport director at the time said in 1998 that "we have talked to a number of regional airlines in both the United States and Canada and we have commitments from these airlines. We expect to see a (new) airline starting at the city centre airport soon."[25]

The snowball was indeed rolling, at least for those in a hurry, those who valued time more than money (including public money). Two studies in the mid-1980s esti-mated that a tunnel would cost between $12 million and $18 million. In 1986 the local commuter airline, citing rapidly increasing numbers of passengers, appealed to the city for a tunnel to be used only by its service vehicles and airport buses; there would be no cars. Some city councilors expressed support, especially if cars continued to be prohibited from the rest of the islands.[26] If the city would back the idea, its proponents apparently reasoned, others were likely to follow. The Ontario provincial government was paying some $600,000 a year to subsidize the ferry between the airport and the mainland. Metro, having shifted from large public works to "partnership" projects with private investors, had already conducted a feasibility study of shutting down winter ferry service to the other parts of the islands and the federal Transportation Department was looking into a major expansion of the airport.

The only question now was who would pay and when the link would be built. Despite the power of the provincial and federal governments, as well as that of the federally designated port authority, the Harbour Commission, which owned most of the airport property, the city retained one element of leverage. The city leased its portion of airport land to the commission in exchange for a limit on noise levels and adherence to the provisions of the Tripartite Agreement, namely, no fixed link and no jets. But what the city could block, others would redefine—or threaten. Frustrated by the city's footdragging on major economic development initiatives and inspired by Metro's support, pro-business leaders began a move to "amalgamate" the city and Metro. Among other things, the "new Toronto" would likely reverse the standing prohibition on airport expansion and a fixed link.

Through the 1990s city officials debated as developers planned and citizens organized. The federal government threatened to settle everything by just taking over the airport and developing it as it saw fit. The Port Authority sued the city over ownership of the airport land, eventually settling for a $48 million cash payout from the city. The city council weighed its options, trying to assess trade-offs and assurances that safeguards against overdevelopment would be enacted. For some, though, it was all economics and civic grandeur. For those "genuinely concerned about the economic vitality of the city centre," wrote one city councilor, the decision is straightforward:

In permitting small commuter aircraft propelled by jet engines access to the airport and providing a fixed link to easily transport commuters to and from the mainland, we would be promoting our City Centre. Promoting these measures would increase passenger movements by an estimated 1.5 million people. These passengers would then stay in the city hotels, eat in the city restaurants, visit the city shops and movie theatres, etc. The airport is also a job creator, employing 345 full and part-time workers, numbers which would certainly increase with the increase in passenger movement. Thirty-eight major and small businesses operate at the airport and depend on its success. These economic spin-offs are not being anticipated by many.[27]

The city council approved the bridge by a 29–11 vote.

Island and waterfront residents were aghast, and outraged. "The life and priorities and civilities of this City have been dealt what is quite likely a death blow," Ward's Island resident Mary Hay told the mayor and executive committee of the City of Toronto in 1997.

With the bridge and, likely, airport expansion now virtually a done deal, the one consolation bridge opponents had were the assurances that the link would only connect the airport, not the rest of the islands. There would be no extension—no roads, no cars, and no development further into the islands. Even that slender thread of hope became questionable, however, when a series of otherwise inexplicable incidents led island and waterfront residents to believe that the tunnel was only the first step. In 1997 Metro rejected a new island school location, stating that it would interfere with "the Gateway to the Island Park." Since the school would not obstruct ferry access, the only "interference," islanders reasoned, would be to a road, to a new road, a "gateway" road. The school was a mile into the islands from Hanlan's Point. At about the same time, the telephone company, Bell Canada, laid a cable under the airport runway and into the island park. Workers said the cable had enough capacity to supply five hotels. And Metro, with its study of canceled winter ferry service, had cost savings well in mind. For its part, the Toronto Port Authority nudged the snowball along: "We're the only city that has a city center airport where tourists and business people can fly right to within walking distance of the major venues. This would be a tremendous advantage in terms of our bid for the 2008 Olympics."[28] Possibly more significantly, it repeatedly announced the imminent construction of the bridge and new airport. In late 2003, for example, it accused bridge opponents of misleading voters in a city election. With all reviews complete and the topic debated to death, the Port Authority issued what it took to be the final statement on the bridge: "There is no legal, procedural or environmental reason to delay the commencement of construction of the bridge. The construction contract has been let and we expect to begin work by month-end once we receive Treasury Board approval."[29]

Nineteenth-century Chicago boosters could hardly have played it better:

• Privately decide what is best for key constituents (here, those desiring quick, inner-city access by air).

• Conduct studies that show great public benefits (easier access, expanded commerce, economic stimulus, jobs, great city status).

• Choose, or create, a decision-making venue that is supportive (a commerce agency or, here, "amalgamated Toronto").

- Then pronounce the inevitability of the entire project (it's the best thing to happen, it *will* happen, so the only role for officials and citizens alike is to improve the project).
- Finally, highlight the "losses" should the project not go forward (no new airlines, no economic vitality, no Olympics, no great city).

So islanders organized again, as did concerned residents and shopkeepers on the waterfront side. Islander and waterfront opponents warned their constituents of all the problems attendant upon a fixed link. With an expanded airstrip, jets would replace turboprops, raising noise levels and air pollution. Some boaters would be cut off from exiting the harbor through the Western Gap, and others would be endangered by the narrowness of the passage. Highway ramping on the mainland side of the bridge would eat up a large portion of the waterfront, including the very promenade the city was trying to promote. Of most significance to the islanders, though, was vehicular access.

With a bridge across the Western Gap and passage across or under the runway (an easy thing to construct), cars and trucks could drive right onto the island. Residents would no longer complain about winter ferry and bus service. Island service workers would no longer have to get permits and wait long hours crossing the ferry. And park visitors would have the best of both worlds: in the summer they could elect to take an idyllic ferry ride, reminiscent of times past or, if they were short on time, just take a quick drive to the park. Of course, all these commuters and workers and visitors would require parking. Some parkland would have to go. Maybe a few buildings, too.

Longtime residents had heard it all before. Just a simple little bridge (or tunnel), a few vehicles, emergency and essential services only. And then, someone would say, just a few more—for the elderly and handicapped. And then a few more—for those who were too poor to risk losing a day's work. And then a few more—for those who didn't have the time to wait, who could pay a premium, a price that would subsidize other essential services. And then, well, everyone should have the choice of ferrying or driving, not the select few. Alternatively, some reasoned, because the bridge would be built only to revitalize the airport, if the airport failed, the public expenditures on the bridge could only be justified by some other commercial development, say a hotel at Hanlan's Point. And condominiums just a bit further into the islands. And then, with revenues flowing into government coffers, a few more. All easily accessible, of course, by bridge and road. And so it goes.

Such would be the slippery slope many islanders imagined, should the bridge be built. The Western Gap always represented more than a few hundred meters of lake water. It was not like that last patch of forest that, everyone agreed, had to be cleared so settlement could proceed, or that last stretch of track before the rail line was complete. No, the Gap, narrow as it is, was always a divide between conventional downtown urban life and unconventional residential life and parkland recreation. For residents, it was a boundary as distinct as national boundaries or formidable mountain ranges. Only what the Gap separated was not peoples but *modes of access*. And from modes of access followed *modes of living*, of residing, of transporting, of caring for one's neighbors, of provisioning and of consuming.

Residents were not alone in their fear of a slippery slope to full auto access. A Toronto Board of Trade study of a buses-only tunnel concluded that cars would inevitably follow. Future Metro councils "would find it impossible to withstand the pressures which would inevitably arise and the tunnel would sooner or later be thrown open for use by private automobiles."[30]

Architecture professor and island resident Jeffery Stinson may have put it best back in the 1970s. Skeptical about any kind of "improved access," he suggested a simple principle. If the islands are to have a special urban character, for visitor and resident, they must remain islands:

We must leave the mainland and we must arrive at the Islands.

Between departure and arrival we must have a trip—an experience that allows us to savor both departure and arrival.

In general, we need not be concerned about "saving time." If the trip is as it should be, it is time well spent.

Everyone, even those of us who love to walk or to cycle or who have large families with tons of picnic paraphernalia, must recognize that easy access to the Islands is not the prime requirement—for making it too easy will eventually make it mainland.

What we want is good access.[31]

Good access is not full access, not open access. Every islander who went through the trauma of the 1950s and 1960s, and all those who learned and appreciated that trauma secondhand, knew this. Good access is access appropriate to a suite of uses, from day trips to lifetime residency. Tourist resorts and convention centers and shopping malls have full access (at least to those who pay), but no residency, no long-term commitment to place. Gated residential compounds may have commitment to place among their homeowners, but they select who has access—residents and service personnel only, read the entryway signs. A vibrant community has *limited access*, enough to allow residents, servicepeople, and visitors to enter, but *not too much*, not so much as to overwhelm residential life itself. Most urban neighborhoods opt for full automobile access, even when the neighborhood is in decline.

So now, in the 1990s and early 2000s, Toronto Island and waterfront residents and a host of others were fighting for "good access." In the past their fights could be understood as fights for residential survival. Now it was for livability, livability as residents experienced it and defined it. It was a fight *against* easy access, access that would be defined by others, particularly those whose gaze on the islands translates to "efficient access" and "saved time" and "valuable real estate." The islanders' foes were no less formidable than the Gardiners and Thompsons of the past. Only now the benefits of the fixed link and a renovated airport could be justified not as a great public need for public parks, but as a great public need for economic growth, for stimulating the economy, for reducing the "transaction costs" of doing business, and, not least, for making efficient use of everyone's time and money.

From across the metropolitan area, some 9,000 individuals petitioned the city to stick to the Tripartite Agreement. They called on their mayor, who had reversed her earlier opposition to the bridge and voted with the majority on the council, to follow the example of one of her predecessors whose name adorns an island ferry. Sam MacBride recognized that a fixed link would change the very character of the islands. In 1937, he took on the federal government and stopped tunnel construction. Now, in the 1990s and early 2000s, citizen groups were mobilized, testifying before the city and Metro, writing memorandums pointing out the deficiencies in government studies and environmental assessments. They wrote letters to the editor and they supported candidates for city council and the mayor's seat. And they helped secure the formation of a "Toronto Island Airport Community Advisory Committee," cochaired by a city councilor and a Ward's Island resident. Perhaps most significantly, they helped elect a mayor opposed to the bridge.

When in 2003 the Toronto Port Authority declared it was proceeding with bridge construction, the newly elected mayor said, in effect, not so fast. As the only candidate to run on an antibridge platform, "I intend to communicate directly with the federal government and request them not to make any approvals until council has had a chance to consider it," he said. "It's up to the citizens of Toronto to decide and by electing me they made a decision." The newly elected prime-minister-in-waiting supported the primacy of city decisionmaking: "very clearly, we will take our cue from the municipal government."[32] It had been a long time since things looked so promising for islanders. That very week, though, the Port Authority began site preparations for the bridge, erecting fences and moving in materials and equipment.

At midcentury, with visions of civic grandeur dancing in the heads of planners and developers, the fate of the Toronto Islands had seemed obvious: recreation for all. Clean air, peace and quiet. Amusements for all comers. Such amenities would be proof positive that Toronto was a great city, a destination spot for visitors and migrants, a congenial environment for investors. The goal was noble. Neither discrimination nor preferential treatment would be countenanced. The Island was a city resource open to everyone, regardless of title or means. In a time of rapid industrial expansion and population growth (both of which were unambiguously good things) such a public resource was clearly underutilized, a "neglected asset" as many described it. Equal and open access, full mobility to and from the islands, all egalitarian and democratically inspired, thus became the necessary condition for enjoyment of this resource.

And, then, late in the twentieth century and early in the twenty-first, the goal became perhaps a little less noble but no less important: economic stimulus via a first-class mode of transport—an executive's airport within minutes of the center of commercial and governmental power. All great cities have such access. From that access would follow investment and jobs and a high quality of life for all. This is not just any access, but efficient access, access that makes the most of people's time, especially the time of those people who seem to have so little of it.

What proponents of these grand public visions did not appreciate—or care about—was that as access becomes more *equal* or more *efficient*, it also becomes more *open*. It is well-established among natural resource managers and scholars that, when demand exists and technologies are available, *open access* tends toward overuse and degradation. The resource, desired by all and free to all, is abused. Also like natural resources, a human-built resource changes as people's needs and expectations change. What was originally only summer residences for most people on Ward's Island, became low-cost, year-round residences. For them, "the resource" was a necessity, a residence and a residential neighborhood. From the planners' perspective at midcentury, by contrast, "the resource" was the "natural beauty" of a piece of land within a mile of central Toronto, surrounded by water and bathed in cool summer breezes. The public good derived from such a resource would increase as more people spent a summer afternoon or day on the island parkland. But even "natural beauty" can be exploited, consumed, used up. To be sure, park advocates noted the possibility of the island being overrun with visitors. But all the rhetoric and all the development plans of the 1950s and 1960s were couched in terms that recognized no such limits. And turn-of-the-century plans were proposed as if residency (islander or mainlander) simply did not exist. Maximum utilization—of a recreational park, of executives' time—was the byword. Much as forests were perceived as unending and fisheries as infinitely abundant, use of the island could always be increased. There was never enough.

Sufficiency in recreational visits, not to mention in revenues from tolls, concession stands, and airport landing fees, was therefore an alien concept for those presiding in high-rise office buildings on the mainland. But for those ensconced in snug little cottages on the islands, those who labored for years and decades and, for some, generations to build a place they could call home, sufficiency in access, "good access," came quite naturally. Although there were always some who wanted the island for their own private, exclusive use (boating and sporting clubs sprang up in the late nineteenth and early twentieth centuries), the great majority held a "multiple-use" perspective on the island, although they probably did not call it that. For the majority, "the resource" was more than the occasional recreational indulgence of natural island beauty. Among other things, residents tended to have a greater sense of history about the islands, certainly more so than visitors and future-oriented, progressive planners. Residents knew that the islands had been used since early European settlement (and maybe before) by *both* the visitor from the mainland *and* the resident fisherman, lighthouse keeper, store owner, and commuter. (See figure 8.2.)

For island residents in the twentieth century, and for many visitors, there were constant reminders of "too muchness." There could be too many boats in the harbor given the limited lighthouse and rescue services; too many fishers crammed into a tiny bay; and too many buildings, especially near the beach where storms, sometimes with six-foot waves, would wash away everything. More generally, on the island it was always possible to have too many representations of city life itself—noise, pollution, congestion, traffic. Residents, both summer and year-round, chose the islands precisely to escape these representations and yet not to escape modern life itself. It may have been this dual desire—having all the benefits and few of the drawbacks of city life—that engendered resentment among city planners and some mainland residents. Summer residents were probably resented the most and, as we have seen, were indeed among the first to lose their homes to the bulldozers. Year-round residents were always less prominent and less visible, especially on Ward's Island served by its own ferry line and removed from the amusements of Central Island. In fact, as noted, much of the discussion of the 1950s and 1960s occurred as if these residents did not exist. But when their leases came up for renewal and when, in the late 1960s and 1970s, people discovered they really could fight city hall, the complacency changed. The long, painful struggle to keep their homes and

Figure 8.2
Ward's Island street; house and community meeting house in background. Photo courtesy Jennifer Clapp.

their neighborhood thus served to redefine "the resource," at least with respect to automobile use. And then the fixed-link controversy forced yet another redefinition, at least for political purposes. It was now "the harbourfront," the mainland and the islands, some combination of commercial and residential that was now the resource. Throughout it all, one technology permeated the planning and destroying and renovating and defending: the automobile.

Automobile use on the Toronto Islands became a defining issue for island residents after World War II. A "national defense" system of freeways was built in the United States and an equivalent system in Canada, each to tie the country together and "get the country moving again." A preferred destination for this new public mobility was parks. Yet while Parisians and Londoners may think of casual strolls in their parks, North Americans thought of "Sunday drives." One drives to, in fact, right *through* the park, stopping for a picnic or ice cream perhaps, maybe a bit of entertainment, but otherwise motoring. A Toronto planner otherwise sympathetic to island residency and restricted auto access put it thus in the 1950s: "It is, of course, undeniable that the most popular and convenient use of recreational facilities is to load the family with all appurtenances and supplies into the car at one's front door and unload them right at the picnic grounds or beach."[33]

But auto driving required auto infrastructure—roads and parking. Access meant consumption, not just of cars and fuel, but of land. Roads and parking had to be carved out of existing parkland, which would contradict the goal of expanding the park itself, or be taken from built land—that is, homes. A few residences could not thwart the larger goal of the greatest good for the greatest number. That goal could never be achieved through residency, the visionaries reasoned, only visitation, especially highly mobile visitation. Residents—and residential life—have always been expendable precisely because there were so few people and, after all, in a mobile society, they could always live somewhere else. On a frontier there's always another place to occupy, another resource to exploit.

In many ways, the threat to residency was always excess mobility, especially as that mobility was defined as automobility. Even airport expansion was not, for islanders, mostly about jet noise and pollution. It was about what an airport or, more precisely, what a bridge to the airport, would bring: easy access by car.

Sufficiency and the Automobile

Industrial societies have had a full century of experience with the automobile. In its first decades, it was a plaything of the rich, a novel form of sport and display. Now it transports people and their goods, getting them to work and school and recreation. And it allows its owners to express their identities through the vehicle's style, mass and speed. In recent decades, the drawbacks of private auto use have become increasingly apparent—injuries and deaths, congestion and pollution.

Public response to these privately generated costs has mostly taken a "production approach": just as the production of cars solves transportation problems of physical drudgery, time use, and access, the production of safety belts, catalytic converters, bumper rails, traffic signals, and widened roads solves the problems of auto use. Production approaches come up short, though, when the problems are a function of the level of use. More efficient engines may burn less gasoline per mile driven, but if motorists drive more and more miles, pollution and reliance on foreign oil continue to increase. More traffic controls may ameliorate congestion at one intersection, but ever more cars compel more roadway and, then, more traffic controls. Enhanced crash worthiness of vehicles may reduce occupants' injuries but the more people drive, the more injuries occur, including injuries to nonoccupants. The problem is not the automobile itself, argue transportation analysts Peter Newman and Jeffrey Kenworthy. After studying transportation patterns in more than 100 cities around the world, they conclude that the automobile problem is "overuse and dependence"; like other such problems—eating and drug abuse for instance—"excessive use arises . . . when we no longer exercise any conscious discretion but become addicted or develop a physical dependence problem."[34]

Two indicators of such dependence is the extent of publicly provided roads and parking, and the percentage of travel by nonauto modes. The United States and Australia have three to four times the road per capita and twice the parking spaces (per 1,000 jobs) as European countries. On average, an American in 1990 drove a private car 16,000 km while taking public transportation for less than 500 km. A European drove less than 7,000 km and took public transit for nearly 2,000 km. Dependence, indeed, excess, sets in when residents have little choice. Newman and Kenworthy call it "Auto City":

Beginning before the Second World War, but really accelerating after it, the automobile, supplemented by the bus, progressively became the transportation technology that shaped the city, particularly in North America and Australia. . . .

Low density housing became more feasible, and as a reaction to the industrial city, town planners began separating residential and business centers by zoning. This also helped to increase journey distances. The city began to decentralize and disperse.

With the availability of cars, it was not necessary for developers to provide more than basic power and water services since people could make the transportation linkages themselves. As this "ungluing" process set in, the phenomenon of automobile dependence became a feature of urban life. Use of an automobile became not so much a choice but a necessity in the Auto City.[35]

But because that choice was framed as "free choice," land-use planning could be deemed unnecessary. Houses and businesses could locate virtually anywhere because individuals could freely drive from one place to the other. "Unfortunately for the engineers and those who felt transportation utopia had arrived," write Newman and Kenworthy, "it was never possible to truly achieve this freedom. Road and parking requirements became a bottomless pit that seemed to absorb any traffic solution and replace it with a new set of congestion constraints. The reality is that individual desires for mobility in a city where individualized locations are not subject to constraint will inevitably mean that traffic rises. . . . If it is possible to travel faster, then people just travel farther."[36] And they consume not just more fuel, but more space. A single-occupancy car traveling at an average of twenty-five miles per hour requires twenty times the space (in roads, parking, and service) of a cyclist and of a passenger in a full bus, and seventy-five times the space of a pedestrian.[37]

The result, Newman and Kenworthy conclude, is that "the biggest threat to the city is automobile dependence."[38] The authors might go a step further, though, and say that if cities, more than any other geographic and political unit, determine humans' draw on resources, the biggest threat to the economy and to ecosystem integrity is automobile dependence.

Production approaches—more roadway, parking, and signaling, more safety gadgets and controls—thus aim to improve automobile use, not change it. They target symptoms, not the underlying structural and behavioral causes of ever-increasing auto use. They ask how automobiles can perform better, how highway systems can be streamlined and connected, how mobility, *automobility*, can be enhanced. They do not ask how public roadway can better serve a range of transport and social needs. And they do not ask how such needs can be met without consuming yet more public space, without causing yet more congestion, more consumption, more deaths, and more climate destabilization.

Such would be a holistic-systems approach, what I will term a "behavioral ecology" of transport. Here "the resource" includes access for all who transport themselves and their goods, as well as the safety and multiple uses of public rights of way. This approach is as likely to ask what is consumed—namely, land, public space, fuel, waste-absorption capacity, personal health—as what is produced. The ecology of such transport is not just the environmental impacts, as huge as they are, but the infrastructure, technologies, and institutions that shape personal and commercial transport. And that shaping is not just technical, nor economic, but political. It recognizes that collective choices, many unseen and unaccounted for, have created the appearance of private choice, at once rational and efficient (chapter 4).

A behavioral ecology of transport requires an ecological and working rationality (chapters 2 and 5), a mode of decision making that makes inherent two kinds of adaptations—first, individual adaptations to one's environment, including to available modes of transport, and, second, collective, systemwide adaptations to the constraints of fuels and land and water, of urban development, and of waste sinks, whether regional airsheds or the global atmosphere. It asks when is it sensible to restrain automobility so as to realize a range of values, transport and other.

These are sufficiency questions. They are not unlike those posed in the timber and fishing cases. But here it is on the consumption side of the economic and material equation. The ultimate environmental benefit is with regard to waste sinks, not the integrity of a forest or fishery. But just as the proximate explanations for sustainable timbering and fishing are found in human material security and well-being, here the proximate causes for restrained auto use are found in quality-of-life issues. The big environmental goals—sustainable resource use, breathable air, climate stabilization—can be invoked for rhetorical purposes. But the proximate drivers are those at the level of daily practice. On the Toronto Islands, that practice was getting to work and to shopping. But it was also engaging government officials so as to provide services for *islander* needs, as *islanders* defined them. And for islanders, it was a secure residential life—one that would not be overrun by bulldozers, touring cars, and jet planes—that was of utmost concern. Restrained mobility was a means to these ends.

Sufficiency in transport, especially automobile transport, helps lay the foundation for addressing the larger issues. Not to address sufficiency at the level of daily practice is to slip into the production approach—technical correction and full-cost pricing, for instance, desirable measures to be sure, but devoid of a politics, a *behavior*, individual and collective, of transport. It all begins with a core value of North American life—mobility—a value increasingly adopted around the world. Like efficiency of which it is a part, mobility is rarely questioned, just assumed. Combined with an exquisite technology—lots of horsepower on four wheels, encased in a protective, often-stylish metal shell, all arranged to enable even the least skilled to move quickly and deftly—mobility, now *automobility*, appears to solve three of life's persistent problems: first, how individuals can transport themselves and their goods, procure supplies, and get to work; second, how they can announce their station in life; and third, how society can achieve well-functioning markets via ever-lower transaction costs—including transport costs—for buyers and sellers.

Mobility

Throughout North America, people with the means choose to live in the country and drive to work in the city. They may have a long commute, but because many enjoy driving or make it enjoyable with built-in sound systems and beverage service, the inconvenience appears minor. Mobility means access to the workaday essentials—home and job—and to the best of two worlds, the rural and the urban.

Some enjoy a vacation by driving to as many sights as possible, traversing rough terrain in an off-road vehicle or "camping" in a motor home. The "work" of driving is offset by the range of sights taken in and the enjoyment of exploring new places. The vacationer is apparently unperturbed by the fact that the experience is mostly inside the car itself. Mobility means more access, which means more car time, and hence more miles and more sights.

In town, car owners have a universal yearning to park right next to their destination, or so it seems. I regularly observe drivers circling block after block, foraging intently for the space nearest the store, all when empty spaces are just a few blocks away. This cannot be explained by time saving, because the searching takes considerable time, nor as an aversion to walking, since so often after parking the individual then walks long distances from shop to shop. The self-directed searching may itself be satisfying. Being autonomously mobile makes door-to-door access an accomplishment.

In a residential neighborhood, pedestrians routinely apologize for slowing a driver, even when they are using a crosswalk. If a ball rolls into the street stopping traffic, everyone apologizes to the car driver. Out of town, farm vehicles moving from one field to another on public roads defer to the automobile driver. Logically, the driver could just as readily apologize to the ball players for interfering with their recreational use of the public right of way or to the farmer for obstructing his business use of the public right of way. But the auto culture puts the interrupted mobility of drivers and their convenience first.

And drivers everywhere expect roads to be clear at all times. Snowstorms and icestorms, even floods and landslides are no excuse for road managers. They must keep the road open; drivers must have access. In frigid climates, a few environmentalists may decry the watershed impacts of de-icing agents (sand and salts), but this is no reason to impede motorists. Call a highway department almost anywhere and they will confirm that they get the most complaints—from motorists and elected officials—when a road is blocked or traffic slowed. Mobility knows no seasons: there are no "acts of God," just temporary and entirely correctable impediments to efficient movement from point A to point B.

Anecdotal those these observations are, they reveal the value of unfettered automobility. With expanded auto access, the range of housing, job, and recreational experiences increases. Because these activities are necessary or rewarding and are freely chosen, the driver's quality of life is seen to improve. Mobility is an unalloyed good. Restricting mobility would be not only anathema but inconceivable, an affront to all that makes a free society so.

The high standing of mobility is also revealed in highway safety policy. Transportation authorities around the world target the traffic death rate for improvement. But that rate—number of deaths per 100 million miles driven—can, like all efficiency ratios, be improved in one of three ways: reduce the deaths, increase the miles driven, or increase both deaths and miles driven with a disproportionate increase in miles driven (chapter 4). By choosing to minimize the deaths:mile ratio, policymakers are implicitly saying that fewer deaths (or proportionately fewer deaths) are better (a contention few would contest) and more miles driven are better (a hugely debatable point). They are not, though, saying that fewer *total* deaths are better. In other words, employing this ratio, traffic death rate, decision makers are saying that fewer deaths are desirable, but so are more miles and if, by driving more, by, indeed, consuming more, society has the same or more deaths, that is acceptable, just the price one pays for more mobility. If transportation authorities really wanted to reduce deaths, total deaths, including the deaths of drivers, occupants, pedestrians, and cyclists, they would seek a "sufficient" quantity of automobile use, not the production fixes that follow the traffic death rate. "Enormous resources and human energy [are] poured into road safety when by far the biggest gains would be made by shifting [transport] to other modes and *reducing the overall level of car use*," write Newman and Kenworthy. "This approach is rarely mentioned in road safety discussions."[39]

Under the value of automobility, and like pollution management and habitat preservation, improvement in the auto death rate is making marginal changes on the side effects, "diddling with the numbers," systems analyst Donella Meadows would say (chapter 2). Only the relevant numbers here are nontrivial: some 40,000 automobile deaths per year in the United States; that is over 100 deaths per day, every day, week after week, month after month, year after year, the equivalent of a September 11 World Trade Center attack every month. In the European Union, 55,000 people are killed a year, 1.7 million injured, and 150,000 permanently disabled. Places like South Africa and Thailand are even higher on a per capita basis.[40]

That such a tragic loss of life (plus the nonfatal injuries, which are generally about ten times the deaths) is implicitly condoned by policymakers via the traffic death rate is evidence enough that mobility is sacrosanct in auto cultures. Mobility, the ability to go where one wishes, as far as one wishes for whatever purpose, and at the fastest possible speed, is a cherished value. As a key subprinciple of that larger social organizing principle, efficiency, mobility has its theoretical pedigree in, once again, economics: *factor mobility*, the ability of workers and machines and financial capital to find their best employment is essential to well-functioning markets, to efficient markets. And so it is that the justification of publicly funded infrastructure—roads and bridges and parking lots—comes from mobility: a productive society is a mobile society; and because everyone—that is, "the public"—benefits from more productiveness, "the public" is obligated to ante up the funds to make it all possible. It is a logic hard to argue with. From it follows a transport system dedicated overwhelmingly to private auto use—after all, nothing is as mobile as the car, certainly not the horse and buggy, not the bicycle, and not the train either, restricted as it is to laid tracks. It is thus a system that depreciates all other modes of transport. "Mobility," write two other transportation analysts, John Pucher and Christian Lefèvre, "has become the key problem. Too much travel means not just congested roads but also excessive noise, air pollution, traffic accidents and energy use. . . . The greater the volume of travel, the more significant the overall magnitude of its social and environmental impacts."[41]

From all this comes a pattern that legitimates personal mobility while relegating traffic deaths and injuries, disruption of residential life, respiratory illnesses, and a destabilized global climate to the margins of public concern. It is a pattern, indeed a *culture*, that implicitly celebrates long-distance commuting, car "camping," door-to-door access, driver convenience, and mileage, all as if the consequences are inconsequential, all as if it were the "cost of doing business," the "price of progress." From a resource perspective, it is as if foresters only managed for board feet, fishers only for the biggest fish, farmers only for one crop. Single use trumps multiple use; one value overrides all other values. Put like this, it is hard to imagine how such a transport system could have come about, how, by any stretch of the imagination, it could be called "rational." Transportation analysts John Whitelegg and Gary Haq construct one "as if" explanation through "backcasting," asking, "What are the policies that would have produced the transport problems we are now dealing with?" They would have been policies that

- encourage people to make as many trips as possible by car;
- subsidize as much as possible car-based transport through publicly funded loans, grants, road building, cheap fuel, health care, policing and courts;
- convert as much land as possible to car-dominance, even if that land is prime agricultural or urban residential land;
- encourage the largest possible cars;
- make buses and trains as unpleasant as possible and walking and cycling as inconvenient and dangerous as possible;
- ensure that cars are never delayed by even a couple seconds;
- make sure children get as little exercise as possible by driving them everywhere;
- ignore the health, aesthetic, ethical and cost advantages of walking and cycling;
- ensure the transport needs of the middle and upper classes are met first.[42]

Another way to explicate the apparent irrationality of the auto culture is to understand it as a system committed to *private choice by sovereign consumers* (chapter

5). "The desire to be master of time and space without dependence on schedules was not invented in an automobile factory," said J. H. Brunn, president of the German Automotive Industry Association in a 1974 speech titled "The Automobile Is Another Bit of Freedom." Nobody really wants to take the bus or train, mingling with strangers and adhering to others' schedules. The desire for independent mobility "accords with the nature of the modern person and comes from the consumer. Everyone should be able to use the means of transit that best suits his or her individual needs."[43] In other words, individuals (consumers) are best positioned to judge what is best for them. The very experience of driving a car on the open road or filling the tank and going in any direction for as long as one wishes is the perfect enactment of this belief. Sure there are costs but, by this belief, they are borne by the drivers themselves via fuel expenditures and purchase taxes, driver's licenses, accident insurance and the like. And even if some public funds are involved in this otherwise private transport, those funds are paid back eventually via road taxes and by the boost to the economy that roads and bridges bring. If injuries and death result, that too is a matter of personal choice—choice in vehicle, safety features, travel route and speed. In a consumer society, just as individuals demand choices in their food, energy, and housing, they demand ready access to jobs, services and amenities. Auto owners want to go wherever there are factories, stores or parks or just open road. They will accept constraints, especially if those "constraints" are perceived to *enhance* access, not restrict it. Driving on the right side of the road, taking turns at intersections, and obeying the speed limit are all "constraints" on otherwise free-for-all driving, yet readily perceived as enhancing the flow of vehicles. The modern person chooses what best suits his or her transit needs. No one else can do it better.

And yet, no one can really do it alone.

However we understand auto-centered transportation systems, the logic of mobility combines with the logic of the consumer economy to produce an overwhelming consensus on the value of personal mobility, the preeminence of the automobile, and the necessity of public subsidy. In fact, ever more mobility makes especially good sense individually when the monetary costs of amelioration and auto infrastructure are dispersed and borne collectively—that is, publicly subsidized. The apparent *in*dependence of private automobility is the *de*pendence of publicly provided roads and parking lots, traffic signals and police, courts and research labs, pipelines and tankers, and oilfields secured by armies all over the world. Studies from many countries find, for instance, that the automobile is subsidized about $3,000 to $4,000 per vehicle per year for roads, parking, health costs, pollution costs and other things.[44] So, in fact, personal choice is only one side of the coin in auto culture. *Collective choice*, the decisions of a few, appealing to the many, and paid for, wittingly or not, by everyone is the other side.

These conditions of private choice—personal expense, constraints that actually enhance access, and publicly financed infrastructure—all contribute to the overwhelming sense in an auto culture that driving *less* than what is possible makes no sense. When the very purpose of private, motorized transport is to enhance mobility and personal choice, access can only be good and more access better. Restraint is an alien concept. And if individuals realize value in enhanced access, then, by simple aggregation, society does as well. From the individual's perspective, there is no reason to have fewer vehicles than one can afford, no reason to drive to fewer destinations than what is possible, no reason to drive fewer miles than what one has time for. It is nearly impossible to ask how much auto use is too much. One can only ask how to make automobility better. To ask the "how much is too much" question would challenge the hegemony of this single use of public rights of way. It would question whether ever-increasing access of this one mode is worth the cost to all other modes, costs well known to experts and an increasing number of lay people. At the level of daily practice, this is the fundamental consumption question, not the purchase of the car or the gasoline, but the *consuming* of physical space and safe space and the vitality of residential and commercial communities. It asks if a "charming" island, broadly valued for both recreation and residency, could be destroyed by easy access. From such a question follows the larger consumption questions—impacts on peoples' health—at times, their very lives—and on the planet's waste sink capacities.

Mobility, in short, is one of the great *myths* of the auto culture, not in the sense of being fictional or wrong, but in the sense of being central to a belief system, one that sees human well-being in terms of ever-increasing movement and personal choice. One practical implication is that if other people's mobility or access is impeded by automobility, if children and parents and the infirm cannot compete, it is of little account. "Unplanned access is not an issue in [conventional] transportation planning," write Newman and Kenworthy. "The only kind of access that can be planned for, or is of any practical relevance in auto-dependent cities, is deliberate access, and this is, and will continue to be . . . by car. . . . Walking and cycling do not figure at all."[45] The *automobile* provides the greatest mobility; its movement must be facilitated, not the movement of the slow and weak; they can adjust: pedestrians can stay on the sidewalk, bicyclists can use the far side of the road, and vendors with pushcarts can rent a storefront.

In the auto culture, then, sufficiency makes no sense. One can never be too independent, have too much personal freedom, exercise too much choice. Mobility, speed, time-saving, comfort. These are the hallmarks of the modern person, of a progressive society. "There is," wrote Lewis Mumford, "only one efficient speed: faster; only one attractive destination: *farther* away; only one desirable size: *bigger*; only one rational quantitative goal: *more*."[46] And, yet, the Toronto case and many more in the literature on alternative transportation and urban planning suggest that some people do question the goal, some do dare ask about purpose and means, some do imagine notions like sufficiency and sustainability. They put a different logic to work, one perfectly intelligible, perfectly rational for the kind of "modern person" they want to be—and the "modern community" they want to be a part of. These are people who have, at one time or another, lived the consequences of unfettered automobility in their daily lives and know perfectly well the private benefits of private auto use on public rights of way. And yet they ask—and act on—the question of enough mobility, of sufficiency in auto use. Importantly, they do so not by eschewing the car altogether, but by carving out islands of respite from the auto-dominant society. They choose to harness the automobile, domesticate it to meet a variety of needs, all to avoid trampling on cherished values such as neighborliness and play and quiet and personal health and safety. The significance of such cases lies not in the numbers of individuals or the extent of their reach nor in the positive environmental and social effects. Rather, it lies in their very existence in the midst of societies with intensely held beliefs about the value of mobility, societies that project powerful images of the good life—all car dependent—and that devote huge resources and defer massive costs to keep it all going.

Harnessing Automobility

If auto culture celebrates personal mobility at the same time it neglects, even destroys, other values, what might be the alternative? What would a holistic, multiple-value, multiple-use approach, a "behavioral ecology of transport" be? How can one usefully distinguish Toronto from Detroit, New York from Los Angeles, or, perhaps the greatest extreme, Stockholm from Bangkok?

A resource-depletion perspective asks what resource is consumed, especially what is irreversibly changed, and under what conditions. The proximate resource consumed by excess auto access, what people experience in their daily lives, is an intangible, quite separate from the gasoline, steel and rubber. It is *public right of way*, which has three spatial attributes: the physical, the psychological, and the social.

Physical Space   Cars and their infrastructure of roadways and parking consume, that is, use up, vast amounts of land, each acre of which could be put to other uses including residential and commercial construction, farming (or grazing or timbering), game preserve, wilderness, or just plain open space. At some time scale, such land can revert to these uses. But for practical purposes, most land conversion to auto use is permanent. The physical space is consumed and, along with it as we have seen, a host of human values and ecosystem services.

Consumption of physical space can be rationalized as a necessary part of life. Like eating the apple and clearing the forest, humans, like all creatures, must consume to sustain themselves. What can not be sustained, though, is *unending* conversion, continuous and permanent diminution of ecosystem services. The U.S. or Australia may be able to "sustain" a much larger population and much more sprawl. They may be able to approach the densities of Europe or Japan. But because Europe and East Asia are currently living with large ecological footprints—maintaining their intensive resource use by importing ecosystem services—they are not models of sustainable resource use.

A city or a nation can overconsume physical space. It can use too much land and water and air. To pursue sustainability is to begin by harnessing one of the biggest consumers of physical space—the automobile. It is to seek sufficiency points in auto use.

Psychological Space   Human cognitive ability to perceive one's environment, including the physical, natural and human-built environment and the social environment, is a major determinant of one's ability to cope with challenges, to work, to live with purpose, and, most generally, to thrive. Recall from chapter 5 that humans employ two mechanisms for processing environmental information, what psychologists call *directed attention* and *involuntary attention*. Directed attention focuses on complex problem solving and demands considerable mental effort. Concentrated problem solving occurs when one is able to *inhibit* other responses to the environment. One result is that directed attention is limited; it is a "psychological resource," a resource that is fragile, that can be depleted, and that must be nurtured. Unlike involuntary attention, it must be restored or the individual experiences stress, impaired judgment, irritability, and a diminished sense of purpose. A range of attributes of the physical environment and of work and play help maintain and restore directed attention. Among them are spending time in savannalike settings such as parks and natural areas and performing routine physical tasks like walking, gardening, and cleaning. A common feature in these "preferred environments" is that individuals are engaged (thus inhibiting more problem solving) and yet, because it is routine, drawing only on involuntary attention.

A second result is that because depleted directed attention was rarely a problem in humans' hunter/gatherer stage, no mechanism simultaneously evolved to alert individuals to its impending depletion, let alone to an understanding of restorative activities. The best we can do in the evolutionarily "novel" setting of modern life is "rest" or "get away." Sleep, relaxation, and vacations can help but they are generally insufficient and sometimes counterproductive. Sleep is not engaging. Relaxing often involves physically restful yet attention-demanding activity—watching television or sporting events, for example. The logistics of a vacation can require considerable problem solving and, hence, deplete more directed attention than is restored. In the auto culture, so many activities, in work and in play, involve driving or dealing with automobiles and the auto-built environment. For drivers and pedestrians alike, negotiating intersections, avoiding vehicles, and dealing with inclement weather all demand considerable directed attention. Driving on the open road with little traffic might be an exception. Possibly even more significant, though, is the impact of the auto-built, physical environment, nearly the antithesis of a restorative environment, especially in congested, urban settings.

So directed attention is a depletable, psychological resource, difficult to anticipate or sense directly, and its restoration requires special environments and activities, both of which are in short supply in the auto culture. A paradox of modern life is that those few people who do enjoy a car-free existence for much of their daily lives are unable to articulate its psychological advantages. Some of my interviewees on Toronto Island would remark how peaceful or how safe their neighborhood is and yet dream about having a car out front. Being experienced themselves with the auto culture, they have opted for restricted access but could hardly say why. Most were not opposed to the automobile per se. Many owned and operated one on the mainland or otherwise depended on cars. They could only say that the inconvenience of not having immediate and complete auto access was worth it. The notion of directed attention helps explain this paradox. More generally, it suggests that, given a choice and given sustained experience with using less than what is possible, people will actually opt for "enough" mobility even when the benefits are intangible and can not be articulated.

Social Space   This third attribute of the public right of way is captured in the term "street life," minus any negative connotations the term may have with such things as gangs, loitering, and prostitution. In the town of Segovia, Spain, residents come out every evening to walk along the main road. Vehicles may pass, but the number and behavior of pedestrians makes it difficult to drive. People stroll up and down, stop for a bite to eat, and talk with fellow passersby. Parents push strollers and older children play games in the street. Elderly saunter or get a push in their wheelchairs. The scene is not a vestige of former times, nor is it created for tourists. It just happens day in and day out, in part, apparently, because it is tradition and in part because people just seem to enjoy it.

In my town, Ann Arbor, Michigan, a tiny, inconspicuous, one-lane, one-way road, Bucholz Lane, is open to vehicles, like all streets. For parts of the day, though, it is controlled by pedestrians, bicyclists, and strollers. The lane is so narrow and the houses so close to the edge that no motorist would dare drive even the posted speed limit of fifteen miles per hour. Instead, drivers enter the lane cautiously, wait for the other users to clear (and stare at them), and then proceed slowly. The lane is open on both ends to more heavily traveled roads and residents use it to drive into their driveways. But there is never a steady stream of traffic, even at the height of rush hour. On the social side, everyone on Bucholz Lane knows each other. All the children (and many from nearby streets) are known. A parent can feel quite secure leaving a youngster on the street to play because the traffic is slow and intermittent and, with adults always nearby, everyone watches out for everyone else's children. A block away in either of several directions, few neighbors know each other and a parent would be terrified to leave a child near, let alone on the street. Between the lane and the nearby streets, the people are no different. The structural conditions that allow for street life are.[47]

Street life in these two examples, like Ward's and Algonquin Islands, combines many activities—talk, play, recreation, child care, and, indeed, transportation. Unlike thoroughfares devoted to the automobile with occasional "interruptions" like cross walks and bicycle lanes, these streets are multiple use. They are places of encounter. And they are profoundly egalitarian: everyone has equal opportunity to transport oneself and use the street as one wishes; there is no membership and no exclusion. They are egalitarian in part because the participants employ technologies that do not exclude others. The automobile, by its very mass and speed, dominates virtually all other modes of transportation, let alone other activities. Here, the automobile assumes a subordinate position. (See figure 8.3.)

The personal interaction in these settings also differs from the means of association common in modern life. There is no schedule, no appointments, no reservations. No one must decide who is to bring the food, the toys, the chairs. There is no requisite special event to call it forth. One need not even have a reason for

Figure 8.3
Residential street in Denmark; cars in foreground and background. Photo courtesy Donna
L. Erickson.

participating nor spend a dime doing so. Participants can converse about anything
from the trivial to the monumental, from the personal to the commercial. They can
come and go as they please. No one is offended if some one is late or leaves early.
It is all spontaneous. As many urbanologists and city planners have argued, such
unplanned interaction is key to a meaningful notion of *community*.[48]

In short, when automobility is harnessed, spontaneous interactions tend to follow;
they become integral to everyday life. They are inclusive, egalitarian, and largely
noninstrumental. They occur because that's what people tend to do, given a chance:
congregate, play, recreate, eat together, tell stories, conduct business, and, not least,
transport themselves and their things. People have the chance when the structural
conditions exist, when streets are places of encounter as much as means of transport, when a public right of way is just that—*public*, for all members of the public,
not just for the fastest and most massive.

The attraction of such settings is evidenced by the comments of those who experience them and by the attempts of others to mimic them, often for commercial

purposes—street fairs, carnivals, and shopping malls for instance. Recall the Toronto planner's Venetian vision, writing in the 1950s, the heyday of unquestioned automobility: " 'Pedestrian Island' has become the term for such areas, even where they are not actually islands, but merely areas free from traffic. The creation of such 'islands' is being attempted all over the world." For many, especially those who know the spontaneous, non-instrumental versions, the facsimiles never match up, not even with climate control, nonstop entertainment, and great shopping deals. These contrived imitations segment street life in time (the "annual" street fair) or space (one street is closed off while everything else continues apace) or by activity (mostly shopping or mostly entertainment). True street life has little segmentation, little specialized functioning that would make for "efficient" use of space and time. The unattraction of a public street's opposite—the freeway—is patent. Drivers traverse long stretches of pavement as fast as possible, shielded from all around them. And no one wants to work or live near such a concrete monstrosity. Instead they throw up sound and visual barriers. "The vitality and attractiveness of urban life in a city's center," Newman and Kenworthy found after collecting data from cities around the world, North and South, seems "to be negatively related to its automobile dependence, in particular the amount of parking and road space provided."[49]

Street life was ubiquitous before automobile culture took hold. Where it exists within the auto culture, it is mostly a quirk, an odd remnant created by decisions made long ago, probably before the rise of auto culture. The Segovia and Bucholz roadways were probably too difficult to widen and traffic was more easily routed elsewhere. Toronto Island, we saw, survived repeated auto incursions in part through resistance, in part through serendipity and shifting political winds. Such "islands and mountaintops" are important, though, because they suggest the possibility of multiple-use, public right of way, even with the automobile. They suggest that sufficiency in automobility can lead to a realization of a range of community needs. What results is reduced consumption, maybe even "sustainable consumption," where land use and fuel burning and waste absorption fit within ecological capacity. (See box 8.1.)

What, then, is the value obtained from the "resource" of physical space, restorative environments and street life? For those of us who find ourselves fully immersed in an automobile culture, street life is nearly nonexistent, invisible, or highly attenuated. Its psychological and social value is little known, let alone appreciated. We get whiffs of it at street fairs and carnivals and indoor malls and historical

Box 8.1
Mobility meets livability: Inner-city Amsterdam

"Unbelievable livability" is how one observer describes Amsterdam's inner city, where 600,000 people live. A major reason is a deliberate city policy, pushed by citizens, to restrict automobility.

For much of its history, the inhabitants of Amsterdam depended on walking and canal boats for transportation, followed by trains, trams, and bicycles. Then the automobile appeared and, as elsewhere, increased dramatically in the 1950s, 1960s, and 1970s. Like all aspiring modern cities, Amsterdam responded with plans to demolish old neighborhoods and build highways through the city. But bicycle riders, historic preservationists, environmentalists and others would have nothing of such a car-intensive vision of their city. They organized protests, wrote pamphlets, and circulated petitions. And they gained seats on the city council.

In 1975 the city government began installing iron posts to block cars from driving or parking on sidewalks, bicycle lanes, and pedestrian areas. It designated new bicycle and pedestrian space and introduced special traffic lights that gave streetcars priority at major intersections. Perhaps most significantly, it regulated parking, a major determinant of traffic volume. Aiming to minimize car trips in the inner city, the city at the same time gave priority to short-term parking for deliveries, business traffic, residents, and the handicapped. Between 1975 and 1989 on-street parking declined significantly.

In a 1992 referendum, the city asked its citizens a question nearly unimaginable in North America: How far should the city go with reducing car traffic in the city center? Fifty-three percent called for a significant reduction in car use (through a 50 percent reduction in parking), while 46 percent voted to maintain current policies allowing for continued growth in car use. As a result, in 1994 the city council instituted a comprehensive "Traffic Arrangement Plan" aimed at removing 7,400 on-street parking spaces (half of which would be replaced with underground parking), increasing parking fees, improving public transportation, and reconfiguring major streets to give more space to alternative transportation.

With an expected 35 percent reduction in auto traffic "the Council's aim, and its hope," writes transport analyst Leo Lemmers, "is that the necessary conditions can be created to give Amsterdam a new kind of accessibility." In Amsterdam, "new" would be to drop yet lower on the industrial world's list of automobile dependency:

Percent of "journeys-to-work" by private automobile

Detroit	95.4
Los Angeles	89.3
New York	66.7
Toronto (Metro)	64.6
Hamburg	49.4
Amsterdam	40.0
Munich	38.0
Stockholm	31.0

Sources: Raven Earlygrow, "Why Is the City So Livable Today? Amsterdam Targets the Car," *Auto-Free Times* 9, Sustainable Energy Institute, Arcata, California, http://www.culturechange.org/issue9/amsterdam.html,   accessed   4/5/2004;   Leo

Box 8.1
(continued)

Lemmers, "How Amsterdam Plans to Reduce Car Traffic," *World Transport Policy & Practice* 1/1 (1995): 25–28 (quote on 27); Peter Newman and Jeffrey Kenworthy, *Sustainability and Cities: Overcoming Automobile Dependence* (Washington, DC: Island Press, 1999), table A.1 Data from the Thirty-Seven-City Study for the World Bank, pp. 344–347; Hans Pruijt, "The Impact of Citizens' Protest on City Planning in Amsterdam," paper presented at the conference "The Future of the Historic Inner City of Amsterdam" in Amsterdam, September 5–7, 2002, http://web.eur.nl/fsw/english/staff/homepages/pruijt/papers/amsterdam, accessed 5/3/2004; Karl Steyaert, "Amsterdam Automobile Case," unpublished manuscript, Ann Arbor, Michigan, October 25, 2000.

recreations, but we don't live it. It is not a part of everyday life. The absence of daily street life thus makes its value hard to assess, let alone to construe as a resource, as an attribute of public right of way, as something that can regenerate but needs maintenance and investment. Yet, like many resources that are essential to our well being, street life is vulnerable to incremental degradation, to encroachment by one use and one set of users, to processes, however logical, however efficient they may appear to individuals and policymakers alike, processes that gradually push aside the many other users and uses.

Automobility is particularly insidious in this respect. The automobile provides such tremendously popular private benefits and, at the same time, is so dangerous with its speed and mass, so consumptive of land and public space. A few such vehicles on an open-access road can quickly overwhelm all other uses. What is more, automobility is difficult to object to when the benefits are so palpable and when the cost to preferred environments and street life is so nebulous and diffuse.

The purpose of mobility is access. But when "the resource" of a public right of way is a combination of physical space, preferred environment, and street life and when resource uses vary from play to work to transport, the *kind* of access—open or regulated—becomes critical. In the natural resource arena, when extraction pressures are high, regulated access, whether of a public forest or a high-seas fishery, is essential for successful management and long-term sustainable use. So too with public rights of way: a set of private and public values centering on transportation but encompassing much more is possible, but only when users recognize that one use can compromise all others. Put in systems terms, if users push one variable to the extreme end of its range the entire system is jeopardized. Maximizing board feet or minimizing labor time risks the productive enterprise. Here, maximizing auto access risks other forms of transport, personal and community health, and ecological integrity. Open access leads to degradation.

Access, so framed, is largely unexamined and unquestioned in the auto culture. Restrictions are readily imposed to increase safety or facilitate traffic flow, but rarely does anyone ask who should have access to a right of way, how much they should use it, and what purposes they should derive from it. The default position in policy debates is that, because access is a good thing, more access is better, and because the auto is the quintessential vehicle for access, more access translates into more auto access. Moreover, because individuals freely choose the automobile, auto access is an expression of free will and, thus, in societies like the United States and Canada, highly valued. Enhancing auto access drives transportation policy; restricting it is anathema except in extreme conditions. Put differently, because access is unexamined, questioning access is to step out of the dominant belief system, to suggest a paradigmatic shift away from the underlying principles of efficiency and mobility.

To illustrate, if a municipality decided to increase auto flow by widening a narrow lane, access would increase. People near and far could now drive through on their way to work or play or shopping. Those who previously walked down the lane could now walk along the new sidewalks and cross at the traffic light. Their inconvenience would be more than offset by the gains achieved by those driving through. This would be a clear efficiency gain in which the greatest good for the greatest number is achieved. And in auto culture, even those who are inconvenienced as pedestrians can benefit, indeed *should* benefit, *as drivers*; they are, after all, members of the same culture, the auto culture: let them drive cars.

In this scenario, what is hard to assess, especially with incremental encroachment over years of widening, new traffic devices, and more automobiles, is the values that are compromised and the distributional effects that are rendered on resident populations. Motorists certainly gain access and, on the face of it, pedestrians and others merely have to route their travel along the sidewalks and crosswalks—or drive themselves. But, as noted, in street life there are many other values associated with passing along a right of way. Pedestrians and bicyclists, let alone strollers and perambulators, are not merely getting from point A to point B. The positive effects of the increase in access are highly visible, the negative invisible. Some gain, mostly motorists from outside the residential street, while others, mostly residents, lose. It is like clear-cutting that gets cheaper lumber to distant consumers while forest-dependent communities fold as their logging, hunting and fishing disappear.

So the users change along with the uses. Outsiders pass through, looking for the most efficient passage to their destination, stopping, if at all, only for a quick purchase. Residents, by contrast, live there, carrying on a portion of their everyday lives on the street. But once cars stake their claim, once use is significantly segmented within the public right of way, then auto passage, indeed, auto *dominance*, is "normal." The cars' speed and mass ensure it. And should their further encroachment ever be questioned, it can always be justified in terms of safety. Recall the Toronto parks commissioner assuring citizens that no one will be hurt by the island road because "random crossing of the roads by pedestrians would not be allowed."[50]

In short, what at first glance appears to be an unequivocal increase in public welfare with an increase in auto access to a public right of way is, in fact, both a redistribution of access and a change in values derived from that access. Net gain can not be assumed, no matter how many people choose to drive through. The use value changes from a diverse set of transport, psychological, and social functions to a single transport function. And because that single function physically dominates the space, the other functions, those intangible, unquantifiable, nonmarket features of everyday life, are shunted off to "community centers," schools, fenced-in parks, shopping malls, child care centers and senior centers. As access for a dominating mode of transport increases, segmentation of everyday life increases. Mobility begets specialization and specialization requires mobility. The positive feedback loop is complete. Life is more efficient. But with benefits redistributed and certain values compromised, net gain for individuals and society at large is ambiguous at best.

This ambiguity in part explains the difficulty of specifying the value of restrained auto access. As noted, for those who, one way or another, have found themselves in car-restricted areas and who like it, it is extremely difficult to put a finger on the value of the absence of something. This difficulty is especially acute when the "something" is auto access and everyone has long personal histories using the car to exploit public rights of way. The benefits of the car are real, personal, and mostly tangible. The benefits of car restriction, by contrast, are almost entirely intangible and, in the auto culture, experienced by few or only experienced as an exotic piece of recreational or historical pleasure. To the extent the car-free aspects of theme parks and historic recreations are experienced, they are done so as a consumable item, not as integral parts of everyday life.

On the Toronto Islands and in many other places we can find both longstanding and incipient forms of resistance to a technology that overwhelms all other means of transport and much of sociability (see box 8.2). In none is the automobile banned. There is no visceral, neo-Luddite rejection of the internal combustion engine or of private, fossil-fuel-based transportation. Rather, in each instance, residents, policymakers, and others have assessed the role of the auto in their respective environments and, for a variety of reasons, judged some level of use as *too much*. *Restraint* in auto access makes sense in these cases because decision makers have deemed other values to be more important than unhindered, ever-increasing auto access. Achieving a sufficiency point in auto use has been neither easy nor can it be presumed permanent. Most of these cases do occur, after all, within auto cultures. The proponents of restrained auto access have, in effect, resisted the expansive nature of the efficiency principle and its operational variants of specialization (segmentation) and mobility. For them, the battle is never won. Specialization of work, family and community and mobility of people and goods is all promoted by the auto culture where the logic of efficiency reigns supreme. But as the costs of hyperspecialization and excessive mobility mount and, especially, as many of those costs come back home (e.g., injuries, loss of community, global warming), a different logic emerges, a logic that says there are limits to how much physical space can be filled with roadway and massive, speedy machines on wheels, how much directed attention can be sapped in everyday activities, how much street life can be compartmentalized and moved elsewhere. That logic says there can be too much automobile use and, depending on the conditions of place, just enough automobile use. It says that a behavioral ecology of transport is multiple use and multiple value, that maximizing any one mode threatens all other modes and functions. It says we do not have to put the automobile back in the barn, but it must be harnessed when it comes out.

From Auto Dominance to Sufficient Transport

What, then, is the beast to be tamed? Consider a spectrum of roadways. At one end, the fastest and most powerful vehicles have exclusive access to the roadway—cars and trucks on a freeway or autobahn, for instance: pedestrians and cyclists prohibited, read the entrance ramp signs. At the other end of the spectrum is a roadway dedicated to *all* modes of transport, motorized and nonmotorized. Here each mode has equal access and equal right to a piece of the right-of-way at any given time. Moreover, the more vulnerable modes—walking, cycling, pushing—have priority when modes compete.

In the earliest years of the automobile, cars dominated not by their numbers or mass, but by their rarity and speed. On a Saturday morning the odd sports car,

Box 8.2
Bogotá confronts automobility

One day in February 2000 Bogotá, Colombia had a car-free day. Road accidents fell by 75 percent and, for the first time in four years, an entire day went by without a traffic fatality. That day 85 percent of all trips were by bus, and 10 percent by bicycle. In a subsequent referendum, a large majority of citizens approved an annual car-free day and the exclusion of cars every weekday between 6 and 9 a.m. and 4:30 and 7:30 p.m. beginning in 2015.

To reduce automobile traffic and improve public access, Bogotá increased its municipal gas tax and instituted a license plate number system aimed at keeping 40% of the car and truck fleet off the street during peak hours on workdays. The city created an inexpensive bus-based mass transit system. Use increased from 312 to 1,807 passengers per bus per day; travel time dropped 32 percent; traffic safety in busway corridors increased dramatically; and all ongoing costs were covered by fares. The city reclaimed some 500 km of sidewalk (which cars had taken over for parking) by raising the sidewalk to prevent cars from climbing the curb. And it built some 350 kilometers of bikeway. For these measures, Bogotá's mayor, Enrique Peñalosa says he "was almost impeached." In time, though, public opinion surveys showed strong support: a 2001 survey gave the bus system an 88 percent approval rating and the bike path program 86 percent.

Excess automobile use continues in Bogotá. But these measures, many quite small, many with unintended results, suggest that the problems of auto dominance are not unique to the North, nor is the potential for alternatives. In the South, writes Mayor Peñalosa, "Road transport absorbs massive public investments . . .; creates congestion which affects the mobility of the bus-riding majority; causes air and noise pollution; and results in road arteries, primarily for private vehicle users, becoming obstacles to lower income pedestrians." Just by asking questions of whose mobility and for what purpose and by experimenting, Bogotá may be a model for many cities in the North.

Sources: Arturo Ardila and Gerhard Menckhoff, "Transportation Policies in Bogotá, Colombia: Building a Transportation System for the People," *Transportation Research Record* 1817 (2002): 130–136; Enrique Peñalosa, "Foreword," in John Whitelegg and Gary Haq, *The Earthscan Reader on World Transport Policy and Practice*, xxv–xxxi (London: Earthscan, 2003) (quote on xxv).

driven by a wealthy, daring young lad, would race along country roads and village streets, sending townspeople and livestock scurrying to get out of the way. "Automobiles resembled untamed animals in the early years, with sudden swings of mood and a tendency to dangerous reactions," writes Wolfgang Sachs in his eloquent cultural history of the automobile in German society. "It took a strong arm to work the crank (which would likely kick back) and so coax a sound from the monster's insides, until it began to roar and shudder and belch its stinking vapors."[51] Driving was an adventure; speed, the conquering of time and space, the reward.

As cars became more common, and as their use shifted from sporting races and pleasure rides to luxury display and then to everyday transport, public sentiment shifted. "The meaning of the automobile is freedom, self-possession, self-discipline, and ease," wrote one German observer in 1903. "In it the traveling coach is revived in all its poetic plenitude, but in a form endlessly enriched by the former's exquisite potential for intensified and simultaneously expanded gratification."[52] Then, with the advent of the "peoples' cars"—the American Model T, the French Citroën, the German Volkswagen—car ownership came to define modern life, especially that centered on mass mobility. The Association of German Automobile Clubs captured the sentiment in its 1965 manifesto: "The automobile is a commodity for everyone for the satisfaction of daily needs, as befits the progressive shaping of our lives in a free world. . . . Social and economic policy [must] create all the preconditions for its sensible use [including] a maximum of technical facilities for insuring smooth traffic flow [and] making the streets once again into a space of humane mobility."[53]

Humane mobility. Something might have been lost in translation, but the logic has been as clear in Germany as in the United States, Canada and Australia after World War II: individuals must satisfy their needs for mobility; the best way to do so is to get everyone in a car; and this requires roadway, roadway unobstructed by wandering pedestrians and animals and cumbersome wagons. Private mobility is a public value and automobile infrastructure a public good. When, in the United States, General Motors (GM), Standard Oil of California, Mac Trucks, Phillips Petroleum and Firestone Tires formed a holding company in the 1930s called National City Lines and conspired to buy up and shut down public transit systems around the United States, hardly a peep was heard when GM was convicted and fined a mere $5,000.[54] Whether or not a GM executive actually said it, the public apparently did agree that what was good for GM (including public subsidies disproportionately allocated to one mode of transport, the automobile) was good for America. And "good" was a public on wheels going wherever people wanted, whenever they wanted.

The beast was no longer the odd sports car temporarily terrorizing a village street. It was a fleet of cars and trucks rolling over public rights of way, penetrating every nook and cranny of daily life, orchestrating the economic and development priorities of national and international policies. It was a transport system overwhelmingly committed to one technology and one value: automobility.

Auto dominance is now nearly complete in North America and many other parts of the world. Faster and farther. And bigger and more powerful. For all the critical analysis over the past few decades, for all the concern about pollution and injury and sprawl, cars just keep rolling off the assembly lines and across the North American landscape, an unstoppable juggernaut. Consumers willingly plunk down the cash (or credit card) spending a fifth or more of their income on their cars.[55] Advertisers present ever more attractive images, conjoining personal freedom and prestige with fun and nature. "The desire for personal mobility seems to be unstoppable," writes transport analyst Charles Lave, an "irresistible force."[56]

To step back and watch the juggernaut is nearly impossible for members of the auto culture. It is all so normal, so natural. But as the juggernauts' wheels roll over yet more victims while sinking ever deeper into its own ruts; as its inner workings—the manipulations of public sentiment and public expenditure—are increasingly exposed; and as people discover that their frantic and unhealthy lives are the logical results of this beast's insatiable appetite, the juggernaut will grind to a halt. Or it will slow to a manageable pace, with a scale and a direction that land and people can support, not through sacrifice, but through service to basic needs for transport and natural resources and sociability. (See box 8.3.)

The issue is not technical—miles per gallon, optimal traffic flow, or seatbelts. And it is not a matter of trade-offs, the economic rationalists' favorite construction when unpleasant outcomes must, by their reasoning, be endured: everything has its costs; people demonstrate the benefits of their choices through their forfeiture of hard-earned income; benefits of car travel must outweigh costs otherwise people wouldn't choose them; automobility is what everyone wants, the socially optimal state of affairs. Sure a road and parking on the Toronto Islands will change things, continue the rationalists, but access for the many, not the few is certainly worth it; sure the airport expansion will serve the investor class, but the economic boost to the entire economy benefits everyone.

No, the real issue is excess. The automobile may, like clear cutting and bottom trawling and the very concept of efficiency, have a place in an ecologically and socially sustainable society. But under present conditions, the juggernaut itself needs brakes, not just the cars. Auto culture must shift to a transport culture, a set of

Box 8.3
King of the road vs. the cautious traveler

Acres of asphalt open before me as I enter the freeway, accelerator pressed nearly to the floor. Six lanes of smooth, endless roadway with concrete barriers and chainlink fences on either side. The message is clear: this is now my space, my territory, just me in my car; make the best of it, waste not a moment. There's no deviation from the task, for there's only one thing to do here—drive. And for that, I'm in charge. I'm king of the road.

Here a narrow lane greets me. I can't quite see around the bend. The houses and trees and playhouse all tell me that people live here. In fact, right there, ahead in the road, children are playing, an elder is walking, and a teenager is cycling. The message is clear: I can cross this space but it belongs to others as much as to me. If I'm not careful, I could damage things, or people, or just the space, at once one of movement and daily life. So here I'm the visitor, the cautious traveler.

norms and principles and rules and practices that locate society at the multiple-use end of the roadway spectrum. The day will come when societies, burdened by the overwhelming costs of automobility and caught in a never-ending cycle of road building and increasing traffic, will "welcome a transport system in which access, not excess, is the predominant feature" of transport systems, writes *WorldWatch* author Marcia D. Lowe. A change in priorities means "improved access [for all users] could replace mobility as the benchmark of future progress in transport."[57] Auto manufacturers and transportation engineers and economists would say that improved vehicles, more bypasses and ring roads, and full-cost pricing will handle the problems of the automobile; what is needed are better cars and better traffic management, that is, incremental changes to existing transportation institutions. Newman and Kenworthy disagree:

There is a limit to how much the local effects of increasing car numbers and car use can be ameliorated through traffic management. Such management can be enduringly effective only in the context of *decreasing*, not increasing, car dependence. Reducing car dependence will be possible only through urban *systems changes* such as area-wide traffic calming, providing inherently less-car-dependent housing and employment arrangements, building new public transportation systems, and giving priority to non-auto modes.[58]

To collect data for their global survey of transportation, Newman and Kenworthy interviewed city officials, public servants, and community groups around the world. "In Auto Cities," they found, "the planners, politicians, and community groups were dispirited and despairing, often saying there was little that could be done. By contrast, in cities where transit was good, with high levels of cycling and walking, and where compact, community-oriented structures continues to be the norm in development, people exuded hope."[59]

Hope. A difficult thing to come by when the predominant urban images are Los Angeles and Detroit or Mexico City and Bangkok. Difficult when the predominant principles underlying urban design, especially transport design, are efficiency and consumer sovereignty and expansion. But when the images are an island neighborhood in Toronto or a street in Segovia or Ann Arbor; when the organizing principles are those that build in ecological and social constraint, that account for human adaptation and human excess; when transport culture is governed by restraint and respite and precaution—then there is reason for hope. This is the promise of sufficiency. Here, it is sufficiency in speed and mass and sufficiency in volume. Earlier it was sufficiency in timber harvesting and lobster fishing. Next, we'll see, it is sufficiency in meat production and a lot more.

Note to reader: If by this point you have read the chapters on timbering and fishing and, now, automobility and, let's say, worked your way though a good share of the conceptual chapters of Part I, sufficiency may seem a self-evident concept. Knowing about just a fraction of the costs of an expansive, frontierlike, efficiency-driven political economy at home and abroad, you may already have the sense, possibly the conviction, that sufficiency is the way to go. Regarding the automobile, for instance, you may say, as many people I know do: Of course we need to harness the automobile! Who can't see that?

In the next and final chapter I will try to reinforce and solidify this sense (or conviction), making the case that sufficiency makes perfectly good sense, common sense, ecological sense, for lots of things, but it makes especially good sense when society is about to hit the ecological wall. Before proceeding, though, allow me to suggest a reality check, as a thought experiment or, if you feel especially daring, a real-life experiment:

Go to your local transportation planning board meeting (or city council or county zoning or company planning meeting) and wait for the issue of parking to arise. After all the proposals for dealing with inadequate parking are aired (parking, conventional understanding has it, is *always* inadequate), stand up and say something like this:

Maybe we have *too much* parking. Or we *will* have too much parking if present trends continue. Maybe what we should be doing, rather than planning for new garages and bigger lots, is deciding how much parking is too much, and then plan everything else around that: bike lanes, pedestrian crossings, public transit and whatnot.

If you live in an auto culture as described in this chapter, brace yourself for the barrage:

What! You want to tell people they should drive endlessly searching for a place to park? Or that they shouldn't even drive into town? They will head for the mall, just the place you despise because it's so "car-dependent." It would be simpler to just shutter the downtown stores and lay off half the workforce, because that's what will happen anyway! Listen, there's plenty of space for new parking. We just have to make more efficient use of space—build up, build down, move some structures, convert the empty lots. And if congestion increases as some predict, we just need to improve traffic flow. Bottom line: *we don't decide lifestyle issues for our citizens*. We provide essential services, the kind they demand and have a right to. Our economy—our jobs, our very way of life—depends on it. So don't tell me or anyone else where to drive!

Fanciful? Try it. I have. The context was slightly different (transporting school children), but the barrage was much the same.

Sufficiency may be perfectly sensible, but it's still completely at odds with contemporary decision making, that which is premised on unending expansion, an omnipresent frontier, a ubiquitous "downstream," consumer sovereignty and, not least, those never-ending, all-popular, eminently scientific, win-win, mutual gains called efficiencies.

9

Making Ecological Sense

There are those who will never see the logic in the logic of sufficiency. Well ensconced in the rationalities of economic, engineering and legal thought, surrounded by an environment that never stops offering its services, sufficiency is an alien concept. If they give it a place—for the odd timber company or the out-of-the-way fishing village—it will always appear second best, a concession to the traditional, the premodern, the unscientific. Sufficiency will be, at best, "good enough," not ideal, not the most, not the maximum possible. For the nonecological rationalists, ideal decision making involves trade-offs, marginal analysis and optimal choice. For the practitioners it involves maximization and minimization. To pick a discount rate and build uncertainty into the decision is real decision making. To get the biggest return on investment, to move data and capital and even people at the fastest speed, that is progress. But to say enough when more is possible, well, that is irrational. To say too much when life is full of uncertainty is to deny the role of risk-taking and exploration and innovation, indeed, human progress.

The rationalists' faith in unending abundance appears unshakable, no more subject to scrutiny than their apparent faith in technological advance and population increase, both presumed beneficial until proven otherwise. Abundance achieved now paves the way for abundance later; the more choice we arrange for ourselves, the more we leave for future generations. Consumption stimulates innovation, expansion opens new frontiers.

This is a curious position for those of us who rest our worldview on scientific discovery, especially that which documents over and over again trends in biophysical deterioration and that which gives credence to threshold effects and cause-effect time lags and irreversibility. It is a curious position when literature and history, as well as, say, psychology and anthropology, show that humans are perfectly adept at confronting and dealing with limits, that maximization makes sense for machines but not organisms and ecosystems. It is an even curiouser position when we examine everyday practices such as redwood timbering and lobster fishing and neighborhood organizing and see common sense, good old-fashioned common sense, however uncommon it may be in the halls of legislatures and trade organizations and corporate headquarters.

It may be enough to conclude this book by stating that the nonecological rationalists will never be convinced. We are talking about two fundamentally opposed worldviews. One sees human potential everywhere, irreversible decline nowhere. The other sees trends that portend permanent diminution of livability, even of life on earth.

There will be no resolution of these competing views, but I offer a few parting words if for no other reason than that advocates of alternative reasoning and alternative choices need all the support they can get. They need a basis, applied and theoretical and beyond the ideological, for taking a different path. Given global ecological constraint, they need more than an ideal, a fantasy, a utopian vision; they need a realistic option. They need an ecological rationality because, for some time, they will be bumping up against economic and engineering and legalistic rationalities, against the presumed benefits of ever-increasing material expansion, against charges of backwardness and parochialism and "doing without."

My experience presenting the ideas and stories in this book over many years attests to this need. In the classroom, with colleagues and the media and members of the public, and among family and friends, I have found that even the most committed environmentalists have a difficult time imagining approaches that do not emphasize taxes and subsidies, lawsuits and boycotts, and, most prevalent perhaps, "environmental education." As an "institutionalist" I attribute this difficulty to a deeper difficulty—sensing the broad principles under which our own society operates, principles that were deliberately constructed to meet the needs of the times and that now appear so natural, even when other needs are more pressing. It is hard to appreciate, for instance, how prevalent efficiency is in everyday decision making and policymaking generally. No one talks about it. It's just there: of course it's better if it's more efficient. For me, one of the big surprises in this study was the absence of a history of the idea of efficiency. There are histories aplenty on the ideas of expansion and progress and conservation, not to mention industrialization and democracy. But the history of an idea so central to the two most dominant disciplines in modern life—engineering and economics—is missing. How can this be? I am still perplexed. I can only surmise that the absence of such a history owes to the very status of the concept: it is indeed the water in which we swim, a given that no fish among us need question, our only challenge being to keep moving, to eat and keep from being eaten, and to multiply. But only a bit of reflection, a bit of detached observation, a glance at the biophysical trends reveals that the water is changing. It is time to make sense of those changes and humans' role in them. And it is time to sketch out alternatives.

In these pages I have implicitly assumed that well-honed argument and good stories will enable a different sense-making, one that allows for rational calculation (economic, engineering, legal *and* ecological), but also intuition and experience, and one that privileges none. I have assumed that if enoughness and too muchness appeal to those seeking something other than maximum return on investment or an optimal basket of consumer goods, these can serve as a foundation for a new way to organize society, especially its economy.

But that may not be enough. If efficiency has been derailed from its classical usages denoting effective and efficacious and from its industrial usages denoting work performed, and if sufficiency is a potential social organizing principle, then the contrast of the two visions ought to be apparent in many places. One is public health. As I bring this study to a close, BSE, bovine spongiform encephalopathy—otherwise known as mad cow disease—has hit North America. The scare to the meat industry and consumers is palpable. The origins of the disease are still a mystery. But its occurrence in a production system committed to never-ending efficiencies is not. This system epitomizes nonecological thinking, compartmentalized decision making that assumes animals and humans can be manipulated as readily as fuels and machines. It epitomizes too much science of one sort, not enough of another. And in the public reaction—some scientifically grounded, some intuitive and experiential—signs of hope are emerging, signs, as I read them, of the logic of sufficiency. With this final case, I set the stage to go beyond the logic of sufficiency to the *ethics of sufficiency*.

Mad Cow

First discovered in Britain in 1986, mad cow disease ravaged British herds and was responsible for some 140 human deaths. It soon spread to 18 other European countries and Japan. In May of 2003 a case appeared in Alberta, Canada, and in December another appeared in the state of Washington in the United States. The disease agent was not at all like the usual suspects, bacteria and viruses, but misfolded proteins—so-called prions—that infect the brain, spinal column, and intestines, and cannot be destroyed by cooking, incinerating, or sterilizing with chemicals. The disease is always fatal. Still, the mechanism for transfer from one individual to another, from one species to another, is unclear. A public debate rages in North America:

• Should we have seen this coming, given the ravaged herds and human deaths elsewhere?
• Were the regulators asleep at the chopping block or were they just pawns of industry?
• Were industry's "it can't happen here" denials mere public relations or reasonable probabilistic assessments of the risks?
• Were the consumer and environmental groups, their voices as shrill as ever, right after all in their calls for tighter regulations or were the two North American cases isolated incidents?
• Is there really a risk given that only a few head of cattle, out of millions, have BSE?
• Is the real issue, as the industry and government regulators said repeatedly, public perception and consumer confidence or is it the uncontrollable spread of a nasty, incurable disease?
• Did BSE come from Canada and, if so, is it the Canadians' fault? Or, because the two countries' herds are highly integrated and the United States dominates, is it the Americans' fault?

These questions are likely to be debated for some time. What is not debatable, at least from the perspective of adaptive, complex systems, ecological rationality, and sufficiency principles, is that the modern meat system is broken. Run as an efficient machine with highly concentrated ownership and a nearly borderless world of cattle exchange and meat and byproduct distribution, this is a system that behaves as if animals and people are just factor inputs, as if disease is only an assembly line defect, correctable with better engineering. A glance at the history of this system shows that what we see today (or, rather, what most of us *never* see) is only an extension of the past, and mad cow disease, or some other "defect," only a logical outcome of a system that knows no bounds, a system committed to ever-more specialization, speed, intensification, and mobility. Efficiency drives production, while abundant products and low prices for the consumer justify that production.

A century and a half ago in places like Cincinnati and Chicago, once meat processing left the local farm and local butcher for the stockyard, it was one efficiency after another, one new cut of meat, one ingeniously devised new byproduct after another. The "stockyard was a triumph of the engineer's craft," writes historian William Cronon in his environmental history of the nineteenth-century Midwest, *Nature's Metropolis*. From it extended fences and railroads and shipping lanes, a great system with "only one purpose: to assemble the animal products of the Great

West, transmute them into their most marketable form, and speed them on their way to dinner tables around the world."[1]

The work of meat production shifted in a matter of decades, even years in some places. On the Great Plains bison hunting shifted to open-range cattle grazing and then, with barbed wire fences, to pasturing on selected grasses and, finally, to confinement—concentrated, intensive feeding; not on grasses, but on grain, mostly corn. Some livestock raisers grew their own corn, but the logic of efficient production meant that others should do that—namely, corn farmers—leaving livestock raisers the opportunity to specialize in breeding young animals or fattening the older ones. With these changes, slaughtering shifted from range to farm to "processing plants." Here the specialization of livestock raising converged with the imperative of processing speed in what became known as the disassembly line, "among the most important forerunners of the mass production techniques that swept American industry in the century to come," writes Cronon.[2] In a description of an assembly line for hogs, one that could have inspired Frederick Winslow Taylor, Frederick Law Olmstead describes the scene in 1857:

We entered an immense low-ceiled room and followed a vista of dead swine, upon their backs, their paws stretching mutely toward heaven. Walking down to the vanishing point, we found there a sort of human chopping-machine where the hogs were converted into commercial pork. A plank table, two men to lift and turn, two to wield the cleavers, were its component parts. No iron cog-wheels could work with more regular motion. Plump falls the hog upon the table, chop, chop; chop, chop; chop, chop, fall the cleavers. All is over. But, before you can say so, plump, chop, chop; chop, chop; chop, chop, sounds again. . . . Amazed beyond all expectations at the celerity, we took out our watches and counted thirty-five seconds, from the moment when one hog touched the table until the next occupied its place.[3]

Celerity, indeed: speed, efficient use of time and resources. This was everything. Today, that scene has only become faster, larger and more specialized and more mechanized, possibly cleaner and shinier, but certainly more thorough in its use of animals and machines and people, more intensive in its production, more extensive in its distribution.

On the disassembly line, workers follow clock time, and, for their increasingly shortened lives, so do the animals. Continuous feeding allows continuous growth, canceling out the seasonal cycling of grazing—growing in times of plenty, resting in between. And with grain and then, later in the twentieth century, growth enhancers, specially formulated feeds and antibiotics, livestock raisers accelerate animals' growth to bring them to market at ever-younger ages. Respite for worker and animal alike is as alien a notion as livestock wandering through wide-open spaces, grazing on a mix of grasses (with the occasional seed and insects ingested along the way) and farmers raising livestock from birth to slaughter while they tend their crops on diversified farms.

The feedlot system "maximized the efficiency of meat production," writes Cronon.[4] As far back as the mid-1800s, "the division of labor allowed packers to accelerate the rate at which workers handled hogs [and cattle], and led to specialized ways of dealing with each constituent body part. . . . The enormous volume of animals meant that even body parts that had formerly been wasted now became commercial products: lard, glue, brushes, candles, soaps."[5] Speed and specialization—ever more efficient. All as if seasons don't matter, a rhythm of work and regeneration is irrelevant; as if the system can always be fixed; as if diseases will never become as effective (on their own terms) as the system is efficient (on its own, mechanical and economic, terms).

To claim that mad cow disease could never happen in North America is to view the constructed food system as a controlled system, complicated to be sure, but not complex, not one that has emergent properties of its own. It is to act as if this grand experiment of ever-more efficient production occurs in a laboratory, sealed tight and completely contained, or as if everything is just a factor input, like the source materials and inventories and waste products at an automobile manufacturing plant. And all this at the same time livestock, feed, meat and by-products increasingly cross every imaginable barrier—political, cultural, climatic, ecological, species.

More than anything, the specialized, speed- and mobility-oriented system of meat production exudes power. A century and more ago "the Chicago packers were ruthless competitors, and had little compunction about selling dressed beef at whatever price would bring customers," writes Cronon. "Market share was the paramount concern, and the packers were willing to do almost anything to gain it. They sold meat below its cost of production to break the resistance of local butchers, raising their prices once they had succeeded."[6] By the late 1880s, the Big Four meatpackers of Chicago dominated American meat production and distribution. "Like the progressive reformers who followed them," concludes Cronon, like the Simon Pattens and Frederick Winslow Taylors and Theodore Roosevelts and Henry Fords, the big meat packers of the late nineteenth century "worshipped at the altar of efficiency, seeking to conserve economic resources by making a war on waste. This was their most important break with the past."[7] So "an industry that had formerly done its work in thousands of small butcher shops around the country must be rationalized to bring it under the control of a few expert managers using the most modern and scientific techniques."[8] Today it is the Big Five, their war on waste even more aggressive, their power even better honed.

Expert managers. It is hard to say whether it has been their scientific management, their much-acclaimed economies of scale, their predatory practices, or their political organizing that has most determined the modern meat system in the United States. All, though, are forms of power, and it is from such power that the rules of the game are written, rules that encourage specialization and speed and concentration, that invoke low consumer prices and abundant choice to justify just about anything, including systematic denial of disease threats. It is clearly power, not true efficiencies, that demeans workers as they fatten and then "disassemble" animals; that distorts those animals, giving them short and brutish lives, stuffed with grains and drugs and rendered body parts of their own species; that makes it all look so neat and clean, so routine, indeed so natural. It is power that allows disease to be construed as a minor risk, just a cost of doing business.

This is a system that is rational—economistically rational—to an extreme, hyperefficient in its animal growing, processing and utilization, hyperdeficient in its attention to natural limits, ecological and human. It is a system that renders humans superfluous as it renders every last bit of meat from a cow carcass and sends its by-products to foodstore shelves, pharmacies and, of all places, the feed of those very same animals. It is a dehumanized, denaturalized system governed by efficiency principles, justified by consumer choice, and carried out under a set of rules largely written by a handful of producers.

The logic of efficient use is a wonderful logic, one that historian Cronon finds reason to celebrate at the same time he documents the destruction of habitats and the alienation of people and their food. The "real achievement" of the big meat packers, he writes, "was to create immense impersonal organizations" where "waste meant inefficiency" that "must be eliminated with every strategy and device that managerial ingenuity could muster against it."[9] But it is a logic that has no bounds. One can never have enough managerial ingenuity, enough meat products, or low enough prices. Taken to its logical extreme, we get cattle, pigs and chickens in their respective "farms," standing shoulder to shoulder unable to escape each other's saliva, urine, and feces. We get a market for "downers," cows too stressed or diseased or injured to walk, that are dragged into slaughter houses and processed, largely for ground meat in the fast food industry. We get dairy cows, their udders so heavy they can barely walk, raised on a diet of antibiotics and high-protein supplements producing every day of their short lives and then, when production declines or they are sick, slaughtered for hamburger. We get "advanced meat recovery" machines that grind up bones, including skeletons, and squeeze out every last shred of meat, along with, occasionally, some nerve tissue, precisely where BSE incubates. And we get one victory after another of the industry, the Big Five blocking preventative measures even after the rest of the meat producing world had taken such measures.

This is efficiency gone awry, a food system "designed to move parts along a conveyor belt, no matter where the parts come from," says writer Verlyn Klinkenborg. "And if one of the parts proves to be fatally defective—a cow with the staggers, for instance—then shutting down the conveyor nearly always comes too late."[10] And the only remedy is to build a better conveyor belt. This is a food system that can be unendingly manipulated, compartmentalized at every stage of animal growth, concentrated and mechanized at every stage of disassembly, and ingeniously configured to create a myriad of products, only one of which is meat. And all as if it were safely contained in a high-security laboratory. This is a food system constructed as if the animals had never roamed open land, grazed on grass, lactated intermittently according to age and season, fended off predators, mated (as opposed to being inseminated with a needle), and dropped their wastes, widely offering nutrients to the very plants and animals that sustain them. It is a system that presumes humans want only two things from farm animals: the highest return on investment among owners, the lowest price with abundant choice among consumers. There are no farmers, just laborers, assembly-line workers and disassembly-line workers. Caring for an animal and its habitat, being humble enough to assume that the system cannot be completely controlled, combining the work of animal husbandry with the work of farming or hunting or teaching or parenting, preparing for limits before limits are reached; all these are irrelevant. It is a system bound to break.

It is in such a system that asking how much is too much is just too much, not just "out of paradigm," but antithetical to the very construction of the system itself, its purposes and methods. Can a system of meat production exist that respects limits and diversity and self-determined work? Of course. Such systems have been around for a long time and across cultures. Recall the centuries-long cattle raising on Marajo Island in the Amazon River (chapter 2). In North America, there are open-range ranches such as those of the Malpai Borderlands Group in New Mexico and Arizona where ranchers protect the land at the same time they raise cattle. There are dairy farmers in New Zealand and Wisconsin who milk seasonally, taking a few months off in the summer or winter to restore both the cows and themselves. There are organic "beefalo" ranchers in Michigan who reject industrialized methods of feeding and slaughtering their cattle. There are ranchers in North Dakota who raise beef without animal byproducts or hormones, have it humanely hand-slaughtered in accordance with Islamic law, and then sell to the halal market.[11]

Sufficiency in meat production is indeed possible, arguably imperative. Getting there seems to be the problem. Perhaps we need a theory.

Reaching for a Theory

Just as every revolution needs a chemist, every shift in social understanding, every economic reorganization, every organizational repositioning needs a theory. And that theory is useful to the extent it addresses contemporary needs and is grounded in well-established behavioral patterns. In the past, society needed theories to organize God's creation, to justify conquest and domination, to spur industrialization, to promote trade and cooperation, to prevent catastrophic economic depression, to explain human's place in the universe. Now we need a theory to guide humans' material appropriation and disposal in an ecologically constrained world. We need a theory that makes patently absurd, indeed unethical, ever-expanding, ever-accelerating, ever-concentrating industrial agriculture and forestry and fishing. We need a theory that makes groundwater overdrafting and dispersion of persistent toxic substances obvious violations of human's environmental trust.

It does not have to be a formal theory, nothing on the order of relativity or quantum mechanics or natural selection. The issue here is human behavior. It is organizing individuals and groups and organizations and nations and international society to operate within the earth's regenerative capacities. On that count, it is as straightforward as balancing a personal checkbook or the company books or a national budget; it is as simple as living off the interest without eating into the principle, as pumping no more water than recharges, as raising livestock in conditions similar to what their ancestors evolved to survive under. And so on. It is really quite simple. And thoughtful people know society will get there one way or another. Infinite material expansion on a finite planet is, quite simply, impossible.

So the only question is how we get there, with how much pain, how much challenge and "rising to the occasion," how much satisfaction and meaning from doing what is necessary and right. And for that we do need a theory, however informal and squishy it might be (theories of human behavior and organization always are).

Unfortunately, with current understanding, we are far from such a theory. Those of us active in academic or policy or activist arenas struggle just to get the questions right: Does saving that species, that forest, that wetland really help? Will better smokestack scrubbers and tighter production loops add up to sustainability? Or is the real problem overpopulation and overconsumption? Is trade good for the environment? Does the Kyoto Protocol limiting greenhouse gasses provide a step forward or an excuse for marginal tinkering?

There is no theory in this book, certainly not in the formal sense, nor even in the sense that there is a theory of cognition in psychology, say, or comparative advantage in economic trade. There are, though, propositions, some more tentative than others. And there is provisional grounding: real decisions by real people trying to make a living or "do their bit" for their society. These are people trying to do good not by doing more and doing it more efficiently, not by controlling yet more land and people and animals, but by functioning within systems that are only partly knowable, and thus only partly controllable. Their actions, indeed their courage, shows that sufficiency is possible. Still, a theory would be nice. So herewith a few thoughts to point in that direction. It all starts with assumptions. (For readers whose eyes glaze over at the very mention of words like *theory* and *assumptions*, I recommend going straight to the next section, "If it exists, it's possible.")

Assume humans are self-interested, shortsighted, insatiable maximizers and, yes, it will take a powerful and enlightened authority, a "Leviathan," to force such creatures to act for the public good and protect the environment. Alternatively, assume that people really can be far sighted and care for their environment and that, as they better understand the problem, they will put aside self-interest for other-interest and, yes, we can be confident things will turn around—all we need to do is wait for prices to correct the distortions and leaders to muster the political will. Both verge on the hopelessly idealistic. But assume that people have tendencies toward *both* self-interest, the short term and the insatiable, on the one hand, *and* toward other-interestedness, the needs of one's society and the distant future, on the other hand, and matters look a lot different. Assume that people can understand "the environment" not just as amenity (a scenic view, a pleasant park) but as life support (the water, the air and the minerals, the organisms and ecosystems we all require to survive and thrive). From this standpoint, environmental protection is no longer a luxury, no longer a trade-off against jobs and prosperity. Once again, matters look different.

These are not heroic assumptions—long-term societal investment, nature as the material undergirding of individuals and their society. Millhands and timber executives at the old Pacific Lumber Company understood that they all did well (and certainly better than timber communities all around them) when they and the company owners invested in timber acquisition, logging techniques, mill operations and retailing, on the one hand *and* in the workers (training and housing and retirement) and Humboldt County and the forest, on the other. They knew their livelihood depended on cutting trees yet, for their children and children's children, on not cutting out. They knew that if the forest degraded, their lives degraded, too. No one had to be converted to environmentally correct thinking to understand these things.

Nor is it heroic to further assume that people can readily sense when an activity is excessive, that indulgence is no more a part of "human nature" than restraint, that participants derive more meaning from active engagement, from productiveness, however unremunerative it may be financially, than from passive absorption, from purchasing and consuming and disposing. Now throw in a few more behavioral assumptions, namely that groups tend not to foul their own nest (but certainly others' nests), that downstream recipients (those very same others) will resist, that people tend to join groups and be responsive to the needs of their groups, and that collectivities are perfectly capable of designing institutions—norms and principles, rules and procedures, some formal, some informal—to ensure their life support and their livelihood and, together, things certainly do look different.

Different, that is, than the prevailing policy environment where the "only way" to reverse the trends in environmental degradation is better science (i.e., more data and better modeling), better pricing (i.e., if markets just worked better all costs will be internalized), and better enforcement (i.e., we know what must be done; we just have to get better at, yes, *forcing* people to do it). This way is not hopeful, or realistic. In fact, it is truly hopelessly idealistic. Bad decisions are rarely a result of inadequate information, however scientifically grounded (witness the continuing promotion of intensified forestry and agriculture and of private automobile transport); markets routinely deviate from the theoretical ideal of "perfect competition," which is to say, power routinely enters market transactions (witness the historical uses and abuses of efficiency, the contemporary meat industry, let alone the manipulations of the Enrons, WorldComs and Parmalattas of the world). And the apparent need for external, often distant and top-down enforcement suggests that the "only way" is not well grounded in established patterns of human behavior. This way is inattentive to the full range of human interests, individual and collective, and it depends on the good will of some (the policymakers and enforcers) at the same time it assumes the narrow self-interest of everyone else.

Indeed, a different mode of reasoning is needed, one consonant with a historically novel condition—global ecological constraint. So the proffered alternative behavioral assumptions—an inclination toward long-term societal investment, an understanding of the environment as life support, a sense of excess, a belief that meaning derives from engagement, a recognition of humans' capacity to self-organize and innovate for collective self-management and restraint—amount to a behavioral framework for a theory of sustainability. They underpin what I have termed ecological rationality. And, yet, as discussed in chapter 2, the hegemony of economistic and legalistic reasoning runs strong. So maybe the best these assumptions can do is give reason for hope, without being idealistic, wishful, or utopian. They are realistically hopeful because, if one takes the evidence presented in these pages as reasonable and accurate, they are reflective of a good part of human behavior. Humans are, if nothing else, problem solvers, not material maximizers. They can, indeed always have, tackled environmental problems at scales relevant to their existence. That has not changed. Pacific Lumber workers and managers struggled for livelihood *in Humboldt County*; Monheganers fought for their livelihood *on Monhegan*; Toronto Island residents resisted excess automobility *on the Toronto Islands*. And yet a more careful look at these cases reveals that their successes depended critically on organizing at higher levels, too: old man Murphy worked with Professor Fritz to reform the industry, not just his company; Monheganers engaged the Department of Marine Resources and went to the Maine legislature; Torontonians lobbied against and worked with the city and the provincial and federal governments. Where there was failure, (most notably Pacific Lumber; still, possibly, the Toronto Islands) it resulted from a failure to organize at a higher level. What has changed, what is indeed novel at this historical juncture, is that such struggles are a result of, and demand attention to much larger scales—to the municipalities and counties, to the states and provinces, to the nation, to "the market," to the regional and international.

So in these pages I have deliberately chosen the case histories, the short stories and anecdotes to highlight the ordinariness of the sufficiency principle. Some of these have highlighted the extraordinariness of the efficiency principle. It would have been rather easy to show sufficiency with isolated or fringe examples—those where religious fervor or an ideology of dissidence and rejection prevail. These are easy but not persuasive. They can be readily dismissed as frivolous or trivial or simply inappropriate for all but an extreme minority. The "hard cases" here are, instead, those that are simultaneously mainstream, everyday, even "modern," and yet take divergent paths. (See box 9.1.)

Can these divergent paths win out over those driven by economistic reasoning, by organizing around specialization and intensification? Can the Marajo and Malpai ranchers, the nine-month dairy farmers, the organic beefalo raiser thrive? Can they, in the terms of game theory, be a dominant strategy? Restraint and respite are, to be sure, vulnerable to the behaviors of exploitation and moving on. Stable,

Box 9.1
What cannot be bigger, faster, cheaper

The nonecological rationalists may scoff at the sufficiency principle just as many industrialists now deride the precautionary principle. The following activities suggest that, despite the dominance of economistic, engineering, and legalistic reasoning in modern industrial life, such reasoning is hardly universal, not even in so-called advanced industrial societies.

If these activities are impossible to make more efficient, to accelerate, to maximize or minimize, then restraint, respite, natural capital primacy, the indefinite future, middle-ground operating, buffering, problem absorption, capacity limits, self-directed work, residential ownership, good access, and ecological security are indeed possible.

Each activity is debatable at some level and in some context. A wetland can be restored expensively or cheaply. But it cannot be restored quickly. A constitution can be physically written quickly or slowly, but it can only be written well with careful deliberation. These activities are not done better, done right, or achieved at all, if they are subject to principles of efficiency and gain. Their purpose is outside the realm of conventional rationalist thought and action, as is much of achieving an ecologically and socially sustainable society.

Listening (really listening) to a child
Restoring a wetland (or forest or prairie)
Building trust in financial markets
Resolving a dispute (especially by probing underlying interests and crafting novel solutions)
Playing (children and adults)
Writing a nation's constitution (or an organization's by-laws)
Having a special meal (e.g., holiday, birthday)
Developing a discipline (e.g., playing a musical instrument, raising livestock, hot rodding, writing, fishing, gardening)
Building camaraderie
Grieving (and consoling a grieved one)
Having a deep conversation (or just a chat)
Conducting a public debate (especially on critical issues that require a decision)
Handling a child's temper tantrum
Experiencing a special or sacred place
Achieving status, prestige, statesmanship

agriculturally based societies have always been susceptible to invading hoards and power-hungry rulers. To organize within ecological constraint is risky in the short term when the dominant political economy is organized for unlimited expansion. Expansionist industrialism in particular is likely to be the most difficult setting to practice ecologically constrained behavior. To find instances of such behavior is truly anomalous. It is most likely to occur where isolation, whether circumstantial or planned, prevails. Remote subsistence peoples in dense forests and Amish farmers and back-to-the-land hippies are examples. Some might look to these cases for example and inspiration. In fact, it is rare when a work on sustainability doesn't cite such groups. But if their defining characteristics are isolation and rejection, they offer little by way of restructuring an entire society for sustainable resource use. To become a dominant mode of organization and interaction, living with ecological constraint must have characteristics that appeal to the great many in society.

So this study has been an exercise in normative theorizing. It would have been more comfortable if it were a descriptive exercise, or a critical exercise. Describe, categorize, explain, analyze, unpack, deconstruct—these are staples of the academic enterprise, necessary endeavors not just for academic freedom and the advancement of knowledge but, arguably, for democracy itself. But academics are generally loath to venture beyond these pursuits, preferring to leave that to others. Or perhaps they fear opening themselves to charges of ideology or social do-gooderism. To do otherwise, to describe, analyze, and deconstruct *and predict, prescribe, and advocate* is to wade into murky waters where vicious beasts—critics and funders and politicians—just wait to attack. Not to do so, though, is to take the academic enterprise only half way. It is to make grand pronouncements about the nature of things, always with a hint, but only a hint, of how things *should* be, leaving it to those who sit in the driver's seat to make the translation from analysis to action. That translation, what leads to real decisions and real outcomes, is itself a matter of inquiry, of establishing an empirical grounding and laying out a set of behavioral assumptions. As such, the translation to action is no less an academic enterprise, and no less an academic *responsibility*, than describing, analyzing, and deconstructing. It's just more daunting, murkier, scarier. Political theorist Paul Wapner puts the academic's moral imperative thus:

Given the many injustices throughout the world, scholarship must not simply content itself with understanding the place of morality in world affairs but must also bring the demands of moral conscience to the study and practice of world politics. Scholars have a responsibility, in other words, to use their work to leave the world a better place than they found it, and this includes, when possible, translating one's scholarly insights into appropriate political action."[12]

So the reader must judge whether my attempt to go beyond the critique is a valid academic endeavor or just an ideological exercise. The reader must decide if my *pre-scription* for sufficiency is a logical outgrowth of the biophysical and social context in which humans find themselves in the early twenty-first century or is just another environmentalist's plea for global stewardship. All I would offer as a preemptive defense should the reader see disguised ideology and environmentalism is three things.

One, as discussed, the underlying behavioral assumptions are hardly heroic. The proverbial "man and woman on the street," the average Joe or Maria, the modestly thoughtful twelve year old, I dare say, will find nothing unusual about restraint and respite, precaution and polluter pays, selectively permeable boundaries, and self-determined work. And they will find utterly bizarre the inner workings of the meat industry, the claims of the timber industry that monocultures save forests, the assumptions of transport planners that automobility is best for everyone, the asser-tions of the leaders of the leading greenhouse gas emitting country that more emis-sions are less emissions.

Two, the biophysical conditions are real, not the figments of the imagination of tens of thousands of scientists and review panels, not the prognostications of modern Malthusians and doomsayers. Many of us may be buying our way out of the con-sequences—for a time. But not everybody can; in fact, the great majority cannot, and no one can indefinitely. No one escapes climate change or groundwater deple-tion or persistent toxics.

Three, the actors I have described who have actually *practiced* sufficiency—the Pacific Lumber executives and workers and foresters, the Monhegan fishers and the Maine fish wardens and legislators, the working class residents of Ward's Island, and others. These people are hardly environmental extremists, let alone pie-in-the-sky social engineers. Their normative innovations made perfectly good sense, given their goals and constraints. Nothing in the logic of sufficiency is endemic to the ivory tower, to activism, to fringe politics. It is not "just a theory."

If It Exists, It's Possible

If it exists, it's possible, Kenneth Boulding, economist, poet and peace activist once said. The context then was international conflict, which seemed pervasive, and the "it" was peace. In this book, the context is global ecological crisis and the "it" is sufficiency, acting on a sense of enoughness and "too muchness." Sufficiency is, I have argued, a necessary condition, a set of decision criteria, a set of principles critical for reversing the biophysical trends and re-organizing society for sustainable resource use. If the resource status of the past was abundance, an ever-present frontier, unending sources and sinks, now it is scarcity. And not just the relative scarcity of economistic reasoning where there is always a trade-off, always a transformation function, always a substitute, but an absolute scarcity in the sense that, with biophysical irreversibilities—species loss, climate destabilization, topsoil erosion, aquifer drawdown—humans cannot just move on to level another forest, plow another grassland, drill another well; they cannot run the conveyor belt faster and expect the disease to go away.

Reversing the trends in ecosystem decline and getting on a sustainable path is most likely to begin with what exists, what we know is possible, whether that be based on intuition or personal experience or good stories or scientific study. If the meat industry or government regulators had asked the public—farmers, scientists, meat eaters, rich, poor, highly educated, poorly educated—whether it makes sense to convert a grazing animal to a meat-eating animal, indeed, to a *cannibal*, and then feed its flesh to humans, there is no doubt in my mind what would be the answer. The proverbial man-and-woman-on-the-street just *knows* this is wrong. One does not need a Nobel Prize in Medicine to come to this conclusion (which one such person—the discoverer of prions—has). There is no issue of uncertainty or incomplete information or questionable science, no "yeah, but that's how it's done . . . and jobs depend on it and . . . consumers would have to pay more"; no "well, if the meat handlers were just more careful . . . the inspectors more thorough . . . if . . ." And yet for all the commonsense revulsion at such a system, agricultural "experts"—industrialists, cost-benefit analysts, food technologists, investors, lawyers, lobbyists, regulators and legislators—constructed just such a system. Right under our noses, so to speak.

So, for those of us who see limits to intensification and cost displacement and the work-and-spend treadmill and the individualization of solutions, the issue is how do we organize a different sense making. How do we guide decision making so as to end up with healthy cows and healthy people and healthy ecosystems? Part of the answer is guidelines, rules-of-thumb, heuristics, decision criteria and, most broadly, social organizing principles. One of the most hopeful signs is the emergence of new environmental principles, notably the precautionary principle.

In just the last decade or two, precaution has attained the status of a global social principle, at least in the context of public health and environmental policy. As discussed in chapter 2, it has the virtue of reversing the priority of economic growth over health and environmental protection. It takes uncertainty in causal explanation as an inadequate reason to avoid acting on threats to public and ecosystem health. Its reception by implicated industries, skeptical, often hostile, suggests how seriously it challenges the primacy of economistic reasoning, unlimited material expansion, and the free and open-access experimentation with the earth's life-support systems that now prevails.

And yet, for all its preventative features, the precautionary principle is reactive in one crucial sense: it only prescribes action *after* the environmental insult has been made. The Montreal Protocol employed the precautionary principle at its inception by acting—that is, deciding to phase out ozone-depleting substances, before the science was conclusive. But as the protocol reads, new, potentially depleting substances can still be made and dumped in the atmosphere. It is the responsibility of others—atmospheric scientists, environmental activists, concerned policymakers—to demonstrate harm, bring the substance to the attention of policymakers, and then add the substance to the list of banned chemicals. In general, decision makers only invoke the precautionary principle *after* the refrigerant is released, after the disease emerges, after the miracle drug is prescribed, after the supercleanser is applied, after, in other words, the experiment has been carried out, after unwitting subjects and vulnerable ecosystems have borne the insult. More "proactive" principles are indeed needed, ones that guide decision making as the experiments are envisioned, not as they are carried out. Reverse onus is one: the burden of proof lies with those who would experiment with critical environmental resources. Zero discharge and virtual elimination (of persistent toxic substances) is another. Proponents of the precautionary principle have, in fact, attempted to absorb reverse onus, zero discharge and prohibitions of various sorts in their more recent formulations. This, too, is a hopeful sign. But principles for sustainability must do more. They must, first and foremost, locate themselves where humans interact directly with the resource, where the ax meets the tree, the net reaches the fish, the pump draws the water. This is where an ecologically based notion of sustainability starts.

The sufficiency principle, or something close to it, is likely to emerge in the coming decades because it meets three conditions. One, it exists. People rarely use the term itself, let alone restraint or respite. But as we saw in the Pacific Lumber Company and the Monhegan fishing community and the cities of Toronto, Amsterdam, and Bogotá, people are very much enacting the sufficiency principle. At the personal level, such a notion is virtually self-evident, even if violated: get enough rest and exercise, eat not too little and not too much. And at the global level, serious students and policymakers of population and AIDS and freshwater scarcity and climate change know that the relevant activities are excessive. And, yet, at virtually every other level—organizational, provincial, national—students and policymakers act as if one can never have enough.

A second condition that enables the adoption of sufficiency is that, in principle and in practice, it is terribly logical. Young children react to a story embodying restraint or respite and they say, of course. Experts steeped in sophisticated mathematical modeling who look for that elegant optimal solution or seek that neat efficiency ratio or cost-benefit balance, concede that biophysical and social systems cannot be so modeled, let alone manipulated to reach such solutions.

Sufficiency is at least as sensible as the logics that prevail in contemporary policymaking, the economistic and engineering and legalistic. Unlike those logics, though, it is well attuned to the defining characteristics of global ecological crisis—threshold effects, ecological "flipping," permanent elimination of a vital resource, emergent diseases. It encourages social analogs to the biophysical facts, facts obtained by scientific study or experience or tradition or intuition: harvest limits and pollution caps follow ecological limits; self-management, buffers and restraint follow limited predictability; respite follows regeneration. Sufficiency encourages a transition from unfettered experimentation and novel insults—processes that risk entire systems—to incremental testing and adaptation. It encourages a shift from unrestrained expansion and intensification to buffering and natural rhythms and downtime.

The third condition underlying a predicted emergence, even ascendance, of the sufficiency principle is that sufficiency is commensurate with biophysical conditions and long-term security. Unlike the efficiency principle which, *as practiced*, fits frontier exploitation and expansion, sufficiency goes straight to the absence of frontiers and the impossibility of ever-increasing human throughput. It is A. S. Murphy, his family's expansionist history deeply embedded in his consciousness, standing on a Pacific Coast mountaintop and saying enough. It is a Monhegan fisherwoman looking at the ocean just a couple miles outside her island waters, littered with buoys, and saying too much. It is residents of cities as diverse as Toronto, Amsterdam, and Bogotá saying that well-constrained automobility is just enough.

Sufficiency works because it makes questions of enoughness and too muchness routine. Risk to *systems*—biophysical and social—rather than to individuals and corporations with their experiments and their investment dollars—are paramount under sufficiency. Limited predictability and surprise are taken as axiomatic rather than human control and unending efficiency gains—"celerity," wars on waste, specialization and mobility. Purpose in material use is integral, examined routinely rather than shunted aside as merely the "personal" or "religious" or "political" or "philosophical." Long-term effects and concerns for human and ecological security stand in contrast to immediate gratification, to time discounting and to concerns for maximum return on investment and maximum consumer choice.

In the past, related principles like frugality and thrift and prudence were significant organizing principles for much of the industrial and industrializing world. Apparently supplanted by efficiency and growth and progress, they actually never died out entirely. Like those little mammals that timidly scurried about amid the dinosaurs, they found protected niches—in the home, in the neighborhood, and in the occasional timber company and fishing operation. They stayed out of harm's way as the juggernaut of industrial development fed by fossil fuels and rationalized by efficiency rolled forward. Those niches made plenty of good sense for their practitioners, this even when global ecological constraint was not bearing down on them.

So, in places, sufficiency does exist, and it is logical, albeit still subordinate to other social organizing principles like efficiency. When conditions change, though, when the larger environment can no longer accommodate endless expansion and freewheeling experimentation, it will, like the mammals, take its place. It is not just possible, it is extremely likely.

Signs of Hope

At times, the task of reversing the biophysical trends and getting on a sustainable path is daunting. As I write, the U.S. administration is dismantling several decades worth of environmental protection and, probably worse, promoting energy production, consumer spending, and just about every other imaginable means of increasing throughput. And all this with considerable public support, it appears. The juggernaut seems unstoppable.

And maybe it is. But I am convinced it will spend itself. The laws of physics and biology supercede the laws of men and women. Problem displacement and debt accumulation (financial and otherwise) may save the day, but only today, not tomorrow.

I take heart not in the occasional environmental law passed, the tightening of one country's automobile efficiency standards, the international agreement on ozone or timber or toxic substances, but in the hard cases, those little-noticed but nontrivial instances of restrained timber cutting or shortened lobster fishing or community rejection of full automobility. And I take heart in, of all places, sites like the Middle

East or Sri Lanka and the Koreas. I discovered in my earlier research on international conflict resolution that however intractable an intersocietal conflict may be, there are always people working on the solution. Pick the direst time in the Middle East conflict, for example, and you can find someone hidden away in a basement drawing up maps for the water and sewer lines, the lines that will connect the two societies and that must be built *when peace is reached*, as inconceivable as that is at the time. Someone else is sketching the constitution for the new country, the one that is also inconceivable at the time. And someone else is outlining the terms of trade for the as yet unproduced goods that will traverse the two societies' border. We do not hear about these people because it is the nature of their work, including the dangers of their activities, that make it so. Surrounded by intense conflict, hatred and violence, these people appear the fool, idealists who do not know or can not accept the reality of their societies' situation. If they really knew that situation, others would say, they would be "realists"; they would concentrate their efforts on hard bargaining, economic incentives, and military force. But, in practice, when a threshold is passed, when leaders shake hands or a jailed dissident is freed or families from the two sides join together, everyone casts about for new ways to organize.

My prognosis, foolish and idealistic as it may seem to some, is that that threshold, that day of biophysical reckoning, is near. And with it, serious questioning about humans' patterns of material provisioning, their production, their consumption, their work and their play. Then, the premises of modern industrial societies—capitalist, socialist, communist—will crumble. Efficiency will provide little guidance because it so readily translates to continuing material throughput. A little intensification here, some specialization there just will not make things better. A feedlot is still a feedlot, a conveyor belt still a conveyor belt. When it becomes obvious that efficiency-driven societies can no longer continue their excesses, displace their costs, postpone their investments in natural capital, when it is obvious they can no longer grow their way out of climate change and species extinctions and aquifer depletions and the bioaccumulation of persistent toxic substances, people everywhere will indeed be casting about. Some will gravitate to the extremes—religious fundamentalism, survivalist homesteading, totalitarian government. Many, though, will seek paths that are familiar, if not prevalent. Notions of moderation and prudence and stewardship will stand up, as if they were just waiting to be noticed, waiting for their time, even though, in many realms they were always there. Model actors will be those who saw limits of some sort—of material expansion, of individualization, of intensification and mobility and specialization—and who fashioned their own means and principles of managing their material needs, however inconsequential they may have appeared to many. Management for these people and their enterprises was less about manipulating things "out there" (the resource, the environment, the employees) and more about managing one's own needs and wants.

So we students of sustainability are the tinkers, hunched over our drawing boards in dark corners, unnoticed by the mainstream, just waiting—and working, and thinking, and, as best we can, living a life more consistent, we hope, with the biophysical and social constraints of the planet. We are collecting the data and constructing the concepts, making sure the cows have plenty of fresh air, the water keeps running, and the wastes keep cycling. We know a few people are listening, and more will be as the contradictions of expansionist societies mount. More will be looking for principles around which to organize their lives and their organizations and their economies. More will be asking, What if we just posed this question, changed that behavioral assumption, established that principle.

What If . . .

So I ask, what if a society committed itself to economic and ecological security? What if, in organizing its economy, its flow of material and energy and wastes, it chose to put the material security of its citizens and the ecological integrity of its resource base front and center?

The very thought is mind-boggling, at least for this member of an efficiency-crazed, growth-manic, technologically freewheeling society. In North America and increasingly elsewhere, the goals of the economy are to maximize return on investment and consumer choice, all at low, low prices. Everything else—even jobs, trade balances, global competitiveness, balanced budgets—is secondary. And ecological integrity is, at best, an afterthought. Environmental protection does enter, but as an amenity, something policymakers can pursue if everything else is going right.

But what if a society embarked on a new direction, spurred perhaps by concern for lost species and distant climate change or, more likely, by fears of emergent diseases and diminishing freshwater? What if a society deemed its primary material concern the sense of security its citizens have with regard to basic needs and the ability of ecosystems to provision those needs?

These are questions virtually unimaginable in mainstream policymaking and public debate, certainly in North America and, I sense, in many other industrial countries and the capital cities of less-industrialized countries. No one in Washington, D.C., Ottawa, Lansing, or Sacramento could pursue such a line and survive politically. No one in the press could base their reporting and editorializing on such notions and avoid being labeled protectionist or socialist or radical.

And yet the underlying ideas and practices are not far fetched at all. They were effectively enacted in the old Pacific Lumber Company, in the Monhegan fishery and village, and on Ward's Island. These are places that struck me as worthy of close inspection, not because they were eccentric, but because they were commonsensical. I suspect there are many more—many, many more. I know that instances of sufficiency are played out every day in people's everyday lives, especially with regard to personal health and family life and neighborhood livability. We just need more looking and more telling. At some point, what is commonsense to some, becomes common sense to all. And then the folks in Washington and Albany and Lansing and Sacramento will catch on.

In 1994 the United Nations Development Programme (UNDP) put forth the concept of human security. Reacting to decades of use of the term *security* for international purposes, primarily military, the authors of the study pointed out that "forgotten were the legitimate concerns of ordinary people who sought security in their daily lives. For many of them, security . . . means, first, safety from such chronic threats as hunger, disease and repression . . . and, second, it means protection from sudden and hurtful disruptions in the patterns of daily life." Such threats are not confined to the poor or the global South, but "exist at all levels of national income and development." The authors stressed that human security is not human economic and political development. Development is a "process of widening the range of choices," as producers, consumers and participants in democratic decision making. By contrast, human security "means that people can exercise these choices safely and freely—and they can be relatively confident that the opportunities they have today are not totally lost tomorrow."[13]

The UNDP authors do not incorporate a notion of ecological security but it is implicit: people must be confident that their actions are not diminishing the potential of ecosystems to provide a secure material base for people's human security and their economic and political development now and into the indefinite future. The authors predict that the idea of human security "is likely to revolutionize society in the twenty-first century." Coupled with ecological security, some good stories illustrating realistic possibilities, and some commonsensical principles around which people can self-organize, not to mention the willingness to ask hard questions and experiment, I think they are right.

So, what if? What if a society sought economic and ecological security as the basis of human security which, in turn, would be the basis of its individual and political development? Among other things, its members would have to ask the right questions. In some settings those questions would be hard to ask, challenging prerogatives and questioning assumptions, as I have found time and again in my own organizations and communities. But they would be simple, too:

What if the timber industry banded together not to weaken regulations or gain preferential access to public forests, but to level the playing field for those who build in policies of restraint, of buffered harvest levels and natural forest regeneration?

What if fishers agreed to extraction technologies that ensured a catch and a livelihood for those who actually did the fishing yet made it deliberately difficult, not easy, to overfish?

What if transport planners included the "time saved" and "time lost" of all who transport themselves—car drivers, bus riders, cyclists, walkers, baby strollers—and included the safety of everyone, not just those encased by a couple tons of steel?

What if farmers were not treated as disposable "workers" because they are "inefficient," but publicly supported because they are the inherent guardians of agriculture's germ plasm and the natural stewards of the land?

What if cattle, pigs, and chickens were treated as animals, however domesticated, that are still grounded in ecological processes including feeding themselves, reproducing, and fending off predators and disease?

What if a river was harnessed not for "maximum beneficial use" ending, inevitably, in a briny stream that rarely reaches its mouth, but for "sufficient" use, enough for *all* uses, commercial, ecological, and aesthetic, plus a bit more as a buffer against the unexpected?

What if personal rhythms of work and nonwork became the norm?

What if emissions were capped and the caps were set according to downstream assimilative capacities, not industry expectations?

What if public livability trumped private mobility?

Wide-eyed musings of an environmental dreamer? I don't think so. These are not environment versus economy questions, not nature versus jobs. That tired dichotomy, simplistic and misleading, implicitly taking "the environment" as an amenity, should have been laid to rest long ago. No, these questions take "the environment" as the biophysical underpinnings of an economy, of all economies. And they elevate human and ecological security over return on investment and consumer choice and low prices; they celebrate work as self-expression and competence and meaning, dismissing jobs and employment as, at best, secondary goals. They presume that material provisioning—harvesting, disposing, transporting—cannot be reduced to monetary measures, that, instead, human provisioning has multiple purposes with multiple and largely incommensurate values. Water security cannot be exchanged for industrial output; safe transport cannot be traded for minutes saved commuting.

And these questions presume that people can organize themselves to achieve multiple purposes. People do not have to wait for their leaders to lead. They do not need precise measures nor experts telling them what the "value" (read, monetary value) is of lives risked, water supplies cut off, forests degraded. In so organizing, principles like precaution and reverse onus and polluter pays and, yes, restraint and respite, make perfectly good sense. They are intuitive, commonplace in contexts as diverse as personal health and inshore fishing and acid rain and climate change. They, indeed, exist and they are possible.

Still, there are those who say impossible. Can't be done. Americans will never get out of their cars. Fossil fuels are the lifeblood of industrial society. And what about the Chinese? And the Indians, huh? Billions of 'em. Besides, people are inherently shortsighted and selfish. And, and, . . . and even if it were possible—*in theory*, of course, only in theory—who can imagine a transition short of absolute cataclysm? Can't happen. Not till it all collapses. Impossible.

Maybe.

But I suspect the impossibility of making a transition from the current overconsumimg society to a sustainable society, from an economy premised on efficiency gains and expansion to an economy premised on human and ecological security conditioned by a sense of enoughness and too muchness is no less possible than other monumental transitions: from privateering to freedom of the seas; from slave holding to abolition; from state-sponsored drug trafficking to state-sponsored "war on drugs"; from South African apartheid to free state; from the medicinal use of sugar to medicine's condemnation of sugar; from smoking as "cool" to smoking as major public health threat. Each in its time seemed impossible, each the starry-eyed vision of a few social do-gooders, idealists who just didn't understand how the world really worked.

Now science is catching up with those who have understood for a long time how ecosystems work, and how humans can either work with or work against those systems. Now people are tired of being demeaned as mere consumers and employees. Now people crave real work, real meaning in their material and social lives. Now citizens are fed up with quick fixes and promises of unending plenty, just as a few get richer (but, arguably, no more secure) and many others get nowhere or get poorer (and—no argument here—a lot less secure). Now men and women and children, with and without specialized knowledge, are seeing that the old expansionist system, legitimated by claims of efficiency and consumer benefit, is broken. The livestock are sharing their diseases; the water tables are dropping; the climate is destabilizing. And they are seeing that things can change, in part with good science, in part with intuition, in part by asking the tough questions, and in part by applying a few good social organizing principles, doing what is logical under global ecological constraint.

Notes

Preface

1. Herman E. Daly, "The Steady-State Economy: Toward a Political Economy of Biophysical Equilibrium and Moral Growth," in Herman E. Daly and Kenneth N. Townsend, eds., *Valuing the Earth: Economics, Ecology, Ethics*, 325–363 (Cambridge, MA: MIT Press, 1993), (quote on 361).

2. Donald Worster, *Rivers of Empire: Water, Aridity, and the Growth of the American West* (New York: Oxford University Press, 1985), 261.

3. Worster, *Rivers of Empire*, 7.

4. Wendell Berry, "Discipline and Hope," in Berry, *Recollected Essays: 1965–1980*, 151–220 (New York: North Point Press, 1998) (quote on 192–193).

5. Berry, "Discipline and Hope," 157–158.

6. Donella H. Meadows, "Places to Intervene in a System (in Increasing Order of Effectiveness)," *Whole Earth* 91 (winter 1997): 78–84 (quote on 81).

Chapter 1

1. Sally Gibson, *More Than an Island: A History of the Toronto Island* (Toronto: Irwin, 1984), 230.

2. Ray Miller and Stan Parker, "Forestry or Forest Management at The Pacific Lumber Company," fifteen-page mimeograph, Pacific Lumber Company files, Scotia, California, undated but likely early 1980s.

3. B. L. Johnson, H. E. Hicks, D. E. Jones, C. Cibulas, A. Wargo, and C. T. De Rosa, "Public Health Implications of Persistent Toxic Substances in the Great Lakes and St. Lawrence Basins," *Journal of Great Lakes Research* 24/2 (1998): 698–772.

4. International Joint Commission, *Seventh Biennial Report under the Great Lakes Water Quality Agreement of 1978 to the Governments of the United States and Canada and the State and Provincial Governments of the Great Lakes Basin* (Windsor, Ontario: International Joint Commission, 1994).

5. Gordon K. Durnil, *The Making of a Conservative Environmentalist: With Reflections on Government, Industry, Scientists, the Media, Education, Economic Growth, the Public, the*

Great Lakes, Activists, and the Sunsetting of Toxic Chemicals (Bloomington: Indiana University Press, 1995), 27; emphasis in original.

6. On the Great Lakes, see Lynton K. Caldwell, *International Environmental Policy* (Durham, NC: Duke University Press, 1984); Jack P. Manno, "Advocacy and Diplomacy: NGOs and the Great Lakes Water Quality Agreement," in Thomas Princen and Matthias Finger, *Environmental NGOs in World Politics: Linking the Local and the Global*, 69–120 (London: Routledge, 1994). On ozone, see Richard Benedick, *Ozone Diplomacy: New Directions in Safeguarding the Planet* (Cambridge, MA: Harvard University Press, 1991); Edward A. Parson, *Protecting the Ozone Layer: Science, Strategy, and Negotiation in the Shaping of a Global Environmental Regime* (Oxford: Oxford University Press, 2002).

7. Certainly population growth and imperialism rank with market-oriented expansionist industrialism as major drivers of ever-increasing throughput. Because these factors only have a distant relation to my central topic, however, I restrict the discussion throughout this book to the efficiency-driven component.

8. William J. Cosgrove and Frank R. Rijsberman for the World Water Council, *World Water Vision: Making Water Everybody's Business* (London: Earthscan, 2000).

9. For development of the concept of overconsumption as distinguished from misconsumption and natural consumption, see Thomas Princen, Michael Maniates, and Ken Conca, eds., *Confronting Consumption* (Cambridge, MA: MIT Press, 2002), especially Thomas Princen, "Consumption and Its Externalities: Where Economy Meets Ecology," 23–42.

10. Herman E. Daly, "The Steady-State Economy: Toward a Political Economy of Biophysical Equilibrium and Moral Growth," in Herman E. Daly and Kenneth N. Townsend, eds., *Valuing the Earth: Economics, Ecology, Ethics*, 325–363 (Cambridge, MA: MIT Press, 1993), (quote on 361).

11. Peter H. Gleick with William C. G. Burns, Elizabeth L. Chalecki, Michael Cohen, Katherine Kao Cushing, Amar Mann, Rachel Reyes, Gary H. Wolff, and Arlene K. Wong, *The World's Water 2002–2003: The Biennial Report on Freshwater Resources* (Washington, DC: Island Press, 2000); Cosgrove and Rijsberman, *World Water Vision*; Sandra L. Postel, *Pillar of Sand: Can the Irrigation Miracle Last?* (New York: Norton, 1999); Sandra L. Postel, "Growing More Food with Less Water," *Scientific American*, February 2001, pp. 46–49; Sandra L. Postel and Aaron T. Wolf, "Dehydrating Conflict," *Foreign Policy* 126 (September/October 2001): 60–67.

12. Peter H. Gleick, "Water and Conflict: Fresh Water Resources and International Security," *International Security* 18/1 (summer 1993): 79–112.

13. Postel and Wolf, "Dehydrating Conflict," 62.

14. Herbert A. Simon, *Administrative Behavior: A Study of Decision-Making Processes in Administrative Organization*, 3rd ed. (New York: The Free Press, 1975), xxvii, xxx.

Chapter 2

1. Elinor Ostrom, *Governing the Commons: The Evolution of Institutions for Collective Action* (Cambridge: Cambridge University Press, 1990); Svein Jentoft and Trond Kristoffersen, "Fishermen's Co-Management: The Case of the Lofoten Fishery," *Human Organization* 48/4 (winter 1989): 355–365; Hugh B. Cott, "Wonder Island of the Amazon Delta,"

National Geographic 74/5 (November 1938): 635–670; Emanuel Adilson, Souza Serrao, and Alfredo Kingo Oyama Homma, "Brazil," in National Research Council, *Sustainable Agriculture and the Environment in the Humid Tropics*, 322–326 (Washington, DC: National Academy Press, 1993).

2. John S. Dryzek, *Rational Ecology: Environment and Political Economy* (New York: Blackwell, 1987); Thomas Princen, "The Zero Option and Ecological Rationality in International Environmental Politics," *International Environmental Affairs* 8/2 (spring 1996): 27–71.

3. For an extended argument in favor of grounding resource regimes, whether small-scale community regimes or international regimes, in on-the-ground practice, see Thomas Princen, "From Property Regime to International Regime: An Ecosystem Perspective," *Global Governance* 4/4 (October–November 1998): 395–413.

4. For an extended discussion, see Thomas Princen, "The Shading and Distancing of Commerce: When Internalization Is Not Enough," *Ecological Economics* 20/3 (March 1997): 235–253.

5. Marginal analysis is a cornerstone of modern economic analysis. In simple terms, it means that in deciding how much to produce (or consume) one evaluates each additional increment (each additional shoe stitched, each additional apple eaten) for its added benefit compared to the next best incremental cost (or benefit). As costs of production increase (or benefits of consumption decrease), there comes a point where it is rational to switch (from shoes to boots, say, or from apples to oranges). Curiously, on the production side, for a fixed capital base, one can produce "too much" under this logic. But on the consumption side, in the larger macroeconomy, although an individual can consume too much of a given item, a society cannot consume too much. Goods are good, so more goods are better. A growing economy is a strong economy, a healthy one. A steady-state economy is a weak economy, an anemic one. Such a view pertains even if the wealth level is high and distribution is fairly even; witness the reports on the Japanese economy through the 1990s (which wasn't declining or even "steady-state," but growing at about a percent a year). See chapter 5.

6. C. S. Holling and Steven Sanderson, "Dynamics of (Dis)harmony in Ecological and Social Systems," in Susan Hanna, Carl Folke, and Karl-Goran Maler, eds., *Rights to Nature: Ecological, Economic, Cultural, and Political Principles of Institutions for the Environment*, 57–85 (Washington, DC: Island Press, 1996) (quotes on 59, 77).

7. Holling and Sanderson, "Dynamics of (Dis)harmony in Ecological and Social Systems," 79.

8. I thank ecologist Paul Webb for clarifying much of the following discussion.

9. Robert Costanza, W. Michael Kemp, and Walter R. Boynton, "Predictability, Scale, and Biodiversity in Coastal and Estuarine Ecosystems: Implications for Management," *Ambio* 22/2–3 (May 1993): 88–96; Stephen H. Schneider and Terry L. Root, "Ecological Implications of Climate Change Will Include Surprises," *Biodiversity and Conservation* 5/9 (September 1996): 1109–1119; Charles Perrings, "Reserved Rationality and the Precautionary Principle: Technological Change, Time, and Uncertainty in Environmental Decision Making," in Robert Costanza, ed., *Ecological Economics: The Science and Management of Sustainability*, 153–166 (New York: Columbia University Press, 1991).

10. James J. Kay and Eric Schneider, "Embracing Complexity: The Challenge of the Ecosystem Approach," *Alternatives* 20/3 (July–August 1994): 32–39 (quotes on 34).

11. Kay and Schneider, "Embracing Complexity," 35.

12. Kay and Schneider, "Embracing Complexity," 34.

13. Kay and Schneider, "Embracing Complexity," 35; emphasis added.

14. Kay and Schneider, "Embracing Complexity," 35.

15. Kay and Schneider, "Embracing Complexity," 36.

16. Donella H. Meadows, "Places to Intervene in a System (in Increasing Order of Effectiveness)," *Whole Earth* 91 (winter 1997): 78–84 (quote on 83).

17. Meadows, "Places to Intervene in a System," 81.

18. Meadows, "Places to Intervene in a System," 81.

19. Kay and Schneider, "Embracing Complexity," 33; emphasis added.

20. Dryzek, *Rational Ecology*.

21. At some level of intensity, even hunting and foraging rearrange ecosystems by disrupting predator-prey relations, for instance, or introducing novel substances via domesticated animals or feed for wild prey. And nonhuman foragers will overexploit if the chance arises.

22. Meadows, "Places to Intervene in a System," 80.

23. Meadows, "Places to Intervene in a System," 80.

24. The economistically oriented reader will be quick to point out that a rational profit maximizer only mines the ore until the cost exceeds the benefits; some amount of ore, however minuscule, will remain. This is optimizing, not maximizing. Yes, among economic values (see the next section in the text) the actor is optimizing, making trade-offs among values established by commodity and capital markets. But an "optimal" decision is made irrespective of waste-sink capacity (in the case of mining minerals) or regenerative capacity (in the case of renewables), getting the most, the maximum of the resource, until values set by commodity and capital markets indicate net benefits no longer accrue.

25. Although the relevant scale in this construction of ecological rationality's worldview is literally the entire world, the rationality itself is relevant at much smaller scales. An isolated, self-reliant, and self-contained community would logically employ such a rationality because it could not solve its resource-scarcity problems by exporting them.

26. Nicholas Georgescu-Roegen, "Selections from 'Energy and Economic Myths,'" in Herman E. Daly and Kenneth N. Townsend, eds., *Valuing the Earth: Economics, Ecology, Ethics*, 89–112 (Cambridge, MA: MIT Press, 1993).

27. James J. Kay, "A Nonequilibrium Thermodynamic Framework for Discussing Ecosystem Integrity," *Environmental Management* 15/4 (1991): 483–495; Gary K. Meffe and C. Ronald Carroll, *Principles of Conservation Biology* (Sunderland, MA: Sinauer Associates, 1994).

28. Dryzek, *Rational Ecology*, 35.

29. Although Dryzek includes social and political rationality in his framework, he dismisses both as of little relevance to the ecological. Moreover, they are subordinate to the economistic and legalistic with respect to the material. Unfortunately, Dryzek appropriates the social and political in one, maybe two of his decision criteria—coordination and flexibility. These criteria are not distinctively ecological, in contrast to what I try to do with the criteria laid out in this chapter.

30. Dryzek, *Rational Ecology*, 44; emphasis in original.

Chapter 3

1. *Oxford English Dictionary*, 2nd ed. (Oxford: Clarendon Press, 1989), vol. 5, p. 84.

2. Frederick Winslow Taylor, *The Principles of Scientific Management* (Minneola, NY: Dover, [1911] 1998), 75.

3. Emily Matthews et al., *The Weight of Nations: Material Outflows from Industrial Economies* (Washington, DC: World Resources Institute, 2000), xi.

4. Gerald Alonzo Smith, "The Purpose of Wealth," in Herman E. Daly and Kenneth N. Townsend, eds., *Valuing the Earth: Economics, Ecology, Ethics* (Cambridge, MA: MIT Press, 1993), 203.

5. *Oxford English Dictionary*, vol. 5, p. 84.

6. *Oxford English Dictionary*, vol. 5, p. 84.

7. Robert L. Heilbroner, *The Worldly Philosophers: The Lives, Times, and Ideas of the Great Economic Thinkers* (New York: Simon and Schuster, 1953), 28–29; Donald Worster, "The Vulnerable Earth: Toward a Planetary History," and Richard G. Wilkinson, "The English Industrial Revolution," both in Donald Worster, ed., *The Ends of the Earth: Perspectives on Modern Environmental History*, 3–20, 80–99 (New York: Cambridge University Press, 1988).

8. Adam Smith, *An Inquiry into the Nature and Causes of the Wealth of Nations* (London: G. Bell and Sons, 1921) (reprint of the 6th ed.).

9. Stephen A. Marglin, "Understanding Capitalism: Control versus Efficiency," in Bo Gustafsson, ed., *Power and Economic Institutions: Reinterpretations in Economic History*, 225–252 (Brookfield, VT: Edward Algar, 1991) (quote on 229).

10. Cheryl Russell, *The Master Trend: How the Baby Boom Generation Is Remaking America* (New York, Perseus, 1993), 32.

11. Stanley Jevons, quoted in Mary E. Clark, *Ariadne's Thread: The Search for New Modes of Thinking* (Basingstoke, UK: Macmillan Press, 1989), 276; emphasis in original.

12. The absence of an intellectual history of efficiency may be one of the more telling features of the concept. It is indeed, as I will soon argue, the water in which we swim; it is an unambiguous good. Why should anyone trace its history?

For the record, I may have missed such a history in some literature—history or linguistics, say. But over several years, several graduate students and I searched high and low. We entered all the suspect keywords, we asked experienced reference librarians, and we asked historians, economists, and others. All to no avail. Hence, consider this chapter a brief, highly incomplete history, a hoped-for incitement to someone with the right skills to do a proper one.

13. Heilbroner, *The Worldly Philosophers*, 22.

14. Clark, *Ariadne's Thread*, 275.

15. Norris A. Brisco, *Economics of Efficiency* (New York: Macmillan, 1914), 6.

16. Vanderveer Custis, *The Foundations of National Industrial Efficiency* (New York: Macmillan, 1923), 10–11.

17. David W. Pearce and R. Kerry Turner, *Economics of Natural Resources and the Environment* (Baltimore, MD: Johns Hopkins University Press, 1990), 27.

18. Marglin, "Understanding Capitalism," 245.

19. Samuel Haber, *Efficiency and Uplift: Scientific Management in the Progressive Era 1890–1920* (Chicago: University of Chicago Press, 1964; quote on 1–2). The discussion of Taylorism in this section also draws on Martha Banta, *Taylored Lives: Narrative Productions in the Age of Taylor, Veblen, and Ford* (Chicago: University of Chicago Press, 1993); Raymond E. Callahan, *Education and the Cult of Efficiency* (Chicago: University of Chicago Press, 1962); Samuel P. Hays, *Conservation and the Gospel of Efficiency: The Progressive Conservation Movement, 1890–1920* (Cambridge, MA: Harvard University Press, 1959); Edward Eyre Hunt, ed., *Scientific Management Since Taylor: A Collection of Authoritative Papers* (New York: McGraw-Hill, 1924); Alf Johansson, "Taylorism and the Rise of Organized Labour: United States and Sweden," in Bo Gustafsson, ed., *Power and Economic Institutions: Reinterpretations in Economic History*, 302–336 (Brookfield, VT: Edward Algar, 1991); Robert Kanigel, "Taylor-Made: How the World's First Efficiency Expert Refashioned Modern Life in His Own Image," *The Sciences* 37/3 (May–June 1997): 18–23; Kevin Whitson, "The Reception of Scientific Management by British Engineers, 1890–1914," *Business History Review* 71/2 (summer 1997): 207–229; Worster, "The Vulnerable Earth."

20. Haber, *Efficiency and Uplift*, 21.

21. Haber, *Efficiency and Uplift*, 23–24.

22. Haber, *Efficiency and Uplift*, 23–24.

23. Haber, *Efficiency and Uplift*, 23–24.

24. Haber, *Efficiency and Uplift*, 55.

25. Haber, *Efficiency and Uplift*, 59.

26. Haber, *Efficiency and Uplift*, 31.

27. Hays, *Conservation and the Gospel of Efficiency*, 124.

28. Haber, *Efficiency and Uplift*, 72–74.

29. "A New Era of Industrial Efficiency," editorial, *The World's Work* 26/4 (August 1913): 380–381 (quote on 381).

30. *Cassier's Monthly* (July 1913), 44, I; cited in Hays, *Conservation and the Gospel of Efficiency*, 125.

31. Haber, *Efficiency and Uplift*, 167.

32. Haber, *Efficiency and Uplift*, 62–63.

33. See "Conclusion: To Confront Consumption," in Thomas Princen, Michael Maniates, and Ken Conca, eds., *Confronting Consumption*, 317–328 (Cambridge, MA: MIT Press, 2002); Mark Edmundson, "On the Uses of a Liberal Education: 1. As Lite Entertainment for Bored College Students," *Harper's Magazine* 295/1768 (September 1997): 39–49; Stanley Aronowitz, *The Knowledge Factory: Dismantling the Corporate University and Creating True Higher Learning* (Boston: Beacon Press, 2000).

34. *A Compilation of Messages and Papers of the Presidents*, 6989; cited in Hays, *Conservation and the Gospel of Efficiency*, 125.

35. Frederick A. Cleveland to C. A. Royse, May 31, 1913, Box 080.2, *Records of the President's Commission on Economy and Efficiency*, National Archives; quoted in Haber, *Efficiency and Uplift*, 114.

36. Haber, *Efficiency and Uplift*, 115.

37. Hays, *Conservation and the Gospel of Efficiency*, 271.

38. Haber, *Efficiency and Uplift*, 116.

39. Haber, *Efficiency and Uplift*, 111.

40. Clark, *Ariadne's Thread*, 293; emphasis in original.

41. Frederick Winslow Taylor, *Testimony of Frederick W. Taylor at Hearings before Special Committee of the House of Representatives, January, 1912: A Classic of Management Literature Reprinted in Full from a Rare Public Document* (New York: Taylor Society, 1926), 104.

42. Frederick Winslow Taylor, "Testimony of Frederick W. Taylor," *Hearings of the U.S. Commission on Industrial Relations*, 64th Congress, 1st Session, Senate Doc. 26 (Ser. Vol. 6929), p. 766; cited in Haber, *Efficiency and Uplift*, 29.

43. Banta, *Taylored Lives*, ix.

44. Callahan, *Education and the Cult of Efficiency*, 23.

45. Haber, *Efficiency and Uplift*, 52.

46. *Bulletin of the Taylor Society*, 1922 or 1923; quoted in Haber, *Efficiency and Uplift*, 164.

47. Haber, *Efficiency and Uplift*, 61–62.

48. John Erwin Hollitz, "The Challenge of Abundance: Reactions to the Development of a Consumer Economy, 1890–1920," unpublished doctoral dissertation, University of Wisconsin—Madison, 1981.

49. See Princen, Maniates, and Conca, *Confronting Consumption*, for further discussion of the insidious nature of consumer sovereignty.

50. Kanigel, "Taylor-Made," 21.

51. Haber, *Efficiency and Uplift*, ix.

52. Percival White, *Atlantic Monthly*, July 1920 (no title, volume, number, or pages), as quoted in "The July Almanac: 75 Years Ago," *Atlantic Monthly* 276/1 (July 1995): 14.

53. Brisco, *Economics of Efficiency*, vii.

54. Hays, *Conservation and the Gospel of Efficiency*, 265.

55. Proceedings of a Conference of Governors in the White House, Washington, DC, May 13–15, 1908 (Washington, DC, 1909), 12; cited in Hays, *Conservation and the Gospel of Efficiency*, 125.

56. Kanigel, "Taylor-Made," 19.

57. Haber, *Efficiency and Uplift*, 57.

58. *Family Planner Handbook 2003–2004*, Forsythe Middle School, Ann Arbor, MI; produced by Premier: A School Specialty Company, Bellingham, WA, 2003, reprinted with permission.

59. Marc Sagoff, *The Economy of the Earth: Philosophy, Law & the Environment* (New York: Cambridge University Press, 1988), 40.

60. Clark, *Ariadne's Thread*, 275.

Chapter 4

1. Michael Maniates, "Individualization: Plant a Tree, Buy a Bike, Save the World?", in Thomas Princen, Michael Maniates, and Ken Conca, eds., *Confronting Consumption*, 43–66 (Cambridge, MA: MIT Press, 2002).

2. Matthew L. Wald, "The World: Oil Crises; Which One Is Worse?" *New York Times*, April 21, 2002, sect. 4, p. 4.

3. Arild Angelsen and David Kaimowitz, "Agricultural Technologies and Tropical Deforestation," as described in The Forest Policy Experts (POLEX) electronic listserve, service of the Center for International Forestry Research; accessed at d.kaimowitz@cgiar.org, August 20, 2001.

4. For an extended treatment of shading and distancing, especially with respect to severing ecological feedback, see Thomas Princen, "The Shading and Distancing of Commerce: When Internalization Is Not Enough," *Ecological Economics* 20/3 (March 1997): 235–253.

5. Although *booster* is often used pejoratively, here I employ the term in a strictly analytic sense. Boosters promote a new technology, a development project, a financial mechanism. They do not actually lay stone or plow land; they sell. Sometimes they boost by the sheer weight of argument, sometimes by clever persuasion, and sometimes by creating conditions that make adoption appear inevitable. See William Cronon, *Nature's Metropolis: Chicago and the Great West* (New York: Norton, 1991), for an eloquent description of boosters in the late-nineteenth-century Midwestern United States.

6. It is possible to construct a scenario whereby fuel-efficiency gains would be so great in society B's conversion, and B's driving habits so entrenched, that efficiencies overwhelmed the driving effects of fewer gas guzzlers. But as long as the original proportion of drivers to walkers is small and total numbers large, the result (increased total consumption and greater environmental impact) is reasonable and most plausible.

7. Andrew Rudin, "DSM: Ten Years Later," *Engineered Systems*, May 2002, pp. 80–82.

8. Horace Herring, "Is Energy Efficiency Environmentally Friendly?", *Energy &Environment* 11/3 (2000): 313–325.

9. Samuel P. Hays, *Conservation and the Gospel of Efficiency: The Progressive Conservation Movement, 1890–1920* (Cambridge, MA: Harvard University Press, 1959), 176.

10. In fact, in what seems to be a much-neglected study, one economist, William Cline, actually used three centuries as his time frame, not the usual three decades or so. Interestingly, he had to conclude, based on the best science at the time and using conventional economic tools, that mitigation was cost effective. Those who choose shorter time frames, whether or not they do so explicitly, often come to the opposite conclusion: mitigation would cost the economy (next year's economy) too much given the uncertainties. See William R. Cline, *The Economics of Global Warming* (Washington, DC: Institute for International Economics, 1992).

Chapter 5

1. Robert Heilbroner, *The Worldly Philosophers: The Lives, Times, and Ideas of the Great Economic Thinkers* (New York: Simon and Schuster, 1953), 27–28, 29, 30; "Development

as Enclosure: The Establishment of the Global Economy," *The Ecologist* 22/4 (July–August 1992): 131–147 (quote on 132–133); E. P. Thompson, *The Making of the English Working Class* (New York: Pantheon Books, 1964), 217, 218, 220.

2. E. P. Thompson, "Time, Work-Discipline, and Industrial Capitalism," *Past and Present* 38 (1967): 56–97, (quote on 80–81).

3. Thompson, *English Working Class*, 292.

4. Jonathan Rose, *The Intellectual Life of the British Working Classes* (New Haven, CT: Yale University Press, 2001), 238.

5. Thompson, *English Working Class*, 357.

6. As will be evident shortly, these characterizations of factory "discipline" and of craftsmanship may be overstatements. But I intend them to highlight the revolutionary shift from independent artisanal work to wage-earning work. The shift was not wholesale, varying considerably from industry to industry, location to location. See Richard Whipp, " 'A Time to Every Purpose': An Essay on Time and Work," in Patrick Joyce, ed., *The Historical Meanings of Work* (Cambridge: Cambridge University Press, 1987), 210–236.

7. Thompson, "Time," 81.

8. Thompson, *English Working Class*, 357.

9. Thompson, "Time," 81. Quoted portions from Rev. J. Clayton's *Friendly Advice to the Poor*, 1775.

10. Powell [no first name], *A View of Real Grievances, with Remedies Proposed for Redressing Them: Humbly Submitted to the Consideration of the Legislature* (London, 1772), 90; quoted in Thompson, "Time," 84.

11. Max Weber, *The Protestant Ethic and the Spirit of Capitalism* (London: Allen & Unwin, 1930), 60.

12. Heilbroner, *Worldly Philosophers*, 24, 31.

13. Thompson, "Time," 91.

14. Wendell Berry, "Discipline and Hope," in *A Continuous Harmony: Essays Cultural and Agricultural* (New York: Harcourt Brace Jovanovich, 1972); reprinted in Berry, *Recollected Essays, 1965–1980* (New York: North Point Press, 1998), pp. 151–220, (quote on 189). Berry is quick to point out that his critique goes beyond the familiar objection to "the ends justify the means." In his words, "We expect ends not only to justify means, but to rectify them as well. . . . Once we have peace, we say, or abundance or justice or truth or comfort, everything will be all right. It is an old dream . . . a vicious illusion. . . . Art does not survive in its revelations, or agriculture in its products, or craftsmanship in its artifacts, or civilization in its monuments, or faith in its relics. . . . It is the obsession with immediate ends that is degrading, that destroys our disciplines, and that drives us to our inflexible concentration upon number and price and size. . . . A good farmer plants, not because of the abstractions of demand or market or financial condition, but because it is planting time and the ground is ready—that is, he plants in response to his discipline and his place. . . . [A poet] writes because he has a poem to write, he knows how, the work pleases him, and he has forgotten all else" (pp. 189, 195).

15. Berry, "Discipline and Hope," 178, 220.

16. Adam Smith, *The Wealth of Nations*; quoted in Heilbroner, *Worldly Philosophers*, 52.

17. Berry, "Discipline and Hope," 165.

18. Berry, "Discipline and Hope," 172.

19. The World Resources Institute, with collaborators in Europe and Japan, found that between 1975 and 1996, a period of "strong economic growth, . . . overall resource use and waste flows into the environment continued to grow" for the five study countries—Germany, Japan, the Netherlands, the United States, and Austria. "Total quantities of conventional wastes, emissions, and discharges"—that is, the actual burden on the environment— "increased by between 16 percent and 29 percent." And this despite the fact that these industrialized countries had become more "efficient"—in other words, their "resource inputs and waste outputs . . . fell dramatically when measured against units of economic output" (Emily Matthews et al., World Resources Institute, *The Weight of Nations: Material Outflows from Industrial Economies* (Washington, DC: World Resources Institute, 2000), vi, vii). Notice that the authors, following convention, use *efficient* to mean that economic output increases for a unit of pollution. Their most important finding, nevertheless, is that overall throughput increases as efficiencies increase. See chapter 4.

20. Thomas Princen, "The Shading and Distancing of Commerce: When Internalization Is Not Enough," *Ecological Economics* 20/3 (March 1997): 235–253.

21. Sidney W. Mintz, *Sweetness and Power: The Place of Sugar in Modern History* (New York: Penguin, 1985), 197.

22. Mintz, *Sweetness and Power*, 204; emphasis added.

23. Thompson, "Time," 56–97 (quotes on 73, 79; reference to women on 59ff).

24. I choose "idiosyncratic regularity" as something of a play on words. Such work is in part "regular"—that is, "normal." And it is "regular" because it is "regulated" not by external agents motivated to make production schedules efficient, but by one's own needs and aspirations.

25. Thompson, "Time," 73.

26. 2003. Raymond De Young, personal communication. See also Raymond De Young, "Why Might People Over-consume? Some Psychological Aspects of Directed Attention Fatigue," unpublished manuscript, Ann Arbor, MI; Steven Kaplan, "The Restorative Benefits of Nature: Toward an Integrative Framework," *Journal of Environmental Psychology* 15 (1995): 169–182.

27. Melvin L. Kohn, "Unresolved Issues in the Relationship between Work and Personality," in Kai Erikson and Steven Peter Vallas, eds., *The Nature of Work: Sociological Perspectives* (New Haven, CT: Yale University Press, 1990), 36–68 (quote on 41–42; emphasis added).

28. A more nuanced treatment of work and consumption would reject the sharp dichotomy of work versus consumption and locate activities along a continuum. The relevant dimensions might be purposefulness (or source of purpose—internal versus external), self-directedness, and restorative potential. Some examples of self-employment might actually score very low (e.g., contract work where the contractor has considerable market power), while some examples of shopping might score high (strategic searching for the perfect item). For the sustainability objective, the challenge would then be to correlate such activities with throughput.

29. An alternative approach, possibly a "first-best" approach, would be to measure the environmental impact of each consumption decision from "cradle to grave." Taxes and other incentives would be imposed to adjust consumption patterns to ecological carrying capacity. This "industrial-ecology" approach can, in principle, be developed. The task is so monumental, though, that it is extremely unlikely to ever be completed, let alone implemented. The emphasis here on work as a link between consumption and environment is thus a "second-best" approach, one that admittedly would lack the measurement assurances of a carrying-capacity approach but would build in a critical behavior (restraint) and organizing principle (sufficiency).

30. Frank Peel, "Old Cleckheaton," *Cleckheaton Guardian*, January–April 1884; cited in Thompson, *English Working Class*, 274.

31. Here I am referring to "owner/workers"—that is, individuals who manage and work at "the business of the enterprise" at the same time that they own it. Today, of course, specialization has gone to such an extreme in the corporate world that even top management is highly specialized, typically in finance, not in the business of the enterprise, and owners are distanced investors. Integration and accountability, especially with respect to the ecological and social underpinnings of such enterprises, are, arguably, extremely low.

32. Thompson, *English Working Class*, 446.

33. Wendell Berry, "Discipline and Hope," 186.

34. Matt Ridley, *The Origins of Virtue: Human Instincts and the Evolution of Cooperation* (New York: Viking, 1998), 209–210.

35. William Leach, *Land of Desire: Merchants, Power, and the Rise of a New American Culture* (New York: Pantheon Books, 1993), 111, 112, xiii.

36. Lizabeth Cohen, *A Consumers' Republic: The Politics of Mass Consumption in Postwar America* (New York: Knopf, 2003), 8–9, 11.

37. David Leonhardt, "Economy's Growth Proves Steadfast although Modest," *New York Times*, April 28, 2001, pp. A1, B3.

38. Leach, *Land of Desire*, 277; italics in original.

39. Leach, *Land of Desire*, 294.

40. Peter Sutherland, chair of Goldman Sachs International and of the Overseas Development Council, and John W. Sewell, president of the Overseas Development Council, "Gather the Nations to Promote Globalization," *New York Times*, February 8, 1998, pp. BU 15.

41. See Thomas Princen, Michael Maniates, and Ken Conca, eds., *Confronting Consumption* (Cambridge, MA: MIT Press, 2002), especially chap. 9, "Conclusion: To Confront Consumption," 321–326, for elaboration of this notion of the sovereign consumer.

42. Leach, *Land of Desire*, 229.

43. Simon Patten, "Reconstruction of Economic Theory" (1912), reprinted in Rexford Tugwell, ed., *Essays in Economic Theory* (New York: Knopf, 1924), 337; Simon Patten, *The Theory of Prosperity* (New York, 1902), 182, quoted in Leach, *Land of Desire*, 239.

44. Angus Deaton in *The Palgrave Dictionary of Economics*, 1987, 599; Heilbroner, *Worldly Philosophers*, 51.

45. Sufficiency in a growing economy may stretch the very concept I am developing. But the point here is that economics, the discipline that most informs policy analysis and prescription, can accommodate something other than maximized gain. Optimality is compatible with sufficiency. It would have ecological content if it applied to growth, too: an economy would grow no faster than ecosystems would adapt and regenerate. See, for instance, Herman Daly, *Beyond Growth: The Economics of Sustainable Development* (Boston: Beacon Press, 1996).

46. Robert Gilpin, *The Political Economy of International Relations* (Princeton, NJ: Princeton University Press, 1987), 17.

47. Christopher Lasch, *The True and Only Heaven: Progress and Its Critics* (New York: Norton, 1991), 184–225.

48. For vivid accounts of the expansionist, progressive ideal in the American Midwest, see William Cronon, *Nature's Metropolis: Chicago and the Great West* (New York: Norton, 1991); in the American arid West, see Donald Worster, *Rivers of Empire: Water, Aridity, and the Growth of the American West* (New York: Oxford University Press, 1985).

49. Lasch, *True and Only Heaven*, 204.

50. Lasch, *True and Only Heaven*, 211.

51. It might be surmised that the producerist ideal was a thing of the past, totally eclipsed by the progressive consensus as Lasch seems to suggest. But I submit that it is alive and well, albeit nearly invisible in mainstream popular culture. Small proprietors still, I believe, outnumber executives and organized labor. And independent farmers still survive despite the aggressions of agribusiness and government agencies.

52. Lasch, *True and Only Heaven*, 531.

53. Dr. Seuss (Theodore Seuss Geisel), *The Lorax* (New York: Random House, 1971); no page numbers.

Chapter 6

1. In the Great Lakes region, for example, a journalist captured the prevailing belief of 1870: "Will our pine timber soon be exhausted? We say no. None of our generation will see our pine forests decimated" (George S. Kaime, "Where Our Lumber Comes From," *Western Monthly* 3 (1870): 191; quoted in William Cronon, *Nature's Metropolis: Chicago and the Great West* (New York: Norton, 1991), 200. A decade later it had become very difficult to make a profit in timber in the region. "Sawmill operators had long been struggling against competitive conditions that encouraged overproduction," writes historian William Cronon of timbering in the Great Lakes region in the late nineteenth century. "In the short term, overproduction meant that they suffered from chronically low prices; in the long term, it meant that they consumed their forest resources and thus undermined their own enterprise." Within two decades, the white pines were completely logged out (Cronon, *Nature's Metropolis*, 190).

On the Pacific Coast, the early loggers probably viewed the coastal redwoods, *Sequoia semperviren*, as similarly inexhaustible. Many of the trees stood more than 250 feet tall and had trunks 15 to 20 feet in diameter. Some were 2,000 years old. Located in moist valleys and coastal mountains from Monterey Bay on the California coast north into southern

Oregon, dense stands of redwoods, along with Douglas fir, probably constituted more timber per acre than any forest in North America.

2. I choose the acronym TPL to denote the "old" Pacific Lumber Company, the company led by the Murphy family and its followers. This conforms with the usage of at least one company historian and the old company's literature. Today, the "new" company, which I refer to later as Maxxam/PL, mostly uses PALCO. TPL also reflects a certain reverence people in the region have for the old company. The "T" is often given emphasis verbally: Did you hear, he works for *The* Pacific Lumber Company.

3. S. R. Black, "California's Newest Crop: The Redwood Tree," *American Review of Reviews*, January 1925, and Addenda, March 1, 1924; both reprinted for the California Redwood Association; no page numbers.

4. Ray Raphael, *More Tree Talk: The People, Politics, and Economics of Timber* (Washington, DC: Island Press, 1994), 170.

5. "History," two-page TPL brochure found in company files, undated but, with the reference to "the hundred years that have passed," probably 1960s.

6. Ben Shannon Allen, *From the Penobscot to the Eel*, "first manuscript, August 31st, 1949"; apparently the property of Pacific Lumber Company, San Francisco; no place or time of publication, or publisher. Page numbering is within chapters. "The New Regime," chap. IV, pp. 2–3, quote on p. 3; pp. 3, 4, "Pacific in High Gear," chap. X, pp. 1–2; "Pacific Plans Boldly for Its Future," chap. XII, p. 3; "Progress—Then Disaster," chap. XIV, p. 2.

7. Frank J. Taylor, "California Redwood," *California: Magazine of Pacific Business*, June 1937, pp. 2–6.

8. Pacific Lumber Company, *1911 Annual Report*.

9. Stan Parker, "Bridge between Strike and 1965," in *PALCO Past: A Social History of Scotia and the Pacific Lumber Company*, unpublished manuscript, Pacific Lumber Company files, Scotia, no chapter or page numbers (all page numbering is within chapters).

10. Taylor, "California Redwood."

11. Stanwood A. Murphy, Jr. testimony, Fields Landing, CA; hearings, U.S. House of Representatives, October 5, 1987, p. 6.

12. Allen, "Down East Goes West," *From the Penobscot to the Eel*, chap. XI, p. 3.

13. J. A. Savage, "The Last of the One-Company Towns," *Business and Society Review* 51 (fall 1984): 26–28 (quote on 26).

14. Blackmun, "More Than Most, This Mill Needs Careful Logging Plan," *Forest Industries*, March 1986, p. 40.

15. Parker, "1934 Interlude: The Company Store," *PALCO Past*, p. 6.

16. Allen, "Scotia Model Community," *From the Penobscot to the Eel*, chap. XIX, pp. 10–11.

17. Parker, "1934 Interlude: Scotia Itself," *PALCO Past*, p. 27.

18. Parker, "The Twenties," *PALCO Past*, chap. 5, p. 2.

19. Raphael, *More Tree Talk*, 172–174.

20. Allen, "Perpetuating the Redwood," *From the Penobscot to the Eel*, chap. XXVIII, p. 1. "TPL" in the original.

21. Allen, "A New Age Dawns," *From the Penobscot to the Eel*, chap. XXV, pp. 9–10.

22. Parker, "The Troubled Years," *PALCO Past*, chap. 6, p. 1; Parker, "The Twenties," *PALCO Past*, chap. 5, p. 1; Parker, "The Penoyer Years," *PALCO Past*, chap. 4, p. 10.

23. Letter from A. S. Murphy to John H. Emmert in Detroit, May 28, 1929. Supplied by Merline Williams from company files either in Scotia or San Francisco.

24. Ray Miller and Stan Parker, "Forestry or Forest Management at The Pacific Lumber Company," fifteen-page mimeograph, Pacific Lumber Company files, Scotia, California, undated but early 1980s, p. 4. Parker was a transportation engineer for TPL, Miller unknown.

25. Parker, "The Twenties," p. 5.

26. Parker, "The Troubled Years," p. 2.

27. Miller and Parker, "Forestry," p. 6.

28. Reforestation in the redwood industry was actually initiated by a number of companies acting together. Six leading companies, including TPL, hired a consultant to study and make recommendations. Nine companies joined these six, representing some 90 percent of all redwood timberland. Although reforestation eventually proved infeasible in the redwood industry, the collective effort did lead to studies of selective logging and increased attention to the idea of sustained yield ("Historical Background of the Forestry Program of the Pacific Lumber Company," unpublished speech in TPL files in Scotia, stamped July 23, 1960, with the initials "A. E. B.," presumably a TPL executive).

29. The selective-cutting policy was motivated in part by a change in California's tax system that encouraged timber companies to leave a portion of their harvested timberlands intact.

30. Emanuel Fritz, quoted without citation in Allen, "Perpetuating the Redwood," pp. 4–5.

31. Henry Gannett, *National Geographic Magazine*, 1899; quoted in Theodore M. Knappen, "The Undying Redwoods of Our Western Coast," *American Review of Reviews*, March 1923, reprinted for the California Redwood Association, no page numbers; Knappen, "Undying Redwoods."

32. Black, "California's Newest Crop."

33. Knappen, "Undying Redwoods."

34. Both headlines are from the Oakland, California, paper *The Post Inquirer*, October 13, 1928, front page.

35. Letter from Emanuel Fritz to Lloyd Wambold, Diamond Match Company, Stirling City, California, September 19, 1947. Bancroft Library.

36. Taylor, "California Redwood."

37. "Historical Background of the Forestry Program of the Pacific Lumber Company."

38. "Pacific Lumber Rakes in the Green," *California Business*, March 4, 1976, pp. 19–21 (quotes on pp. 19, 20).

39. Parker, " 'The Trader' Triumphant," *PALCO Past*, chap. 7, p. 6.

40. TPL did grow throughout A. S. Murphy's tenure and those of his successors. But the acquisitions were almost entirely nontimber enterprises—welding equipment and commer-

cial rental properties, for instance (*Moody's Industrial Manual*, 1979, vol. 2, p. 4055; 1984, vol. 2).

41. Parker, "'The Trader' Triumphant," p. 9.

42. Parker, "'The Trader' Triumphant," p. 9.

43. Howard Brett Melendy, "One Hundred Years of the Redwood Lumber Industry, 1850–1950," unpublished doctoral dissertation, Stanford University, 1952, 217.

44. Letter from Emanuel Fritz to G. B. McLeod, head of a major redwood company in the California Redwood Association, probably Dolbeer & Carson, dated January 14, 1946. Bancroft Library.

TPL did add a third mill in Fortuna in the early 1970s. But the effect was not to expand capacity so much as to adjust it. As the big old-growth logs diminished and smaller young growth came online, mill B was slowly becoming obsolescent, designed as it was strictly for huge logs. The Fortuna mill was designed specifically for small logs and therefore allowed TPL to make a gradual transition out of old growth and into second growth and to do so over several decades. More telling was the purchase of an additional mill immediately after the buyout by Maxxam Corporation. This mill, located nearby in Carlotta, was acquired in 1986 not for the timberland that came with it but, as far as the evidence suggests, to increase mill capacity. And this at the same time Maxxam/PL was increasing the cut and, to some extent, looking for yet more timberland.

45. Miller and Parker, "Forestry." Indications of such restraint appeared earlier in TPL documents as well: "It is the policy of the Company to control the harvesting of its timber in order to operate on a sustained yield basis" (Form 10-K Annual Report Pursuant to Section 13 or 15(d) of the Securities Exchange Act of 1934, received from The Pacific Lumber Company, March 31, 1976; no page numbers).

46. Greg S. Biging, "Independent Review of Methods Used in LTSY Projection," appendix L to Pacific Lumber Company's *Sustained Yield Plan*, December 12, 1996.

47. Pacific Lumber Company, *1981 Annual Report*.

48. Letter dated March 7, 1994, from P. L. Tedder, timber consultant at Resource Economics Incorporated, Corvallis, Oregon, as supplement to Tedder's report, *An Estimate of the Fair Market Value of Pacific Lumber Company Timber and Timberlands as of October, 1985*; TPL company files.

49. Blackmun, "More Than Most," p. 39.

50. Testimony of John Campbell, executive vice president, Pacific Lumber Company; hearings, U.S. Congress, October 5, 1987, p. 28.

51. Blackmun, "More Than Most," pp. 39–41.

52. "Pacific Lumber Rakes in the Green," p. 20. Capitalization in original.

53. Consultancy report to John Campbell, The Pacific Lumber Company, signed by Kass Green and Warren S. Halsey of Hammon, Jensen, Wallen & Associates, Incorporated, Oakland, California, October 1, 1987, five pages. Referred to in congressional testimony of John Campbell, executive vice president, Pacific Lumber Company; hearings, U.S. Congress, October 5, 1987, p. 27.

54. Pacific Lumber Company, *1980 Annual Report*, 4; emphasis added.

55. Lisa H. Newton, "Chainsaws of Greed: The Case of Pacific Lumber," in W. Michael Hoffman, Robert Frederick, and Edward S. Petry, Jr., eds., *The Corporation, Ethics, and the Environment* (New York: Quorum Books, 1990), 96; David Harris, "The Last Stand," *Rolling Stone* 727 (February 8, 1996): 38–43, (quote on 41); Pacific Lumber Company, *1980 Annual Report*, 4; George Brown and Pete Stark, "The Last Stand," *New York Times*, December 1, 1995, p. A33. For accounts sympathetic to the environmentalists and opponents of the takeover, see David Harris, *The Last Stand: The War between Wall Street and Main Street over California's Ancient Redwoods* (New York: Times Books, 1995). For accounts sympathetic to Maxxam/Pacific Lumber, see Alston Chase, *In a Dark Wood* (New York: Houghton Mifflin, 1995); also see Michael V. Russo, "Pacific Lumber Company," teaching case, 1997.

56. "The company had planned to cut its enormous old-growth redwoods over a period of at least 40 years, never taking more timber than the forest produced in any one year. Now the new owners intend to double the rate of harvest, cutting the forest in 20 years or less" (Jane Easter Bahls, "A Timber Takeover's High Toll," *Sierra*, September-October 1988: 32–33, 37–38 (quote on 32).

57. John Campbell, personal interview, Scotia, 1997.

58. Letter from Emanuel Fritz to G. B. McLeod, January 14, 1946. Bancroft Library.

59. Handwritten note from Emanuel Fritz describing a set of his own files; no date or location. Bancroft Library.

60. Taylor, "California Redwood."

61. Letter from Emanuel Fritz to Gordon Manary, The Pacific Lumber Company, San Francisco, November 26, 1948. Bancroft Library.

62. Memorandum from Emanuel Fritz to Kenneth Smith of the CRA, February 2, 1948. Bancroft Library.

63. Lumber Code Authority of August 19, 1933, article 10, schedule C, section 2; as quoted in unpublished speech in company files in Scotia, titled "Historical Background of the Forestry Program of the Pacific Lumber Company, July 23, 1960, with the initials "A. E. B.," presumably a TPL executive.

64. Memorandum from Emanuel Fritz to CRA, May 12, 1947.

65. Letter from Emanuel Fritz to T. D. Woodbury of the U.S. Forest Service, March 5, 1937. Bancroft Library.

66. Letter from Emanuel Fritz to Erle Kauffman of the American Forestry Association, September 29, 1949. Bancroft Library.

67. Letter from Emanuel Fritz to T. D. Woodbury of the U.S. Forest Service, March 5, 1937. Bancroft Library.

68. Memo from Fritz to K. Smith, CRA, February 2, 1948.

69. Memorandum from Emanuel Fritz to Kenneth Smith, CRA, February 7, 1947. Bancroft Library.

70. Franklin D. Roosevelt and F. A. Silcox, quoted in *California Ranger* newsletter, Region Five, vol. 9 no. 7, January 7, 1938.

71. "U.S. Forester Silcox Says—'Public Regulation of Private Forests Is Essential,'" *West Coast Lumberman* 65/3 (March 1938): no page number available.

72. Handwritten note from Emanuel Fritz describing a set of his own files; no date or location. Bancroft Library.

73. Memo from Fritz to K. Smith, CRA, February 7, 1947.

74. Melendy, "One Hundred Years of the Redwood Lumber Industry," 114.

75. Memo from Fritz to major redwood producers, February 7, 1946. Bancroft Library.

76. Memo from Fritz to K. Smith, CRA, February 7, 1947.

77. Melendy, "One Hundred Years of the Redwood Lumber Industry," 220, 301.

78. Emanuel Fritz, "What's Ahead for The Redwood Industry?", unpublished paper, marked "1949, To California Redwood Association" and attached to letter from Fritz to Sherman Bishop of the CRA, June 8, 1949, p. 14. Bancroft Library.

79. Fritz, "What's Ahead for the Redwood Industry?", p. 14.

80. Fritz, "What's Ahead for the Redwood Industry?", p. 25.

81. Charles McCoy, "U.S. Regulators Sue Financier Hurwitz over Failed Thrift," *Wall Street Journal*, August 3, 1995, p. B10.

82. One scholar of the redwood industry wrote in 1952 that "while charges of monopoly have been hurled at the redwood industry and at the California Redwood Association, only once has the industry been hauled into court for anti-trust violations." The Redwood Lunch Club, six of the largest redwood companies including TPL, was fined $5,000 for price fixing (Melendy, "One Hundred Years of the Redwood Lumber Industry," 313).

83. In reconstructing the reasoning of A. S. Murphy, therefore, one needn't show that Murphy had sustainability in mind to argue that he developed elements of a long-term resource-management regime. One need only assume that, in this particular historical context, Murphy's primary motive was to stay in the timbering business while making adjustments for the biophysical constraint of limited forests. Lessons can be derived because in different contexts it is precisely the self-motivated social adjustment to ecological constraint for which insight is needed, not, as in the prevailing approaches today, more biophysical precision or better rewards and penalties.

84. Catherine M. Mater, "Emerging Technologies for Sustainable Forestry," and Jeff Romm, "The Pursuit of Innovation," in Michael B. Jenkins, *The Business of Sustainable Forestry: Case Studies* (Chicago: The John D. and Catherine T. MacArthur Foundation, 1998).

85. *Sustainable Forestry: Principles and Implementation Guidelines* (Washington, DC: American Forest and Paper Association, 1997), 5–8.

86. *Sustainable Forestry*, 9.

87. Merline Williams, draft of doctoral dissertation chapter, unpublished. TPL company files, Scotia.

88. Fritz, "What's Ahead for the Redwood Industry?", p. 21.

89. Cronon, *Nature's Metropolis*.

90. Williams, unpublished doctoral dissertation.

91. Fritz, "What's Ahead for the Redwood Industry?", p. 6.

92. For an accessible explanation of the tyranny of interest rates in timbering, see Ray Raphael, *More Tree Talk: The People, Politics, and Economics of Timber* (Washington, DC:

Island Press, 1994). Raphael concludes that "from an economic standpoint, the time frame for growing pulp—say 15 to 30 years—can be handled within a capitalist economy; the time frame for regenerating a real forest—say 70 to 300 years—is incompatible with capital investments that must produce competitive rates of return"—that is, that must compete with the economy's overall "guiding rate of return," a rate "that has nothing at all to do with silviculture or ecosystem management" (p. 169).

93. Pacific Lumber Company, *1980 Annual Report*, 4.

94. Fritz, "What's Ahead for the Redwood Industry?", p. 25.

95. U. S. Congress. House. Committee on Energy and Commerce. *Hearings before a subcommittee on oversight and investigations of the Committee on Energy and Commerce*, 100th Congress, October 5, 1987, and February 8, 1988, 7–8.

96. Williams, unpublished doctoral dissertation.

Chapter 7

1. Letter from Jo Stevens to Senator Jill Goldthwait, Senate of Maine, Augusta, January 14, 1998.

2. James A. Acheson, *The Lobster Gangs of Maine* (Hanover, NH: University Press of New England, 1988).

3. George Brown Goode, *The Fisheries and Fishery Industries of the United States* (Washington, DC: GPO, 1887), 696.

4. Goode, *Fisheries*, 697.

5. Goode, *Fisheries*, 697.

6. "Article on the Lobster followed by Some Observations on the Clam," *Bulletin of the State Department of Sea and Shore Fisheries of Maine*. 1/1 (Rockland, March 1920): 1.

7. Harold B. Clifford, *The Boothbay Region, 1906 to 1960* (Freeport, ME: Bond Wheelwright Co., 1961), 124.

8. The 1920 quote reflects the "bust" of the 1920s and 1930s. And yet in the "boom" years of the 1990s, after considerable increase in fishing pressure, catches were eight times those levels. "I am now convinced, along with many fishermen," writes anthropologist James Acheson, the leading authority on the traditional social organization of lobster fishers, "that some of the predictions of scientists are not based on the best information—and the predictions of fishermen are buttressed by far more than folklore. . . . People who live from the sea know a great deal about the life cycles of the species they exploit, including spawning behavior, nursery grounds, migration routes, growth rates and predation" (Jim Acheson, "Needing Each Other: Fishermen and Scientists Share a History of Conflict, But Peace Could Be Breaking Out," *Island Journal* 15 (1998): 74–75.

9. Notes of Monhegan lobster fisher John Murdock, around 1997–1998.

10. Sydney Davis, letter to the editor, *Courier-Gazette*, news clipping file, Sea and Seashore Fisheries Commission, no date but probably about 1945.

11. Quoted in Ted Bernard and Jora Young, *The Ecology of Hope: Communities Collaborate for Sustainability* (Gabriola Island, BC: New Society Publishers, 1997), 49.

12. News clipping file, Sea and Seashore Fisheries Commission, no publication information available.

13. Richard W. Judd, "Saving the Fisherman as Well as the Fish: Conservation and Commercial Rivalry in Maine's Lobster Industry, 1872–1933," *Business History Review* 62 (Winter 1988): 596–625.

14. Jim Doherty, "Claws: In Down East Maine, the Lobster Means More Than Seafood," *Smithsonian* 28/7 (October 1997): 47–55 (quote on 50).

15. Legislative Record of the Seventy-Third Legislature of the State of Maine, 1907, Augusta, Maine; chaps. 61, 352, 357, 380. The additional communities were the towns of Harrington, Milbridge, Steuben, Gouldsboro, Lubec, and Trescott.

16. Goode, *Fisheries*, 699.

17. Quoted in Goode, *Fisheries*, 729.

18. *Express*, Portland, news clipping file, Sea and Seashore Fisheries Commission, no publication information available. File date July 21, 1962.

19. Susan Pollack, "The Lobster Trap," *Sierra* 83/4 (July–August 1998): 46–52 (quote on 48).

20. Letter from Lewellyn Joyce, Correspondence, Sea and Seashore Fisheries Commission, 1965 folder, received February 9, 1965.

21. Nicholas G. Pitarys, "Animosity toward 'Hogging' Seen behind Trap Cutting," *Express*, stamped July 21, 1962, by clipping service, no page numbers.

22. Wallace Moore, letter to the editor, *Portland Press-Herald*, Portland, Maine, news clipping file, Sea and Seashore Fisheries Commission, 1965 folder, stamped February 25, 1965.

23. Letter from George K. Norwood of Saco, Maine, Correspondence, news clipping file, 1965 folder, Sea and Seashore Fisheries Commission, dated February 5, 1965.

24. Doherty, "Claws," 54.

25. Sydney Davis, letter to the editor, *Courier-Gazette*, news clipping file, Sea and Seashore Fisheries Commission, no date but probably about 1945.

26. The definitive text, confirmed for its accuracy in capturing the social dynamics of lobstering by one of my interviewees, a boat captain, is Acheson's *The Lobster Gangs of Maine*.

27. Much of the literature on lobster fishing tends to ignore this aspect of the self-management of fishing and, consequently, the importance of restraint. Analysts tend to frame the traditional forms of management as a question of territorial defense. Acheson, for example, calls one set of territories "nucleated." A harbor, usually along the mainland, has a core fishing area that is staunchly defended. As one goes farther and farther from the home harbor, the boundary becomes muddled or fluid and the bottom is more often shared. Other territories, which Acheson calls "peripheral," generally center on an island and maintain rigid boundaries with no sharing of bottom. Monhegan is a prime example.

   This framing appears to have both economic and biological roots. It asks how profit-maximizing resource users can efficiently divide up a fixed resource given the transaction costs of transport and defense. It does not tend to ask about the conditions for long-term resource use, except to note that the territories that break down, whether nucleated or peripheral, tend to be overharvested. The implicit causal relationship with respect to the sustainability question is that territories lead to, or are necessary conditions for, long-term use. This may be true as far as it goes. But it tends to lump together what I have distinguished as the "hogs" and the "real fishers." That is, hogs can successfully defend their territory but exercise little restraint in resource use. They are in it only for the short term.

By contrast, the sufficiency perspective, with its roots in the long-term functioning of both the biophysical and social systems, does ask about the conditions for restraint *within* the defended territory. That is, the logic of sufficiency compels an identification of sources of limits not just as carrying capacity and maximum yield, but as elements of individual and collective action—in other words, as patterns of behavior and institutions of self-management. A sustainable resource system can never be built where hogging is the rule, no matter how successful the territorial defense. The nature of lobster fishers' work on the water and in the fishhouse (and sometimes in the agency offices and legislative halls) is integral to the assessment of sustainable resource practices.

28. Letter addressed to Commissioner Robin Alden, Department of Marine Resources, and signed by twenty-two fishermen from Matinicus Island, Maine; accessed at http://www.monhegan.com/oldstuf/lobster/lobwar/matini.htm.

29. For example, the state of Maine licensed some 2.6 million traps in 1996 and fishermen caught 36.2 million pounds worth more than $107 million. Lobster catches and profits were at an all-time high in the 1990s ("Worries About Lobster in Maine Rise by the Pound," *New York Times*, November 28, 1997, p. A17).

30. Legislative testimony on LD 2021; no date.

31. Letter in Marine Resources Committee file, 1998; no date or signature.

32. Letter from Bill Payne, Marine Resources Committee file, 1998; no date.

33. Letter in Marine Resources Committee file, 1998; no date or signature.

34. Quoted without citation in Ronald P. Formisano, *The Great Lobster War* (Amherst: University of Massachusetts Press, 1997), 141.

35. See, for example, James R. McGoodwin, *Crisis in World's Fisheries: People, Problems, and Policies* (Stanford, CA: Stanford University Press, 1990); Karyn L. Gimbel, ed., *Limiting Access to Marine Fisheries: Keeping the Focus on Conservation* (Washington, DC: Center for Marine Conservation and World Wildlife Fund US, 1994); Simon Fairlie, guest ed., "Overfishing: Its Causes and Consequences: A Special Double Issue," *The Ecologist* 25/2–3 (March–June 1995).

36. Acheson, *The Lobster Gangs of Maine.*

37. "Maine and the Lobster Catch," editorial, *New York Times*, June 2, 2001, p. A22.

38. James M. Acheson and James A. Wilson, "Order out of Chaos: The Case for Parametric Fisheries Management," *American Anthropologist* 98/3 (September 1996): 579–594; Acheson, "Needing Each Other."

39. Office of Policy and Legal Analysis, Maine State Legislature, "Summary of LD 2021: An Act Concerning Commercial Fishing in the vicinity of Monhegan Island," January 1998, pp. 1–2.

40. State of Maine, Interdepartmental memorandum, November 25, 1997, Subject: Adopted Rule—Monhegan Island Conservation Area and Prohibitions, pp. 2, 5–9; approved by the DMR advisory Council November 25, 1997.

41. "Monhegan postpones opening of its lobster season," *Working Waterfront/Inter Island News*, November 1997; accessed online at http://www.monhegan.com/oldstuf/lobster/lobwar/iin11.htm, June 15, 1998.

42. Mrs. Clarence Davis, "Island Trap Day Described by Correspondent," *Courier Gazette*, January 12, 1963; no page number.

43. "Threat from Rivals Prompts Lobstermen to Delay Season," *Bangor Daily News*, October 8, 1997; accessed online at http://www.bangornews.com/News/971008threatfrom-rivalsprom.html, June 15, 1998.

44. Ibid.

45. Testimony of E. Penn Estabrook, acting commissioner of the Department of Marine Resources, Committee on Marine Resources, January 27, 1998.

46. Letter to Senator Jill Goldthwait from Robin Alden, January 12, 1998.

47. Joseph Cyr, "Lawsuit Looms over Lobsters," *Courier-Gazette*, February 5, 1998, pp. A1, A5.

48. John Richardson, "Monhegan Lobstermen Fight for Waters," *Portland Press Herald*, January 28, 1998; accessed online at http://www.monhegan.com/oldstuf/lobster/lobwar/pph0128.htm, June 15, 1998.

49. Letter to Marine Resources Committee, 1998 session, from Eugene M. Harrington, Jr.; no date.

50. Letter to "legislator" from Monhegan Island Lobstermen, winter 1997.

51. Letter to Senator Jill Goldthwait from Robin Alden, January 12, 1998.

52. Written testimony provided to the Maine Marine Resources Committee, 1998 file; no date or name.

53. Letter to Marine Resources Committee from Douglas Boynton, LD 2021 file; no date.

54. Sherman Stanley, written testimony provided to the Maine Marine Resources Committee, 1998 file, January 27, 1998.

55. Alison Rieser, director of the Marine Law Institute of the University of Maine School of Law; quoted in "King Signs Monhegan Conservation Zone Law," *Bangor Daily News*, February 28, 1998; accessed online at http://www.monhegan.com/oldstuf/lobster/lobwar/bdn0229.htm, June 15, 1998.

56. Some observers raised constitutional questions. Could the state grant exclusive harvesting rights to a public resource? Could they prohibit others from entering and, at the same time, prohibit these fishers from fishing in other state waters? Could they stop them from lobstering in federal waters? The director of the Marine Law Institute of the University of Maine School of Law, Alison Rieser, argued that both Maine state courts and the U.S. Supreme Court have affirmed a government's right to protect natural resources. "It is within the sovereign power of the state to promote conservation of resources and limit access to fishing grounds," Rieser said. "It's a management approach and the courts have said it is legitimate to create special conservation districts and limit who fishes them" (*Bangor Daily News*, February 28, 1998; accessed online at http://www.monhegan.com/oldstuf/lobster/lobwar/bdn0229.htm, June 15, 1998).

57. James A. Acheson, personal communication, October 3, 2003, Ann Arbor, Michigan.

58. "Lobstering Moratorium," editorial, *Kittery-Eliot Star*, news clipping file, Sea and Seashore Fisheries Commission, 1960s; no date or page number.

59. Doherty, "Claws," 48.

60. Study and quote cited in Trevor Corson, "Stalking the American Lobster," *Atlantic Monthly* 289/4 (April 2002): 61–81 (quote on 70).

61. Joe Fessenden, quoted in David Grima, "State Gears Up for Pan Bay Turf Battle," *Courier-Gazette*, September 23, 1997; accessed online at http://www.monhegan.com/oldstuf/ lobster/lobwar/lob9-23.htm, June 15, 1998.

62. Gimbel, Limiting Access to Marine Fisheries.

63. "The Monhegan Zone," editorial, *Bangor Daily News* February 2, 1998; accessed online at http://www.monhegan.com/oldstuf/lobster/lobwar/bdn0202.htm, June 15, 1998.

64. Letter to Marine Resource Committee from Willard J. Boynton and Jacqueline Boegel of Monhegan, January 25, 1998.

Chapter 8

1. A note on the sustainability goal that informs this entire study: unlike the timber and lobstering cases, nothing in the following automobile cases can support a claim of "sustainable practice." I doubt that any adjustment to auto use—engine efficiencies, closed-loop production methods, pollution-control devices—can make such a claim. Such adjustments and the cases presented here necessarily fall within the realm of "environmental improvement," as discussed in chapter 2. The advantage in explicating conditions for self-imposed restraint in auto use is that, unlike the institutional and behavioral adjustments to production we saw in the timbering and fishing cases, this is one realm in which the question of end-use consumption of resources can be examined directly. The timber and lobster cases can be seen as representing restraint in production with their attendant, yet indirect, curtailment of consumption and, hence, total throughput. The auto cases focus the analytic gaze directly on consumption.

2. Alexander Ross, untitled article in *The Telegram*, Toronto, July 31, 1965, p. 13. Italics and lowercase in original.

3. Sally Gibson, *More Than an Island: A History of the Toronto Island* (Toronto: Irwin, 1984), 188.

4. Gibson, *More Than an Island*, 220.

5. Gibson, *More Than an Island*, 220.

6. Ross, untitled article, 1965.

7. Testimony of Hans Blumenfeld before the Metropolitan Toronto Planning Board, November 1, 1955, p. 4. Metro files.

8. Ross, untitled article, 1965.

9. Margery L. Greene, "Enjoys Island Trip," letter to the editor, *Toronto Star*, February 15, 1957. Metro files, no page numbers.

10. Testimony of Hans Blumenfeld, 1955, p. 7; "Toronto Island Park," Metro Parks and Culture, the Municipality of Metropolitan Toronto, undated brochure but about 2000.

11. Gibson, *More Than an Island*, 226.

12. "Is Island Tunnel Idiocy or Averting Another Zoo?", *The Telegram*, January 7, 1953. Metro files, Toronto.

13. Gibson, *More Than an Island*, 227.

14. Gibson, *More Than an Island*, 230.

15. Gibson, *More Than an Island*, 230.

16. Gordon Bleasdell, "Park, Family Resort to Cost $14,500,000 Toronto Island Plan," *Toronto Daily Star*, February 10, 1956, p. 5. Metro files.

17. Testimony of Hans Blumenfeld, 1955, p. 2.

18. Ross, untitled article, 1965.

19. Gibson, *More Than an Island*, 245.

20. "Need Bridge to Island," editorial, *Toronto Star*, August 26, 1960: Metro files, no page numbers.

21. "Need Bridge to Island," 1960.

22. Gibson, *More Than an Island*, 245.

23. Arthur W. Henschel, "Footbridge or Tunnel across the Gap," *Toronto Star*, May 28, 1973. Metro files, no page numbers.

24. Testimony by Mary Hay of the Toronto Waterfront Coalition to Mayor and Executive Committee of the City of Toronto, May 5, 1997.

25. Joseph Hall, "Fixed Link to Benefit Airport Experts Say," *Toronto Star*, August 6, 1998. Metro files, no page numbers.

26. Geoffrey York, "Tunnel to Island Airport Called Likely," *The Globe and Mail*, January 11, 1986, p. A19. Metro files.

27. Councillor John Adams, "What's Wrong with Toronto City Council?", *Our Toronto*, November 1995.

28. "Toronto Island Residents Resist Bridge to City," CNN.com, November 22, 1998; accessed at http://www.cnn.com/WORLD/americas/9811/22/toronto.island/.

29. Lisa Raitt, CEO and Harbourmaster, Toronto Port Authority, "Miller Campaign Deliberately Misleads Voters on Fixed Link, City Centre Airport," October 16, 2003; accessed online at http://www.torontoport.com/thc/notices/miller_letter.htm, December 16, 2003.

30. "Board of Trade Opposes Island Bus Tunnel Plan," *Telegram*, May 18, 1965. Metro files, no page numbers.

31. Jeffrey Stinson, "Islands Must Remain Islands," *Toronto Star*, May 28, 1973. Metro files, no page numbers available, paragraphing in original.

32. "Missing Permits Delay Airport Bridge-Toronto," November 13, 2003; accessed at http://archives.californiaaviation.org/airport/msg28317.html

33. Testimony of Hans Blumenfeld, 1955, p. 1.

34. Peter Newman and Jeffrey Kenworthy, *Sustainability and Cities: Overcoming Automobile Dependence* (Washington, DC: Island Press, 1999), 60.

35. Newman and Kenworthy, *Sustainability and Cities*, 31.

36. Newman and Kenworthy, *Sustainability and Cities*, 59.

37. John Whitelegg, "Time Pollution," *The Ecologist* 23/4 (July–August 1993): 131–134.

38. Newman and Kenworthy, *Sustainability and Cities*, 237.

39. Newman and Kenworthy, *Sustainability and Cities*, 119.

40. John Whitelegg and Gary Haq, "The Global Transport Problem, Same Issues But a Different Place," in John Whitelegg and Gary Haq, eds., *The Earthscan Reader on World Transport Policy and Practice* (London: Earthscan, 2003), 21–22; M. M. Peden, *World Report on Road Traffic Injury Prevention* (Geneva: World Health Organization, 2004).

41. John Pucher and Christian Lefèvre, *The Urban Transport Crisis in Europe and North America* (London: Macmillan Press, 1996), 1–2.

42. Whitelegg and Haq, "The Global Transport Problem," 3–25.

43. J. H. Brunn, "Das Auto ist ein Stück mehr Freiheit" (The auto is another piece of freedom), speech to the VDA-Mitgliederversammlung, Baden-Baden, Germany, September 27, 1974; quoted in Wolfgang Sachs, *For Love of the Automobile: Looking Back into the History of Our Desires*, translated from the 1984 German original by Don Reneau (Berkeley: University of California Press, 1992), 97.

44. Newman and Kenworthy, *Sustainability and Cities*, 142.

45. Newman and Kenworthy, *Sustainability and Cities*, 46.

46. Lewis Mumford, *The Myth of the Machine: The Pentagon of Power* (New York: Harcourt Brace Jovanovich, 1970), 173; quoted in Sachs, *For Love of the Automobile*, 120; emphasis in original.

47. Comparing three San Francisco residential streets, Donald Appleyard and colleagues found that, as traffic volume increased, so did noise and pollution, while safety, neighborliness, and a sense of ownership in the neighborhood decreased. Inhabitants of the lightly trafficked street had three times the number of local friends and twice the number of acquaintances as those on a heavily traveled street (Donald Appleyard, M. Sue Gerson, and Mark Lintell, *Livable Streets* (Berkeley: University of California Press, 1981)).

48. Jane Jacobs, *The Death and Life of Great American Cities* (New York: Random House, 1961); Ray Oldenburg, ed., *Celebrating the Third Place: Inspiring Stories about the "Great Good Places" at the Heart of Our Communities* (New York: Marlowe, 2001).

49. Newman and Kenworthy, *Sustainability and Cities*, 319.

50. Bleasdell, "Park, Family Resort to Cost $14,500,000 Toronto Island Plan."

51. Sachs, *For Love of the Automobile*, 6.

52. Otto Julius Bierbaum, *Eine empfindsame Reise im Automobil. Von Berlin nach Sorrent und zurück an den Rhein* (Munich, 1903), p. 268f; in Sachs, *For Love of the Automobile*, 8.

53. "Association of German Automobile Clubs Manifesto on Motorized Travel," *ADAC Motorwelt*, 1965, no. 5; quoted in Sachs, *For Love of the Automobile*, 76–79.

54. Bradford C. Snell, "American Ground Transport: A Proposal for Restructuring the Automobile, Truck, Bus & Rail Industries: Presented to the Subcommittee on Antitrust and

Monopoly of the Committee on the Judiciary, United States Senate, February 26, 1974";
posted online by Car Busters, March 2001; accessed online at http://www.carbusters.org/
freesources/AmericanGroundTransport.rtf, June 11, 2004.

55. Surface Transportation Policy Project, "Consumer Expenditures in 2002," citing the U.S.
Bureau of Labor Statistics Consumer Expenditure Survey, November 21, 2003; accessed at
http://www.bls.gov/news.release/cesan.nr0.htm.

56. Charles Lave, "Cars and Demographics," *Access* 1 (1992): 4–11; cited in Newman and
Kenworthy, *Sustainability and Cities*, 108.

57. Marcia D. Lowe, "Re-Inventing Transport," in Lester R. Brown et al., eds., *State of the
World 1994* (London: Earthscan, 1994), 98; in Newman and Kenworthy, *Sustainability and
Cities*, 67.

58. Newman and Kenworthy, *Sustainability and Cities*, 45; emphasis added.

59. Newman and Kenworthy, *Sustainability and Cities*, 319.

Chapter 9

1. William Cronon, *Nature's Metropolis: Chicago and the Great West* (New York: Norton,
1991), 211.

2. Cronon, *Nature's Metropolis*, 229.

3. Frederick Law Olmstead, *A Journey Through Texas: Or, A Saddle-Trip on the
Southwestern Frontier; with a Statistical Appendix* (New York: Dix, Edwards & Co.,
1857), 9.

4. Cronon, *Nature's Metropolis*, 223.

5. Cronon, *Nature's Metropolis*, 229.

6. Cronon, *Nature's Metropolis*, 243.

7. Cronon, *Nature's Metropolis*, 249.

8. Cronon, *Nature's Metropolis*, 255.

9. Cronon, *Nature's Metropolis*, 255.

10. Verlyn Klinkenborg, "Coming to Terms with the Problem of Global Meat," *New York
Times*, January 10, 2004, p. A30.

11. Christopher Shirley, "Going Seasonal: Take Time Off from Milking to Boost Profits
and Herd Health, Say These Farmers," *The New Farm*, May–June 1993, pp. 28–34,
46; Jon Christensen, "Environmentalists Hail the Ranchers: Howdy, Pardners!", *New York
Times*, September 10, 2002, p. D3; Tom Wolf, "The Malpai Borderlands Group: Science,
Community, and Collaborative Management," Workshop on Collaborative Resource
Management in the Interior West, October 18 to 22, 2001; accessed online at http://www.
redlodgeclearinghouse.org/stories/malpai.pdf, June 15, 2004; Dan Gunderson, "North
Dakota Ranchers Market Beef to Muslims," Minnesota Public Radio, January 17, 2002;
accessed online at http://news.minnesota.publicradio.org/features/200201/17_gundersond_
dakhalal-m/, June 15, 2004; Hwaa Irfan, "The Halal Meat Industry: Was Your Eid Sheep

Really Halal?", Islam Online, July 3, 2002; accessed online at http://www.islamonline.net/english/Science/2002/03/article3.shtml, June 15, 2004.

12. Paul Wapner, "The Resurgence and Metamorphosis of Normative International Relations: Principled Commitment and Scholarship in a New Millennium," in Paul Wapner and Lester Edwin J. Ruiz, eds., *Principled World Politics: The Challenge of Normative International Relations* (Lanham: Rowman & Littlefield, 2000), 1–21 (quote on 4–5).

13. United Nations Development Programme, "New Dimensions of Human Security," excerpted in Ken Conca and Geoffrey D. Dabelko, eds., *Green Planet Blues: Environmental Politics from Stockholm to Kyoto*, 2nd ed. (Boulder, CO: Westview Press, 1998), 298–303 (quotes on 298, 300).

Index